古代小說

Kodae Sosŏl: A Survey of Korean Traditional Style Popular Novels

W.E.Skillend

Acknowledgements

There is little in this work, other than the basic concept and the labour of the compilation of it, which I would claim to be my own, and I have tried to acknowledge to whom I am indebted for each item of information given. However, it has almost certainly happened more than once that I have received ideas from others, forgotten their origins and come to regard them as my own. It seems therefore fairest to acknowledge here that virtually all that I know about Korean literature has been taught to me by one or other of the body of Korean scholars whose perseverance in the face of apathy and disinterest in the world at large moves one to deep admiration, and whose friendliness and helpfulness towards foreigners who do take an interest in Korea make Korean studies as enjoyable as they are interesting.

For this publication itself I wish to thank the Publications Committee of the School of Oriental and African Studies, University of London, which has generously agreed to bear the whole cost.

W. E. Skillend,
London, August 1967.

Introduction

1. The Scope and Aims of This Work

1.1 This work is concerned with 古代小說 *kodae sosŏl*, particularly with investigating what *kodae sosŏl* exist or have existed in texts in Korean in a traditional style. *Kodae sosŏl* comprise almost all prose works of traditional literature in Korean, and they include not only fictional stories, fables, myths, legends and so on, but also very factual anecdotes from history, biographies, and even memoires, diaries and autobiographies. They are generally considered to be the traditional equivalent or the predecessor of the modern novel, but it has seldom been suggested that they were composed with the serious literary intent that can mark a modern novel. They appear to be rather a response to a popular demand for entertaining and/or edifying stories, and in this sense they may be regarded as popular novels in a traditional style.

1.2 The same category has been established within Chinese literature, and many *kodae sosŏl* in Korean are translations of, or are less directly derived from Chinese works. Even those which are usually regarded as purely Korean compositions, such as **229 심청전 Sim Ch'ŏng chŏn,** can be very difficult to distinguish in atmosphere, mood, content and even setting from those which are Chinese in origin. In addition there are *kodae sosŏl* in *hanmun* (漢文, classical Chinese written by Koreans), and, while these appear as a group to be more seriously intended than those in Korean, certain particular *kodae sosŏl* in Korean are translations of, or are less directly derived from works in *hanmun*. It is also believed that in some cases *kodae sosŏl* in *hanmun* are translations of works in Korean.

1.3 It is therefore not suggested that the writing of *kodae sosŏl* in Korean can be considered in isolation from the writing of *kodae sosŏl* in *hanmun*. Indeed, it is clear that no full appreciation of *kodae sosŏl* in Korean is possible without reference to the framework of the whole China-based culture which Korea was proud to accept in the past. Nor, on the other hand, is it suggested that the writing of popular novels in a modern style can be considered in isolation from the writing of popular novels in a traditional style. The two overlap considerably in theme and in date, and changes in style are fitful. It does, however, seem that *kodae sosŏl* in Korean in a traditional style may be regarded as the reading of a large and fairly homogeneous group of people over a considerable period. They are presented here as a group of works of literature which can be identified by fairly simple and fairly objective criteria, in the belief that some continuity can be seen in the history of Korean literature by considering what was read by groups of people over periods of time, as well as by considering what was written by individuals at particular times.

1.4 The information on these *kodae sosŏl* presented here is intended to be factual rather than critical, and the whole work is intended to serve as a basic point of reference for westerners who wish to investigate the subject in general, any aspect of the subject, or any particular story or work of literature. It consists of general information on each story, and a listing of such texts as have been found or reported to tell each story.

2. The Selection of Titles.

2.1 The list of titles given is based on a complete list of titles found in Korean spelling and of spellings in Korean of titles found written with Chinese characters. In the second category are included a few titles of Chinese or *hanmun* works which have not been found in old Korean versions, but which are mentioned by others in close connection with works in Korean. The complete list has been reduced by more than half by omitting from it titles which would only be referred to adjacent title entries. For example, 토귀전, 토기젼 and 토끼의간 are all omitted because they would simply be referred to the next entry on the list, **468 토끼전 T'okki chŏn,** and the titles which would immediately follow this, 토끼타령, 토별가, 토별산수록, 토생원전, 토석사젼, 톡긔젼, 톳기젼 and 톳기젼, are also omitted because they too would only be referred to the same entry. Further reductions have been made by not listing separately variations with ㆍ (아래아) *ă (arae a)* for ㅏ(아) *a* and ㆎ(아래아이) *ăe* for ㅐ *ae*, and by giving only one entry where a number of titles begin with the same minor variation of spelling which places them in a very different position in the list. For example, 녀 ..... **Nyŏ** .....: see 여 ..... Yŏ..... means that any of the titles which begin with this common, and easily recognized, variation in Korean spelling can be found under the standard spelling.

2.2 The number of main entries has been kept to a minimum by assembling under each numbered main entry all texts which are known or thought to have some relationship to each other. The entries are made under those titles which appear to be most likely to be referred to, but in some cases it has been necessary to select arbitrarily for a main entry one title under which a group of

6

stories may most conveniently be described, as with the entry 133 병자록 **Pyŏngja rok,** for instance. It is hoped that the system of cross-references will be adequate to lessen the inconvenience caused in such cases.

2.3 This policy has meant that under some entries, **208** 소학사전 **So Haksa chŏn,** for instance, on which considerable work has been done, a great variety of works is assembled together, but the total length of the list is swollen by separate numbered entries for those works on which there is not sufficient information to relate them to any others. It is sometimes clear that accidental variations in title have arisen as titles are passed from one literary historian, critic or bibliographer to another. I have tried to note all such cases, as, for instance, with the "So or Su Families" group, on which there is a long note following **195** 소문록 **So Mun nok.** Such notes are not intended as criticisms of other writers, and it is only hoped that the present work does not add too many accidental variations of its own. The purpose of such notes is simple to serve the convenience of other westerners for whom minor misprints in Korean are often a major obstacle to understanding.

3. The Arrangement of the List of Titles.

3.1 The listing is of titles for stories in (Korean) alphabetical order, and an **Index** of titles in Chinese characters in radical-stroke order is appended. Listing by author or date is impossible, since no more than a handful of stories is of known authorship or date of origin, the conjectured or reported origins of stories hardly ever coincide with their use in texts, and the earliest texts are mostly anonymous and undated. Listing by theme or type of story is rejected as involving too subjective and arbitrary a judgement.

3.2 The alphabetical order used follows exactly that used in the Minjung Sŏgwan's Kugŏ Taesajŏn (이희승편 : 국어대사전, 민중서관, Seoul, 1961). It should be noted particularly that the double letters follow all uses of the corresponding single letters, for example that 꼭 follows 김 and 쌍 follows 심.

4. General Information on Stories.

4.1 The information given is either provided by the texts listed or attributed to its source. Only one exception has been generally and intentionally made to this rule, and that is when titles are given of Chinese or *hanmun* works which are the same as, or very similar to those of works in Korean on which little information is available. If only the title is given, no source is mentioned, since there are many sources for such titles and the information contained in them is largely common knowledge. If any further information is given on the Chinese or *hanmun* work without any indication of source, it may be assumed that the source for it is a text of the work in question. In such cases the mention of the title of the Chinese or *hanmun* work is in any case intended as a suggestion for further investigation only.

4.2 Where there is sufficient information on any story, a brief indication of its nature has been given, including a translation of the title and any explanation of the title that seems to be needed. Where the events or characters in a story can be identified with historical events or characters, or with events or characters found in Chinese or *hanmun* works, a special note of this has been made, since it may give an indication of the source of the story. The information given is always brief, since its chief purpose is to enable a quick check to be made to discover whether any text not listed here might carry the same story as texts which are listed, and if it often appears facile to the expert on Korean literature, such an expert is requested to bear in mind the westerner who wishes to study Korean literature but is still puzzled by certain elementary facts which have never actually been explained in published works.

4.3 To supplement the meagre information given, reference is made to the fullest descriptions and discussions which have been found elsewhere of each story. These are given most commonly to the five general works on *kodae sosŏl* by **Kim T'aejun, Kim Kidong** (two), **Pak Sŏngŭi** and **Sin Kihyŏng**, full titles, etc., of which are given under those names in the **Index of Brief References** at the end of this introduction.

5. Sources of Information.

5.1 **Kim T'aejun** was the pioneer in this field with his <u>Chosŏn Sosŏl sa</u>, "A History of the Korean Novel" (1930-31, 1933 and 1939), and all who have followed him, including myself, owe him a very great debt. Neither the fact that his historical account may now be questioned at almost every point, as far as *kodae sosŏl* in Korean are concerned, nor the fact that almost every word which he wrote has been quoted by at least one subsequent critic, should deter anyone from reading his work, but it is not easy to find now, and the same two facts do at least mean that one misses little factual information of importance if one cannot read it.

5.2 **Kim Kidong's** first work, Han'guk Kodae Sosŏl Kaeron, "A Survey of Korean *Kodae Sosŏl*" (1956), is in a sense only a draft for his later work, but it does contain descriptions of one or two stories which are not in his later work, and the simpler approach of this earlier work may be found more helpful in some cases. His second work, Yijo Sidae Sosŏllon, "On the Novéls of the Yi Dynasty Period" (1959), is essential reading for any study of the subject at all. It gives descriptions of seventy five or so of the most important *kodae sosŏl* in Korean, as well as of several in *hanmun*. These descriptions are always fac- tually accurate, based on indentified texts in most cases, and accompanied by full discussions of the stories. Some two hundred other titles are also men- tioned, most of them in the table, pages 568-601, where the arrangement by date is inconvenient, but the acknowledgement of his sources of information is extremely useful. It would also be difficult to improve on his general introduc- tion to the subject.

5.3 **Pak Sŏngǔi's** work, Kodae Sosŏl sa, "A History of *Kodae sosŏl*" was apparently first published in 1958, but unfortunately I did not see it until some time after the second edition came out in 1964, and I have therefore not made enough use of it to be able to assess it confidently. It is clearly reliable, but I have the impression, formed mainly by looking up individual stories in it, that it is far less original than other work which he has done.

5.4 **Sin Kihyŏng's** work, Han'guk Sosŏl Paltal sa, "A History of the Develop- ment of the Korean Novel" (1960), reached me even later, when I had practi- cally completed this survey of the subject, and so again I cannot assess it fairly. It appears to be orthodox and full of factual information on the whole, but no great reliance should be placed on the brief notes on the works which he gives in his table, pages 473-486.

5.5 There is one more general survey of this subject, 周王山 Chu Wangsan: 朝鮮古代小說史 Chosón Kodae Sosŏl sa, "A History of Korean *Kodae sosŏl*" (正音社 Chŏngǔm sa, Seoul, 1950, 319 pages), but this is not easily obtainable nowadays, seems to contain no information that is not available elsewhere, and in any case has an index which makes reference to it easy enough should any- one wish to consult it.

5.6 All general surveys of Korean literature of course give some information on *kodae sosŏl*, but almost everything of value in them has been incorporated into the works just described. Reference to general surveys of Korean litera- ture is, however, occasionally useful because they publish information derived from texts in their authors' private possession. This is particularly often the case with two works by **Yi Pyŏnggi,** which are given in the **Index of Brief References,** his **Kungmunhak Kaeron,** "A Survey of Korean Literature" (1961), and, together with **Paek Ch'ŏl, Kungmunhak Chŏnsa.** "The History of Korean Literature" (1957 and 1961). Slightly different is the case of **Yi Nŭngu's Kungmunhak Kaeron,** "A Survey of Korean Literature" (1954 and 1955). Yi Nŭngu is one of the few fortunate Koreans who has seen the collections described below in London, Paris and Tokyo, as well as the Asami collection, now in Berkeley, and the section of his work on *kodae sosŏl* is essentially a list of some of the texts in those collections. Therefore, if one can trace any reference to a story back to a mention of it by Yi Nŭngu in this work, one knows the precise value of the reference.

5.7 There is one more general survey of Korean literature which needs to be mentioned here, not only because fairly frequent reference to it is necessary and its short chapter on novels is one of the best organized accounts which I have read, but also because the circumstances surrounding it are too complicated to be indicated briefly at every mention of it. Kim Kidong gives as the source of some of his information 우리어문학회 Uri Ŏmunhak hoe, compiled: 國文學概論 **Kungmunhak kaeron,** "A Survey of Korean Literature", published, he reports, by 一成堂書店 Ilsŏngdang Sŏjŏm, presumably in Seoul, in 1949. I have been given to understand that some of the compilers of this work went to North Korea in 1950, either taking with them or losing during the war a number of texts which were the only sources for some of the information given in their work, but I have not been able to find a copy of that work. A second edition was put out by three remaining members of the society, **Ku Chagyun, Son Nakpŏm and Kim Hyŏnggyu,** and the same publishers in 1955, and I have given references to this where Kim Kidong refers to the 1949 edition, but I have no means of knowing how much the two editions may differ.

5.8 Books devoted to particular stories are all given under the appropriate entries, if only because they carry full texts, but of the hundreds of articles which I have read, I have listed only the few which give factual information on any story or text which is not available elsewhere, or which reprint a text. The articles which are not listed tend to be critical assessments of the better known stories. They are all written from a far deeper appreciation and wider experience of Korean literature than I ever expect to achieve, and i hope that westerners who take up the subject will be able to find their way to them through the excellent bibliographies of scholarly work which are available.

6. Stories Known by Title Only.

6.1 In all too many cases, about one third of the entries, the only information given is a bare mention of the title in one or more sources. Nearly one hundred of the titles given by **Courant** in his bibliography (1894-1901, see the **Index of Brief References**) have not been found in any text. This compares with some fifty of his titles given from identified texts and a further twenty or so found in other texts, notably texts in the Palace Library, described below §12, 10. The mention of a title by Courant cannot be lightly disregarded. In many cases his mention of a text is the best information we have for the dating of a work, and we may suppose, knowing the number of works which have been lost in the last twenty years or so, that many more may have disappeared in the last seventy years. On the other hand, Courant does make some demonstrable mistakes, such as giving a separate entry, 짐흥전 <u>Chim Hŭng chyŏn</u>, for one identified text of a story which he gives elsewhere correctly as **64** 김홍전 **Kim Hong chŏn**. Therefore, at least when Courant himself expresses doubt about a title, as he does with the last twelve in his first volume, we may share that doubt, and we may have reservations about others too if we cannot find any supporting evidence for the existence of stories of those titles.

6.2 **Kim T'aejun** seldom mentions a title without giving at least a short note on the work, though it is equally seldom that he identifies a text. There are about sixty titles mentioned by him which have not been found in texts, about half of which are quoted from Courant.

6.3 **Kim Kidong** quotes about forty of these sixty titles from Kim T'aejun without giving any further information. Besides these, he has another seventy titles, approximately, which he describes as 未發表 (I translate this "not made known before" at each relevant entry), and which I have not found on any text. His source for most of these is, I understand, texts in the National Library in Seoul (see §13.2, below), mostly modern printings, but also a few manuscripts. These may therefore be fairly confidently accepted as titles of works existing in the form which he indicates, paperback (see §11.2, below) or manuscript.

6.4.1 Another source for many titles on which no information appears to be available is the catalogue of an exhibition of works of Korean classical litera-ture (朝鮮古典文學作品展覽會目錄 <u>Chosŏn Kojŏn Munhak Chakp'um Chŏllamhoe Mongnok</u>) held at Seoul University under the auspices of its Department of Korean Language and Literature on October 24th, 25th and 26th, 1947. I refer to this briefly as the **1947 exhibition**, and am much indebted to Professor

Chŏng Pyŏnguk for a copy of this catalogue, with his correction of some of the entries and his notes on what was and was not shown. About three hundred items are listed for exhibition, one hundred and seventy of which are classi-fied as *sosŏl*. Eighteen of the *sosŏl* texts which are described as being in *hanmun* are of stories which I have not found in old Korean. Of the remaining *sosŏl* texts, forty five were not actually shown, including all twenty eight noted as belonging to 趙潤濟 Cho Yunje, the authority on Korean literature who has described his feelings on being forced to sell his books in **Hyŏndae Munhak**, 99-105, March-September 1963.

6.4.2 Some forty of the titles given as of *sosŏl* in this catalogue have not been found even mentioned elsewhere. These forty belong, or, in most cases, unfortunately, belonged to a number of individuals and institutions, but one curious group is the five texts, items 178-182, which are all the texts of *sosŏl* noted as belonging to 通文舘 T'ongmun'gwan. The only well known T'ongmun-gwan today is the business of one of the best publishers and book-dealers in Seoul, Mr Yi Kyŏmno (李謙魯), who is reputed also to have an extensive private library. The five items are four manuscripts, of 264 영소전역대 **Yŏngsojŏn Yŏktae**, 393 적성호연 **Chŏk Sŏng Hoyŏn**, 471 평등관 **P'yŏng-dŭng-gwan** and 520 황명배신전 **Hwangmyŏng Paesin chŏn**, none of which I can even romanise with confidence, and one movable type print (活版), the only such shown in the exhibition, of a story on which I have more questions than facts, 458 최충전 **Ch'oe Ch'ung chŏn**.

6.4.3 Other exhibitors in 1947 included 方鍾鉉 Pang Chonghyŏn and 李秉岐 Yi Pyŏnggi, whose collections, subsequently, alas, much reduced, are now in Seoul University as the **Ilsa** and **Karam collections** respectively (see §12.13, and the **Index of Brief References**); 李海晴 Yi Haech'ŏng, of the Royal Yi family and owner of many texts from a royal household, who was at Seoul Uni-versity between 1945 and 1950; 鄭炳昱 Chŏng Pyŏnguk, whose collection as in 1962 is included in my list of texts, see §12.4; 李熙昇 Yi Hŭisŭng, now Emeri-tus Professor of Korean at Seoul University (one text only, of 222 수호지 **Suho chi**); 宋錫夏 Song Sŏkha, who published works on folklore; 李明善 Yi Myŏngsŏn and 金三不 Kim Sambul, two eminent literary scholars who went to North Korea in 1950; and 金益煥 Kim Ikhwan and 金慶春 Kim Kyŏngch'un, on whom I have no further information. Texts from Seoul University, Ewha Woman's University and the **Palace** library were also shown.

7. The Origins of the Stories.

7.1 When stories are well represented by texts, which hardly ever go back beyond the middle of the nineteenth century, there is always considerable speculation as to where the story came from before that. There is usually very little factual evidence, unless the characters or events can be identified as historical, and therefore what little there is tends to take on an exaggerated importance, as is the case with **500 홍길동전 Hong Kiltong chŏn**, for instance, and, as a result, to be difficult to reject without denying a wide range of accepted opinions, as is shown by 丁奎福 Chŏng Kyubok's work on **31 구운몽 Kuun mong**. However, all indications which have been given by others of any history to a story before the date of the earliest text which carries it are mentioned under the relevant entry. In addition it is necessary to describe here one early Japanese work to which considerable importance has been attached by Korean literary historians, and also a group of sources which give information on the oral tradition of certain stories in *p'ansori* form.

7.2 Shōsho Kibun

7.2.1 The Japanese work is 象胥紀聞 Shōsho Kibun, "Notes Made by Interpreters". This is described in Japanese reference works as a work compiled as a result of the visits of delegations from abroad to Japan. It is said to exist in manuscripts of three volumes and to have been compiled by 小田幾五郎 Oda Ikugorō, with a preface dated 寛政六年, 1794. I have not seen any copy of this.

7.2.2 **Kim T'aejun**, 216, has the following reference to it:

日本의 象胥記聞及 拾遺에 依하면 (喜永三年傳寫本에 依함) 조선의 通俗物語條
下에 「崔忠傳 林慶業傳 伯龍傳 其他宋代物語 玉嬌梨傳 淑香傳 李白慶傳 三國志等
通俗物多」라고 하였으니 그 象胥紀聞이 純祖時代의 作이라고 假定할지라도 .....

"According to the Japanese 'Notes Made by Interpreters', with 'Supplement' (manuscript copy made in 1850), under the section 'Popular Tales in Korea': 'There are many popular ones, such as Ch'oe Ch'ung chŏn, Yim Kyŏngŏp chŏn, Paengnyong chŏn, other stories from the Sung period, Okkyori chŏn, Sukhyang chŏn, Yi Paekkyŏng chŏn and Samgukchi.' If we assume that 'Notes Made by Interpreters' is a work of the early nineteenth century....."

The 'Supplement' is described by Japanese sources as a Meiji manuscript, and it seems clear that Kim T'aejun had not seen the preface mentioned above.

7.2.3 Kim Tonguk, 382 (1960: 41, see the **Index of Brief References**), makes the following reference:

正祖十八年 山田士雲의 「象胥記聞」에 「張豊雲傳 九雲夢 崔賢傳 蘇大成傳 張朴傳 林將軍忠烈傳 蘇雲傳 崔忠傳 泗(謝)氏傳 淑香傳 玉橋(梨)傳 李白慶傳 三國誌」등이 諺文으로 쓰여졌음을 밝히고 있음으로써도 .....

".... and since it is made clear in 'Notes Made by Interpreters' by Yamada Shiun, 1794, that Chang P'ungun chŏn, Kuun mong, Ch'oe Hyŏn chŏn, So Taesŏng chŏn, Chang Pak chŏn, Yim Changgun Ch'ungnyŏl chŏn, So Un chŏn, Ch'oe Ch'ung chŏn, Sa-ssi chŏn, Sukhyang chŏn, Okkyo(ri) chŏn, Yi Paekkyŏng chŏn and Samgukchi had been written in Korean ....."

He also gives 山田士雲：象胥記聞 in the list of works consulted (page 401, 1960:67)

7.2.4 The actual date of this Japanese work as between 1794 and 1850 might be immaterial since (according to George M. McCune: "The Exchange of Envoys between Korea and Japan during the Tokugawa Period", Far Eastern Quarterly, V 3, May 1946, 308-325) there was no official delegation from Korea to Japan between 1763 and 1876, but if the Supplement is earlier than 1876 the date might be critical, and the discrepancies between the two quotations from the work are in any case puzzling. Apart from the difference between "there are many popular ones" and "it is made clear that ..... had been written in Korean", the titles do not agree.

7.2.5 Four titles appear in both quotations:

崔忠傳: see **458** 최충전 **Ch'oe Ch'ung chŏn**. This is based on the life of an historical Korean person of the ninth century, one text in *hanmun* is said to be of the early seventeenth century, and there are texts in Korean from at least the second half of the nineteenth century.

三國誌: see **156** 삼국지연의 **Samgukchi Yŏnŭi**. This is the title of one of the best known works of Chinese fiction. It is said that the work was known in Korea from about 1600 on, and the earliest dated Korean text is 1859.

李白慶傳: listed as **343** 이백경전 **Yi Paekkyŏng chŏn**, this title is known only from these quotations.

淑香傳: see **225** 숙향전 **Sukhyang chŏn**. The derivation of this story is not known but reference was made to it in the 1754 *hanmun* version of **460** 춘향전 **Ch'un-hyang chŏn**, there are texts in Korean dated 1858, and there are texts in *hanmun* which may be earlier.

7.2.6 Two more titles appear in slightly different forms in the two quotations: 林慶業傳 (Kim T'aejun) and 林將軍忠烈傳 (Kim Tonguk): these are both clearly **363** 임경업전 **Yim Kyŏngŏp chŏn**. There are many accounts in *hanmun* of the life of Yim Kyŏngŏp (1594-1646), probably with varying amounts of fictional embellishments, including one dated 1711, and many texts in Korean from about 1880 on.

玉嬌梨傳 (Kim T'aejun) and 玉橋(梨)傳 (Kim Tonguk): listed as **271** 옥교리전 **Okkyori chŏn**. This is clearly the Chinese novel 玉嬌梨(小傳) Yü-chiao-li (Hsiao-chuan), but it is not known otherwise in Korean.

7.2.7 Kim T'aejun gives one title which is not given by Kim Tonguk: 伯龍傳: listed as **124** 백룡전 **Paengnyong chŏn**, but known only from this mention of it. It is followed in the quotation given by Kim T'aejun by "[and?] other stories from the Sung period", which is also not given by Kim Tonguk.

7.2.8 Kim Tonguk gives seven titles which are not given by Kim T'aejun: 張朴傳: listed as **376** 장박전 **Chang Pak chŏn**, which is known only from this mention of it.

崔賢傳: this has the same form in Korean, see **459** 최현전 **Ch'oe Hyŏn chŏn**, as the title of a text which was shown in the 1947 exhibition, but which now seems to be lost. The story is not known.

九雲夢 and 泗(謝)氏傳: see **31** 구운몽 **Kuun mong** and **149** 사씨남정기 **Sa-ssi Namjŏng ki**. These two works have been long supposed to have been written in Korean about 1700, but it is doubtful whether any of the texts which we now have can confidently be regarded as works of earlier than about 1800.

蘇大成傳, 蘇雲傳 and 張豊雲傳: see **194** 소대성전 **So Taesŏng chŏn**, **208** 소학사전 **So Haksa chŏn** and **385** 장풍운전 **Chang P'ungun chŏn**. These works may be Chinese in origin, but their history as works in Korean previous to the dates of the earliest known texts, of the middle and late nineteenth century, is not known.

7.2.9 Thus the evidence of these quotations cannot be regarded as unimpeachable, and the information given which is not given elsewhere is slight. Their value, if they can be verified, is that they might confirm the supposition, which is in any case not unreasonable, that some stories existed in Korean, perhaps in written form, at a date earlier than is shown by extant texts, and that other stories existed which are not now extant.

7.3 Stories in P'ansori.

7.3.1 The evidence for the currency of twelve stories in the repertoire of the *kwangdae* (廣大, etc., strolling players) is rather more diffuse. The style of singing which *kwangdae* use is called 판소리 *p'ansori*, and while it is clear what *kwangdae* and *p'ansori* are now, the precise meaning which the two terms might have had in the past, and exactly how long they have been around in Korea, is not certain. The fullest sources of information on the subject are two articles:

7.3.2 李惠求 Yi Hyegu: 宋晚載의 觀優戲 Song Manjae ŭi Kwan-u-hŭi, " 'At the Play', by Song Manjae" (Seoul, Chungang University: 中央大學校三十周年紀念論文集 Chungang Taehakkyo Samsip Chunyŏn Kinyŏm Nonmun chip, "Theses Collected in Commemoration of the Thirtieth Anniversary of Chungang University", 1955, 93-119. This is also separately paginated, but the references I give are to the pagination of the volume as a whole). The work Kwan-u-hŭi, "At the Play", is a poem, with preface and postface, in *hanmun* which refers to all twelve stories in the repertoire of the *kwangdae*. A manuscript of it was discovered in Yonsei University library, Seoul, in 1954, and Yi Hyegu suggests that it is probably a work of the early nineteenth century. The work is reprinted in full in this article, with the stanzas numbered. I give references to these also. The information on each story is slight, the nature of the material mades this study extremely exacting to read, and Kim Tonguk takes full account of it in his article, described next, but the discovery of this source has given us firm knowledge of a period on which there was previously only speculation, and Yi Hyegu's study is masterly.

7.3.3 金東旭 Kim Tonguk: 판소리發生攷 P'ansori Palsaeng ko, "A Consideration of the Origins of *P'ansori*" (Seoul, Seoul University: 서울大學校論文集, 人文社會科學, Sŏul Taehakkyo Nonmun chip, Inmun Sahoe Kwahak, "Seoul University Theses, Humanities and Social Sciences", 2, June 1955, 167-205, and 3, April 1956, 239-301) is the most complete survey of the subject which I know. All the references which I give are in fact to section three, where the stories are discussed individually, in volume 3 of the journal, between pages 250 and 287, but the whole study is thoroughly to be recommended.

7.3.4 There are apparently other works similar to Kwan-u-hŭi, such as 觀劇絕句 Kwan-gŭk Chŏlgwi, " 'At the Play', a *Chüeh-chü*", of 1826 by 申緯 ·Sin Wi (1769-1845, see Kim T'aejun, 198, Kim Tonguk, 13), 觀劇詩 Kwan-gŭk Si, " 'At the Play', a *Shih*", by 李裕元 Yi Yuwŏn (1814-1888, see Kim T'aejun, 126,

16

134, 136, 153, 197, **Kim Tonguk** 13-14), and 春陽打詠 Ch'unyang T'ayŏng,
(= Ch'unhyang T'aryŏng, "The Ballad of Ch'unhyang") by 趙在三 Cho Chaesam,
dated 1855 (See **Kim T'aejun**, 198-199, **Kim Tonguk**, 14), but the chief work of
reference before the two articles just given were published seems to have
been 鄭魯湜 Chŏng Nosik: 朝鮮唱劇史 Chosŏn Ch'anggŭk sa, "A History of
Korean Opera" (朝鮮日報社 Chosŏn Ilbo sa, Keijō, 1940). This is frequently
quoted in works on Korean literature, and seems to give slightly different information from that given in Kwan-u-hŭi, but I have not seen it and do not give
references to it.

7. 3. 5 Of the twelve stories which formed the repertoire of the *kwangdae* early
in the nineteenth century, three are known only from the brief references to
them in Kwan-u-hŭi and similar sources or in other oral traditions. These
three are listed, under **3** 가짜신선타령 **Katcha Sinsŏn T'aryŏng, 98** 매화전 **Maehwa
chŏn** and **296** 왈짜타령 **Waltcha T'aryŏng,** but only because they are mentioned
in most works on *kodae sosŏl.* All three are known by other titles as well, and
the first of them was later replaced by the story of **224** 숙영낭자전 **Sugyŏng
Nangja chŏn.**

7. 3. 6 Two of the stories, described under **121** 배비장전 **Pae Pijang chŏn** and
293 옹고집전 **Ong Kojip chŏn,** are popular satirical stories which originated in
Korea in the distant past. They were introduced into prose literature in Korean
from their *p'ansori* forms in the twentieth century. One more, described under
375 장끼전 **Changkki chŏn,** is a fable of which we have written forms in Korean
from the end of the nineteenth century which have not yet been fully investigated, but there seems to be little doubt that the current versions of the fable
have at least been influenced by the *p'ansori* forms.

7. 3. 7 The remaining six stories are known to have been rewritten for and
taught to particular singers by 申在孝 Sin Chaehyo (1812-1884) between 1866
and 1884. These occupy a unique position in that we have texts of Sin Chaehyo's
works, that is texts of these stories of known authorship. Though these are in
rhythmic style used in *p'ansori,* it is generally held by Korean literary historians that his work is of a very high quality, and it may be due to his mastery
that the *p'ansori* versions have now replaced any earlier prose versions in
the tradition of most of these stories.

7. 3. 8 The stories described under **229** 심청전 **Sim Ch'ŏng chŏn, 460** 춘향전
Ch'unhyang chŏn and **531** 흥부전 **Hŭngbu chŏn** are the three firm favourites
among the stories of *kodae sosŏl.* The first two seem to be completely Korean
in origin, and, although the third is similar to stories known elsewhere in the

17

Far East, it circulates in Korea in a distinctively Korean form. In each case there are other traditions which can be found in prose versions in Korean from about the time at which Sin Chaehyo was composing his version or earlier, but a *p'ansori* version is the source of what is now the dominant tradition of all three.

7.3.9 In the case of the fable described under **468 토끼전 T'okki chŏn**, there are prose versions in Korean from the last decade of the nineteenth century and later, which are still to be investigated, but there seems to be little doubt that what is now the dominant tradition of this story has its source in a *p'ansori* version.

7.3.10 The story described under **391 적벽가 Chŏkpyŏk ka** is derived from the Chinese novel San-kuo-chih Yen-i (see **156 삼국지연의 Samgukchi Yŏnŭi**). A *p'ansori* version of this is probably the source for the story printed in Chŏnju under the title **514 화용도 Hwayongdo**, and the separate tradition of this is still continued. However, there have been several other traditions of stories from San-kuo-chih Yen-i, which can be found in prose versions in Korean from both before and after Sin Chaehyo made his version of Chŏkpyŏk ka, and the current practice is rather to derive the whole work from a Chinese version.

7.3.11 The story described under **1 가루지기타령 Karujigi T'aryŏng** seems to have been widely regarded as being in bad taste. There are other oral traditions, but it has never, as far as is known, been taken as the story of a novel. There are several texts of it in the story-tellers' rhythmic style, all of which probably derive from Sin Chaehyo's version.

7.3.12 For the texts of Sin Chaehyo's works, we now have, according to the catalogue of the **Karam collection:** "申五衛將本集 Sin Owijang Pon chip, 'The Collected Texts of Sin Chaehyo's Works', a work of the late nineteenth century, manuscript, 6 vols, compiled by his grandson (申)燦泳 (Sin) Ch'anyŏng in the year 壬午". Among the contents are given: in vol. 1: 春香歌 Ch'unhyang ka (=**460 춘향전 Ch'unhyang chŏn**); in vol. 2: 沈晴歌 Sim Ch'ŏng ka (=**229 심청전 Sim Ch'ŏng chŏn**), and 赤壁歌 (=**391 적벽가**) Chŏkpyŏk ka; in vol. 3: 橫負歌 Hoengbu ka (= **1 가루지기타령 Karujigi T'aryŏng**); in vol. 5: 兎鱉歌 T'obyŏl ka (= **468 토끼전 T'okki chŏn**); and in vol. 6: 박타령 Pak T'aryŏng (= 531 흥부전 Hŭngbu chŏn). It would seem, then, that there should be no further problems in ascertaining the texts of Sin Chaehyo's works. However, it has not been published yet, and it may be as well to go into the subject a little more here.

18

7.3.13 This text was in Yi Pyŏnggi's private collection before he presented his collection to Seoul University library, and the information on the texts of Sin Chaehyo's works which has appeared here and there in publications before the catalogue was published in 1966 raises several questions. As to the title, that given in the catalogue is unusual, and one wonders whether 本集 is not a single word, *ponjip*, "Original Collection", indicating perhaps that it is an authoritative version intended to correct other, unauthorized versions. In the 1947 exhibition, item 82, from Yi Pyŏnggi's collection, was 申五衛將全集 Sin Owijang Chŏnjip, which is a more usual form of title (and possibly therefore less likely to be correct), "The Complete Works of Sin Chaehyo". This text also differs, apparently, in size and in content from the "Collected Texts". It is described as a manuscript of 5 vols, and it would appear that these are equivalent to vols 1, 2, 5, 3 and 4 of the "Collected Texts" as in the 1966 catalogue. No such work as is given in the catalogue of the 1947 exhibition appears now in the catalogue of the Karam collection, and one wonders whether the two are not the same. Then there is the question of its date. If the "Collected Texts" is a "a work of the late nineteenth century", one might expect the year 壬午 to be 1882. However, such compilations by descendants are not usually made during the author's lifetime, and there are indications that Sin Chaehyo might still have been working on his compositions in 1882 (see, for instance, **Kim Tonguk**, 111, on the date of Sin Chaehyo's Karujigi T'aryŏng). In addition, although I have no clear information on Sin Ch'anyŏng, **Kim Tonguk**, 110, dates his obituary of his grandfather as 1932, and it would therefore not be entirely unreasonable to suppose that the "Collected Texts" (or "Authorized Version of the Works") was compiled in 1942. If this is correct, the discrepancies of title, size and contents as given in 1947 and 1966 is puzzling, and the source of a text of 1942 would also have to be sought.

7.3.14 When 姜漢永 Kang Hanyŏng first published the text of Sin Chaehyo's Ch'unhyang ka (in **Kugŏ Kungmunhak**, 5-9, June 1953-January 1954), he gave as the source for his text a copy made in 1907 by 柳寵錫 Yu Nongsŏk of a text owned by Sin Chaehyo's only son (who must also therefore be Sin Ch'anyŏng's father) 申錫卿 Sin Sŏkkyŏng. He reported that Yu Nongsŏk had already made another copy of this work in 1904 or earlier, and that he had made copies of Chŏkpyŏk ka in 1904 and of Pak T'aryŏng in 1903. These, he stated, are known as 柳氏本 *Yu-ssi pon* or 星斗本 *Sŏngdu pon*. When Kang Hanyŏng republished Ch'unhyang ka in 1959, it was described as the first volume in a series which would reprint all Sin Chaehyo's works (as described in the catalogue of the

Karam collection), and he has also republished separately texts of works which are to be found in each of the six volumes except volume 5. It would therefore seem that Kang Hanyŏng either owns or at least has access to copies of all Sin Chaehyo's works made from a family source in the first decade of this century. One would like to know, then, what is the relationship between these and the texts in the Karam collection.

7.3.15 Furthermore, there seem to be other sources, or possible sources, for texts of Sin Chaehyo's works. One work which is referred to in several studies is 李善有 Yi Sŏnyu's 五歌全集 Oga Chŏnjip, "Complete Collection of the Five Songs". A copy of this was shown in the **1947 exhibition**, item 12, as a modern printing of one volume, owned by Yi Pyŏnggi, and containing all the stories which were rewritten by Sin Chaehyo except Karujigi T'aryŏng. **Yi Pyŏnggi: Kungmunhak Kaeron**, 153, describes it as published by Yi Sŏnyu of Chinju in 1933, and suggests that the text had been taken from the singing of a certain *kisaeng* of Chinju who had been trained by Sin Chaehyo. The differences which he shows between passages from this and from the "Collected Texts" on the following pages are considerable. If there are oral traditions of Sin Chaehyo's works which differ from the written traditions, then one might also examine the modern versions of the stories which are also derived from oral traditions to see whether they throw any light on the question.

7.3.16 In short, while one must accept the view of contemporary Korean literary historians on the importance which the works of Sin Chaehyo have in the history of certain stories of *kodae sosŏl*, what the Sin Chaehyo version of any work was exactly is still not clear.

8. The Texts.

8.1 The texts which tell each story in Korean in a traditional style are listed. No limit has been set in respect of their dates. The descriptions of them are taken mainly from notes made on visits to various collections, described below, §12, between 1961 and 1965. These notes have been compared, where possible, with published catalogues and other descriptions of the texts in question, and any discrepancies noted, and the texts which I have not seen, but which are mentioned by others, are also given, with an acknowledgement of the source of the information, see §13 and the **Index of Brief References**, and such description of the texts as they give. Where some connection has been established or can be suggested with Chinese or *hanmun* works, I have tried to discover what texts of those Chinese or *hanmun* works there might be, but the notes given on this point are not the result of any persistent investigation or close scrutiny.

8.2 In the few cases in which the relationship between various texts has been clearly established, for instance in the case of **485 한중록 Hanjung nok**, they are presented in accordance with that relationship. However, in most cases this has not been established, and the texts are listed with manuscript copies first, then old prints, from engraved wood blocks, and lastly modern printed editions. Within each group the texts are generally listed in order of date. Undated copies are listed after dated copies, unless there is sufficient indication of date to make it preferable to list undated copies in probable date order.

9. Manuscripts.

9.1 Manuscripts are placed first because there might be among them copies which are older than those of the more surely dated printed texts. It should be stressed, however, that there is not a single manuscript which is explicitly dated as earlier than the 1880's, while there are many which are explicitly dated as twentieth century, and it is only very rarely that there is any external evidence at all on the texts themselves, such as the seal prints on some texts in the Palace library, for any dating earlier than the middle of the nineteenth century. For the dating of most manuscripts a much closer examination of the internal evidence would be necessary than I could possibly have given in the course of this investigation, but where such close examinations have been made by Korean scholars, as with **31 구운몽 Kuun mong** and **485 한중록 Hanjung nok**, for instance, not a single case of a manuscript being earlier than the middle of the nineteenth century has yet been proved. Indeed, I know of only one case, that of the Seoul University manuscript of <u>Kuun mong</u>, where an earlier date has even been suggested from a close study of the internal evidence, and there is no agreement in this case. It would therefore seem reasonable to stipulate that any suggestion of an earlier date for a manuscript be proved beyond all doubt before it is accepted. However these general circumstances cannot be decisive in the dating of any particular text. The problem of dating is most specific in the cases of the many manuscripts which are dated only as one of the the years of the sixty year cycle. In such cases I have only given them a definite date A.D., for instance "신히 (辛亥, 1911)", when I have found positive indications of the actual date. These can range from the text in question being written on the back of paper which has already been used for the writing or printing of a dated text to a feeling based on the total appearance of a text, but

I have tried not to be positive about such dates, if the evidence is not clearly definable, without taking expert Korean advice. Where I have finally felt any doubt at all myself, I have given what seems to be the latest possible date, followed by "etc.". Thus "무인 (戊寅 1878, etc.)" means that the date might be 1818, or even any earlier date which might be so indicated, but that 1938 is very unlikely and 1878 the most likely date.

9.2 In some cases it has been possible to indicate the nature of a manuscript in a brief note. There is often a great deal of detail in the colophon of a manuscript which I have not given, such as the name of the copyist, his address, age, and so on, the day, even the hour, when he began and finished copying it out, and almost always an apology for the quality of the work. Such things must be investigated more thoroughly one day, but for the moment I have considered it sufficient to give the location, title(s), date and size of any manuscript, the size in terms of number of volumes, double leaves per volume, columns of writing on the average single side of a leaf, and syllables in the average column. However, I have tried to note those manuscript copies which were made by Japanese, usually by adding "by Hashimoto [橋本]" or "by Nakamura [中村]", and also those copies which were made for use in lending libraries. These last tend to be of a uniform size, about 30 leaves to a volume, and their leaves are usually numbered. They are generally rather poorly written in the first place, and nearly always in very worn condition, and they seem as a rule to carry much longer versions of the stories than any other texts.

10. Block Prints.

10.1 The block prints (xylographs is a widely used term for them) fall into three groups, those made in Seoul, those made in Ansŏng (安城) in Kyŏnggi Province, about 40 miles south of Seoul, and those made in Chŏnju (全州), capital of Chŏlla North Province, which is about another 80 miles in the same direction, and the centre of an area in which the performances of *kwangdae* were particularly popular. Those made in Chŏnju are very distinctive, mainly because of the triangular shape of the circles in the letters *iŭng* and *hiŭt*, and the titles are usually followed by the verb *(i)ra*: "This is . . . . .". Their colophons when they have them, identify them as having been made in 完山 or 완산 Wansan, an old name for Chŏnju, usually in a particular district of Wansan, and they are usually therefore now called 完板本 *Wanp'an pon*, "Chŏnju block prints". Seoul and Ansŏng block prints are so similar to each other in appearance that no one claims to be able to identify any particular copy as one or the other unless it has an identifying colophon. Since Seoul block prints are by far the more commonly found, it is usually assumed that any copy is a Seoul block print unless there is a definite indication to the contrary. Seoul block prints (called 京板本 *Kyŏngp'an pon*) indicate their place of origin as a district of Seoul, without, however, any word for Seoul itself. The names for the districts are not those in official use now, but some of them continue in unofficial use and most of the others have been found in historical documents. Ansŏng block prints (安城板本 *Ansŏngp'an pon*) have only one form of colophon: 안셩동문이신판 "Newly engraved at Tongmun-ni, Ansŏng".

10.2 About fifty stories have been found in Seoul block print editions, some of them in several editions, giving something like a hundred known editions altogether. Perhaps as many as a dozen stories can be found in Ansŏng block print editions, all of them also found in Seoul block print editions. Among the Chŏnju block prints one can find about fifteen stories, some in several editions, but the information on this subject is not clear enough to be summarised here.

10.3 The study of these block prints is very much hampered by the smallness of the number of actual copies that survive. It is true that there may be as many as five hundred copies of Seoul block prints, and others are still coming to light, even being offered for sale in Seoul, but they are mainly to be found in small numbers in various collections scattered literally right round the world. Even so, in most cases it is obvious that every single copy of one story is from a different engraving, more often than not from a completely different edition. With the Chŏnju block prints, the number of known copies is so small that it is difficult to form any complete picture of the printing of texts there, and with the Ansŏng block prints there are so few that no one even seems to have tried to go into the question deeply. There is, however, one outstanding study of the whole subject, **Kim Tonguk**'s article 한글小說坊刻本의成立에對하여 Han' gŭl Sosŏl Panggak pon ŭi Sŏngnip e tae hayŏ, "On the Rise of the Locally Printed Texts of Novels in Korean". This was first published in 鄕土서울 Hyangt'o Sŏul, journal of 서울特別市史編纂委員會 Sŏul T'ŭkpyŏlsi sa P'yŏnch'an Wiwŏnhoe, "Committee for the Compilation of the History of Seoul City", no. 8, July 1960, pages 38-67, but it was reprinted, with some revisions, in his Ch'unhyang chŏn Yŏn'gu, "A Study of the Ch'unhyang Story", and it is to this work, full details of which are given in the **Index of Brief References** which follows this Introduction, that I refer, by its author's name only, for information on block prints. In this second publication, Kim Tonguk gives a reference, page 401, to 李能雨 Yi Nŭngu: 이야기册"古代小說"板本誌略 Iyagi ch'aek "Kodae Sosŏl" P'anbon Chiryak,

Introduction: 10.4-11.2

"A Note on the Block Prints of the Popular Novels '*Kodae Sosŏl*'", 淑大論文集 <u>Suktae Nonmunjip</u>, "Sungmyŏng Women's University Theses", 4, July 1964, but unfortunately I have not seen this.

10.4 By far the greater number of these block prints bear no date, and those which do have a date are dated only by the designation of one of the sixty years of the cycle. Nevertheless Kim Tonguk seems not to doubt that all surviving copies date from about the middle of the nineteenth century or later, even well into the twentieth century, and such evidence as there is points very clearly to this conclusion. The coincidence with the earliest established dates for manuscripts both emphasizes the need for extreme caution in dating any manuscripts as earlier than the middle of the nineteenth century, and indicates that, if novels were written before that date, they were at least not very widely circulated and read.

11. Modern Printings.

11.1 Modern printings in movable type are of various sorts, and it is obvious that all scholarly editions of old texts have had to be included in this list of texts. One can include in this the **Ewha Series** (see the **Index of Brief References**), with its facsimile reproductions of seventeen old texts, but in other cases some judgement has had to be exercised. I have tried to follow the rule of including modern texts only if they preserve the traditional style of the stories, but this style is made up of a variety of features, plot, form, wording and grammar, for instance, and it is open to debate how much a work can be altered without being considered as a modern rewriting. Since the list is designed primarily to make known to westerners where they may find texts of these stories, I have tended to include doubtful cases, but, as a general rule, probably nothing is included which shows more sign of having been rewritten than the **Hŭimang Series** (again in the **Index of Brief References**). This virtually had to be included because of the number of stories which it makes available, and the status of the editors of the various stories.

11.2 Even with this liberal interpretation of the notion of a text of a *kodae sosŏl* in traditional form, one cannot but have serious misgivings about including the many editions which I refer to as "paperbacks". They are not very prepossessing to look at, with their gaudy covers, and the texts tend to be almost exact reprints of each other, with only the covers changed, and even on the front of the cover the picture tends to be reproduced very accurately however often the publisher's and author's names change. They are often published in one and

24

the same copy by more than one publisher, and attributed to more than one author in different copies, the permutations and combinations for some identical texts being almost endless. The texts themselves are usually printed in the large, squarish type known in Korean as 新活字 *Sin-hwalcha*, "New Movable Type", which came into use with "New Literature" in the early years of the twentieth century, but was generally replaced by the styles of type now commonly in use during the late nineteen twenties. The Sammun sa, Taejo sa and Sech'ang Sŏgwan recent paperbacks (after about 1957) have changed to more modern styles. What I call paperbacks seem first to have been called in Korean 六錢小說, *Yuk chŏn Sosŏl*, "Sixpenny Novels", when 崔南善 Ch'oe Namsŏn published them, from about 1911 on, with the aim of making literature in Korean widely available, but they have since been called 딱지小說 *Ttakchi Sosŏl*, "Pulp Novels", or generally included in the term 이야기冊 *Iyagi ch'aek*, literally "Story Books", but often used in the sense of "popular novels". Still, whatever prejudices one might have against the paperbacks, prejudices which have a most respectable ancestry in well-bred Koreans' attitudes to all literature in Korean in the past, there is something to be said in their defence. They seldom give any indication that they are deliberate rewritings of old stories. Indeed comparison often shows that they are very faithful copies of old texts, and so, since they both indicate a continuing readership for *kodae sosŏl* and are the most widely available texts of the stories, I have listed all I have found.

11.3 The titles of these paperbacks as given are taken, without, as a rule, the descriptive pre-titles which are often used, from the first page of the text, and if there is any statement there of authorship or publication, this is also given. The information given on the covers is less useful, and has therefore not been fully copied. The titles on the covers have not been mentioned unless they contain information which is not available elsewhere, the names of the publishing houses have been given in romanised form only, the names of the authors given on the back covers have been omitted, and the place of publication has not been given. This last is in every case Seoul, sometimes under the name 漢城 Hansŏng in the earliest days, shortly after 1910, nearly always 京城 Keijō (Kyŏngsŏng in Korean) during the Japanese occupation, 1910-1945, occasionally 漢陽 Hanyang after 1945, and since then simply 서울 Sŏul (Seoul).

11.4 The following is a list, in ABC order, of the publishers of paperbacks given in texts which I have seen, together with those mentioned by Kim Kidong (see especially **Kim Kidong**, 28-35). I have not listed the agents (發賣所, 分賣店, etc.) given when they differ from the publishers as given, but I have

Introduction: 11.4

listed all the different publishers given together, except in the case of those associated with Sechʻang Sŏgwan, see below. The dates given are those on texts which I have seen or which Kim Kidong gives, and the names in brackets after some dates are those of the authors as given on the back covers. These are listed in the next paragraph.

Chinhŭng Sŏgwan 振興書館: between 1945 and 1950.

Chʻŏngsongdang Sŏjŏm 靑松當書店: 1916.

Chosŏn Sŏgwan 朝鮮書館: 1915.

Chosŏn Tosŏ Chusik Hoesa 朝鮮圖書株式會社: 1923, 1925 (two), 1928 (all Hong Sunpʻil).

Chungang Chʻulpʻansa 中央出版社: 1945 (two, Min Myŏngsŏn); also Chungang Insŏgwan 中央印書舘 and Chungang Sŏrim 中央書林, mentioned in several sources.

Haedong Sŏgwan 海東書館: 1918.

Hanhŭng Sŏrim 韓興書林: 1924, 1925 (Kang Ŭiyŏng).

Hannam Sŏrim 翰南書林: 1916, 1917, 1924. Also published many lithographic reprints of Seoul block prints, which I do not count as paperbacks.

Hansŏng Sŏgwan 漢城書館: 1915 (four, Namgung Sŏl), 1916, 1917, 1918 (Namgung Sŏl), 1920.

Hanyang Sŏjŏgŏp Chohapso 漢陽書籍業組合所 (see also Kyŏngsŏng.....): 1918 (Hyŏn Kongnyŏm).

Hoedong Sŏgwan 滙東書館: 1912, 1915 (Yi Kyuyong), 1916 (two, Yi Kyuyong), 1918, 1921 (Kim Tongjin), 1925, 1932 (Kang Ŭnhyŏng).

Imundang 以文堂: 1918.

Kongdong Munhwasa 共同文化社: 1954.

Kwangdong Sŏguk 光東書局: 1914 (Hyŏn Kongnyŏm), 1919 (Yi Chongjŏng), 1920, 1921 (Kim Tongjin), 1923.

Kwangmun Sŏsi 廣文書市 (or 光文書市): 1914, 1917, 1918, 1922.

Kyŏngsŏng Sŏgwan 京城書館: 1925 (Fukuda Shōtarō).

Kyŏngsŏng Sŏjŏgŏp Chohapso 京城書籍業組合所 (sometimes Sŏjŏk for Sŏjŏgŏp and Chohap for Chohapso, and see also Hanyang.....): 1916 (Hong Sunpʻil), 1920 (Kim Tongjin), 1924 (Hong Sunpʻil), 1926 (four, Hong Sunpʻil).

Pangmun Sŏgwan 博文書館: 1916 (two), 1917 (three, Kim Yongjun), 1919 (two, No Ikhyŏng), 1920, 1921 (Kim Tongjin), 1923 (three, Pak Kŏnhoe), 1924 (No Ikhyŏng), 1933 (No Ikhwan).

Pogŭp Sŏgwan 普及書館: 1918 (Hyŏn Kongnyŏm), 1918 (Pak Kŏnhoe), 1922.

Sammun sa 三文社 : in 1953 issued a volume called 朝鮮文學全集 Chosŏn
Munhak Chŏnjip, "The Complete Works of Korean Literature, Volume 5":
小說集 Sosŏl chip, "Collected Novels, Volume 1", containing several
kodae sosŏl. The texts are exactly as in other paperbacks, and the
author of the whole volume is given as Sin T'aehwa. There was also a
Sammunsa Sŏjŏm 三文社書店, which published in 1932 (Kang Ŭnhyŏng).

Sech'ang Sŏgwan 世昌書館 : 1915 (two), 1917, 1933 (Sin T'aesam), 1935 (Sin
T'aesam). These publishers are also the main publishers of paperbacks
today. They had over one hundred titles in stock in 1962, about sixty of
which were *kodae sosŏl*. Most of these bear the date 1952, but a few
have later dates, and the author is alway Sin T'aesam. Most of the
volumes give 文昌書館 Munch'ang Sŏgwan and 天一書館 Ch'ŏnil Sŏgwan
as joint publishers, but I have not seen any works published independently by either of these.

Sin'gu Sŏrim 新舊書林 : 1912, 1913 (two), 1914, 1915 (two, Pak Kŏnhoe), 1916
(two), 1917 (three), 1918 (Pak Kŏnhoe), 1919, 1922 (Chi Songuk), 1923
(one Chi Songuk, one No Ikhwan, and one other), 1926 (two), 1933 (No
Ikhwan).

Sinmun'gwan 新文舘 : founded by 崔南善 Ch'oe Namsŏn in 1911, and run in
the name of his brother 崔昌善 Ch'oe Ch'angsŏn, is reported to have
published many *kodae sosŏl*, but I have only seen one or two dated 1911
and 1913. In addition, Sinmun'gwan is given as the printer in some later
paperbacks from other publishers which I have seen.

Taech'ang Sŏwŏn 大昌書院 : 1917, 1918 (two, Pak Kŏnhoe), 1919, 1920
(Katsumoto Ryōkichi), 1921 (Kim Tongjin), 1922 (Hyŏn Kongnyŏm), 1923,
1926 (Hyŏn Kongnyŏm).

Taejo sa 大造社 : issued a three volume 小說集 Sosŏl chip, "Collected
Novels", containing sixteen *kodae sosŏl* in 1958. I have also seen their
separate publications of most of these dated 1959. No author is given
in any.

Taesan Sŏrim 大山書林 : 1925 (Yi Myŏnu), 1926 (Yi Myŏnu).

Taesŏng Sŏrim 大成書林 : 1925 (Kang Ŭnhyŏng), 1929 (Kang Ŭnhyŏng).

Tŏkhŭng Sŏrim 德興書林 : 1913, 1914 (two), 1916 (Kim Tongjin), 1921 (Kim
Tongjin), 1923 (Kim Tongjin), 1924 (Kim Tongjin), 1925 (two, Kim
Tongjin), 1931.

Tonga Sŏgwan 東亞書館 : 1916 (three, Kim Yŏn'gyu), 1917.

Tongmi Sŏsi 東美書市 : 1915 (one Pak Kŏnhoe, one Yi Yonghan), 1923.

Tongmun Sŏrim 同文書林: 1918.

Tongmyŏng Sŏgwan 東明書舘: 1915.

Tongyang Sŏwŏn 東洋書院: 1925 (two, Cho Namhŭi).

Yŏngch'ang Sŏgwan 永昌書舘: 1917, 1918 (two), 1924 (Kang Ŭiyŏng), 1925
   (Kang Ŭiyŏng), 1928, also several undated, some clearly before 1945,
   others probably after 1951.

Yŏnghwa Ch'ulp'ansa 永和出版社: 1958 (Kang Kŭnhyang), also several undated, probably after 1951. Several sources also mention a Yŏnghwa
   Sŏgwan 永和書舘.

Yŏngp'ung Sŏgwan 永豊書舘: 1913, 1914.

Yŏngp'ung Sŏsi 永豊書市: 1914 (Yi Chuhwan).

Yuil Sŏgwan 唯一書舘: 1912 (two, Namgung Chun), 1913 (Namgung Chun),
   1915 (two, Namgung Sŏl).

11.5 None of the authors given are recognized writers of *kodae sosŏl*. They
may perhaps be regarded as editors, though there is no sign in these publications that any significant amount of editing was done. The authors are sometimes described as "author and publisher", and occasionally given as the owner
of the publishing house. Sin T'aesam of Sech'ang Sŏgwan was still alive when I
was in Seoul in 1962, but I was not able to visit him. I was told that he was "an
old man in the country with a large collection of books", which may, of course,
have been earlier paperbacks. The following is a list, again in ABC order, of
these authors with the characters for their names and the dates or ranges of
dates of the books in which their names have been seen:

Chi Songuk 池松旭 1922-23

Cho Namhŭi 趙男熙 1925

Fukuda Shōtarō 福田正太郎 1925

Hong Sunp'il 洪淳泌 1916-28

Hyŏn Kongnyŏm 玄公廉 1914-26

Kang Kŭnhyang 姜槿響 1958

Kang Ŭiyŏng 姜義永 1918-25

Kang Ŭnhyŏng 姜殷馨 1925-32

Katsumoto Ryōkichi 勝本良吉 1920

Kim Tongjin 金東縉 1916-25

Kim Yongjun 金容俊 1917

Kim Yŏn'gyu 金然奎 1916

Min Myŏngsŏn 閔明善 1945

Namgung Chun 南宮濬 1912-13

Namgung Sŏl 南宮楔 1915-18

No Ikhwan 盧益煥 1923-33

No Ikhyŏng 盧益亨 1919-24

Pak Kŏnhoe 朴健會 1915-23

Sin T'aehwa 申泰和 1953

Sin T'aesam 申泰三 1933-61

Yi Chongjŏng 李鍾楨 1919

Yi Chuhwan 李柱浣 1914

Yi Kyuyong 李圭瑢 1915-16

Yi Myŏnu 李冕宇 1925-26

Yi Yonghan 李容漢 1915

Fukuda Shōtarō and Katsumoto Ryōkichi are, of course, Japanese names, but whether the persons are Japanese or Korean I cannot say. There is also another name which looks Japanese, but for which I cannot suggest a reading 木竟樵夫, in an undated publication by Yǒngch'ang Sǒgwan. For Namgung Chun, see Yi and **Paek: Kungmunhak Chǒnsa,** page 242. Pak Kǒnhoe also appears often at the beginning of texts as the author, and there his *ho* is sometimes given as 快齋 K'waejae.

11.6 The back cover of most paperbacks also gives a list of the titles currently available from the publishers. When I have had sufficient time in any place to check these lists, I have noted the titles advertised. A note has been given under each entry of the dates on which the titles have been advertised by various publishers, unless the actual publications have been seen or have been reported. Each list contains between fifty and one hundred and twenty titles, approximately, most about one hundred, giving altogether over one hundred and fifty titles in the lists which I have seen. No title appears in more than about two thirds of the lists which I have seen, and some in only one, two or three.

11.7 I have seen altogether about one hundred and fifteen *kodae sosǒl* in paperback publications, seventy five of which, approximately, have also been found in manuscript or block print copies. A further fifty or more titles have been seen in advertisements in paperbacks, one third of which have also been found in other texts. **Kim Kidong** mentions more than sixty more titles as having been published in paperbacks, of which less than a quarter have been found in any text at all. It would therefore seem that I have seen only between a half and two thirds of the *kodae sosǒl* which are to be found in paperback editions, and only a very small proportion of what purport, on their covers, to be different editions. While this last point may not be serious, since such different paperback editions tend to be very close to each other in text, it is clearly not easy to find any texts at all of many of the *kodae sosǒl* which have been mentioned in the literary histories, and extremely difficult to find any old texts, using "old" even in the sense of "before 1910", of the vast majority of the stories. One can only hope that this list of texts will be speedily replaced by one which is not only more authoritative, but also more complete, since, if this cannot be done, it will be very difficult indeed to verify the historical accounts of *kodae sosǒl* which have been given.

Introduction: 12.1-12.5

12. Locations of Texts.

12.1 No locations are given for modern printed texts. The following are the locations of the manuscripts and block prints which I have seen myself, which are given after each text in the lists under each story in square brackets:

12.2 Asami Collection, Berkeley:

This is the private collection of 淺見倫太郎 Asami Rintarō, and it is now in the East Asiatic Library, University of California. It is reputed to be one of the best private collections of Korean books yet made, and although it contains only two old texts of *kodae sosŏl*, its 503 홍백화전 Hongbaekhwa chŏn may be valuable.

12.3 British Museum:

The Department of Oriental Printed Books and Manuscripts, British Museum, London, has thirty five Seoul block prints of *kodae sosŏl* and three manuscripts, one of which, of 292 옥환기봉 Okhwan Kibong may be valuable. The records which show that these books were purchased in 1889 are also a valuable piece of evidence. For this information, and for a great deal of personal help, I am indebted to Mr Eric Grinstead of the Museum.

12.4 Chŏng Pyŏnguk:

鄭炳昱 Chŏng Pyŏnguk, Professor of Korean Literature at Seoul University, spent much time and showed unbelievable patience in showing me his private collection, explaining what were to me the many mysteries of Korean literary history, and giving me the opportunity to learn the techniques of dealing with its materials in the only possible way, by apprenticeship under a master. In addition his collection contains so many manuscripts of value that one tends, in going through the list, to regard as ordinary a large number of texts which would be outstanding in other surroundings. The texts listed here show how much I owe to him.

12.5 Dr Doo Soo Suh:

徐斗銖 Sŏ Tusu, now teaching at the University of Washington, Seattle, has only one text in his private collection of the sort which I list here, but that is one of only two old texts of 95 두껍전 Tukkop chŏn. He also gave much time to helping me see and appreciate the works in the Far East Library at his University, and his experience in Korean literary studies is of great value to anyone who comes into contact with him.

12.6 Harvard:

The collection of Korean books in the Harvard-Yenching Institute Library was not only one of the largest collections in the west when I last saw it, in April 1965, but it was also growing at a rate which anyone outside the United States would find difficult to believe. The librarian, Mr Sung-ha Kim (金聖河), was extremely helpful to me. The many Seoul block prints and manuscripts here appear to be of rather late dates, but are of great interest in total.

12.7 Imanishi Collection, Tenri:

The collection made by 今西龍 Imanishi Ryu was in the Oyasato Research Institute, Tenri University, when I saw it in February 1962. It was only provisionally catalogued then, and I was greatly assisted in examining it by several members of the staff, but particularly by Mr Nakamura Tamotsu (中村完). The dozen or so of its texts which I list here are all of interest.

12.8 Kaai Bunko, Kyoto:

In Kyoto University Library I was given every courtesy and help in examining the Korean books, and regret that, of the many texts which I saw there, only one, a manuscript of **363 임경업전 Yim Kyŏngŏp chŏn,** is of the sort which I list here.

12.9 Ogura Collection, Tokyo:

At the time I saw this, in March 1962, it consisted of unsorted piles of books in a temporary store-room in Tokyo University, but it was well worth making the effort to look through the collection made by 小倉進平 Ogura Shimpei. Since his interest was in the Korean language, a higher proportion of his books than is usual in Japanese collections is in Korean. All of the texts listed here are of interest, and a more thorough study of them than I was able to make in the circumstances would probably show items of real value.

12.10 Palace:

The Former Royal Palace Library (舊王宮圖書館, etc.) in Seoul, also known as the 樂善齋 Naksŏnjae library, after the palace building in which it was originally housed, is how housed in the grounds of the 昌慶 Ch'anggyŏng Palace. It has a unique atmosphere, and the librarian, Mr Hwang, personally conducted me round all the stacks, explaining the collection to me. It is the most valuable single collection for the study of *kodae sosŏl,* of which it has about one hundred works in over two thousand beautiful volumes of manuscripts. Many of the works now exist only here, and, while this may only mean that they were never of interest ouside the palace in the past, they are clearly of great interest today.

Introduction: 12.11-12.14

One looks forward with great anticipation to the publication of the results of a study of the *kodae sosŏl* in this collection which has been made recently by Chŏng Pyŏnguk and his colleagues at Seoul University.

12.11 School of Oriental and African Studies, University of London:

This library contains only two manuscripts of *kodae sosŏl*, both of moderate interest only.

12.12 Seattle:

The Far East Library, University of Washington, has a Korean collection which, though apparently not long established, was growing quickly when I saw it in April 1965. Six of its manuscripts are listed here, all of interest.

12.13 Seoul University:

In 1961-62, all the books so referred to were in the Department of Korean Language and Literature, (國語國文學硏究室), College of Liberal Arts and Sciences. I spent a great deal of time there in 1961 and 1962, having the benefit of the advice of many members of that department, including Professor Chŏng Pyŏnguk, already mentioned, and Professor Ki-moon Lee (李基文 Yi Kimun). Professor Lee gave weeks of his valuable time to coaching me on the general subject of texts in Korean before I began work on them, and, since his authority on the history of the Korean language is beyond dispute, his advice on particular texts was a lesson in itself. Seoul University also houses the 奎章閣 Kyujanggak, a most important collection of Korean books. A catalogue of this collection has been published, and it does not seem to contain any texts of what one might call popular novels, but two other collections in Seoul University are of great importance for the study of *kodae sosŏl*. These are the **Ilsa and Karam collections**, the catalogue of which is given in the **Index of Brief References** which follows this Introduction. The libraries, the personnel and the close proximity of the Palace Library make Seoul University the best possible centre for the study of *kodae sosŏl*.

12.14 Tōyō Bunko:

The Tōyō Bunko (東洋文庫), Tokyo, contains what appears to be one of the most comprehensive collections of Korean books outside Korea. There is a published catalogue of these, and many of the books in it are also described in **Maema Kyōsaku: Kosen Sappu** (given in the **Index of Brief References**). The collection includes about fifty *kodae sosŏl*, mainly block prints and lending library manuscripts. None is of outstanding interest by itself, but our picture of *kodae sosŏl* would certainly be very much further from complete if we did not have this collection. The organisation of this library is most efficient.

12.15 **1961 Exhibition:**

An exhibition of old books written by or primarily for women was held at Sungmyŏng Women's University (淑明女子大學校), Seoul, on October 26th, 27th and 28th, 1961. Although this is not strictly speaking a location, it was here that I saw several texts which I did not see in their proper locations. These included fifteen from the National Library, one from the Ilsa collection, and twelve from the private collections of 姜漢永 Kang Hanyŏng, 金東旭 Kim Tonguk, 李能雨 Yi Nŭngu and 張德順 Chang Tŏksun. If my memory serves me right, all of these scholars accompanied me around the exhibition, but whoever it was who provided the additional information which I noted in my catalogue, I am most grateful.

13. Collections Not Seen.

13.1 There are two collections in Europe which contain valuable materials, and which fortunately have been very fully reported. The first is that in l'École des Langues Orientales Vivantes in Paris, on which **Courant** provided much information in his bibliography, and the second is the Aston collection in the Institute of the Peoples of Asia in Leningrad, for which we have **Petrova's** catalogue. Both these works are referred to very frequently by their authors' names only, and will be found under those names in the **Index of Brief References**. Both are extremely valuable tools for the study of *kodae sosŏl*.

13.2 There is one more library which I wished to examine more closely, the National Library in Seoul, but in 1961-62 it was impossible to make use of it for various reasons, among which was certainly not any unwillingness on the part of the librarian or his staff to help. The library contains mainly works published in this century, and it could be used to give a very full picture of Korean literary activity since the early years of this century, including the publishing and republishing of *kodae sosŏl*.

13.3 I do not know of any other large public or semi-public collections of *kodae sosŏl*. University libraries in Korea all certainly have a few texts each which have been published or described, but is there any body of evidence on the history of *kodae sosŏl* still to be given? One cannot press for private collections to be made public while so much that is already public is virtually unread, but it is to be hoped that no further losses, such as have been suffered by private collectors recently, will affect the remaining private collections before their contents become public knowledge.

I cannot leave this introduction without adding that *kodae sosŏl* were written to give pleasure, and that they can still give pleasure. The fact that one dull book can be written about them should not discourage anyone else from picking up one or two and reading them. One aim of this dull catalogue of titles is to make it more widely known what there is to be read. It is hoped that those who can read them will do so, and perhaps even agree that they ought to be made easier, by reprinting, annotation or translation, for others to read.

Index of Brief References

Courant:

Maurice Courant: <u>Bibliographie Coréenne</u>, 3 vols and Supplément. Ecole des Langues Orientales Vivantes (Publications XVIII-XXI), Paris, 1894-1901. References given are to entry numbers. Numbers below 945 are in volume 1 (1894), and numbers above 3347 are in the supplement (1901). Texts referred to as in Paris are in l'École des Langues Orientales Vivantes. I have not been able to discover where the other collections which he mentions as containing texts of *kodae sosŏl* are now, and so if any text is given by him as in Paris and another collection, I have noted this as "Paris, etc.". For further comments see Introduction, § 6.1.

Ewha Series:

Seoul, 梨花女子大學校韓國文化研究院 Yihwa Yŏja Taehakkyo Han'guk Munhwa Yŏn'guwŏn, "Korean Culture Research Institute, Ewha Woman's University", compiled: 韓國古代小說叢書 Han'guk Kodae Sosŏl Ch'ongsŏ, "Korean *Kodae Sosŏl* Series". 通文館 T'ongmun'gwan, Seoul, 1958-1961. 4 vols.
Facsimile reproductions of eight Seoul block prints, four Chŏnju block prints and five manuscripts. The notes referred to are mainly summaries of the stories.

Hŭimang Series:

Seoul, 韓國古典文學全集編輯委員會 Han'guk Kojŏn Munhak Chŏnjip P'yŏnjip Wiwŏnhoe, "Committee for the Compilation of the Collection of Korean Classical Literature", compiled: 韓國古典文學全集 Han'guk Kojŏn Munhak Chŏnjip, "Collection of Korean Classical Literature". 希望出版社 Hŭimang Ch'ulp'ansa, Seoul, 1965. 5 vols.

Reprints texts of thirty six *kodae sosŏl* in Korean, slightly modernised, mainly in respect of the spelling and certain grammatical points, and occasionally adds short notes. There are also translations of some *kodae sosŏl* in *hanmun*.

Hyŏndae Munhak:

現代文學 Hyŏndae Munhak, "Contemporary Literature", published monthly since January 1955 by 現代文學社 Hyŏndae Munhak sa, Seoul.

In spite of its title, this journal seems to have printed more articles on *kodae sosŏl* than any other single journal, and it has run serialised versions of many texts of *kodae sosŏl*, including some which are not easily to be found elsewhere.

References: Ilsa-Kim

Ilsa collection, and

Karam collection:

These collections, of the late 方鍾鉉 Pang Chonghyŏn and of 李秉岐 Yi Pyŏnggi, respectively, are now in Seoul University Library, and a catalogue of them has been published: Seoul, 서울大學校附屬圖書館 Sŏul Taehakkyo Pusok Tosŏgwan, Seoul University Library, compiled and published: 일사·가람文庫古書著者目錄 Ilsa, Karam Mun'go Kosŏ Chŏja Mongnok, An Author Catalogue of Rare Books of the Ilsa and Garam Collections in Seoul University Library, 1966, 344 pages. Most entries for *kodae sosŏl* will in fact be found under their titles, but there is also a title index.

Kim Kidong:

金起東 Kim Kidong: 李朝時代小說論 Yijo Sidae Sosŏllon, "On the Novels of the Yi Dynasty Period". 精研社 Chŏngyŏn sa, Seoul, 1959. 608 pages.

If reference to this is followed by "(1956: 000)", this indicates a reference to **Kim Kidong (1956)**, listed next. See Introduction, §5.2.

Kim Kidong (1956):

金起東 Kim Kidong: 韓國古代小說概論 Han'guk Kodae Sosŏl Kaeron, "A Survey of Korean *Kodae Sosŏl*". 大昌文化社 Taech'ang Munhwasa, Seoul, 1956. 399 pages. See **Introduction**, §5.2.

Kim T'aejun:

金台俊 Kim T'aejun: (增補) 朝鮮小說史 (Chŭngbo) Chosŏn Sosŏl sa, "A History of the Korean Novel (Revised)". 學藝社 Hagye sa, Keijō, 1939. 272 pages.

This work is reported to have been first published in 東亞日報 Tonga Ilbo, November 1930 — February 1931, and the first book edition by 清進書館 Ch'ŏngjin Sŏgwan in 1933. From the references given by others it would appear that the two editions are very different. See **Introduction**, §5.1.

Kim Tonguk:

金東旭 Kim Tonguk: 春香傳研究 Ch'unhyang chŏn Yŏn'gu, "A Study of the Ch'unhyang Story". 延世大學校出版部 Yŏnse Taehakkyo Ch'ulp'anbu, Yonsei University Press, Seoul, 1965. 14, 432 [6] pages.

This is referred to most frequently for its reprint of his article on block printing, and if reference to it is followed by reference to **1960** or to Hyangt'o Sŏul, this is a reference to the first publication of this article. See **Introduction**, §10.3.

Ku, Son and Kim: Kungmunhak Kaeron:

具滋均 Ku Chagyun, 孫洛範 Son Nakpŏm and 金亨奎 Kim Hyŏnggyu: (改訂版)
國文學概論 (Kaejŏngp'an) Kungmunhak Kaeron, "A Survey of Korean Literature
(Revised Edition)". 一成堂書店 Ilsŏngdang Sŏjŏm, Seoul, 1955. 360 pages.
See Introduction, §5.7.

Kugŏ Kungmunhak:

국어국문학 Kugŏ Kungmunhak, The Korean Language and Literature, published
irregularly since 1952, first in Pusan, then Seoul, by 국어국문학회 Kugŏ Kung‑
munhak hoe, The Society of Korean Language and Literature.

Maema Kyōsaku: Kosen Sappu:

前間恭作 Maema Kyōsaku: 古鮮册譜 Kosen Sappu, "A Bibliography of Old Korean
Books". 東洋文庫 Tōyō Bunko (叢刊 Sōkan 11), Tokyo, 1944-57. 3 vols.

Reference has not been given to this work for those texts which I have seen
myself, but it is often a convenient point of reference for *hanmun* works.

Mibalp'yo Kodae Sosŏl ko:

朴晟義 Pak Sŏngŭi: 未發表古代小說攷 — 高大圖書舘藏本 Mibalp'yo Kodae Sosŏl
ko - Kodae Tosŏgwan Changbon, "A Study of Unpublished *Kodae Sosŏl* Texts in
Korea University Library" (Seoul, 高麗大學校 Koryŏ Taehakkyo, Korea University: 文理論集 (文學部篇) Mulli Nonjip (Munhakpu p'yŏn), The Humanities,
(Literature), 7, November 1963, pages 279-301).

"Unpublished" means also "which have not been made known before", and this
description of five *kodae sosŏl* from manuscripts is a valuable source of information.

Mongyu rok Sogo:

張德順 Chang Tŏksun: 夢遊錄小考 Mongyu rok Sogo, "A Note on Records of
Dream Journeys" (Seoul, 延世大學校 Yŏnse Taehakkyo, Yonsei University:
東方學志 Tongbang Hakchi, Journal of Far Eastern Studies, 4 June 1959, pages
131-148).

This gives useful information on several novels which are barely mentioned
elsewhere.

References: Pak-Yi

Pak Sŏngŭi:
朴晟義 Pak Sŏngŭi: (韓國) 古代小說史 (Han'guk) Kodae Sosŏl sa, "A History of (Korean) *Kodae Sosŏl*". 日新社 Ilsin sa, Seoul, 1964. 458 pages. The first edition is given as 1958.
See Introduction, §5.3.

Petrova:
O. P. Petrova: Opisanie Pis'mennuikh Pamyatnikov Koreiskoi Kul'turui. Izdatel'stvo Vostochnoi Literaturui, Moscow. Vol. 1 1956, Vol. 2 1963.

A catalogue of Korean books in the Institute of the Peoples of Asia, Leningrad. All works referred to are from the collection formed by W. G. Aston about 1890. Reference is to the entry numbers, and also, where applicable, to the illustrations at the end of volume 2.

Sin Kihyŏng:
申基亨 Sin Kihyŏng: 韓國小說發達史 Han'guk Sosŏl Paltal sa, "A History of the Development of the Korean Novel". 彰文社 Changmun sa, Seoul, 1960. 549, 26 pages.
See Introduction, §5.4.

Yi and Paek: Kungmunhak Chŏnsa:
李秉岐 Yi Pyŏnggi and 白鐵 Paek Ch'ŏl: 國文學全史 Kungmunhak Chŏnsa, "The History of Korean Literature". 新丘文化社 Sin'gu Munhwasa, Seoul, 1961. 6, 15, 557, 22 pages. The first edition is given as 1957.
See Introduction, §5.6.

Yi Nŭngu: Kungmunhak Kaeron:
李能雨 Yi Nŭngu: 國文學概論 Kungmunhak Kaeron, "A Survey of Korean Literature". 국어국문학회 Kugŏ Kungmunhak hoe, Seoul, 1954, and 以文堂 Imundang, Seoul, 1955. 4, 164 pages.
See Introduction, §5.6.

Yi Pyŏnggi: Kungmunhak Kaeron:
李秉岐 Yi Pyŏnggi: 國文學概論 Kungmunhak Kaeron, "A Survey of Korean Literature" 一志社 Ilchi sa, Seoul, 1961. 11, 280 pages.
See Introduction, §5.6.

1947 exhibition: see Introduction, §6.4.

(1956): see **Kim Kidong,** above.

(1960): see **Kim Tonguk,** above.

1961 exhibition: see Introduction, §12.15.

In addition, well known Korean, Chinese and Japanese proper names, and a few words which are usually accepted in romanised form, rather than translated or explained, are not explained or further identified in this work.

A List of Kodae Sosŏl by Titles

1. 가루지기타령 Karujigi T'aryŏng "The Ballad of the Load Across the Back"

"The load across the back" is a euphemism for the corpse of a commoner. The story involves necrophily and also violence to a *changsŭng* by the lecherous couple 卞강쇠 Pyŏn Kangsoe and 雍女 Ongnyŏ. This was one of the twelve stories sung in *p'ansori* and one of the six rewritten by Sin Chaehyo, this one between 1881 and 1884, see **Introduction**, §7.3, and the articles described there, Song Manjae ŭi Kwan-u-hŭi, 104-105 (Kwan-u-hŭi stanza 13), and P'ansori Palsaeng ko, 274-276. The latter states that Hoengbu ka, the title given for the Sin Chaeyo version, is a "*hanmun* translation", but this may mean of the title only, not the text, and that the story is also known as 송장가 Songjang ka, "The Song of the Corpse(s)'. Yi Pyŏnggi: Kungmunhak Kaeron, 149, gives the titles of *p'ansori* version as 변광쇠타령 Pyŏn Kwangsoe T'aryŏng, 가루지기타령 Karujigi T'aryŏng and 橫負歌 Hoengbu ka.

本秉岐 Yi Pyŏnggi, ed.: 가루지기타령 Karujigi T'aryŏng, 國際文化舘 Kukche Munhwagwan, Seoul, 1949, 72 pages, is given in several bibliographies and studies.

姜漢永 Kang Hanyŏng: 변강쇠打令 Pyŏn Kangsoe T'aryŏng (**Hyŏndae Munhak**, 75-77, March-May 1961), is in modern spelling, without introduction or notes.

가루지기打令 Karujigi T'aryŏng in the **Hŭimang Series**, I 215-245, appears to be very similar to the last.

2. 가인기우 Kain Kiu

Kim Kidong, 33, gives 佳人奇遇 Kain Kiu (presumably) "The Miraculous Meeting of the Lovers" as a paperback publication of a *kodae sosŏl*. This title was advertised by Taech'ang Sŏwŏn and Hanyang Sŏjŏgŏp Chohapso in 1918, by Taech'ang Sŏwŏn and Pogŭp Sŏgwan in 1919 and 1920, and by Sech'ang Sŏgwan in 1933. On page 596 **Kim Kidong** lists 佳人奇逢 Kain Kibong as a love story in Korean set in China, existing in paperback edition(s), but not made known before.

3. 가짜신선타령 Katcha Sinsŏn T'aryŏng

This was one of the stories sung in *p'ansori*, but all that is known of it now is the summary in Kwan-u-hŭi, stanza 18, see Song Manjae ŭi Kwan-u-hŭi, 106-107 and 118, and P'ansori Palsaeng ko, 278-279, as described in the **Introduction**, §7. 3. The title presumably means "The Ballad of the Pseudo-Fairy", and it was apparently a story of a simpleton who was deceived into thinking that he had been turned into a fairy or magician. The two articles mentioned above both give a similar legend, and both point out that the place of this story in the repertoire of the *kwangdae* was taken by a version of 224 숙영낭자전 **Sugyŏng Nangja chŏn**.

4. 감용전 Kamyong chŏn

감용전 Kamyong chyŏn (or Kam Yong chyŏn), manuscript, 35 leaves, given as in the **Ilsa collection.**

5. 강감찬전 Kang Kamch'an chŏn "The Story of Kang Kamch'an"

The hero is an historical person (947-1030).

姜邯贊傳 Kang Kamch'an chŏn, Kwangdong Sŏguk, 1914 (reprinted from 1908), 33 pages.

(고려명장) 강감찬실긔, (高麗名將) 姜邯贊實記 (Koryŏ Myŏngjang) Kang Kamch'an Silgŭi, "The True Story of Kang Kamch'an (A Famous General of Koryŏ)", Yŏngch'ang Sŏgwan, not dated (but before 1945), 45 pages.

There is a version in English of a story about him in Zong In-sob: Folk Tales from Korea (Routledge and Kegan Paul, London, 1952), 56-58.

강능추월 **Kangnŭng Ch'uwŏl**, etc.: see 279 옥소전 Okso chŏn

6. 강도몽유록 Kangdo Mongyu rok

Kim Kidong, 588, lists 江都夢遊錄 Kangdo Mongyu rok (presumably) "Record of a Dream Journey to Kanghwa" as an historical story in both Korean and *hanmun* set in Korea, existing in manuscript(s). He refers to Kim T'aejun. On page 37 he states that it exists in manuscript(s) in *hanmun* only. **Kim T'aejun**, 70, seems to imply fairly clearly that it is in *hanmun*. The work is mentioned, but not described, in **Mongyu rok Sogo.** I have found only one manuscript in *hanmun* [Tōyō Bunko], and no confirmation that there is a version in Korean.

강도일기 **Kangdo Ilgi:** see 133 병자록 **Pyŏngja rok**

강릉매화전 **Kangnŭng Maehwa chŏn:** see 98 매화전 **Maehwa chŏn**

강릉추월 **Kangnŭng Ch'uwŏl:** see 279 옥소전 **Okso chŏn**

7. 강산기우 Kangsan Kiu

Kim Kidong, 33, has 江山奇遇 Kangsan Kiu in a list of paperback editions of *kodae sosŏl*.

강산련 **Kangsannyŏn**, and
강상련 **Kangsangnyŏn:** see 229 심청전 **Sim Ch'ŏng chŏn**

8. 강유실기 Kang Yu Silgi "The True Story of Chiang Wei"

(大膽) 姜維實記, (디담) 강유실긔 (**Taedam**) **Kang Yu Silgŭi**, currently available from Sech'ang Sŏgwan, 160 pages. The title was also advertised by Sinmyŏng Sŏrim in 1930. This follows San-kuo-chih Yen-i (see 156 삼국지연의 **Samgukchi Yŏnŭi**) from the end of chapter 92 fairly closely, and states at the beginning and at the end that it is taken from that Chinese work. *Taedam* means "the Brave".

9. 강태공전 Kang T'aegong chŏn "The Story of Grand Duke Chiang"

The story concerns the supposedly historical Chinese 姜尚 Chiang Ch'ang, a minister of the first king of the Chou dynasty (twelfth century B.C.). See **Kim Kidong** (1956), 146-149.

강티공젼 Kang T'ăegong chyŏn, manuscript, 63 leaves, given as in the **Karam collection**.

강티공젼 Kang T'ăegong chyŏn, Taech'ang Sŏwŏn and Pogŭp Sŏgwan, 1920, 77 pages.

강태공전 Kang T'aegong chŏn, currently available from Sech'ang Sŏgwan, 68 pages, and title advertised by Tongmi Sŏsi, 1915, Sin'gu Sŏrim, 1918 and 1925, Yŏngch'ang Sŏgwan and Hanhŭng Sŏrim, 1925, and Tŏkhŭng Sŏrim, 1935.

10. 개벽연의 Kaebyŏk Yŏnŭi "The Creation, a Romance"

기벽연의 Kăebyŏk Yŏnŭi, manuscript from the Maenghyŏn 孟峴 royal household, 2 vols, 60, 75 leaves (12 columns, 23 syllables), dated 갑진 (甲辰 1904).
[Chŏng Pyŏnguk]

Courant, 306 and **Kim T'aejun**, 77, 97, both mention 開闢演義 (**Kaebyŏk Yŏnŭi** in Korean) **K'ai-p'i Yen-i**, a Chinese work printed in 1635 and reprinted in 1830, which covers the period from the creation of the world to the end of the Chou Dynasty.

11. 개소문전 Kaesomun chŏn

Kim Kidong, 589, lists 蓋蘇文傳 **Kaesomun chŏn** (presumably) "The Story of Kaesomun" as an historical novel in Korean set in Korea, existing in paperback edition(s), but not made known before. The title was advertised by Tŏkhŭng Sŏrim in 1935.

淵蓋蘇文, in modern Korean **Yŏn Kaesomun**, but there are several different spellings of his name, and the original form of it is a matter of conjecture, was a minister of Koguryŏ at the time of its defeat by T'ang and Silla, about 660 A.D. **Hsüeh Jen-kuei**, who figures in 185 설인귀전 **Sŏl In'gwi chŏn** and other stories, led the T'ang armies at the time.

12. 견한록 Kyŏnhan nok "Records to Fill Idle Moments"
A collection of historical stories.

견한녹 **Kyŏnhan nok**, manuscript from the Maenghyŏn 孟峴 royal household, 1 vol. (vol.1 only), 69 leaves (10 or 11 columns, 20 syllables). Title on the cover 遣閑錄 **Kyŏnhan nok.** [**Chŏng Pyŏnguk**]
1947 exhibition, 153: 遣閑錄 **Kyŏnhan nok**, manuscript, 2 vols. (Yi Haech'ŏng).

13. 경애전 Kyŏngae chŏn

1947 exhibition, 115: 경이전 **Kyŏngae chyŏn**, manuscript, 1 vol. (Cho Yunje, not shown).

14. 계상국전 Kye Sangguk chŏn

See 朴晟義 · **Pak Sŏngŭi**: 桂相國傳小攷 **Kye Sangguk chŏn Sogo**, "A Note on the Story of the Minister Kuei" (Seoul, 高麗大學校 **Koryŏ Taehakkyo**, Korea University: 文理論集 (文學部篇) **Mulli Nonjip (Munhakpu p'yŏn)**, The Humanities (Literature), 6, December 1962, 39-72). This article describes this work in great detail from a manuscript in Korea University Library, titles 계상국전 **Kye Sangguk chyŏn** (vols 1 and 2), 계월선전 **Kye Wŏlsyŏn chyŏn** (vols 3 and 4), and 桂月仙傳 **Kye Wŏlsŏn chŏn** on all covers, 4 vols, 36, 37, 40, 39 leaves (13 columns, 27-28 to 34-35 syllables), dated 乙酉 (1885). The story is apparently that one of the stars of the plough is born in Ming China, about 1500, as 桂月仙 Kuei Yüeh-hsien and marries ten women, who are the moon goddess and nine stars born as human beings. **Courant**, 830, gives the title as in vols 3 and 4 above.

15. 계심쌍환기봉 Kyesim Ssanghwan Kibong

Courant, 848: 계심쌍환긔봉 桂心雙環奇逢 <u>Kyesim Ssanghwan Kŭibong</u>, "The Miraculous Encounter of the Two Rings of Kyesim". He does not mention any texts, but suggests that Kyesim (Chinese: Kuei-hsin) is the name of a woman. **Kim T'aejun**, 229, quotes the title from Courant, and **Kim Kidong**, 595, quotes it from Kim T'aejun, adding that it is a love story in Korean set in China, existing in paperback edition(s).

계월선전 **Kye Wŏlsŏn chŏn**: see 14 계상국전 **Kye Sangguk chŏn**

16. 계축일기 Kyech'uk Ilgi "Diary of the Year of the Black Ox [1613]"

The form is that of a diary covering the years 1602-1621 by a servant of the Queen Mother Inmok (仁穆大妃), widow of King Sŏnjo, but most critics take it as a novel in diary form. There is an excellent edition by Kang Hanyŏng, below, but see also **Kim Kidong**, 356-360, **Pak Sŏngŭi**, 253-256, and **Sin Kihyŏng**, 421-424.

1947 exhibition, 239: 癸丑日記 <u>Kyech'uk Ilgi</u>, manuscript, 2 vols (Palace).

This is said to have been lost during the Korean War. In 1947 Kang Hanyŏng made a copy of it, which I saw in the **1961 exhibition**, as item 58. This text was reprinted, without any notes, in **Hyŏndae Munhak**, 25-30, January — June 1957, and it is again reprinted, with very full notes, in:

姜漢永 Kang Hanyŏng, ed.: 癸丑日記 <u>Kyech'uk Ilgi</u>. 靑羽出版社 Ch'ŏngu Ch'ul·p'ansa, Seoul, 1958, and 新古典社 Sin'gojŏn sa, Seoul, 1960, both 252 pages.

The full title is 계튝일긔서궁녹 <u>Kyet'yuk Ilgŭi Sŏgung nok</u>, "Diary of the Year of the Black Ox, Record of the West [now the Tŏksu] Palace". Some critics prefer to take 西宮錄 <u>Sŏgung nok</u> as the title on the grounds that the work is not a true diary.

癸丑日記 <u>Kyech'uk Ilgi</u> in the **Hŭimang Series**, III 57-125, could be taken from the same text.

Kang Hanyŏng, in the postface of his edition, page 230, states that 任昌淳 Yim Ch'angsun has a variant text entitled 西宮日記 <u>Sŏgung Ilgi</u>, "Diary of the West

Palace.", and that a Kyech'uk Ilgi was reproduced photographically in 閔丙燾 Min Pyŏngdo, ed.: 朝鮮歷代女流文集 Chosŏn Yŏktae Yŏryu Munjip, "Collected Writings of Women through the Ages in Korea" (乙酉文化社 Ŭryu Munhwasa, Seoul, 1950). 17 계해반정록 Kyehae Panjŏng nok is a sequel to Kyech'uk Ilgi.

17. 계해반정록 Kyehae Panjŏng nok "Record of the Restoration of the Year of the Black Pig [1623]"

계히반정녹 Kyehăe Panjyŏng nok, manuscript, 26 (+6) leaves (11 columns, 22 syllables). [Chŏng Pyŏnguk]

This is in diary form, beginning from the date at which 16 계축일기 Kyech'uk Ilgi finishes, and covering the end of the reign of Kwanghae-gun, to 1623. See also perhaps 334 윤지경전 Yun Chigyŏng chŏn. The six leaves in the text above are 홍원빈입궐초일긔 Hong Wŏnbin Ipkwŏl Ch'o Ilgŭi, "Diary Notes on Miss Hong, Wŏnbin, Taking up Residence in the Palace". There does not appear to be any such person around 1623, but the records relevant to Kwanghae-gun are very deficient.

18. 계화몽 Kyehwa mong "The Dream of the Cinnamon Flower"

The story is set in fifteenth century China (Ming, Ch'eng-hua). A sprig of cinnamon flowers is presented in a dream by a fairy to the wife of one Ts'ui (최운 Ch'oe Un in Korean) as an announcement of the birth of their third daughter.

계화몽 桂花夢 Kyehwa mong, Taech'ang Sŏwŏn and Pogŭp Sŏgwan, 1922, 129 pages.
See 442 채련전 Ch'aeryŏn chŏn.

19. 고금비원 Kogŭm Piwŏn

1947 exhibition, 194: 古今秘苑 Kogŭm Piwŏn (presumably) "The Secret Garden Yesterday and Today", manuscript, 2 vols (Palace).
This did not appear to be in the Palace library in 1962.

20. 고려보감 Koryŏ Pogam

고렷보감 Koryŏt Pogam, lending library manuscript, 10 vols, 319 leaves (11 columns, 14 syllables) in all, dated 무술 (戊戌 1898). Title on the cover 高麗寶鑑 Koryŏ Pogam. [Tōyō Bunko]

I found this extremely difficult to read, and was not able to identify any historical figures in it. I have noted that the opening passages appears to concern a family of T'ang China, yet the title appears to mean "Precious Mirror of Koryŏ".

21. 고성효행록 Kosŏng Hyohaeng nok

Kim T'aejun, 161, includes 雇星孝行錄 Kosŏng Hyohaeng nok in a list of similar titles which seems to be derived largely from **Courant**, but this particular title does not appear in Courant. **Kim Kidong**, 599, quotes it from Kim T'aejun, and describes it as a moral story in Korean set in China, existing in manuscript(s). *Kosŏng* gives no obvious sense, but it may be a pseudonym of some sort: "Record of the Filial Piety of Ku-hsing". It is possible to read 雇 *ho,* but not usual, and **Sin Kihyŏng**, 473, gives the reading *Kosŏng*.

22. 고후전 Kohu chŏn "Stories of Illustrious Empresses"

高后傳 Kohu chŏn, manuscript, 4 vols. [Palace]
1947 exhibition, 154: 高后傳 Kohu chŏn, manuscript, 2 vols (Yi Haech'ŏng).

I have not been able to identify the subjects of the few stories whose names, in Korean, I noted.

공명선생실기 Kongmyŏng Sŏnsaeng Silgi: see 156 삼국지연의 Samgukchi Yŏnŭi

23. 공작행 Kongjak Haeng

1947 exhibition, 118: 孔雀行 Kongjak Haeng (presumably) "The Behaviour of the Peacock", manuscript, 1 vol. (Cho Yunje, not shown).
This text was listed as a *sosŏl*, but the work of the same title which is reprinted in full in **Yi and Paek: Kungmunhak Chŏnsa**, 188-196, is a poem in *hanmun* with Korean transcription and translation.

곽당낭문녹 Kwak Tyang Nyangmun nok: see 25 곽장양문록 **Kwak Chang Yangmun nok**

24. 곽분양전 **Kwak Punyang chŏn "The Story of Kuo Fen-yang"**

The story concerns 郭子儀 Kuo Tzu-i (697-781), a general who defeated An Lu-shan (see **244** 안녹산전 **An Noksan chŏn**), and was given the title of Prince of Fen-yang.

Courant, 788: 곽분양젼 郭汾陽傳 Kwak Punyang chyŏn, block print, 2 vols, in Paris, etc.; 3351: same, 3 vols, in Paris; **1947 exhibition,** 129: 郭汾陽傳 Kwak Punyang chŏn, Seoul block print, 3 vols (Chŏng Pyŏnguk: he did not seem to have this in 1962); **Kim Tonguk,** 386: Seoul block prints of 3 vols, 23, 24, 22 leaves, and of 2 vols, 35, 34 leaves.

곽분양젼 Kwak Punyang chyŏn, Sin'gu Sŏrim and Pangmun Sŏgwan, 1923 (reprinted from 1913), and, with identical text, currently available from Sech'ang Sŏgwan, 86 pages. The title was advertised by the first publishers above in 1918, 1919, 1925 and 1932, by Yŏngch'ang Sŏgwan and Hanhŭng Sŏrim in 1925, and by Kwangdong Sŏguk in 1926.

Courant, 789: 곽분양충힝록 郭汾陽忠行錄 Kwak Punyang Ch'yunghăeng nok, "Record of the Loyal Behaviour of Kuo Fen-yang" (title only)

곽성의전 **Kwak Sŏngŭi chŏn:** see **392** 적성의전 **Chŏk Sŏngŭi chŏn**

25. 곽장양문록 Kwak Chang Yangmun nok

1947 exhibition, 95: 곽댱냥문녹 Kwak Tyang Nyangmun nok, manuscript, 1 vol. (Pang Chonghyŏn: no such title is given as in the **Ilsa collection**).

Courant, 910: 곽쟝냥문녹 郭張兩門錄 Kwak Chyang Nyangmun nok, "Record of the Two Families Kwak [Chinese: Kuo] and Chang" (title only). **Kim T'aejun,** 160: 郭氏兩門錄 Kwak-ssi Yangmun nok does not give as easy sense as Courant's title, and is presumably a mistake for it. He implies that it is imitative of a Chinese work. Kim Kidong, 594, follows Kim T'aejun, and describes it as a love story in Korean set in China, existing in paperback edition(s).

26. 곽재우전 **Kwak Chae'u chŏn**

Kim Kidong, 589, lists 郭再祐傳 Kwak Chae'u chŏn (presumably) "The Story of Kwak Chae'u" as an historical story in Korean set in Korea, existing in manuscript(s). He refers to **Kim T'aejun,** who mentions it, page 70. Kwak Chae'u was a leader of a righteous army in the wars of 1592-1597 (see **366** 임진록 **Imjin nok**).

27. 곽해룡전 Kwak Haeryong chŏn

A war story set in Yüan China. **Kim T'aejun**, 99, 108, includes it among the best of such war tales, in which as a group, however, he finds little literary interest. See **Kim Kidong (1956)**, 173-175.

곽히룡전 Kwak Hǎeryong chyŏn, lending library manuscript, 3 vols, 30, 30, 30 leaves (11 columns, 12-13 syllables), dated 을사 or 을스 (乙巳 1905). Title on the cover 郭海龍傳 Kwak Haeryong chŏn. [**Tōyō Bunko**]

곽히룡전 Kwak Hǎeryong chyŏn, manuscript, 2 vols, 33, 32 leaves (11 columns, 13 syllables). Title on the cover 郭海龍傳 Kwak Haeryong chŏn. [**Seoul University**]

郭海龍傳 곽해룡전 Kwak Haeryong chŏn, currently available from Sech'ang Sŏgwan (but text as composed before 1945), 40 pages. The title was advertised by Tŏkhŭng Sŏrim in 1935.

28. 관운장실기 Kwan Unjang Silgi "The True Story of Kuan Yün-ch'ang"

Kuan Yün-ch'ang, or 關羽 Kuan Yü, is one of the leading figures in San-kuo-chih Yen-i (see 156 삼국지연의 Samgukchi Yŏnŭi), and this story is a free translation into traditional Korean novel form of the opening chapters of that work.

관운장실긔 (關雲長實記) Kwan Unjang Silgǔi, currently available from Sech'ang Sŏgwan, 68 pages. The title was advertised by Pangmun Sŏgwan and Sin'gu Sŏrim in 1919, 1923, 1925 and 1932, by Yŏngch'ang Sŏgwan and Hanhŭng Sŏrim in 1925, and by Kwangdong Sŏguk in 1926.

광한루기 Kwanghallu ki: see 460 춘향전 Ch'unhyang chŏn

29. 괴화기록 Koehwa Kirok

槐花記錄 Koehwa Kirok, manuscript, 1 vol. (vol. 2 only), dated 을축 (乙丑 1925, etc.), given as in the **Ilsa collection**.

30. 구래공전 Kuraegong chŏn

구리공정츙직절긔 寇萊公貞忠直節記 Kurǎegong Chyŏngch'yung Chikchyŏl kǔi, manuscript, 31 vols. [**Palace**]

구리공정츙직절긔 Kurǎeong Chyŏngch'yung Chikchyŏl kǔi, manuscript, 19 vols, dated 졍유 (丁酉 1897). Title on the cover 구리공전 Kurǎegong chyŏn. [**Seoul University**]

The longer titles presumably mean "Record of the Virtuous Loyalty and Perfect Honour of K'ou, Duke of Lai" (see below), but I have no further note on these texts than is given above.

Courant, 796: 구공청힝록 蘧公淸行錄 Kugong Ch'yŏnghǎeng nok, "Record of the Purity of Duke K'ou", and, 797: 구릭공츙효록 寇萊公忠孝錄 Kurǎegong Ch'yunghyo rok, "Record of the Filial Piety of K'ou, Duke of Lai". He mentions no specific texts, but suggests that both concern 寇準 K'ou Chun, Duke of Lai, died 1023.

31. 구운몽 Kuun mong "The Nine Cloud Dream"

For the story, of a man and the eight women he is destined to meet, which is set in a dream, see Gale's translation, and for the texts see Chŏng Kyubok's study of them, both of which are listed below. There are also good annotated editions, also listed below. Literary critics regard it as artistically the best of the *kodae sosŏl*. In general they base such comments on the *hanmun* version by 金春澤 Kim Ch'unt'aek (1670-1717), but treat it as a work written in Korean by 金萬重 Kim Manjung (1637-1692). See Kim T'aejun, 108-119, **Kim Kidong,** 276-289 (**1956: 223-233), Pak Sŏngŭi,** 270-293, Sin Kihyŏng, 172-192, and, in fact, the appropriate passage in almost any work on Korean Literature.

The most widely used text in *hanmun* is the 3 volume block print 九雲夢 Kuun mong dated 崇禎後三度癸亥 (1803). This is found very commonly in libraries, and was also reprinted, with Japanese translation, in 謝氏南征記 · 九雲夢 Sha-shi Nansei ki, Kyūun mu, 朝鮮研究會 Chōsen Kenkyū kai, Keijō, 1914. **Harvard** has a 3 volume manuscript which the catalogue dates "ca, 1670". Yi Kawŏn (in his 1955 edition, listed below) states that he has three manuscripts in *hanmun*. Chŏng Kyubok (in his study of the texts, listed below) states that he has one manuscript in *hanmun*. There appear to be several *hanmun* texts in the **Ilsa and Karam collections,** as noted below.

Kim Ch'unt'aek's *hanmun* version is usually regarded as a translation from Korean, but Chŏng Kyubok, in his study of the texts, below, points out that there is no evidence for this assumption. However, all critics give quotations for the history of this work which indicate that Kim Manjung did write a work of this title, possibly in Korean, and that it was in circulation, in some form and to some extent at least, about a century earlier than 1803, the earliest established date for any *hanmun* text of the story. It is given as in Shōsho Kibun by Kim Tonguk, 382, see the Introduction, §7. 2.

구운몽 <u>Kuun mong</u>, manuscript, 4 vols, 63, 64, 53, 68 leaves (9 columns, 19 syllables. [**Seoul University**]

This is a most beautiful manuscript, and is widely regarded as the oldest extant text of this story in Korean, but it has not been dated, and the opinion that it may be very close in date to the supposed original work by Kim Manjung (i.e. about 1690) must certainly be treated with caution. 鄭炳昱 Chŏng Pyŏnguk has been preparing an annotated edition of it for some years.

Title not known, manuscript, 2 vols, said by Chŏng Kyubok (in his study of the texts, below) to be in the possession of 李在秀 Yi Chaesu. He describes it as in a language of a date earlier than that of his own text of 1846 (next), but a poor text derived from a *hanmun* version.

Title not known, manuscript, 3 vols, 75, 57, 52 leaves (10 columns, 18-20 syllables), dated 병오 (丙午 1846), described by Chŏng Kyubok (in his study of the texts, below) as being in his own possession. This early date for the text seems to be incontestable, but he does not rate it very highly, finding it a much abridged version of a *hanmun* text.

Title not known, manuscript, 1 vol., in the possession of Yi Kawŏn, and published by him with notes in 1955, see below. He dates it about 1880, and it is generally very highly regarded as a text of this story.

Title not known, manuscript, 3 vols, 35, 40, 31 leaves (10-15 columns, 25-40 syllables), described by Chŏng Kyubok (in his study of the texts, below) as in the possession of 姜允浩 Kang Yunho. It is reported to be dated 을유 (乙酉) in vol. 1 and 光緒十二年乙酉 in vol. 2. 光緒十二年 is 1886 and 乙酉 could be 1885. Chŏng Kyubok gives 1885 as the date, without comment on the discrepancy. He says that it is an embellished translation of a *hanmun* text, but that the language is older than that of his own text of 1846 (above).

Title not known, manuscript, 10 vols, described by Chŏng Kyubok (in his study of the texts, below) as being in the library of Ewha Women's University, Seoul. He states that it is dated 丁未 1907. The size and date would seem to indicate that it is a lending library copy. This text was apparently so badly damaged in the Korean War that it is now virtually illegible, but a small part of it was reprinted in 李熙昇 Yi Hŭisŭng, ed.: 歷代國文學精華 <u>Yŏktae Kungmunhak Chŏnghwa</u>, "The Quintessence of Korean Literature through the Ages" 博文出版社 Pangmun Ch'ulp'ansa, Seoul, 1938, and reprints), 231-239.

구운몽 Kuun mong, lending library manuscript, 7 vols, about 30 leaves (12 columns, 13-14 syllables) per volume, dated 긔유 (己酉 1909). Title on the cover 九雲夢 Kuun mong. [Tōyō Bunko]

1961 exhibition, 60: 구운몽 Kuun mong, manuscript, 1 vol. (National Library).

1947 exhibition, 83: 九雲夢 Kuun mong, manuscript, 1 vol. (Palace). This appears to have been lost during the Korean War, but Yi Myŏnggu seems to have had a good look at it for his study, listed below.

구운몽 Kuun mong, manuscript, 93 leaves, given as in the **Karam collection**.

구운몽 Kuun mong, Seoul block print, 32 leaves, 孝橋新刊 "newly engraved at Hyogyo". [**British Museum**]

Courant, 771, gives the same as also in Paris, etc.; **Petrova**, 196, gives the same as in Leningrad; same, but no colophon and apparently a later printing [**Harvard**]; this was also reprinted lithographically by 翰南書林 Hannam Sŏrim, Keijō, 191- and 1920.

구운몽 Kuun mong, Seoul block print, 29 leaves, 丁亥季春布洞 "P'odong, third month 1887". [**British Museum**]

This is identical with the 32 leaf edition as far as leaf 28, and leaf 29 is a much shorter ending to the story.

1961 exhibition, 59: 九雲夢 Kuun mong, Chŏnju block print, 2 vols, 35, 50 leaves, in vol. 1: 壬戌孟秋完山開板 "engraved at Chŏnju, seventh month 1862", and in vol. 2: 丁未仲春完南開刊 "engraved at Chŏnju South, second month 1907". (Kang Hanyŏng).

The same, reprinted by 多佳書舖 Taga Sŏp'o, Chŏnju, 1916, is given as in the **Karam collection**.

Kim Tonguk, 397, gives the same, but queries 1907 and suggests 1847. Compare Hyangt'o Sŏul, 8, 1960, page 60.

The catalogue of the **Ilsa and Karam collections** gives several more entries under 김만중: 九雲夢, Kim Manjung: Kuun mong, but there is no clear indication that any but the one manuscript listed above and the Chŏnju block print are in Korean.

Chŏng Kyubok (in his study of the texts, below) gives an edition by Kyŏngsŏng Sŏjŏk Chohap, 1916, 1 vol., 3 kwŏn, in which Hong Sunp'il added Korean particles to the hanmun text of 1803, and the same was advertised by Chosŏn Tosŏ Chusik Hoesa in 1925.

演訂九雲夢 <u>Yŏnjŏng Kuun mong</u>, Yuil Sŏgwan, 1913, 2 vols, 118, 118 pages.

Chŏng Kyubok (in his study of the texts, below) describes this and states that all subsequent paperback editions are derived from it, with the exception of the 1916 edition from the *hanmun*, above. The pre-title *Yŏnjŏng* appears to be used in all paperback editions of this work, but not in those of any other work. It may mean "revised for popular reading", and Chŏng Kyubok suggests that the Yuil Sŏgwan edition was based on a collation of earlier texts and slightly modernised in language.

Several sources report a publication by Pangmun Sŏgwan, 1917, 2 vols.

연명구운몽 <u>Yŏndyŏng Kuun mong</u>, Chosŏn Tosŏ Chusik Hoesa (vol. 1 only seen, 96 pages), and Tongyang Sŏwŏn (vol. 2 only seen, 93 pages), both 1925.

연명구운몽 <u>Yŏndyŏng Kuun mong</u>, currently available from Sech'ang Sŏgwan, 176 pages.

The title has also been advertised by Taech'ang Sŏwŏn and Pogŭp Sŏgwan in 1920, by Pangmun Sŏgwan and Sin'gu Sŏrim in 1923, 1925 and 1932, by Yŏngch'ang Sŏgwan and Hanhŭng Sŏrim in 1925, and by Tŏkhŭng Sŏrim in 1933. Chŏng Kyubok also mentions paperback editions by Hoedong Sŏgwan and Yŏnghwa Sŏgwan.

An edition by 國立서울大學校文理科大學國文學研究室 Kungnip Sŏul Taehakkyo Mullikwa Taehak, Kungmunhak Yŏn'gusil, "Department of Korean Literature, College of Liberal Arts and Sciences, Seoul National University", was advertised by 國際文化舘 Kukche Munhwagwan, Seoul, in 1950, but I have not seen it, nor seen any report of it.

李家源 Yi Kawŏn, ed.: 九雲夢 <u>Kuun mong</u>. 德基出版社 Tŏkki Ch'ulp'ansa, Seoul, 1955. 335, 44 pages.

This is the most useful edition of this work that I have seen. The text is that of Yi Kawŏn's manuscript, above, and there are full notes.

九雲夢 <u>Kuun mong</u> in: 朴晟義 Pak Sŏngŭi, ed.: 九雲夢・謝氏南征記 <u>Kuun mong</u>, <u>Sa-ssi Namjŏng ki</u>, 正音社 Chŏngŭm sa, Seoul, 1959, pages 7-88. This is annotated for use in schools.

九雲夢 <u>Kuun mong</u> in the **Hŭimang Series**, IV 9-154

James S. Gale, translated: <u>The Cloud Dream of the Nine; A Korean Novel</u>..... <u>by Kim Man-choong</u>. Daniel O'Connor, London, 1922. xl, 307 pages.

It is generally thought that this is a translation from the *hanmun* version of 1803, probably with reference also to an edition in Korean.

李明九 Yi Myŏnggu: 九雲夢攷 <u>Kuun mong ko</u>, "A Study of The Nine Cloud Dream" (Seoul, 成均館大學校 Sŏnggyun'gwan Taehakkyo, Sŏnggyun'gwan University: ·成均學報 <u>Sŏnggyun Hakpo</u>, "Sŏnggyun Journal", 2, July 1955, 114-178, and 論文集. 人文社會科學編 <u>Nonmunjip</u>, Inmun Sahoe Kwahak p'yŏn, "Theses, the Humanities and Social Sciences", 3, June 1958, 108-121).

This is the fullest and most careful general study of this work that I have seen. On the texts, only the eight most important are considered, with the well argued conclusion that the Seoul University manuscript, the first listed above, is the nearest to the original that we have.

丁奎福 Chŏng Kyubok: 九雲夢異本攷 <u>Kuun mong Ibon ko</u>, "A Study of the Variant Texts of the Nine Cloud Dream" (Seoul, 高麗大學校亞細亞問題硏究所 Koryŏ Taehakkyo Asea Munje Yŏn'guso, Asiatic Research Center, Korea University: 亞細亞硏究 <u>Asea Yŏn'gu</u>, The Journal of Asiatic Studies, 8, December 1961, 1-43, with an English summary of the whole, 45-49, and 9, May 1962, 133-159).

The conclusion, from a comparison of most of the texts listed above, is that all the texts in Korean, except perphaps for the Seoul University copy, which he was not able to examine closely, are derived from the *hanmun* text as in the 1803 edition. It is also argued that it is mere supposition that the *hanmun* text was a translation from Korean, and some weaknesses in the traditional account of Kim Manjung's writing of the story are pointed out. The direct comparison of the texts is one of the best that has been made of any *kodae sosŏl*, and one certainly could not reject the conclusions without performing the task oneself, but the arguments from the language of the Korean texts could probably not be supported, and there are many points which are not precisely dealt with, especially the early references to this work.

32. 국조고사 Kukcho Kosa "Tales from the Court"

Collected historical stories.

     국됴고사 國朝故事 <u>Kuktyo Kosa</u>, manuscript, 5 vols. [**Palace**]

     국됴고ᄉ 國朝故事 <u>Kuktyo Kosă</u>, manuscript, 5 vols. [**Seoul University**]

     國朝故事 <u>Kukcho Kosa</u>, manuscript, 112 leaves, in the **Karam collection**, is described as in Korean, but the manuscript of 87 leaves in the **Ilsa collection** is not so described.

권선동 **Kwŏn Sŏndong**: see 35 권익중전 **Kwŏn Ikchung chŏn**

33. 권용선전 **Kwŏn Yongsŏn chŏn "The Story of Ch'üan Lung-hsien"**

A love story set in Ming China. See **Kim Kidong**, 435-440 (1956: 242-248).

權龍仙傳 권용선전 <u>Kwŏn Yongsyŏn chyŏn</u>, currently available from Sech'ang Sŏgwan, 87 pages. The title was advertised by Pangmun Sŏgwan and Sin'gu Sŏrim in 1919 and 1925, by Chosŏn Tosŏ Chusik Hoesa in 1925, and by Yŏngch'ang Sŏgwan and Hanhŭng Sŏrim in 1925. **Kim Kidong**, 32, gives a publication by Sin'gu Sŏrim, 1918, 98 pages.

34. 권율장군전 **Kwŏn Yul Changgun chŏn**

Kim Kidong, 589, lists 權慄將軍傳 <u>Kwŏn Yul Changgun chŏn</u> (presumably) "The Story of General Kwŏn Yul" as an historical story in Korean set in Korea, existing in manuscript(s). He also mentions, pages 16 and 225, 都元帥權慄傳 <u>Towŏnsu Kwŏn Yul chŏn</u> (presumably) "The Story of Kwŏn Yul, the Commander-in-Chief". Kwŏn Yul was a general in the wars of 1592-1597 (see **366** 임진록 **Imjin nok**). Kim Kidong refers to **Ku, Son and Kim: Kungmunhak Kaeron**, where the title is mentioned, page 251.

35. 권익중전 **Kwŏn Ikchung chŏn "The Story of Ch'üan I-chung"**

A story of love and war set in Ming China. See **Kim Kidong** (1956), 170-172.

權益重傳 (권익중전) <u>Kwŏn Ikchung chŏn</u>, currently available from Sech'ang Sŏgwan, 40 pages. On the cover 一名權仙童 <u>Ilmyŏng Kwŏn Sŏndong</u>, "Also Called 'Ch'üan Hsien-t'ung'" (Hsien-t'ung is the son of I-chung in the story).

련익즁젼 <u>Kwŏn Ikchung chŏn</u>, Taejo sa, 1959, 51 pages.

귀매 **Kwimae**: see **448** 청구야담 **Ch'ŏnggu Yadam**

36. 규중칠우 **Kyujung Ch'iru "The Seven Friends of the Housewife"**

An allegorical story of a dispute as to their relative importance between a needle, thread, a pair of scissors, a small and a large iron, a tape-measure and a thimble.

閨中七友 <u>Kyujung Ch'iru</u> in: 李秉岐 **Yi Pyŏnggi**, ed.: 要路院夜話記 <u>Yorowŏn Yahwaki</u>, 乙酉文化社 **Ŭryu Munhwasa**, Seoul, 1949, and reprints, 47-56.

An introductory note gives the title of this story as 閨中七友爭論記 Kyujung Ch'iru Chaengnon ki, "Record of the Dispute between the Seven Friends of the House-wife", and states that it is included in 忘老却愁記 Mangno Kaksu ki. Yi Pyŏnggi's one volume manuscript of poetry of this latter title was shown in the 1947 exhibition, as item 34, and the catalogue notes that it has as appendices this story and two others (given under 42 금산사창업연몽유록 Kŭmsan-sa Ch'angŏpyŏn Mongyu rok and 162 삼설기 Samsŏlgi, story no. 1). None of the titles mentioned is given as in the Karam collection. Two other manuscripts, entitled 閨中七友爭功記 Kyujung Ch'iru Chaenggong ki, "Record of the Dispute as to Merit between the Seven Friends of the Housewife", one belonging to Cho Yunje (not shown) and one belonging to Yi Haech'ŏng, are in the catalogue of the 1947 exhibition, but as item 246, under "Essays, Travel Diaries, etc.". I have been told that these were both in metrical form, but Yi Pyŏnggi's text of 1949, above, is not.

37. 규합록 Kyuhap nok

1947 exhibition, 202: 閨閤錄 Kyuhap nok (presumably) "Record of the Women's Quarters", manuscript, 3 vols. (Seoul University).

I did not see this in **Seoul University** in 1962.

그안해 Kŭ Anhae: see **448** 청구야담 Ch'ŏnggu Yadam

38. 금강취유기 Kŭmgang Ch'wiyu ki

金剛聚遊 Kŭmgang Ch'wiyu, Tongmi Sŏsi, 1915, 94 pages.

I read only the opening passage of this paperback, which shows that the story is about a Chŏng Tarhong (뎡달홍) of Sŏrhak-ch'on (셜학촌) in the time of King Kongmin of Koryŏ (1352-1374), and took the title to mean "A Party Outing to the Diamond Mountains", without being able to see its relevance to the story. **Kim Kidong**, 596, lists 金剛聚遊記 Kŭmgang Ch'wiyu ki as a love story in Korean set in Korea, existing in paperback edition(s), but not made known before. On page 561 he prefers not to classify it as to type of story.

39. 금고기관 Kŭmgo Kigwan "Strange Tales New and Old"

今古奇觀 Chin-ku-ch'i-kuan is a Ming collection of forty short stories. I have referred to the reprint of a Ming edition by 人民文學出版社 Jen-min Wen-hsüeh Ch'u-pan-she, Peking, 1957, 2 vols, edited by 顧學頡 Ku Hsüeh-chi. The order

56

of the stories sometimes varies in other editions. Twelve of the stories were translated in E. B. Howell: (Chin Ku Ch'i Kuan) The Inconstancy of Madam Chuang and Other Stories from the Chinese (T. Werner Laurie, London, [1925]) and The Restitution of the Bride and Other Stories from the Chinese (T. Werner Laurie, London, 1926).

There is a manuscript in the **Palace** library entitled on the cover 今古奇觀 **Kŭmgo Kigwan,** one volume, which begins with 둥대윤귀단가ᄉ **Tŭng Taeyun Kwi-dan Kasă.** This will be a translation of story no. 3, 滕大尹鬼斷家私 **T'eng Ta-yin Kuei-tuan Chia-szu,** "The Superior Magistrate T'eng Settles a Case of Private Property through a Ghost" (translated by Howell, 1925, 169-207, as The Judgement of Magistrate T'eng), but unfortunately I did not note what else the volume might contain.

Kim T'aejun, 96, states that the work in Korean called **Kŭmgo Kigwan** which he had seen contained translations of story no. 27, 錢秀才錯占鳳凰儔 **Ch'ien Hsiu-ts'ai Ts'o-chan Feng-huang-ch'ou,** "The Failure to take Possession of Mr. Ch'ien's Fiancee" (Howell, 1925, 211-259: Marriage by Proxy; this may also be 395 전수재전 **Chŏn Sujae chŏn)** and of story no. 7, 賣油郎獨占花魁 **Mai-yu-lang Tu-chen Hua-kuei,** "The Oil Merchant who Took Sole Possession of Hua-Kuei". He also states that **356** 이태백실기 **Yi T'aebaek Silgi** is derived from story no. 6, 李謫仙醉草嚇蠻書 **Li Chai-hsien Tsui-ts'ao Hsia-man-shu,** "Li Po, Drunk, Drafts a Message to Terrify the Barbarians" (Howell, 1925, 65-99: The Diplomacy of Li T'ai-po), that "one version of" **443** 채봉감별곡 **Ch'aebong Kambyŏl kok** is derived from story no. 35, 王嬌鸞百年長恨 **Wang Chiao-luan Pai-nien Ch'ang-hen,** "Wang Chiao-luan's Long Resentment of One Hundred Years", that stories nos. 2 and 4 are to be found in "Hyŏn Pyŏngju's recent compilation **Pak Munsu chŏn"** (see **116** 박문수전 **Pak Munsu chŏn),** and that Hyŏn also translated stories nos. 19 and 20. Story no. 19 is 俞伯牙摔琴謝知音 **Yü Po-ya Shuai-ch'in Hsieh-chih-yin,** "Yü Po-ya Smashes his Lute as a Tribute to One who Understood his Music" (Howell, 1925, 37-61: The Minister, the Lute and the Woodcutter). 伯牙琴 **Paega Kŭm,** "Po-ya's Lute", was advertised by Taech'ang Sŏwŏn and Hanyang Sŏjŏgŏp Chohapso in 1918, and by Taech'ang Sŏwŏn and Pogŭp Sŏgwan in 1919. Story no. 20 is 莊子休鼓盆成大道 **Chuang-tzu Hsiu Ku-pen Ch'eng-ta Tao,** "Chuang-tzu Stops Playing the Drum on a Bowl and Perfects his Magic Powers" (Howell, 1925, 11-34: The Inconstancy of Madam Chuang).

It seem likely that **199** 소소매전 **So Somae chŏn** will have some connection at least with story no. 17 in this collection, 蘇小妹三難新郎 **Su Hsiao-mei San-nan Hsin-lang,** "Miss Su's Three Difficult Marriages"

Many other stories in this popular collection must have either been translated into Korean or have been the inspiration for Korean stories. It should be noted that they are often difficult to identify in that they open with a summary of a story which is similar to the main story being told. This common Chinese practice in story-telling does not seem to have been widely followed in Korea, but it can be seen in the Korean version of story no. 4, which is given under 116 박문수전 Pak Munsu chŏn.

금낭이산 Kŭmnang Isan: see 134 보심록 Posim nok

40. 금대옥환전 **Kŭmdae Okhwan chŏn**

Courant, 851: 금듸옥환젼　金帶玉環傳 Kŭmdăe Okhwan chyŏn, "The Story of the Golden Sash and the Jade Ring" (title only).

금덕전 Kŭmdŏk chŏn, and
금독전 Kŭmdok chŏn: see 43 금송아지전 Kŭm Songaji chŏn

41. 금방울전 **Kŭm Pangul chŏn "The Story of the Golden Bell"**

The story is extremely difficult to follow in detail, and so to summarise, but the bell appears to be born of a woman and to end as a women itself, acting between as the magic guardian of the hero, 張海龍 Chang Hai-lung, during the troubled times at the end of the Yüan Dynasty and the beginning of the Ming Dynasty. See Kim Kidong, 127-130, and Sin Kihyŏng, 428-431. Kim Kidong, 34, gives 能見難思 Nŭnggyŏn Nansa, "One Can Hardly Believe One's Eyes" as the title of a modern rewriting of this story.

금방울젼 Kŭm Pangul chyŏn, lending library manuscript, 3 vols, 29, 31, 29 leaves (11 columns, 14 syllables), dated (vols 1 and 2) 무술 (戊戌 1898). Title on the cover 金鈴傳 Kŭmnyŏng chŏn. [Tōyō Bunko]

금방울젼 Kŭm Pangul chyŏn, Seoul block print, 28 leaves. [British Museum]

There are two such prints in the British Museum, apparently identical as texts, but clearly from different blocks. Courant, 804, gives the same as also in Paris, etc., and Petrova, 192, gives the same, but of 22 leaves, as in the Aston collection in Leningrad.

금방울젼 Kŭm Pangul chyŏn. 翰南書林 Hannam Sŏrim, Keijō, not dated [about 1920]. 16 single leaves. This is a lithographic reprint of a Seoul block print, and what appears to be the same is reproduced facsimile in the **Ewha Series,** I 325-355, with a note 432-433.

Kim Tonguk, 387, gives three Seoul block prints:

(1) 宋洞新刊 "newly engraved at Songdong", 20 leaves; (2) 16 leaves; (3) 28 leaves.

Kim Kidong gives publications by Sin'gu Sŏrim, 1916, 59 pages, and Sech'ang Sŏgwan, 1917, 61 pages, the latter entitled <u>Nŭnggyŏn Nansa</u>. This was advertised by Pangmun Sŏgwan and Sin'gu Sŏrim in 1923, 1925 and 1932.

금방울전 (金鈴傳) <u>Kŭm Pangul chŏn</u> (<u>Kŭmnyŏng chŏn</u>), currently available from Sech'ang Sŏgwan (but text as composed before 1945), 37 (+4) pages. This was advertised by Yŏngch'ang Sŏgwan and Hanhŭng Sŏrim and by Sin'gu Sŏrim in 1925.

금방울전 <u>Kŭm Pangul chŏn</u>, Taejo sa, 1959, 27 pages.

金鈴傳 <u>Kŭmnyŏng chŏn</u> in the **Hŭimang Series**, I 131-160.

鈴 *-nyŏng* is *pangul* "bell".

42. 금산사창업연몽유록 **Kŭmsan-sa Ch'angŏbyŏn Mongyu rok** "Record of a Dream Journey to the Foundation Feast at Chin-shan Temple"

The story is always of several founders of Chinese dynasties, but it varies from text to text, with the setting sometimes in fourteenth century China (Yüan, Chih-cheng) and sometimes in eighteenth century China (Ch'ing, K'ang-hsi). All the texts seen give the impression of being translations from *hanmun* (see **Courant**, 776 and 777). See **Mongyurok Sogo**, 136-137 and 143-144, **Pak Sŏngŭi**, 287-288, and **Sin Kihyŏng**, 431-432.

금산ᄉ창업연의 <u>Kŭmsan-sǎ Ch'angŏp Yŏnŭi</u>, "The Romance of the Foundation Feast at the Chin-shan Temple", manuscript, 3 vols, 24, 24, 26 leaves (12 columns, 18 syllables), dated 병진 (丙辰 1856). Title on the cover 金山寺夢遊錄 <u>Kŭmsan-sa Mongyu rok</u>, "Record of a Dream Journey to the Chin-shan Temple". [**British Museum**]

금산ᄉ <u>Kŭmsan-sǎ</u>, "The Chin-shan Temple", manuscript, 62 (+3) leaves (12 columns, 21 syllables), dated 임술 (壬戌 1862). [**Chŏng Pyŏnguk**]

금산ᄉ창업연몽류록 <u>Kŭmsan-sǎ Ch'angŏbyŏn Mongnyu rok</u>, manuscript, 49 leaves (16 columns, 21 or 22 syllables). Titles on the cover 금산사 <u>Kŭmsan-sa</u> and 金山寺創業宴夢遊錄 <u>Kŭmsan-sa Ch'angŏbyŏn Mongyu rok</u>. On a leaf inside the cover 壬寅七月日孟峴 "at Maenghyŏn, seventh month 1902". [**Chŏng Pyŏnguk**]

Chŏng Pyŏnguk thought that the text was either earlier than the date given or a very faithful copy of something earlier.

금산ᄉ창업연녹 Kŭmsan-să Ch'angŏbyŏn nok, "Record of the Foundation Feast at the Chin-shan Temple", manuscript, 71 leaves (10 columns, 23 syllables). [**Harvard**]

1947 exhibition, 158: 金山寺創業宴錄 Kŭmsan-sa Ch'angŏbyŏn nok, manuscript, 1 vol. (Yi Haech'ŏng).

金山寺創業宴會錄 Kŭmsan-sa Changŏp Yŏnhoe rok was given as one of the appendices (see also **36** 규중칠우 Kyujung Ch'iru and **162** 삼설기 Samsŏlgi, story no. 1) to 忘老却愁記 Mangno Kaksu ki, a one volume manuscript of poetry shown in the 1947 exhibition (item 34, Yi Pyŏnggi), but none of the titles mentioned is given as in the **Karam collection.**

금산ᄉ몽유록 金山寺夢遊錄 Kŭmsan-să Mongyu rok, Hoedong Sŏgwan, 1915, 59 (+15) pages.

금산사몽유록 金山寺夢遊錄 Kŭmsan-sa Mongyu rok, currently available from Sech'ang Sŏgwan, 50 (+13) pages.

The texts appear to be identical in these two paperbacks, and the extra pages are 삼사기 三士記 Samsa ki, story no. 1 in **162** 삼설기 **Samsŏlgi.** The title was advertised by Taech'ang Sŏwŏn and Pogŭp Sŏgwan in 1920, and by Chosŏn Tosŏ Chusik Hoesa in 1925.

43. 금송아지전 **Kŭm Songaji chŏn "The Story of the Golden Calf"**

Kim T'aejun, 45-46, summarises the story as told in a Buddhist work 地行錄第七地 Chihaeng nok, Che Ch'il Chi, which I have not been able to identify. **Kim Kidong,** 114-119, quotes almost all of this, and gives a longer summary of the story as in a publication by Sin'gu Sŏrim, 1923, 35 pages. On page 29 he gives the publishers as Tongmi Sŏsi. Both critics give 金犢傳 Kŭmdok chŏn, which also means "The Story of the Golden Calf", and 金牛太子傳 Kŭmu T'aeja chŏn, "The Story of the Prince of the Golden Cow" as alternative titles. The story is apparently of the incarnation of the Buddha as a prince who is eaten by a cow, which subsequently gives birth to a wondrous calf of golden colour. He is restored to his rightful position by the faith of a princess.

Courant, 926: 금덕젼 Kŭm Tŏk chyŏn may be a mistake for this.

44. 금수전 Kŭmsu chŏn

금수전 <u>Kŭmsu chŏn</u>, block print (?), 20 leaves (枚), is given as in the **Karam collection**. The query is in the catalogue.

Kim Tonguk, 387, gives 禽獸傳 <u>Kŭmsu chŏn</u> (presumably) "The Story of the Beasts" as a Seoul block print of 20 leaves. **Kim Kidong**, 596, lists 禽獸奇夢 <u>Kŭmsu Kimong</u> (presumably) "The Miraculous Dream of the Beasts" as a love story in Korean set in China, existing in paperback edition(s), but not made known before. This was advertised by Sin'gu Sŏrim in 1918.

금우태자전 **Kŭmu T'aeja chŏn**: see **43** 금송아지전 **Kŭm Songaji chŏn**

45. 금향정기 Kŭmhyang-jŏng ki

금향졍긔 <u>Kŭmhyang-jyŏng kŭi</u>, lending library manuscript, 7 vols, 231 leaves (10 columns, 14 syllables) in all, dated 신묘 (辛卯 1891). Title on the cover 錦香亭記 <u>Kŭmhyang-jŏng ki</u>. [**Seoul University**]

금향졍긔 <u>Kŭmhyang-jyŏng kŭi</u>, lending library manuscript, 7 vols, 207 leaves (11 columns, 13-14 syllables) in all, dated 임주 (壬子 1912). Title on the cover 錦香亭記 <u>Kŭmhyang-jŏng ki</u>. [**Tōyō Bunko**]

Courant, 791: 금향뎡긔 金香亭記 <u>Kŭmhyang-dyŏng kŭi</u>, Seoul block print, 2 vols, "engraved at 由洞 Yudong", in Paris, and, 3352: same, 3 vols, also "engraved at Yudong". He describes it as a love story set in the tenth century. **Kim Tonguk**, 390, gives much the same information, adding that the two volume edition is of 36 and 32 leaves. There is a copy of a vol. 2 (of two), 32 leaves, 由洞新刊 "newly engraved at Yudong", in the **British Museum**.

Kim Kidong, 32 and 597, states that it exists in paperback editions, and the title was advertised by Pangmun Sŏgwan and Sin'gu Sŏrim in 1923, 1925, 1928 and 1932.

A novel of the title 錦香亭 <u>Chin-hsiang-t'ing</u>, "The Chin-hsiang Pavilion", is known in China.

46. 금환기봉 Kŭmhwan Kibong.

금환긔봉 金環奇逢 <u>Kŭmhwan Kŭibong</u>, manuscript, 6 vols. [**Palace**]

The meaning of this title is presumably "The Miraculous Encounter of the Gold Ring". The nearest title referred to elsewhere seems to be, **Courant**, 850: 금환지합연 金環再合緣 <u>Kŭmhwan Chăehap yŏn</u>, "The Double Encounter of the

Gold Ring" (title only). **Kim T'aejun,** 229 quotes this as 金環再合錄 <u>Kŭmhwan Chaehap nok,</u> and **Kim Kidong,** 595, quoting this from Kim T'aejun, describes it as a love story in Korean set in China, existing in paperback edition(s).

긔봉..... **Kŭibong.....** : see 기봉..... **Kibong.....**

47. 기몽성취록　Kimong Sŏngch'wi rok

1947 exhibition, 152: 奇夢醒醉錄　Kimong Sŏngch'wi rok (presumably) "Record of Awakening from a Strange Dream", manuscript, 10 vols (Yi Haech'ŏng).

48. 기봉쌍룡기　Kibong Ssangnyong ki

Courant, 837: 긔봉쌍뇽긔 奇逢雙龍記 <u>Kŭibong Ssangnyong kŭi,</u> "Record of the Miraculous Encounter of the Two Dragons" (title only).

49. 기봉장애　Kibong Changae

Courant, 853: 긔봉쟝ᄆᆡ 奇逢長涯 <u>Kibong Changae,</u> "The Miraculous Encounter of the Stream Changae (or Changmae)" (title only). **Kim T'aejun,** 229, quotes 奇逢長涯 <u>Kibong Changae</u> from Courant, and **Kim Kidong,** 595, quoting Kim T'aejun, describes it as a love story in Korean set in China, existing in paperback edition(s).

50. 기봉정취록　Kibong Chŏngch'wi rok

Courant, 843: 긔봉졍취록 奇逢正聚錄 <u>Kŭibong Chyŏngch'ywi rok,</u> "Record of the Miraculous Encounter and the Favourable Assembly" (title only). **Kim T'aejun,** 229, quotes this from Courant as 奇逢正聚譜 <u>Kibong Chŏngch'wi po.</u> **Kim Kidong,** 595, quotes this from Kim T'aejun, and adds that it is a love story in Korean set in China, existing in paperback edition(s).

51. 김길동전　Kim Kiltong chŏn

1947 exhibition, 74: 金吉童傳 <u>Kim Kiltong chŏn</u> (presumably) "The Story of Kim Kiltong", manuscript, 1 vol. (Yi Myŏngsŏn). The catalogue notes that "the contents are by and large the same as" 500 홍길동전 **Hong Kiltong chŏn.**

52. 김덕령전 **Kim Tŏngnyŏng chŏn**

Ku, Son and Kim: Kungmunhak Kaeron, 251, mentions 金德齡傳 Kim Tŏngnyŏng chŏn, "The Story of Kim Tŏngnyŏng" as one of the stories set in the wars of 1592-1597 (see **366** 임진록 **Imjin nok**). **Kim Kidong,** 589, quotes this from the 1949 edition, and adds that it exists in manuscript(s). On page 225 he dismisses it as an embellished biography. See also **Kim T'aejun,** 69-70. The title was advertised by Tŏkhŭng Sŏrim in 1935.

Kim Tŏngnyŏng was a leader of a righteous army in the wars of 1592-1597. There is a version in English of a story about him in Zong In-sob: Folk Tales from Korea (Routledge and Kegan Paul, London, 1952), 58-59.

53. 김상서재세록 **Kim Sangsŏ Chaese rok**

Courant, 867: 김샹셔지셰록 金尙書再世錄 Kim Syangsyŏ Chăesye rok, "The Second Existence of the Minister Kim [Chinese: Chin]" (title only). **Kim T'aejun,** 229, quotes this from Courant as 金尙書再合錄 Kim Sangsŏ Chaehap nok. **Kim Kidong,** 595, quoting this from Kim T'aejun, describes it as a love story in Korean set in China, existing in paperback edition(s). **Kim Kidong (1956),** 11, suggests that it was inspired by **208** 소학사전 **So Haksa chŏn.** Compare also **54** 김상서전 **Kim Sangsŏ chŏn** and **63** 김학사전 **Kim Haksa chŏn.**

54. 김상서전 **Kim Sangsŏ chŏn**

Kim Kidong, 36, includes 金尙書傳 Kim Sangsŏ chŏn (presumably) "The Story of the Minister Kim [or Chin]" among the stories in Korean existing in manuscript(s) which he was not able to discuss. Compare **53** 김상서재세록 **Kim Sangsŏ Chaese rok.**

55. 김씨효문록 **Kim-ssi Hyomun nok**

Courant, 879: 김시효문록 金氏孝門錄 Kim-si Hyomun nok, "The Filial Piety of Kim [or Chin]" (title only). **Kim T'aejun,** 161, has 金氏奉孝錄 Kim-ssi Ponghyo rok in a list of titles of this type which seems to be derived largely from Courant, but the nearest title to this which Courant has is the one just given. **Kim Kidong,** 599, quotes Kim T'aejun's title, and describes it as a moral tale in Korean set in China, existing in manuscript(s).

56. 김원전　Kim Wŏn chŏn "The Story of Chin Yüan"

In fifteenth century China (Ming, Ch'eng-hua), the hero rids his country of a monster, but only gains his reward by the aid of the Dragon King. See **Kim Kidong**, 125-127, and **Sin Kihyŏng**, 354-356.

김원전 <u>Kim Wŏn chyŏn</u>, manuscript, 43 (+1) leaves (10 columns, 22-23 syllables), dated 갑오 (甲午 1894). [**Harvard**]

Courant, 810: 김원전 金圓傳 <u>Kim Wŏn chyŏn</u>, block print, 33 leaves, in Paris, etc. Kim Tonguk, 387, gives the same as a Seoul block print. **Kim Kidong**, 29, gives a publication by Tonga Sŏgwan, 1916, 59 pages, and, on page 125, 1917, 76 pages.

　　　　김월향전 **Kim Wŏrhyang chŏn**: see 58 김인향전 **Kim Inhyang chŏn**

57. 김유신전　Kim Yusin chŏn

Kim Kidong, 209, mentions 金庾信傳 <u>Kim Yusin chŏn</u> as a story modelled on the life of Kim Yusin (593-673). He also includes it in a list, page 33, of *kodae sosŏl* published in paperback editions which he was not able to discuss. The title was advertised by Taech'ang Sŏwŏn and Hanyang Sŏjŏgŏp Chohapso in 1918 and by Taech'ang Sŏwŏn and Pogup Sŏgwan in 1919.

58. 김인향전　Kim Inhyang chŏn "The Story of Kim Inhyang"

The heroine is the elder of two step-daughters at Anju, P'yŏngan Province, early in the fifteenth century. See **Kim Kidong**, 333-336 (1956:313-316).

인향전 <u>Inhyang chyŏn</u>, 박승엽져 "by Pak Sŭngyŏp", currently available from Sech'ang Sŏgwan, 33 (+7) pages, with a title on the cover as given by Kim Kidong, 金仁香傳 <u>Kim Inhyang chŏn</u>. The text ends, after the seven page short story, with an advertisement from before 1945 by a 덕창서관 Tŏkch'ang Sŏgwan. The title was also advertised by Hansŏng Sŏgwan and Yuil Sŏgwan in 1915 and by Pangmun Sŏgwan and Sin'gu Sŏrim in 1923, 1925 and 1932.

Ku, Son and Kim: Kungmunhak Kaeron, 244: 金月香傳 <u>Kim Wŏrhyang chŏn</u> is probably a mistake for this.

59. 김진옥전　Kim Chinok chŏn "The Story of Chin Chen-yü"

The hero, in Ming China, is separated from his parents, has difficulties in making the marriage he wishes, performs deeds of valour in attempting to suppress a rebellion, serves under the Dragon King, etc. See **Kim Kidong**, 264-268, and **Sin Kihyŏng**, 304-305.

김진옥젼 <u>Kim Chinok chyŏn</u>, lending library manuscript, 4 vols. about 30 leaves (11 columns, up to 15 syllables) per volume, dated 긔유 (己酉 1909) in vols 1 and 3. Title on the cover 金振玉傳 <u>Kim Chinok chŏn</u>. [**Tŏyŏ Bunko**]

Kim Kidong, 264, gives publications by Tŏkhŭng Sŏrim, 1916, 70 pages, and Taech'ang Sŏwŏn, 1920, 64 pages, and the title has been advertised by these publishers since the same dates, and by Tongmyŏng Sŏwŏn in 1925 and Taesan Sŏrim in 1926.

60, 김취경전 Kim Ch'wigyŏng chŏn

Kim Kidong, 339-344, describes 金就景傳 <u>Kim Ch'wigyŏng chŏn</u>, "The Story of Kim Ch'wigyŏng", as a "wicked step-mother" story set in Koguryŏ. He describes his text as a manuscript of 4 *kwŏn*, 2 vols, 130 and 128 pages (10 columns, 22 syllables).

61. 김태자전 Kim T'aeja chŏn "The Story of the Crown Prince Kim"

See 梁在淵 Yang Chaeyŏn: 金太子傳評說 <u>Kim T'aeja chŏn P'yŏngsŏl</u>, "A Critical Study of The Story of the Crown Prince Kim" (**Kugŏ Kungmunhak**, 25, June 1962, 175-192). The only other work which gives this story more than a passing mention is **Kim T'aejun** (page 143), and Yang Chaeyŏn seems justified in his criticism that Kim T'aejun's information is not entirely accurate. The story is that Sosŏn (簫仙), son of King Sosŏng (799-800) of Silla, goes searching for a herb to cure his father's illness, is blinded and shipwrecked, but ends up holding high office in China before returning to succeed to the throne. The story seems to bear little relation to the known history of the period.

김틱ᄌ젼 <u>Kim T'äejä chyŏn</u>, manuscript, 3 vols, 107, 118, 95 leaves (12 columns, 17 syllables), dated 디명삼년갑인 (大正三年甲寅 1914) and 디명사년을묘 (大正四年乙卯 1915). [**Seoul University**]

金太子傳 <u>Kim T'aeja chŏn</u>, manuscript, 4 vols, given as in the **Karam collection**.

Yang Chaeyŏn gives a publication by Yuil Sŏgwan, 1915. This is the only text in Korean which he mentions, and he concludes rather hesitantly that it is probably derived from the nineteenth century *hanmun* texts entitled 普陀奇聞 <u>Pot'a Kimun</u>, "Miraculous Report from P'u-t'o", and 六美堂記 <u>Yungmidang ki</u>, "Record of the Hall of Six Beauties", which seem to be the same work. <u>Kim T'aeja chŏn</u> was advertised by Chosŏn Tosŏ Chusik Hoesa in 1925 and by Pangmun Sŏgwan in 1928.

62. 김학공전 **Kim Hakkong chŏn** "The Story of Chin Hao-kung"

A conventional biography of a virtuous and superhuman hero in Sung China. See **Kim Kidong,** 394-397 **(1956: 270-274).** He states that **226** 신계후전 **Sin Kyehu chŏn** is a very close imitation of this story, with the scene shifted to Korea. He gives a publication by Kyŏngsŏng Sŏjŏgŏp Chohap, 1926, 60 pages.

김학공견 (金鶴公傳) Kim Hakkong chyŏn, currently available from Sech'ang Sŏgwan, 60 pages. The title was advertised by Taech'ang Sŏwŏn and Hanyang Sŏjŏgŏp Chohapso in 1918.

63. 김학사전 **Kim Haksa chŏn**

1947 exhibition, 90: 金學士傳 Kim Haksa chŏn (presumably) "The Story of the Minister Kim [or Chin]", manuscript, 1 vol. (Yi Pyŏnggi).

김학ᄉ제생녹 Kim Haksǎ Chǎesaeng nok (presumably) "Record of the Second Existence of the Minister Kim [or Chin]", manuscript, 17 leaves, dated 무인 (戊寅 1878, etc.), given as in the **Karam collection.**

See also **53** 김상서재세록 **Kim Sangsŏ Chaese rok.**

64. 김홍전 **Kim Hong chŏn** "The Story of Chin Hung"

A story of a filial son, set in early fifteenth century China (Ming, Yung-lo).

김홍전 Kim Hong chŏn, lending library manuscript, 4 vols, 31, 30, 31, 32 leaves, dated 경인 (庚寅 1890). Title on the cover 金鴻傳 Kim Hong chŏn. [**Seoul University**]

김홍젼 Kim Hong chyŏn, Seoul block print, 2 vols, 29, 28 leaves. [**British Museum**]

Courant, 808, gives what appears to be the same as this last as in Paris, but, 827, he describes the British Museum text under 짐홍젼 Chim Hŭng chyŏn. **Kim Kidong,** 597, states that it exists in paperback edition(s). All sources except the Seoul University manuscript above give as characters for the title 金紅傳 Kim Hong chŏn.

65. 김효증전 **Kim Hyojŭng chŏn**

Kim Kidong, 592, lists 金孝曾傳 Kim Hyojŭng chŏn (presumably) "The Story of Chin Hsiao-tseng" as a moral story in Korean set in China, existing in paperback edition(s). He refers to **Kim T'aejun,** but I have not found the reference. The first story in **333** 육효자전 **Yuk Hyoja chŏn** concerns one Kim Hyojing, and may be the same story.

66

66. 김희경전 **Kim Hŭigyŏng chon "The Story of Chin Hsi-ching"**

Concerns the difficult course of the hero's love. There are several markedly different versions, as below.

김희경전 Kim Hŭigyŏng chyŏn, manuscript, 2 vols, 45, 67 leaves (vol. 1: 10 columns, 23 syllables, vol. 2: 11 or 12 columns, 19-20 syllables). There is a title leaf with the title 金喜景傳 Kim Hŭigyŏng chŏn and the date 光緒八年壬午 (1882). Title on the cover 金喜慶 Kim Hŭigyŏng (= Chin Hsi-ch'ing). [**Chŏng Pyŏnguk**]

Mibalp'yo Kodae Sosŏl ko: 김희경전 Kim Hŭigyŏng chyŏn, manuscript, 1 vol., two *kwŏn*, 59 leaves (10 columns, 25-30 syllables), probably deficient, characters given 金熙敬傳 Kim Hŭigyŏng chŏn, setting in Yüan China.

女子忠孝錄 (녀ᄌ튱효록) Nyŏjǎ Ch'yunghyo rok, "Record of the Girl's Loyalty and Filial Piety", currently available from Sech'ang Sŏgwan, 71 pages, also same, with identical text, probably about 1945, but with no details of publication. The same was advertised by Tŏkhŭng Sŏrim in 1935.

For this version, set in Ming China, see **Kim Kidong (1956)**, 248-252.

녀즁호걸 (女中豪傑) Nyŏjyung Hogŏl, "The Woman Hero", currently available from Sech'ang Sŏgwan, 113 pages. This title was advertised by Taech'ang Sŏwŏn and Pogŭp Sŏgwan in 1920 and by Pangmun Sŏgwan and Sin'gu Sŏrim in 1923, 1925 and 1932.

This shows considerable differences of text when compared with the other paperback text, and in this the setting is in Sung China, but the story appears to follow essentially the same course in the two, and the characters in the two appear to be all the same.

67. 꼭두각시전 **Kkoktu Kaksi chŏn**

1961 exhibition, 50: 쏙쏙각씨젼 Kkokttok Kakssi chyŏn, manuscript, 1 vol. (National Library). According to the catalogue, the story tells of the loyalty of Kkoktu Kaksi to her crippled and weak-minded husband.

Choe Sangsu: A Study of the Korean Puppet Play (Korean Folklore Studies Series, 4), Korean Books Publishing Company and the Korean Folklore Society, Seoul, 1961, 2, 124, 7 pages (and parallel Korean text, 4, 145 pages), gives the text of the puppet play 꼭두각시놀음 Kkoktu Kaksi Norŭm and discusses it in detail. It differs markedly in general theme from the story given as in the National Library copy above. On pages 14-17 (English; Korean: 10-14) he discusses the word *Kkoktu* and its many variations, see 496 호독각씨전 **Hodok Kak-ssi chŏn**. **Kim T'aejun**, 153, mentions the title 꼭둑각시傳 Kkoktuk Kaksi chŏn.

68. 낙성비룡록　Naksŏng Piryong nok

낙셩비룡 洛城飛龍 Naksyŏng Piryong, manuscript, 2 vols. [**Palace**]

落星傳 낙성젼 Naksŏng chyŏn, manuscript, 1 vol., 55 (+11) leaves (10 columns, 21 syllables), dated 계미 (癸未 1883). [**Chŏng Pyŏnguk**]

I have only noted that these two are the same work, a story set in 16th century China (Ming, Cheng-te).

1947 exhibition, 144: 洛星飛龍錄 (in the catalogue 洛成非龍錄) Naksŏng Piryong nok, manuscript, 2 vols (Yi Haech'ŏng).
Recent press reports on work done on the Palace collection describe this as a tale of marvels.

　　　　낙양삼사기 **Nagyang Samsa ki**: see 162 삼설기 **Samsŏlgi**

69. 낙천등운 Nakch'ŏn Tŭngun

낙쳔등운 落泉登雲 Nakch'yŏn Tŭngun, manuscript, 5 vols. [**Palace**]

70. 난조재세기연록 Nanjo Chaese Kiyŏn nok

Courant, 866: 난조지셰긔연록 鸞鳥再世奇緣錄 Nanjo Chăesye Kŭiyŏn nok, "The Miraculous Destiny of the Phoenix in its Second Existence" (title only). **Kim T'aejun**, 229, quotes this from Courant. **Kim Kidong**, 595, quotes it from Kim T aejun as 鸞鳥再世奇緣 Nanjo Chaese Kiyŏn, and describes it as a love story in Korean set in China, existing in paperback edition(s).

71. 난학몽 Nanhak mong

난학몽 .Nanhak mong, manuscript, 4 vols, 62, 59, 49, 49 leaves (10 columns, 25 syllables), dated 융희이년무신 (隆熙二年戊申 1908), "compiled by 悟軒 Ohŏn, 鄭泰運 Chŏng T'ae'un, translated by 肯齋 Kŭngjae, 李敏濟 Yi Minje". [**Seoul University**]

When this text was shown in the **1947 exhibition**, as item 208, its title was given wrongly as 남학몽 Namhak mong.

72. 남계연담 Namgye Yŏndam

남계연담 南溪演談 Namgye Yŏndam, manuscript, 2 vols (vols 2 and 3 only).
[Palace]

1947 exhibition, 159: 南溪讌談 Namgye Yŏndam (in the catalogue 南燕讌談 Namyŏn Yŏndam), manuscript, 3 vols (Yi Haech'ŏng).

The title would appear to mean "Namgye's Lectures", and there is a famous scholar Namgye, 朴世采 Pak Sech'ae (1632-1695), but if this is taken literally it is difficult to see why this work should be classified as a *sosŏl*.

남뎡일긔 **Namdyŏng Ilgŭi**: see **76** 남행록 **Namhaeng nok**

73. 남송연의 Namsong Yŏnŭi

Courant, 765: 남송연의 南宋演義 Namsong Yŏnŭi, "Romance of the Southern Sung". Southern Sung is 1127-1280. Works of similar titles are known in China.

남원고亽 **Namwŏn Kosă**: see **460** 춘향전 **Ch'unhyang chŏn**

74. 남윤전 Nam Yun chŏn

Kim Kidong, 569-575, describes 南胤傳 Nam Yun chŏn, "The Story of Nam Yun", from a late Yi Dynasty manuscript of 86 pages (12 columns, 26 syllables), as the story of the love of Nam Yun during the wars of 1592-1597 (see **366** 임진록 **Imjin nok**). He does not appear to be historical.

남정기 **Namjŏng ki**: see **149** 사씨남정기 **Sa-ssi Namjŏng ki**

남정일기 **Namjŏng Ilgi**: see **76** 남행록· **Namhaeng nok** and **133** 병자록 **Pyŏngja rok**

75. 남정팔난기 **Namjŏng P'allan ki** "Record of Eight Trials on the Journey to the South".

The story is set in Sung China, and the traveller is 황극 , for which **Courant, 824**, suggests 黃極 Huang Chi. No extended description or discussion of this work appears to have been published.

남정팔난긔 <u>Namjyŏng P'allan kŭi</u>, manuscript, 6 vols. about 60 leaves (10 col-umns, 21 syllables) per volume, dated 신ᄉ (辛巳 1881, etc.). Title on the cover 南征八難記 <u>Namjŏng P'allan ki</u>. [Chŏng Pyŏnguk]

This is a very nice "palace style" manuscript, but Chŏng Pyŏnguk was very doubtful about dating it any earlier than 1881.

남정팔난긔 <u>Namjyŏng P'allan kŭi</u>, manuscript, 5 vols, 76, 82, 71, 73, 61 leaves (10 columns, 23 syllables). Title on the cover 南征八難記 <u>Namjŏng P'allan ki</u>. [**Seoul University**]

This text is also in "palace style" script. It appears to be dated 빅호, which might be 庚寅 1890.

남정팔난긔 <u>Namjyŏng P'allan kŭi</u>, lending library manuscript, 3 vols (vols 1, 3 and 11), 28, 29, 26 leaves, dated 긔히 (己亥 1899) in vols 1 and 11. Title on the cover of vol. 1 南征八亂記 <u>Namjŏng P'allan ki</u>, "Record of the Eight Wars on the Journey to the South". [**Harvard**]

남정팔난긔 <u>Namjyŏng P'allan kŭi</u>, lending library manuscript, 14 vols, about 30 leaves (11 columns, up to 15 syllables) per volume, dated 신히 (辛亥 1911) in all vols except vol. 9. Title on the cover 南征八難記 <u>Namjŏng P'allan ki</u>. [**Tōyō Bunko**]

남정팔난긔 <u>Namjyŏng P'allan kŭi</u>, Seoul block print, 2 vols, 30, 30 leaves. [**British Museum**]

Courant, 824, gives what appears to be the same as this as in Paris.

남정긔**Namjyŏng kŭi**: see 149　사씨남정기　**Sa-ssi Manjŏng ki**

남학몽 **Namhak mong**: see 71　난학몽 **Nanhak mong**

남한일기**Namhan Ilgi**: see 133　병자록 **Pyŏngja rok**

76. 남행록　Namhaeng nok

南行錄 <u>Namhaeng nok</u> (presumably) "Record of a Journey to the South", manu-script, 33 leaves, title on the first leaf 남명일긔 <u>Namdyŏng Ilgŭi</u>, given as in the **Karam collection**. The title as on the first leaf would be the same in modern Korean as one title given as of a story set in the wars of 1636-1637, see **133 병자록 Pyŏngja rok,** but I have been told that this work in the **Karam collection** is a record of a banishment which might be either fictional or autobiographical.

77. 낭자전 **Nangja chŏn**

1947 exhibition, 167: 娘子傳 <u>Nangja chŏn</u> (presumably) "The Story of the Maiden", manuscript, 1 vol. (Ewha). This may be known under another title, perhaps **224** 숙영낭자전 **Sugyŏng Nangja chŏn.**

냥 . . . . . **Nyang. . . . .** : see 양 . . . . . **Yang. . . . .**

녀 . . . . . **Nyŏ. . . . .** : see 여 . . . . . **Yŏ. . . . .** , but for

녀와뎐 **Nyŏwa tyŏn:** see **113** 문창진군탕평록 **Munch'ang Chin'gun T'angp'yŏng nok,** for

녀장군전 **Nyŏ Changgun chyŏn:** see **403** 정수정전 **Chŏng Sujŏng chŏn,** and for

녀즁호걸 **Nyŏjyung Hogŏl,** and

녀조충효록 **Nyŏjă Ch'yunghyo rok:** see **66** 김희경전 **Kim Hŭigyŏng chŏn**

년국지 **Nyŏn'gukchi,** and

녈국지 **Nyŏlgukchi:** see **261** 열국지 **Yŏlgukchi**

노셤샹좌긔 **Nosyŏm Syangjwa kŭi,**

노쳐녀가 **No Ch'ŏnyŏ ka,** and

녹쳐ㅅ연회 **Nok Ch'yŏsă Yŏnhoe:** see **162** 삼셜기 **Samsŏlgi**

놀부전 **Nolbu chŏn:** see **531** 흥부전 **Hŭngbu chŏn**

농문전 **Nyongmun chyŏn:** see **305** 용문전 **Yongmun chŏn**

뉴 . . . . . **Nyu. . . . .** : see 유 . . . . . **Yu. . . . .**

뉵 . . . . . **Nyuk. . . . .** : see 육 . . . . . **Yuk. . . . .**

눙견난사 **Nŭnnggyŏn Nansa:** see **41** 금방울전 **Kŭm Pangul chŏn**

니 . . . . . **Ni. . . . .** : see 이 . . . . . **Yi. . . . .**

님 . . . . . **Nim. . . . .** : see 임 . . . . . **Yim. . . . .** , but for

님장군전 **Nim Changgun chyŏn:** see **363** 임경업전 **Yim Kyŏngŏp chŏn**

다람의쇼지 **Taram ŭi Syoji:** see **431** 쥐전 **Chwi chŏn**

78. 단장록 **Tanjang nok**

Kim Kidong gives 斷腸錄 <u>Tanjang nok</u> (presumably) "Record of Heartbreak" as existing in paperback edition(s) (page 32), but not made known before (page 597). **Sin Kihyŏng,** 475, adds that it is a love story in Korean set in China. **Kim T'aejun,** 242, mentions it as a work of the early years of the twentieth century by 一齋 Ilchae, 趙重桓 Cho Chunghwan.

단틱죵전 **Tan T'ǎejyong chyǒn:** see 83 당태죵전 **Tang T'aejong chǒn**

79. 담낭전 Tamnang chǒn "The Story of T'an-nang, the Walking Encyclopaedia"

담낭뎐 <u>Tamnang tyǒn</u>, manuscript, 25 leaves (11 columns, 22 syllables), dated 계히 (癸亥 1923, etc.), is reproduced in the **Ewha Series**, II 381-430. The story is set in 12th century China (Sung, Cheng-ho), but, as the note, pages 442-445, points out, the story is only a setting for the recital of some elementary learning. Tamnang (談囊, T'an-nang in Chinese) is both the personal name of the "hero" and an indication of his role: "story-bag". See also **162** 삼셜기 **Samsǒlgi**.

80. 담화사기 Tamhwa Sagi

담화ᄉ긔 <u>Tamhwa Sǎgǔi</u>, manuscript, (4½+) 16½ leaves (11 columns, 16 syllables). [**Chǒng Pyǒnguk**]

The 4½ leaves are **120** 방흘동자전 **Panghul Tongja chǒn**, dated 1915, and both stories are about small children. The title of this one will probably be something like "A History Told as a Story".

81. 당씨츙효록 Tang-ssi Ch'unghyo rok

Courant, 887: 당셰츙효록 唐氏忠孝錄　Tang-ssi Ch'yunghyo rok, "The Loyalty and Filial Piety of the Tang [Chinese: T'ang] Family" (title only). **Kim T'aejun,** **161,** has this in a list of titles of this type which seems to be derived largely from Courant. **Kim Kidong,** 599, quotes it from Kim T'aejun, and describes it as a moral tale in Korean set in China, existing in manuscript(s).

82. 당진연의 Tang Chin Yǒnǔi

당진연의 唐秦演義 <u>Tang Chin Yǒnǔi</u>, manuscript, 6 vols. [**Palace**]
당진연의 唐晉演義 <u>Tang Chin Yǒnǔi</u>, manuscript, 13 vols. [**Palace**]
당진연의 <u>Tang Chin Yǒnǔi</u>, lending library manuscript, 17 vols, about 30 leaves (11 columns, 15 syllables) per volume. This text is formed from two copies, vols 1-5 and vols 6-17. Vol. 4 is dated 신츅 (辛丑 1901) and vols 6-16 are dated 임자 (壬子 1912). Title on the cover 唐秦演義 <u>Tang Chin Yǒnǔi</u>. [**Tōyō Bunko**]

These texts all presumably cover the same period of Chinese history, but I did not determine what that was in any case. **Courant,** 762, who mentions no specific texts, suggests that this title refers to the revolt of 秦宗權 Ch'in Tsung-ch'üan against T'ang in 883. This would be supported by the title in

Chinese on two of the three texts above, but the second text above suggests that Chin is 後晉 Hou-chin, one of the Five Dynasties, which followed T'ang.

83. 당태종전 Tang T'aejong chŏn "The Story of T'ai-tsung of T'ang"

The story mainly concerns the conversion of the Emperor to Buddhism by one 雲水先生 Yün-shui Hsien-sheng. See **Kim Kidong**, 119-125, and **Sin Kihyŏng**, 408-412. **Kim T'aejun**, 97, suggests that the story is near to that of the Chinese story 唐太宗洞冥記 T'ang T'ai-tsung Tung-ming-chi, "Record of T'ai-tsung of T'ang's View of Hell", which is among the texts found at Tun-huang and also exists in several later versions.

Courant, 786: 당틱종젼 唐太宗傳 Tang T'ǎejong chyŏn, block print, 26 leaves, in Paris, etc. **Petrova, 208:** 단틱종젼 唐太宗傳 Tan(g) T'ǎejyong chyŏn, block print, 31 leaves, in the Aston collection in Leningrad. **Kim Tonguk, 387:** 唐太宗傳 Tang T'aejong chŏn, Seoul block print, 紅樹洞戊午 "Hongsudong, 1858", 26 leaves.

당틱종젼 Tang T'ǎejyong chyŏn. 翰南書林 Hannam Sŏrim, Keijō, 191-, 26 single leaves. A lithograph of a Seoul block print.

Kim Tonguk, 398, gives a Chŏnju block print 太宗傳 갑ᄌ즁춘의곤샨은각셔라 "T'aejong chŏn, engraved .... second month 1864".

Kim Kidong, 119, gives a publication by Tongmi Sŏsi, 1915, 30+ pages.

唐太宗傳 당태종젼 Tang T'aejyong chyŏn, currently available from Sech'ang Sŏgwan, 32 pages. It was advertised by Yŏngch'ang Sŏgwan and Hanhŭng Sŏrim in 1925.

대담강유실기 **Taedam Kang Yu Silgi:** see 8 강유실기 **Kang Yu Silgi**

84. 대명영렬전 **Taemyŏng Yŏngnyŏl chŏn**

대명영렬뎐 大明英烈傳 Taemyŏng Yŏngnyŏl tyŏn, manuscript, 8 vols. [**Palace**]

1947 exhibition, 156: 大明英烈傳 Taemyŏng Yŏngnyŏl chŏn, manuscript, 1 vol. (Yi Haech'ŏng).

The title presumably means "Stories of the Heroes of Ming". There are several Chinese works of very similar titles, usually telling of the founding of the Ming Dynasty.

대성용문전 **Taesŏng Yongmun chŏn:** see 194 소대성전 **So Taesŏng chŏn**

85. 대성훈몽전 **Taesŏng Hunmong chŏn**

디성훈몽전 <u>Tăesyŏng Hunmong chyŏn</u>, manuscript. [**Ogura collection, Tokyo**]
The only note I have on this is that it "looks recent".

86. 대송흥망록 **Taesong Hŭngmang nok**

대송흥망녹 大宋興亡錄 <u>Taesong Hŭngmang nok</u> (presumably) "Record of the Rise and Fall of Sung", manuscript, 2 vols. [**Palace**]

Chinese works of similar titles seem to be concerned primarily with 岳飛 Yüeh Fei, see 111 무목왕정충록 **Mumok Wang Chŏngch'ung nok**.

87. 대의각미록 **Tae'ŭi Kangmi rok**

1947 exhibition, 143: 大意各美錄 <u>Tae'ŭi Kangmi rok</u>, manuscript, 1 vol. (Yi Haech'ŏng.

    댱 . . . . . **Tyang**. . . . . : see 쟝 . . . . . **Chang**. . . . .

    뎍셩의젼 **Tyŏk Syŏngŭi chyŏn** : see 392 젹셩의젼 **Chŏk Sŏngŭi chŏn**

    뎐우치젼 **Tyŏn Uch'i chŏn**, etc.: see 396 젼우치젼 **Chŏn Uch'i chŏn**

    뎡 . . . . . **Tyŏng**. . . . . : see 졍 . . . . . **Chŏng**. . . . . , but for

    뎡일남뎐 **Tyŏng Illam tyŏn**: see 351 이언총림 **Iŏn Ch'ongnim**

88. 도앵행 **To-aeng-haeng**

도잉힝 <u>To-ăeng-hăeng</u>, manuscript, 2 vols, 80, 92 leaves. (10 columns, 17 or 18 syllables), dated 긔히 (己亥 1899). [**Imanishi collection, Tenri**]

도잉힝 <u>To-ăeng-hăeng</u>, manuscript, 1 vol. (vol. 1 only, incomplete), 29 leaves (12 columns, 12 or 13 syllables). [**Chŏng Pyŏnguk**]

Both of these are extremely difficult to read, but they appear to begin in a very similar way, setting the story in the reign of the Emperor Wu of Liang, that is in sixth century China. The catalogue of the Imanishi collection suggests the characters 桃櫻杏 **To-aeng-haeng** very tentatively for the title, which would then presumably mean "The Peach, the Cherry and the Apricot". Two manuscripts of this title were shown in the **1947 exhibition**, item 141 (Yi Haech'ŏng, 2 vols, and Pang Chonghyŏn). Another (Kim Kyŏngch'un) was not shown.

도잉횡 <u>To-ăeng-hoeng</u>, manuscript, 2 vols, dated 갑인 (甲寅 1914, etc.), in the **Ilsa collection** could be Pang Chonghyŏn's text above from the 1947 exhibition.

89. 도원결의록   Towŏn Kyŏrŭi rok "Record of the Oath of Brotherhood in the Garden of Peaches"

도원결의녹 Towŏn Kyŏrŭi nok, Seoul block print, 1 vol. (vol. 1 only), 18 leaves, 南谷新板 "newly engraved at Namgok". Subtitle 일명은별삼국지 Ilmyŏng ŭn Pyŏl Samgukchi, "Also Called A Version of San-kuo-chih". Title on the cover 桃園結義 Towŏn Kyŏrŭi. [**Imanishi collection, Tenri**]

I did not note the contents specifically, but this is obviously a version of the opening passages of San-kuo-chih Yen-i (see **156** 삼국지연의 **Samgukchi Yŏnŭi.**

도원수권율전 **Towŏnsu Kwŏn Yul chŏn**: see **34** 권율장군전 **Kwŏn Yul Changgun chŏn**

90. 동국사기 **Tongguk Sagi** "Historical Records of the Eastern Kingdom"

동국ᄉ긔 Tongguk Săgŭi, manuscript, 63 leaves (12 columns, 16 syllables), dated inside the front cover 甲辰 (1904). [**Chŏng Pyŏnguk**]

This came from the Maenghyŏn 孟峴 royal household. It contains historical stories from the Koryŏ and Yi Dynasties.

동상기 **Tongsang ki**: see **169** 서상기 **Sŏsang ki**

91. 동선기 **Tongsŏn ki**
Kim T'aejun, 123: "The 記 *ki* of 南征記 Namjŏng ki [= **149** 사씨남정기 **Sa-ssa Namjŏng ki**] is also the same as the *ki* of the anonymous 洞仙記 Tongsŏn ki. Tongsŏn ki tells the story of the love affair of 洞仙 [Tung-hsien?] and 西門勗 [Hsi-men Chi?]. In it there are many exchanges of letters between these two, and the tradition that it was written in one night by the author to console his sick mother raises the question of whether this is not also a work by 金萬重 Kim Manjung."

Kim Kidong, 594, lists it as a love story in both *hanmun* and Korean set in China, existing in manuscript(s). He refers to Kim T'aejun.

92. 동야휘집 **Tongya Hwijip**
1947 exhibition, 100: 東野彙集 **Tongya Hwijip**, manuscript, 1 vol. (Pang Chonghyŏn). No such text is given as in the **Ilsa collection.**

The title means something like "Classified Stories from Korean History", and
is fairly generally known as that of an 8 volume *hanmun* work of the mid-
nineteenth century (see **Maema Kyōsaku: Kosen Sappu,** III 1503, the catalogue of
the **Karam collection,** and, for reference to a story in it which is similar to that
of **121 배비장전 Pae Pijang chŏn,** P'ansori Palsaeng ko, 268-269, as described
in the **Introduction,** §7.3.3, **Kim Kidong,** 536-538, etc.). The catalogue of the
1947 exhibition does not state that Pang Chonghyŏn's text is, or was, in *hanmun,*
and the fact that it is apparently so much shorter than other known texts indicates that it may be the sort of partial translation which is often found of such
works.

93. 동유기　Tongyu ki

Petrova, 218: 東遊記 동유긔　Tongyu kŭi, "Record of a Trip to the East", manuscript, 4 vols (vols 2, 3, 4, 6), 51, 48, 52, 50 leaves (10 columns), dated 戊寅 (Petrova: 1758 or 1818), in the Aston collection in Leningrad. The quotation from
the colophon suggests that it is a private copy. The contents are summarised
as: "A novel, in which travellers undergo adventures in a journey to the east,
i.e. Korea." A novel of this title is known in China, but that does not seem to
touch upon Korea.

　　동주열국지 **Tongju Yŏlgukchi:** see **261** 열국지 **Yŏlgukchi**

　　동진긔 **Tongjin kŭi:** see **369** 자치통감 **Chach'i T'onggam**

94. 동한연의　Tonghan Yŏnŭi

Courant, 754: 동한연의 東漢演義 Tonghan Yŏnŭi, "Romance of the Eastern Han".
The text is not identified, but is described as of 6 vols. Eastern Han is 25-
220 A.D. Compare **292 옥환기봉 Okhwan Kibong,** and see **Kim T'aejun,** 86 and
92. The title was advertised by Hangsŏng Sŏgwan and Yuil Sŏgwan in 1915.

　　도..... **Tyo.....:** see 조..... **Cho.....**

95. 두껍전　Tukkŏp chŏn "The Story of the Toad"

A fable in which certain human characteristics are embodied in several animals, primarily a toad and a fox. Various versions of it are given by the
critics, see **Kim T'aejun,** 130-131, **Kim Kidong,** 161-165 **(1956:** 366-370), **Pak
Sŏngŭi,** 307-310, and **Sin Kihyŏng,** 385-387, and also in a number of works on
folk-lore.

독겁전 Tukkŏp chyŏn, manuscript, 6 columns and 9 leaves (12 columns, 28 sylla-bles), dated 경술 (庚戌 1910). [Dr Doo Soo Suh] The whole manuscript is entitled 郎君歌 Nanggun ka on the cover, and contains first a *kasa* 낭군가 Nanggun ka of 17½ leaves and 4 columns.

노셤 샹좌귀 Nosyŏm Syangjwa kŭi, "Old Toad in the Seat of Honour", the third story in the third volume of the 1848 Seoul block print of 162 삼셜기 Samsŏlgi.

독겁전 蟾同知傳 Tukkŏp chyŏn, Sŏm Tongji chŏn, Tŏkhŭng Sŏrim, 1916 (reprinted from 1914), 39 pages.

셤동지젼 (독겁젼) Sŏm Tongji chyŏn (Tukkŏp chyŏn), currently available from Sech'ang Sŏgwan (but text as composed before 1945), 24 pages.

셤동지젼 (蟾同知傳) Sŏm Tongji chŏn, Taejo sa, 1959, 27 pages.

One or other of these two titles has been advertised in almost every catalogue of paperback publications.

두겁傳 Tukkŏp chŏn in the **Hŭimang Series**, IV 287-305,

Various sources also give the title as 蟾處士傳 Sŏm Ch'ŏsa chŏn. Both 同知 *tongji* and 處士 *ch'ŏsa* are old official titles which are used very loosely and may be translated "Mr". 蟾 *sŏm* is *tukkŏp*, "toad".

96. 등하미인젼 **Tŭngha Miin chŏn**

Kim Kidong, 597, lists 燈下美人傳 Tŭngha Miin chŏn (presumably) "The Story of the Beauty under the Lamp" as a love story in Korean set in China, existing in paperback edition(s) (also page 33, without *chŏn*), but not made known before.

림..... **Rim.....** : see 임..... **Yim.....** , but for

림장국전 **Rim Changgun chyŏn:** see 363 임경업전 **Yim Kyŏngŏp chŏn**

97. 매당편 **Maedang p'yŏn**

Courant, 918, lists 미당편 梅棠篇 **Măedang p'yŏn, "**The Compositions of Maedang" (title only) as a novel. It seems on the face of it to be unlikely title for a
novel, and he also lists, 744, not as a novel, 梅堂遺稿 Maedang Yugo, but I have
not been able to discover who Maedang might be.

매유랑독점화괴 **Maeyurang Tokchŏm Hwagoe:** see 39 급고기관 **Kŭmgo Kigwan**

98. 매화전 **Maehwa chŏn**

梅花傳 Maehwa chŏn, "The Story of Plum-blossom" or 江陵梅花傳 Kangnŭng
Maehwa chŏn, "The Story of Plum-blossom of Kangnŭng" was one of the stories
sung in *p'ansori*, see **Introduction,** §7.3, but all that is known of the *p'ansori*
version(s) now is the summary in the twelfth stanza of Kwan-u-hŭi, see Song
Manjae ŭi Kwan-u-hŭi, 103-104 and 118, and P'ansori Palsaeng ko, 276-277.
Both give a number of stories about *kisaeng* called Maehwa or from Kangnŭng.

명듀보월빙 **Myŏngdyu Powŏl Ping:** see 102 명주보월빙 **Myŏngju Powŏl Ping**

명사십리 **Myŏngsa Simni:** see 134 보심록 **Posim nok**

99. 명월기함록 **Myŏngwŏl Kiham nok**

Courant, 922: 명월긔함록 明月起涵錄 Myŏngwŏl Kŭiham nok, "The Stagnant
Water Stirred up by the Moon" (?) (doubtful title only: the query is Courant's
own).

명월부인전 **Myŏngwŏl Puin chyŏn:** see 117 박씨부인전 **Pak-ssi Puin chŏn**

100. 명의록 **Myŏngŭi rok**

1947 exhibition, 160: 明義錄 Myŏngŭi rok (presumably) "Record of Splendid
Righteousness", manuscript, 1 vol. (Yi Haech'ŏng). The *hanmun* work of this
title is factual, and there is a well known version of this explained in Korean,
明義錄諺解 Myŏngŭi rok Ŏnhae, in a print of 1777.

101.　명주기봉 Myŏngju Kibong

명쥬긔봉 明珠奇逢 <u>Myŏngjyu Kŭibong</u>, manuscript, 24 vols. [**Palace**]
When this text was shown in the **1961 exhibition**, as item 68, the catalogue noted: "A novel which portrays the troubled fortunes of Hsüan Shou-wen." He is the subject of **492 현수문전 Hyŏn Sumun chŏn. Courant**, 842, has the same title, "The Miraculous Encounter of Myŏngju". **Kim Tʻaejun**, 229, quotes both 明珠奇逢 <u>Myŏngju Kibong</u> and 明珠奇緣 <u>Myŏngju Kiyŏn</u> from Courant. I cannot find the second separately listed in Courant, though he does have 명쥬옥연 明珠玉緣 <u>Myŏngju Ogyŏn</u>, "The Precious Destiny of Myŏngju" (entry 859), which is not quoted by any Korean critic. **Kim Kidong,** 594 and 595, quotes both titles from Kim Tʻaejun, and describes them as love stories in Korean set in China, existing in paperback edition(s). <u>Myŏngju Kibong</u> was advertised by Hansŏng Sŏgwan and Yuil Sŏgwan in 1915 among a number of translations from Chinese. The two titles would mean virtually the same, but, other than Courant's translation and suggestion that Myŏngju may be the name of a woman, I have not been able to see the meanings of them. There does not appear to be any such name in the texts of any other story about Hsüan Shou-wen that I have seen, or any reference which would explain the title. The same word or name Myŏngju appears in the next two titles.

102.　명주보월빙 Myŏngju Powŏl Ping

명듀보월빙 明珠寶月聘 <u>Myŏngdyu Powŏl Ping</u>, manuscript, 100 vols. [**Palace**]
The title would appear to mean "The Betrothal of Myŏngju and Powŏl [Chinese: Ming-chu and Pao-yüeh]". Recent press reports of work done on the Palace collection mention this as a story of a family in 99 vols, and state that **335 윤하정삼문취록 Yun Ha Chŏng Sammun Chʻwirok** is a sequel to it. **Courant**, 921, gives the title 명쥬보월 明珠寶月 <u>Myŏngjyu Powŏl</u>, "The Clear Pearl and the Precious Moon". On Myŏngju, see **101 명주기봉 Myŏngju Kibong.**

103.　명주보은록 Myŏngju Poŭn nok

Courant, 864: 명쥬보은록 明珠報恩錄 <u>Myŏngjyu Poŭn nok</u>, "Myŏngju's Returning Favours" (title only). On Myŏngju, see **101 명주기봉 Myŏngju Kibong.**

　　명쥬옥연 **Myŏngjyu Ogyŏn: see 101 명주기봉 Myŏngju Kibong**

104. 명행정의록　Myǒnghaeng Chǒngŭi rok

명힝정의록 明行貞義錄　Myǒnghǎeng Chyǒngŭi rok, manuscript, 70 vols.
[Palace]

1961 exhibition, 43: 명행의록　Myǒnghaeng Chǒngŭi rok, manuscript, 94 vols
(National Library).

On the second text, the catalogue noted: "A compilation to encourage loyalty,
filial piety, virtue and good speech and behaviour." Courant, 875, gives the title,
Kim T'aejun, 161, probably quotes it from Courant, and Kim Kidong, 599, referring to Kim T'aejun, describes it as a moral tale in Korean set in China, existing
in manuscript(s). He gives a slightly different title, 明行正義錄　Myǒnghaeng
Chǒngŭi rok, which means essentially the same: "Record of Exemplary Acts of
Righteousness".

모란졍긔 Moran-jyǒng kǔi: see 374　쟝국진젼　Chang Kukchin chǒn

105. 목시룡형제충효젼 Moksirong Hyǒngje Ch'unghyo chǒn

목시룡형졔츙효견 Moksirong Hyǒngjye Ch'yunghyo chyǒn, manuscript by Hashimoto,
1 vol. (vol. 1 only), 37 leaves. Title on the cover 牧忠孝傳　Mok Ch'unghyo chǒn,
date on the cover 庚子 (1900). [Harvard]

There are many elementary mistakes in this text. I could not see the meaning
of *Moksirong*, though Mok can be a surname, and the rest of the title presumably
means "The Story of the Loyalty and Filial Piety of the Brothers . . . . ."

몽결초한송 Monggyǒl Ch'ohan song: see 413　제마무젼　Che Mamu chǒn

106. 몽린록　Mongnin nok

夢麟錄 Mongnin nok, manuscript, 12 vols, given as in the Ilsa collection.

107. 몽옥쌍룡기　Mongok Ssangnyong ki

Courant, 835: 몽옥쌍룡긔 夢玉雙龍記　Mongok Ssangnyong kǔi, "Record of the Two
Dragons and the Jade Seen in a Dream" (title only).

108. 몽옥쌍봉련록 Mongok Ssangbong(n)yŏn nok

Kim Kidong, 600, lists 夢玉雙峰練錄 Mongok Ssangbongnyŏn nok (or Ssangbong yŏn nok) as a moral tale in Korean set in China, existing in manuscript(s) (also page 37), but not made known before.

109. 몽옥쌍환기봉 Mongok Ssanghwan Kibong

Courant, 846: 몽옥쌍환긔봉 夢玉雙環奇逢 Mongok Ssanghwan Kŭibong, "The Miraculous Encounter of the Two Jade Rings seen in a Dream" (title only).

110. 무릉도원기 Murŭng Towŏn ki

Kim Kidong, 596, lists 武陵桃源記 Murŭng Towŏn ki (presumably) "Record of the Peach Spring at Wu-ling" as a love story in Korean set in China, existing in paperback edition(s), but not made known before. The title at least must be derived from 桃花源記 T'ao-hua-yüan-chi, an allegory written about 400 A.D. by 陶潛 T'ao Ch'ien (陶淵明 T'ao Yüan-ming). It was advertised by Yŏngch'ang Sŏgwan before 1945, with the pre-title 五美人 O Miin, "The Five Beauties"

111. 무목왕정충록 Mumok Wang Chŏngch'ung nok

무목왕정퉁록 武穆王貞忠錄 Mumok Wang Chyŏngt'yung nok, manuscript, 7 vols (vols 1, 2, 6, 7, 8, 10 and 12). [**Palace**] According to the librarian, a seal print on this text is of " the wife of King Yŏngjo", i.e. the text may be eighteenth century.

Chinese works of the same and similar titles concern 岳飛 Yüeh Fei (1103-1141), and the title presumably means "Record of the Virtue and Loyalty of King Wu-mu". **Courant**, 935: 무목왕명총뉵 Mumok Wang Myŏngch'yong nyuk (doubtful title only) is presumably a mistake for a title of the same work. See also **86** 대송흥망록 Taesong Hŭngmang nok.

무송타령 Musong T'aryŏng, and
무숙이타령 Musugi T'aryŏng: see 296 왈짜타령 Waltcha T'aryŏng
무신창의사실 Musin Ch'angŭi Sasil: see 133 병자록 Pyŏngja rok

112. 문장풍류삼대록 Munjang P'ungnyu Samdae rok

문장풍뉴삼디록 文章風流三代錄 Munjang P'ungnyu Samdăe rok, manuscript, 2 vols. [**Palace**]

문쟝풍뉴삼디록 文章風流三代錄 Munjyang P'ungnyu Samdăe rok, manuscript, 2 vols. [**Palace**]

I was told that these were two copies of a *sosŏl*, but made no note of their contents.

113. 문창진군탕평록 Munch'ang Chin'gun T'angp'yŏng nok "Record of Saint Wen-ch'ang's Righteous Battles"

문챵진군탕평녹 Munch'yang Chin'gun T'angp'yŏng nok, manuscript, 22 leaves (18 or 19 columns, 20 syllables) and 2 columns, dated 긔스 (己巳 1869, etc.). [**Chŏng Pyŏnguk**]

녀와뎐 문챵셩탕평요얼 Nyŏwa tyŏn, Munch'yang-syŏng T'angp'yŏng Yoŏl, manuscript, 47½ (+20) leaves, dated 계튝 (癸丑 1913). [**Chŏng Pyŏnguk**] The 20 leaves are 199 소소매전 So Somae chŏn and some poems.

These two are very similar stories, which I found very difficult to understand. Apparently 문챵진군 (文昌眞君) or 문챵셩 (文昌聖) is 文昌帝君 Wen-ch'ang Ti-chün, patron saint of men of letters, etc.; 녀와 is 女媧 Nü-wa, a female saint; 탕평 is 蕩平, referring in this case to strife between Taoism and Buddhism; and 요얼 is 妖孽, which seems to mean something like "the works of the devil". See also **473 평요기 P'yŏngyo ki**.

女媧錄 Yŏwa rok, manuscript, 53 leaves, given as in the **Ilsa collection**, may be the same or a similar work.

114. 미소명행록 Miso Myŏnghaeng nok

Courant, 874: 미소명힝록 湄蘇明行錄 Miso Myŏnghăeng nok, "The Exemplary Behaviour of Miso" (title only).

민셩왕후덕행록 Min Sŏngwanghu Tŏkhaeng nok: see 362 인현왕후전 Inhyŏn Wanghu chŏn

115. 민시령전 Min Si(r)yŏng chŏn

민시령전 Min Siryŏng chyŏn, manuscript by Hashimoto, 33 (+8) leaves, dated 己亥 (1899). Title on the cover 閔時榮傳 Min Siyŏng chŏn. **[Harvard]** The story is set in China, but I could not examine the text far enough to correct its obvious mistakes or gain any accurate knowledge of the story in detail.

      쌍천긔봉 Psangch'yŏn Kŭibong: see 241 쌍천기봉 Ssangch'ŏn Kibong

116. 박문수전 Pak Munsu chon "The Story of Pak Munsu [and Other Stories]"

어스박문슈 (御史朴文秀) Ŏsă Pak Munsyu, "The Government Inspector Pak Munsu", 금슈호연성현령션병쥬즙 錦水胡然生玄翎仙丙周輯 "compiled by Kŭmsu Hoyŏnsaeng, Hyŏn Yŏngsŏn, Pyŏngju". Title on the cover 朴文秀傳 박문슈젼 Pak Munsyu chyŏn. Kyŏngsŏng Sŏjŏgŏp Chohap, 1926. 43 pages.

Kim T'aejun, 96, mentions this collection of three stories as "Hyŏn Pyŏngju's recent compilation Pak Munsu chŏn". The compiler also edited one text of 燕의脚 Yŏn ŭi Kak (a modern rewriting of 531 흥부전 Hŭngbu chŏn) in 1920, and in that text he is given as 錦江漁父 Kŭmgang Ŏbu 玄翎仙 Hyŏn Yŏngsŏn. I have not found any further information on him.

The title story concerns the historical Pak Munsu (1691-1756), and is described by **Pak Sŏngŭi**, 385-386. The second story is set in Pyŏn Han, and tells of the fate of the daughter of an official who dies while still responsible for the loss of a granary. Kim T'aejun has pointed out, page 96, that this is derived from 兩縣令競義婚孤女 Liang Hsien-ling Ching-i Hun Ku-nü, "The Two County Magistrates, Rivals in Justice, Arrange a Marriage for an Orphan Girl", story no. 2 in Chin-ku-ch'i-kuan, see 39 금고기관 **Kŭmgo Kigwan**. The third story is about 裴度 P'ei Tu, in T'ang China, and is a translation of the fourth story in Chin-ku-ch'i-kuan, 裴晋公義還原配 P'ei Chin-kung I-huan Yüan-p'ei, "P'ei, Duke of Chin, Justly Restores the Wife" (translated in E. B. Howell: The Restitution of the Bride ....., T. Werner Laurie, London, 1926, 7-32).

The three stories are all very nicely told in traditional style, but it seems fairly clear that they are modern compositions. The texts below all follow that given above, but without the attribution to Hyŏn Pyŏngju or Yŏngsŏn, and largely without the explanatory characters which are used in the above text.

御史朴文秀傳 어사박문수전 Ŏsa Pak Munsu chŏn, Chinhŭng Sŏgwan, not dated [probably about 1945-1950], 32 pages.

御史朴文秀傳 어사박문수전 Ŏsa Pak Munsu chŏn, currently available from Sech'ang Sŏgwan, 31 pages.

御史朴文秀傳 (어사박문수전) Ŏsa Pak Munsu chŏn, Taejo sa, 1959, 32 pages.

朴文秀傳 Pak Munsu chŏn in the **Hŭimang Series**, IV 241-262.

The various titles were advertised by Pangmun Sŏgwan and Sin'gu Sŏrim in 1919, by Sin'gu Sŏrim in 1925, by Yŏngch'ang Sŏgwan and Hanhŭng Sŏrim in 1925, and by Kwangdong Sŏguk in 1926.

117. 박씨부인전 **Pak-ssi Puin chŏn** "The Story of the Lady Pak"
The heroine, who appears to be completely fictional, renders magical aid to her husband, the historical 李時白 Yi Sibaek, a military leader during the Manchu invasions of 1637 (see **133** 병자록 `Pyŏngja rok`). See **Kim T'aejun**, 99-103, **Kim Kidong**, 225-232 (1956: 128-133), **Pak Sŏngŭi**, 261-267, **Sin Kihyŏng**, 343-349. The assumption among the critics seems to be that this work dates from not long after the period of the action, since it is widely suggested that this novel was written to appeal to women readers of novels at the end of the seventeenth century. Since this has coloured more than one general survey of Korean literature, it may be as well to stress here the very late dates of all the texts below. No old texts are found in any of the older established collections, the title is not in **Courant,** and the work has not been found in any block print edition. On the evidence now available it would be more reasonable to connect its composition with the war of 1894 than the war of 1637.

朴氏傳 **Pak-ssi chŏn**, manuscript, 62 leaves, dated 임신 (壬申 1872, etc.), given as in the **Karam collection.**

朴氏傳 **Pak-ssi chŏn**, manuscript by Hashimoto, 65 leaves, copied in 己亥 (1899) from a text dated 丁酉 (1897, etc.). [**Harvard**]

박씨젼 **Pak-ssi chyŏn**, manuscript, 73 leaves (9 columns, 23 syllables). Title on the cover 박시젼 **Pak-si chyŏn.** [**Harvard**] This had not been catalogued when I saw it in March 1965, and although it is a nice looking manuscript, it appeared to me to be in the same hand as the copy of **318** 유소제전 **Yu Soje chŏn,** which is fairly certainly 1915-1918.

박씨젼 **Pak-ssi chyŏn**, manuscript, 31 leaves, dated 을축 (乙丑 1925, etc.). Title on the title page 朴夫人傳 **Pak Puin chŏn.** [**Seattle**] This manuscript was also not catalogued when I saw it in March 1965, but my impression from its general style, especially taken in conjunction with the other manuscripts acquired at about the same time, was that it was unlikely to date from 1865 or any earlier date.

명월부인젼 Myŏngwŏl Puin chyŏn, "The Story of the Lady of Myŏngwŏl", manuscript, 71 leaves. Title at the end of the story 박씨뎐 Pak-ssi tyŏn. Reproduced in the **Ewha Series**, III 273-413, with a note 424-426. This is possibly the manuscript reported to be owned by 孫洛範 Son Nakpŏm, and to be the basic text for his annotated edition 朴氏夫人傳 **Pak-ssi Puin chŏn**, 豊國學園 P'ungguk Hagwŏn, Seoul, 1956, 174 pages, which I have not been able to find.

朴夫人傳 **Pak Puin chŏn**, manuscript, 36 leaves, given as in the **Karam collection**.

1947 exhibition, 137: 朴氏傳 **Pak-ssi chŏn**, manuscript, 1 vol. (Yi Myŏngsŏn).

Kim Kidong, 226, gives 朴氏傳 **Pak-ssi chŏn**, Hansŏng Sŏgwan, 1915, 62 pages, and 朴氏夫人傳 **Pak-ssi Puin chŏn**, Taech'ang Sŏwŏn, 1917, 52 pages.

박씨젼 **Pak-ssi chyŏn**, currently available from Sech'ang Sŏgwan, 47 pages. Also the same, but 46 pages, no publisher, not dated, and frequent advertisements of the title in paperbacks.

朴氏傳 **Pak-ssi chŏn** in 李慶善 Yi Kyŏngsŏn, ed.: 壬辰錄・朴氏傳 **Imjin nok, Pak-ssi chŏn**, 正音社 Chŏngŭm sa, Seoul, 1962, pages 101-216. This is rewritten as a school text. No source for the text is given.

朴氏傳 **Pak-ssi chŏn** in the **Hŭimang Series**, IV 155-193.

박타령 **Pak T'aryŏng: see 531 홍부전 Hŭngbu chŏn**

118. 박태보실기 Pak T'aebo Silgi

Kim Kidong, 38, mentions 朴泰輔實記 **Pak T'aebo Silgi**, "The True Story of Pak T'aebo". Pak T'aebo (1654-1689) was one of those who opposed King Sukchong's banishing of the queen and his remarriage (see **362 인현왕후전 Inhyŏn Wanghu chŏn**). The only advertisement of the title which I have seen, by Tŏkhŭng Sŏrim in 1935, places it among the modern novels.

박흥보가 **Pak Hŭngbo ka: see 531 홍부전 Hŭngbu chŏn**

119. 반씨전 Pan-ssi chŏn

Kim T'aejun, 123-124: " 潘氏傳 **Pan-ssi chŏn** was probably suggested by 南征記 **Namjŏng ki** [=**149 사씨남정기 Sa-ssi Namjŏng ki**]." **Kim Kidong,** 592, refers to Kim T'aejun and describes it as a domestic story in Korean set in China, existing in paperback edition(s). The title was advertised by Taech'ang Sŏwŏn and Pogŭp Sŏgwan in 1919 and 1920.

120. 방휼동자전　Panghul Tongja chŏn

방휼동ㅈ전 <u>Panghul Tongjă chyŏn</u>, manuscript, $4\frac{1}{2}$ $(+16\frac{1}{2})$ leaves (11 columns, 16 syllables), dated. 을뫼乙卯 (1915). [**Chŏng Pyŏnguk**]

A very short story about a small child. 동ㅈ is 童子, but 방휼 is not clear. The $16\frac{1}{2}$ leaves are **80 담화사기 Tamhwa Sagi.**

121. 배비장전　Pae Pijang chŏn "The Story of the Aide-de-camp Pae"

A pleasantly amusing story of the discomforture of a gentleman who swears to his wife, as he leaves for a tour of duty on Cheju Island, that he is above taking an interest in other women. See <u>Song Manjae ŭi Kwan-u-hŭi</u>, 106, and <u>P'ansori Palsaeng ko</u>, 266-274, as described in the **Introduction**, §7.3, for a very full statement and study of the evidence for the currency of this story in the reper- toire of the *kwangdae* almost continuously from the mid-eighteenth to the early twentieth century, and of similar stories from even earlier. Part of the evi- dence is <u>Kwan-u-hŭi</u>, stanza 16. Most of this will also be found in **Kim Kidong,** 534-542 (see also **1956**: 216-219), **Pak Sŏngŭi,** 452-455, and **Sin Kihyŏng,** 436-438. All critics are agreed that it was only turned into a novel at a very late date.

金三不 Kim Sambul, ed.: 裴裨將傳・雍固執傳　Pae Pijang chŏn, <u>Onggojip chŏn</u> 國際文化舘 Kukche Munhwagwan, Seoul, 1950, contains a very convenient anno- tated text of this story, pages 13-86. The spelling is modern, but the text is said to be taken from a manuscript, which was in the editor's possession, of 75 leaves, the last 16 of which were a later addition. No date is suggested for it. It was shown in the **1947 exhibition,** as item 162, and it is thought that it must have been lost in the Korean War. It would appear to be a text such as might have been used in the reciting of *p'ansori.*

裴裨將傳 <u>Pae Pijang chŏn</u> in the **Hŭimang Series,** I 247-280, seems to follow Kim Sambul's text.

裴裨將傳 빅비장젼 <u>Păe Pijang chyŏn</u>, currently available from Sech'ang Sŏgwan, 72 pages. This text differs considerably from Kim Sambul's in wording.

Kim Kidong, 32 and 534, gives publications by Sin'gu Sŏrim, 1916 and 1920, 112 pages, and the title was advertised by Pangmun Sŏgwan and Sin'gu Sŏrim in 1919, by Tongyang Sŏwŏn in 1925, by Kwangdong Sŏguk in 1926, and by Tŏkhŭng Sŏrim in 1935.

One or two of the less reliable reference works give 稗將 *p'aejang* for the 裨將 *pijang* of the title. The two words mean much the same if *p'aejang* is 牌將, but

稗將 gives no sense. In Kwan-u-hŭi the office is given as 婢將 , which is also *pijang*, but which I have not been able to find as an official title. A deliberate pun may be intended.

122. 배시황전 **Pae Sihwang chŏn**

Kim Kidong, 589, lists 裴是愰傳 Pae Sihwang chŏn as an historical story in Korean set in Korea, existing in manuscript(s), but not made known before. On page 37, he mentions 裴是惺傳 Pae Sisŏng chŏn in the same terms. No other source mentions this, and it may be a misprint, but on the other hand there is hardly any other reference to the first title above either, and I have not found any historical person either Pae Sihwang or Pae Sisŏng.

배정승 **Pae Chŏngsŭng**: see 448 청구야담 **Ch'ŏnggu Yadam**

배진공의환원배 **Pae Chin-gong Ŭihwan Wŏnbae**: see 116 박문수전 **Pak Munsu chŏn**

123. 백극지 **Paekkŭkchi**

1947 exhibition, 151: 빅극지 Păekkŭkchi, manuscript, 1 vol. (Yi Haech'ŏng).

124. 백룡전 **Paengnyong chŏn**

Kim T'aejun quotes 伯龍傳 Paengnyong chŏn (or Paek Yong chŏn) from Shōsho Kibun, see **Introduction**, §7. 2. **Kim Kidong**, 594, referring to Kim T'aejun, describes it as a love story in Korean set in China, existing in paperback edition(s).

125. 백복전 **Paekpok chŏn**

1947 exhibition, 161: 百福傳 Paekpok chŏn, manuscript, 2 vols (Kim Sambul).

백아금 **Paega Kŭm**: see 39 금고기관 **Kŭmgo Kigwan**

백옥루 **Paegong-nu**: see 276 옥루몽 **Ongnu mong**

126. 백학선전 **Paekhaksŏn chŏn** "The Story of the White-Crane Fan"

In fourteenth century China (Ming, Hung-wu), the hero gives the fan to his sweetheart as a token. **Kim T'aejun**, 219-220, **Kim Kidong**, 432-435, **Pak Sŏngŭi**, 442-443, and **Sin Kihyŏng**, 301-302, (also **Kim Tonguk**, 388) all summarise the story with little comment.

빅학선견 **Păekhaksyŏn chyŏn**, manuscript in pen and ink, 46 leaves, dated 明治三十五年 (1902). Title on the cover 白鶴扇傳 Paekhaksŏn chŏn. **[Harvard]**

빅학선견 **Păekhaksyŏn chyŏn**, Seoul block print, 24 leaves. **[British Museum]**

Courant, 807, gives the same as also in Paris, etc., **Petrova**, 200, gives the same as in the Aston collection in Leningrad, and 翰南書林 Hannam Sŏrim, Keijŏ, published the same in a lithographic reproduction in 1920.

빅학선견 **Păekhaksyŏn chyŏn**, Seoul block print, 20 leaves, 宋洞新刊 "newly engraved at Songdong". **[Ogura Collection, Tokyo]**

The same, or a very similar block print is reproduced in the **Ewha Series**, II 341-380, with a note 441.

(증슈) 빅학선 (增修) 白鶴扇 (Chŭngsyu) Păekhaksŏn, "The White Crane Fan (Revised)", 박건회편 "compiled by Pak Kŏnhoe", Sin'gu Sŏrim, 1915, 48 (+29) pages. Also the same, currently available from Sech'ang Sŏgwan, 44 (+27) pages. The extra pages in these two are 태상감응편 T'aesyang Kamŭng p'yŏn, a translation of the Chinese collection of moral tales 太上感應篇 T'ai-shang Kan-ying-p'ien, for which see **Kim T'aejun**, 16, 97 and 159.

李明九 Yi Myŏnggu, ed.: 白鶴扇傳 Paekhaksŏn chŏn in **Hyŏndae Munhak**, 32, August 1957, 289-297, and 35, November 1957, 263-270.

白鶴扇傳 Paekhaksŏn chŏn in the **Hŭimang Series**, V 283-319.

127. 번이화정서전 **Pŏn Yihwa Chŏngsŏ chŏn** "The Story of Fan Li-hua's Subjugation of the West"

번리화정서전 **Pŏn Rihwa Chyŏngsyŏ chŏn**, Pangmun Sŏgwan and Sin'gu Sŏrim, 1933 (reprinted from 1932), 83 pages, title on the cover 樊梨花征西傳 **Pŏn Yihwa Chŏngsŏ chŏn**, and the same currently available from Sech'ang Sŏgwan, but title on the cover 梨花征西傳 Yihwa Chŏngsŏ chŏn.

This is a sequel to **186** 설정산실기 **Sŏl Chŏngsan Silgi**, and the fourth, and apparently the last, in the series which begins with **185** 설인귀전 **Sŏl In'gwi chŏn**.

128. 범문저연별전 **Pŏm-mun Chŏyŏn Pyŏlchŏn**

Courant, 855: 범문져연별전 范門諸緣別傳 **Pŏm-mun Chyŏyŏn Pyŏlchyŏn**, "The Story of the Happy Destiny of the Pŏm Family" (title only). Neither the form nor the translation of the title is very convincing.

129. 범문정충절언행록 Pŏm Munjŏng Ch'ungjŏl Ŏnhaeng nok

범문졍츙졀언힝녹 范文正忠節言行錄 Pŏm Munjyŏng Ch'yungjyŏl Ŏnhăeng nok, manuscript, 30 vols (vols 2-31). [**Palace**] The title presumably means "Record of the Loyal and Virtuous Words and Actions of Fan, Wen-cheng".

Courant, 764: 범문정공츙렬록 范文正公忠烈錄 Pŏm Munjyŏng-gong Ch'yungnyŏl lok, "Record of the Heroism and Loyalty of Fan, Duke Wen-cheng". He mentions no texts, but suggests that it concerns 范仲淹 Fan Chung-yen (989-1052).

130. 벽주금천쌍환 Pyŏkchu Kŭmch'ŏn Ssanghwan

Courant, 849: 벽쥬금천쌍환 碧珠金川雙環 Pyŏkchyu Kŭmch'yŏn Ssanghwan, "The Two Rings of Pyŏkchu and Kŭmch'ŏn". He mentions no texts, but suggests that Pyŏkchu and Kŭmch'ŏn are names of women.

131. 벽파금천쌍환기봉 Pyŏkp'a Kŭmch'ŏn Ssanghwan Kibong

Courant, 932: 벽파금쳔쌍환긔봉 碧坡金川雙環奇逢 Pyŏkp'a Kŭmch'yŏn Ssanghwan Kŭibong, "The Miraculous Encounter of the Two Rings of Pyŏkp'a and Kŭmch'ŏn (title only). **Kim T'aejun,** 229, quotes this as 碧坡金川雙環 Pyŏkp'a Kŭmch'ŏn Ssanghwan, and **Kim Kidong,** 595, quoting Kim T'aejun, describes it as a love story in Korean set in China, existing in paperback edition(s).

132. 벽허담 Pyŏkhŏdam

벽허담관제언녹 碧虛談關帝言錄 Pyŏkhŏdam Kwanjye Ŏnnok, manuscript, 26 vols. [**Palace**]

벽허담 Pyŏkhŏdam, manuscript, 29 vols, dated 무신 (戊申 1908) in vols 1 and 29. Title on the cover 碧虛談 Pyŏkhŏdam. Title on the first leaf of vol. 29 벽허담관제언녹 Pyŏkhŏdam Kwanje Ŏnnok. [**Seoul University**]

關帝 Kuan-ti (Kwanje in Korean) is the spirit of 關羽 Kuan Yü, a hero of San-kuo-chih Yen-i (see **156 삼국지연의 Samgukchi Yŏnŭi**), and the patron saint of soldiers. A religious sect centred on his worship published scriptures in Korean in 1855 and 1884 (see 최현배 Ch'oe Hyŏnbae: 한글갈 Han'gŭl Kal, 정음사 Chŏngŭm sa, Seoul, 1961, page 185). Kwanje Ŏnnok means "The Words of Kuan-ti". For Pyŏkhŏdam, Courant, 919, suggests "Conversations on the Blue Sky", but with a query, and I can offer no more certain translation.

변강쇠전 Pyŏn Kangsoe chŏn, etc.: see **1 가루지기타령 Karujigi T'aryŏng**

별 .... **Pyŏl** ..... "A Version of ....." is a common prefix to titles, which can usually be readily referred to in their form without the Pyŏl....., but for

별주부전 **Pyŏl Chubu chŏn,**

별토전 **Pyŏlt'o chŏn,** etc.: see **468** 토끼전 **T'okki chŏn**

133. 병자록　**Pyŏngja rok "Record of the Year of the Red Rat [1636]"**

Kim Kidong, 589, lists 丙子錄 Pyŏngja rok as an historical novel in both *hanmun* and Korean set in Korea, existing in manuscript(s). He refers to **Kim T'aejun,** but Kim T'aejun appears to have only a passing reference to the title, page 99. **Kim Kidong,** 17, states specifically that it is a novel inspired by the Manchu invasions of 1636-1637, but on page 226 he states that he had not read it. The only texts of this title which I have seen are either straightforward modern historical accounts of the invasions, or translations-cum-explanations of 羅萬甲 Na Man'gap's contemporary diary in *hanmun,* 丙子日記 Pyŏngja Ilgi.

Kim T'aejun, 69, mentions as titles of works concerned with the wars of 1636-1637, **363** 임경업전 **Yim Kyŏngŏp chŏn,** and also the following, on which I have no supporting evidence, or even some conflicting evidence: 丙子湖南倡義錄 Pyŏngja Honam Ch'angŭi rok (presumably) "Record of the Righteous in the Southern Provinces in the Year of the Red Rat"; 丁卯兩湖擧義錄　Chŏngmyo Yanghogŏ Ŭirok (presumably) "Record of Righteousness in the Invasions of the South-West in the Year of the Red Hare [1627]"; 西征錄　Sŏjŏng nok (presumably) "Record of the Subjugation of the West [i.e. P'yŏngan Province, so presumably referring to the revolt of 1624]"; 江都日記 Kangdo Ilgi "Kanghwa Diary"; 南征日記 Namjŏng Ilgi, perhaps a mistake for 南漢日記 Namhan Ilgi, which appears in a similar list on page 99, and is presumably the same as **152** 산성일기 **Sansŏng Ilgi,** but see also **76** 남행록 **Namhaeng nok;** 戊申倡義事實 Musin Ch'angŭi Sasil, "Facts of the Righteous of the Year of the Yellow Monkey", which is known as a record of the suppression of a revolt of 1728; 永陽四難倡義錄 Yŏngyang Sanan Ch'angŭi rok, "Record of the Righteous in the Four Difficulties at Yŏngyang", apparently, but the reference is not obvious; and 三學士傳 Sam Haksa chŏn, "The Story of the Three Ministers", which is known as a *hanmun* work on the three strongest opponents of an accomodation with the Manchu, 洪翼漢 Hong Ikhan, 吳達濟　O Talche and 尹集 Yun Chip. See also **117** 박씨부인전 **Pak-ssi Puin chŏn.**

It is perhaps significant that even such a thorough study as 張德順 Chang Tŏksun: 丙子胡亂을 前後한 戰爭小說 Pyŏngja Horan ŭl Chŏnhu han Chŏnjaeng

Sosŏl, "War Tales of about the Time of the Manchu Invasions of 1636" (Seoul, 延世大學校文科大學 Yŏnse Taehakkyo Munkwa Taehak, College of Liberal Arts, Yonsei University: 人文科學 Inmun Kwahak, Journal of the Humanities, 3, January 1959, 1-16), while very interesting on war tales in general, gives no further titles of sosŏl in Korean specifically arising from these wars, and no additional evidence for the existence of any of the above.

In short, all references to the wars of this period by critics and literary historians have led to only three kodae sosŏl in Korean with stories set in them: **117** 박씨부인전 **Pak-ssi Puin chŏn, 152** 산성일기 **Sansŏng Ilgi** and **363** 임경업전 **Yim Kyŏngŏp chŏn.**

134. 보심록 Posim nok

Kim Kidong, 390-394, describes a meandering story of virtuous acts rewarded under the title 報心錄 <u>Posim nok</u>. He gives 錦囊二山 <u>Kŭmnang Isan</u> as an alternative title, and 明沙十里 <u>Myŏngsa Simni</u> as the title of a modern rewriting. On page 34 he states that both these are titles of modern rewritings of the story. **Sin Kihyŏng,** 360-364, gives much the same information. **Kim T'aejun,** 160, 164-165, suggests that it is derived from a Chinese work 趙氏孤兒 <u>Chao-shih Ku-erh</u>.

Kim Kidong, 390, gives a paperback, title not given, by Hoedong Sŏgwan, 1912, 140 pages, and, on page 32, 報心錄 <u>Posim nok</u> by Kyŏngsŏng Sŏjŏgŏp Chohap, 1926, 118 pages. The two texts which I have seen are:

明沙十里 명사십리 <u>Myŏngsa Simni</u>, Kyŏngsŏng Sŏjŏgŏp Chohap, 1926, 93 pages, and currently available from Sech'ang Sŏgwan, 88 pages, and:

금낭이산 (錦囊二山) (一名報心錄) <u>Kŭmnang Isan (Ilmyŏng Posim nok)</u>, currently available from Sech'ang Sŏgwan, 118 pages.

The first of these is in traditional kodae sosŏl form, and appears to be the story as described by Kim Kidong. The second has the episodes in a completely different order, and is modern in style. This does not accord exactly with Kim Kidong's information, but he is certainly right in his view that it is difficult to see the literary value of the work through its heavy moralising, and that the story is extremely complicated. My own impression is that anyone who cares to read the stories may hazard his own guess at the meanings of the titles.

The advertisements which I have seen, by almost all publishers of paperbacks, are, for <u>Posim nok</u> 1919, 1923 and 1928, for <u>Myŏngsa Simni</u> several between 1919 and 1935, and for <u>Kŭmnang Isan</u> several between 1923 and 1925.

135. 보은기우록 Poŭn Kiu rok

보은긔우록 報恩奇遇錄 <u>Poŭn Kŭi'u rok</u>, manuscript, 18 vols. [Palace]

보은긔우록 <u>Poŭn Kŭi'u rok</u>, manuscript, 18 vols, 563 leaves (10 columns, 20 syllables) in all, reported by **Petrova**, 220, under the title 報恩記偶錄 <u>Poŭn Kiu rok</u>, to be in the Aston collection in Leningrad. She gives a reproduction of the first page in table 4.

Courant, 862: 보은긔우록 報恩奇遇錄 <u>Poŭn Kŭi'u rok</u>, "The Miraculous Returning of a Favour" (title only).

The story is set in sixteenth century China (Ming, Chia-ching), and appears to concern the fortunes of a 위 (衛 , 魏, etc., Wei) family.

보흥루몽 **Po Hongnu mong**: see 501 홍루몽 Hongnu mong

136. 봉선루기 Pongsŏl-lu ki

Kim Kidong, 596, lists 逢仙樓記 <u>Pongsŏl-lu ki</u> (presumably) "Record of the Pongsŏn Pavilion" as a love story in Korean set in Korea, existing in paperback edition(s), but not made known before.

137. 봉황금 Ponghwang kŭm

Kim T'aejun, 228, describes 鳳凰琴 <u>Ponghwang kŭm</u> (presumably) "The Phoenix Lute" as derived from the stories about Su Yün. See 208 소학사전 **So Haksa chŏn**. The title was advertised by Pangmun Sŏgwan and Sin'gu Sŏrim in 1923, 1925 and 1932, by Sinmyŏng Sŏrim in 1930, and by Tŏkhŭng Sŏrim in 1935.

봉황대 **Ponghwang-dae**: see 341 이대봉전 Yi Taebong chŏn

138. 봉황전 Ponghwang chŏn

Kim Kidong, 598, lists 鳳凰傳 <u>Ponghwang chŏn</u> (presumably) "The Story of the Phoenix" as a love story in Korean set in China, existing in manuscript(s), but not made known before.

139. 부담 Pudam "Tales of Hearsay"

1947 exhibition, 244: 淨淡 Pudam, manuscript, 1 vol. (Palace). I could not find this in the **Palace** collection in 1962.

李秉岐 Yi Pyŏnggi, in 要路院夜話記 Yorowŏn Yahwa ki (乙酉文化社 Ŭryu Munhwasa, Seoul, 1949), pages 69-97, describes Pudam as an outstanding collection of good stories, and prints three stories from it: 신방초일 (新房初日) Sinbang Ch'oil, "The First Day of Marriage", 불효부전 (不孝婦傳) Purhyobu chŏn, "The Story of the Unfilial Wife", and 해서긔문 (海西奇聞) Haesŏ Kŭimun, "A Strange Report from Hwanghae".

140. 부부화락록 Pubu Hwarak nok

1947 exhibition, 188: 부부화락녹 Pubu Hwarak nok (presumably) "Record of Harmony between Man and Wife", manuscript, 1 vol. (Kim Ikhwan).

141. 부용상사곡 Puyong Sangsa kok

Kim Kidong, 492-495, describes 芙蓉想思曲 Puyong Sangsa kok, "Puyong's Song of Love", from a publication by Sin'gu Sŏrim, 1914, 87 pages, as a relatively straightforward story of the love of a *kisaeng* and a *yangban*, in the best traditions of such stories. He states that the story was "introduced briefly" by Kim T'aejun, but I cannot find the reference, and this may be a mistake, since on page 601 he refers to **Ku, Son and Kim: Kungmunhak Kaeron,** and this does summarise the story, on page 257.

142. 북송연의 Puksong Yŏnŭi "Romance of Northern Sung"

북송연의 北宋演義 Pŭksong Yŏnŭi, manuscript, 5 vols. [**Palace**]
북송연의 Puksyong Yŏnŭi, lending library manuscript, 13 vols, about 30 leaves (11 columns, 15 syllables) per volume, dated 임인 (壬寅 1902). Title on the cover 北宋演義 Puksong Yŏnŭi. [**Tōyō Bunko**]

Courant, 763, gives the title only, as on the first text above. Northern Sung is 960-1126. Works of this title are known in China. See also **Kim T'aejun,** 86, 92.

143. 빙빙전 **Pingbing chŏn**

빙빙뎐 聘聘傳 <u>Pingbing tyŏn</u>, manuscript, 4 vols (vols 2-5). [Palace]

꼭쏙각씨젼 **Kkokttok Kakssi chyŏn**: see 67 꼭두각시전 **Kkoktu Kaksi chŏn**

144. 사각전 **Sa Kak chŏn** "The Story of Hsieh Chüeh"
Mibalp'yo Kodae Sosŏl ko describes this story from a manuscript of 48 leaves (11-12 columns, 25-30 syllables), apparently fairly old, in Korea University Library. It is reported to have on the cover 史客傳 <u>Sa Kaek chŏn</u>, but inside 사각젼 <u>Sa Kak chyŏn</u>, with the hero's name in the text as 사각 Sa Kak, and it is suggested that the title should be as in:

사각젼 (謝角傳) <u>Sa Kak chyŏn</u>, 永昌書舘版 "published by Yŏngch'ang Sŏgwan", currently available from Sech'ang Sŏgwan, 45 pages.

In this text the story is a conventional biography, much as that described above, but with the setting in Yüan China, not Ming.

145. 사대장전 **Sa Taejang chŏn**

Kim T'aejun, 229, mentions 史大將傳 <u>Sa Taejang chŏn</u>, "The Story of General Shih", as a pseudo-biography in six episodes of " 史安 Shih An (謝安 Hsieh An?) of 紹興 Shao-hsing in 晉 Chin". The only historical Shih An lived in Ming times. Hsieh An (died 385) suits the date given for the setting of the story, but neither of these persons came from a place called Shao-hsing. There are several far more famous generals with the surname Shih from T'ang, Yüan and Ming times, and at least two of these could have been born in the era Shao-hsing (1131-1162). **Kim Kidong**, 590, adds only that the work exists in paper-back editions. The title was advertised by Taech'ang Sŏwŏn and Hanyang Sŏjŏgŏp Chohapso in 1918.

146. 사명당전 **Samyŏngdang chŏn** "The Story of Samyŏngdang"

四溟堂 Samyŏngdang is the name taken by 任惟政 Yim Yujŏng when he became leading priest in succession to his master Sŏsan Taesa, see **168** 서산대사전 **Sŏsan Taesa chŏn**. In this position he led righteous armies in the wars of 1592-1597, and this story is usually mentioned as an historical story connected with those wars, see **366** 임진록 **Imjin nok**, for example by **Kim Kidong**, 16, 209, 225, 589, etc. (he uses the characters 泗溟堂傳 <u>Samyŏngdang chŏn</u>), and **Kim T'aejun**, 69-70. Samyŏngdang does figure in the works called <u>Imjin nok</u>, but the two texts which I have seen with the title Samyŏngdang chŏn tell mainly of his unsuccessful marriage and his training as a priest. The Japanese invasions, and the part which he played in fighting them are mentioned only very briefly, almost incidentally, towards the end.

西山大師와 四溟堂傳 서산대사와 사명당전 Sŏsan Taesa wa Samyŏngdang chyŏn, "The Story of Sŏsan Taesa and Samyŏngdang", currently available from Sech'ang Sŏgwan, 56 pages, short title on each page 사명당전 Samyŏngdang chyŏn. The title was advertised by Sin'gu Sŏrim in 1925.

사명당전 Samyŏngdang chyŏn, Taejo sa, 1959, 40 pages. These publishers issued the same text several times, sometimes in a separate volume, sometimes in conjunction with Sŏsan Taesa chŏn.

Kim Kidong, 589, states that Samyŏngdang chŏn exists in manuscript(s). There are also completely modern stories about him.

사설춘향가 Sasŏl Ch'unhyang ka: see 460 춘향전 Ch'unhyang chŏn

147. 사성기봉 Sasŏng Kibong

Kim Kidong, 276, mentions 四姓奇逢 Sasŏng Kibong (presumably) "The Miraculous Encounter of the Four Surnames" as if 368 임화정연 Yim Hwa Chŏng Yŏn were an alternative title for it. On page 593 he lists it as an idealistic story in Korean set in China, existing in paperback edition(s). He refers to Kim T'aejun, but I cannot find the reference.

148. 사수몽유록 Sasu Mongyu rok

1947 exhibition, 128 泗水夢遊錄 Sasu Mongyu rok (presumably) "Record of a Dream Journey to Szu-shui", manuscript, 1 vol. (Yi Myŏngsŏn).

Mongyurok Sogo, 136 and 148, deals with this story, and mentions a text in Korean. Kim Kidong, 37 and 588, adds that it exists in manuscript(s) in both *hanmun* and Korean.

149. 사씨남정기 Sa-ssi Namjŏng ki "Record of the Lady Hsieh's Journey to the South"

In sixteenth century China (Ming, Chia-ching), the wife, née 謝 Hsieh, is displaced by a concubine, who subsequently brings the husband to ruin. When the wife and husband are reunited, all ends happily. See Kim T'aejun, 108-112 and 122-123, Kim Kidong, 303-307 (1956: 291-294), Pak Sŏngŭi, 288-293, Sin Kihyŏng,

172-177 and 192-195, and the appropriate passage in almost any work on
Korean literature. The primary evidence quoted for the history of this work
is a statement by 金萬重 Kim Ch'unt'aek (1670-1717) that he translated into
hanmun the story in Korean of this title by his great-uncle 金春澤 Kim
Manjung (1637-1692). There is also quoted a later suggestion that the work
was written as a rebuke to King Sukchong for having dismissed his queen in
1689 (see 362 인현왕후젼 **Inhyŏn Wanghu chŏn**). There is some conflict of evidence, and the texts have not been thoroughly compared. In fact this work does
not seem to have received half the attention given to the other work attributed
to Kim Manjung, **31 구운몽 Kuun mong,** in spite of Kim Ch'unt'aek's reported
opinion that this work is "incomparable".

There are several *hanmun* manuscripts, which I have not examined in detail,
and on which I have not found any precise information. One is reprinted, with
Japanese translation, in 謝氏南征記 九雲夢 Sha-shi Nansei ki, Kyūun mu,
朝鮮研究會 Chōsen Kenkyū kai, Keijō, 1914. **Kim Tonguk**, 383, states that a
hanmun text was printed from wood blocks at 由洞 Yudong in [1815, mistake
for] 1851. He also quotes Shōsho Kibun (see **Introduction**, §7.2) for the title
泗氏傳 Sa-ssi chŏn, which he suggests is 謝氏傳 Sa-ssi chŏn, a version of this
story.

남정긔 南征記 Namjyŏng kŭi, manuscript, 3 vols. [**Palace**]

A manuscript, title not given, of two or three vols, three *kwŏn*, dated
광무십년병오 (光武十年丙午 1906) is reported by 金敏洙 Kim Minsu as being
the source for his annotated version 謝氏南征記 Sa-ssi Namjŏng ki in **Hyŏndae
Munhak**, 11, 12, 14, 18 and 20, November 1955—August 1956 (apparently not complete).

사씨남정긔 Sa-ssi Namjyŏng kŭi, manuscript, 2 vols, 38, 47 leaves (10 columns,
25 syllables). Title on the cover 謝氏南征記 Sa-ssi Namjŏng ki. [**Seattle**]

This text is almost certainly later than 1910.

1947 exhibition, 138: 南征記 Namjŏng ki, manuscript, 1 vol. (Yi Haech'ŏng).

스뎨남졍긔 Să-tsăe Namjyŏng kŭi, manuscript, 1 vol. (vol.1 only), dated 졍미
(丁未 1907, etc.), given as in the **Karam collection**.

謝氏南征記 Sa-ssi Namjŏng ki, manuscript, 1 vol.(last vol. only), given as in the
Ilsa collection.

Courant, 773: 샤시남졍긔 Sya-si Namjyŏng kŭi, Seoul block print, 2 vols, engraved at 由洞 Yudong in 辛亥 (1851), in Paris; and, 3348: same, 3 vols, engraved

at Yudong in 1851, also in Paris. **Kim Tonguk,** 391, gives the Seoul block print, 2 vols, 22, 34 leaves, 歲在辛亥季冬由洞新板 "newly engraved at Yudong, twelfth month 1851". The same date and place are given for the printing of a *hanmun* text, see above.

謝氏南征記 Sa-ssi Namjŏng ki, Yŏngp'ung Sŏsi, 1914, 120, 2 pages. This is a *hanmun* text put into Korean by the addition of particles.

사시남졍긔 Sa-si Namjyŏng kŭi, currently available from Sech'ang Sŏgwan, 77 pages.

사씨남졍긔 (謝氏南征記) Sa-ssi Namjŏng ki, Sammun sa, 1953, 92 pages.

Kim Kidong, 31 and 303, reports publications by Yŏngp'ung Sŏgwan, 1913, 109 pages, and 1914, 91 pages, and by Pangmun Sŏgwan, 1917, 81 pages, and it has been frequently advertised by almost all publishers of paperbacks.

謝氏南征記 Sa-ssi Namjŏng ki in: 朴晟義 Pak Sŏngŭi, ed.: 九雲夢 · 謝氏南征記 **Kuun mong,** Sa-ssi Namjŏng ki, 正音社 Chŏngŭm sa, Seoul, 1959, pages 89-257. This is annotated as a school text-book.

謝氏南征記 Sa-ssi Namjŏng ki in the **Hŭimang Series,** III 175-241.

150.   사씨행록 Sa-ssi Haengnok

1947 exhibition, 80: 샤시힝녹 Sya-si Hăengnok, manuscript, 2 vols. (Song Sŏkha). The title presumably means "Record of the Actions of Sa". It could be the same as **325** 유한당사씨언행록 **Yuhandang Sa-ssi Ŏnhaeng nok.**

151.   사은기우록 Saŭn Kiu rok

Kim Kidong, 595, lists 私恩奇遇錄 Saŭn Kiu rok as a love story in Korean set in China, existing in manuscript(s). As a source he adds "introduced by 李秉岐 Yi Pyŏnggi". I have not found any published reference by him to such a work.

152.   산성일기 Sansŏng Ilgi "Diary in the Hill Fort"

산셩일긔 山城日記 Sansyŏng Ilgŭi, two manuscripts, each of 1 vol. After the title in each is 병ㅈ Pyŏngjă (丙子 "the year of the red rat" = 1636). [Palace]

One of these was shown in the **1961 exhibition,** as item 19, and the catalogue notes that there is another copy in the National Library.

姜漢永 **Kang Hanyŏng**, ed.: 山城日記 (丙子) <u>Sansŏng Ilgi (Pyŏngja)</u> in **Hyŏndae Munhak**, 46, 50, 51, 53, 54, October 1958—June 1959. The introduction seems to indicate that it was not one of the Palace texts which was used, but the text is not described. The first two instalments are in old spelling, the last three in modern.

The hill fort is 南漢山城 Namhan Sansŏng, to which the court escaped during the Manchu invasions of 1636-1637, see **133** 병자록 **Pyŏngja rok**. It is not clear just how factual these versions of this diary are.

153. 산양대전 **Sanyang Taejŏn "The Great Battle of Shan-yang"**

Kim T'aejun, 92, and **Kim Kidong**, 210, mention 山陽大戰 (記) <u>Sanyang Taejŏn (ki)</u> as a story derived from <u>San-kuo-chih Yen-i</u> (see **156** 삼국지연의 Samgukchi Yŏnŭi). This is true of the story in the text below, but I cannot identify it with any particular passages in that work.

山陽大戰 산양대전 <u>Sanyang Taejyŏn</u>, currently available from Sech'ang Sŏgwan, 38 pages. The title was advertised by Taech'ang Sŏwŏn and Pogŭp Sŏgwan in 1920, by Pangmun Sŏgwan and Sin'gu Sŏrim in 1923, 1925 and 1932, by Chosŏn Tosŏ Chusik Hoesa in 1925, by Yŏngch'ang Sŏgwan and Hanhŭng Sŏrim in 1925, and by Tŏkhŭng Sŏrim in 1935.

154. 삼강명행록 **Samgang Myŏnghaeng nok**

Courant, 305: 삼강명힝록 三綱明行錄 <u>Samgang Myŏnghăeng nok</u> "Excellent Actions Due to Observing the Three Principles" (title only, and not as a novel). **Kim Kidong**, 600, lists 三綱名行錄 (but on page 37 as Courant) <u>Samgang Myŏnghaeng nok</u> as a moral story in Korean set in China, existing in manuscript(s), but not made known before.

155. 삼국대전 **Samguk Taejŏn "The Great War of the Three Kingdoms"**

Kim Kidong, 210, mentions 三國大戰記 <u>Samguk Taejŏn ki</u> as a story derived from <u>San-kuo-chih Yen-i</u>, see **156** 삼국지연의 **Samgukchi Yŏnŭi**. The story as in the text below appears to be a general rewriting, though still in traditional *kodae sosŏl* form, of the story of that work.

三國大戰 삼국대젼 <u>Samguk Taejyŏn</u>, currently available from Sech'ang Sŏgwan, 100 pages. The title has been frequently advertised in paperbacks since 1918.

삼국....., **Samguk.....**, "..... of the Three Kingdoms" is common in pre-titles of works derived from San-kuo-chih Yen-i (**156** 삼국지연의 **Samgukchi Yŏnŭi**), but for

삼국리대장전 **Samguk Ri Taejang chyŏn**: see **355** 이태경전 **Yi T'aegyŏng chŏn**

156.   삼국지연의 **Samgukchi Yŏnŭi** "Romance of the Three Kingdoms"

三國志 San-kuo-chih, "Chronicles of the Three Kingdoms", was a near contemporary account of the fall of the Han Dynasty and the wars which followed in third century China, which is itself of interest for the information which it gives on Korea. However, the fictional works sometimes called by this title, 삼국지 **Samgukchi** in Korean, are taken from fictionalised Chinese versions usually called by the one name 三國志演義 San-kuo-chih Yen-i, 삼국지연의 **Samgukchi Yŏnŭi** in Korean, and often attributed to 羅貫中 Lo Kuan-chung (1330-1400), though it is by no means simply one work by one man. (See, for instance, J.R. Hightower: Topics in Chinese Literature, Harvard University Press, Cambridge, 1950, 93-94.) There is a full English translation of one Chinese version by C.H. Brewitt-Taylor: San Kuo or Romance of the Three Kingdoms, Kelly and Walsh, Shanghai, 1925, 2 vols, vi, 638, 623 pages. All Korean critics are agreed that it was introduced to Korea about 1600, and that it had an almost immeasurable effect on Korean prose fiction. See **Kim T'aejun**, 67 ff., 86, 89 ff., 105-106, and, for briefer mentions, **Kim Kidong**, 21, 23, etc., **Pak Sŏngŭi**, 207-208. It is given as in Shōsho Kibun by both Kim T'aejun and Kim Tonguk, see **Introduction**, §7.2.

삼국지통쇽연의 三國志 Samgukchi T'ongsyok Yŏnŭi, Samgukchi, "Popular Romance from the Chronicles of the Three Kingdoms", manuscript, 39 vols. **[Palace]**

When this text was shown in the **1961 exhibition**, as item 63, the catalogue noted: "About 1884 李鍾泰 Yi Chongt'ae translated nearly a hundred Chinese novels by royal command, and this may be one of them."

삼국지 Samgukchi, lending library manuscript, 69 vols, about 30 leaves (11 columns, 14 syllables) per volume, dated 임인 (壬寅 1902) in vols 54, 69, and perhaps others, 신히 (辛亥 1911) in vol. 1, and perhaps others, and 임자 (壬子 1912) in vol. 29. Several volumes are undated, including vol. 50, which looks rather older than the rest. Title on the cover 三國志 Samgukchi. **[Tōyō Bunko]**

삼국지 Samgukchi, manuscript, 18 vols (vols 1-7 and 9-19), 791 leaves in all, dated 디한광무칠연감진 (大韓光武七年 1903 甲辰 1904) in vols 6, 7, 9 and 10, and 디한광무십연병오 (大韓光武十年丙午 1906) in all other volumes. [Harvard]

1947 exhibition, 228: 三國誌 Samgukchi, manuscript, 30 vols, and, 229: 正本三國誌 Chŏngbon Samgukchi, "The True Text of the Chronicles of the Three Kingdoms," manuscript, 18 vols, and, 230: 三國誌 Samgukchi, manuscript, 2 vols. (all Seoul University, the last not shown). I could not find any of these in 1962.

삼국지 Samgukchi, Seoul block print, 5 vols, 25, 27, 20, 26, 28 leaves. [**British Museum**]

1961 exhibition, 64: 三國誌 Samgukchi, Seoul block print, 3 vols. (Kang Hanyŏng, not shown). The catalogue noted: "The quarto volume, which is not uniform, has 美洞新版 'newly engraved at Midong' and one other volume has 紅樹洞己未板 'engraved at Hongsudong in 1859'". **Courant,** 756, gives the same information on an apparently identical text in Paris.

Petrova, 213 and 214, gives two vol. 3's; one of 20 leaves 己未孟夏紅樹洞新刊 "newly engraved at Hongsudong, fourth month, 1859", and one of 22 leaves, 己未石橋新刊 "newly engraved at Sŏkkyo in 1859".

Kim Tonguk, 389, gives as the only Seoul block print: 3 vols, 35 leaves, 美洞新板 "newly engraved at Midong", 35 leaves, and 30 leaves, 咸豊己未孟夏紅樹洞新刊 "newly engraved at Hongsudong, fourth month 1859."

삼국지 Samgukchi. 翰南書林 Hannam Sŏrim, Keijō, 1917. Vol. 1 only, 35 leaves, seen. A lithograph, probably from the three volume edition as described by Kim Tonguk.

삼국지 Samgukchi, Ansŏng block print, 1 vol. (vol. 3 only), 20 leaves. Title on the cover 三國志 Samgukchi. [Tōyō Bunko]

Kim Tonguk, 395, gives the same. **Kim Tonguk,** 397, gives three Chŏnju block prints: (1) 언삼국지 Ŏn Samgukchi (presumably) "The Chronicles of the Three Kingdoms in Korean", 47 leaves, bound with 공명선생실기 Kongmyŏng Sŏnsaeng Silgi (presumably) "The True Record of Kung-ming", 18 leaves; (2) 삼국지 Samgukchi, 2 vols, 47, 38 leaves (presumably it is the first page of this edition which is reproduced in Hyangt'o Sŏul, 8, page 62); (3) with the colophon 님신완산신판이라 "newly engraved at Chŏnju in 1872". In Hyangt'o Sŏul in 1960, page 61, he indicated that this last was the last volume of a three volume edition, but neither description is very clearly set out.

Many other sources mention these block prints, but all their factual information is given above. All the versions in Korean in modern editions which I
have seen seem to be taken directly from Chinese texts, and so are not included here. The following titles which are listed in this index are of stories
set in the wars which form the subject of San-kuo-chi Yen-i:

8 강유실기 Kang Yu Silgi

28 관운장실기 Kwan Unjang Silgi

89 도원결의록 Towŏn Kyŏrŭi rok

153 산양대전 Sanyang Taejŏn

155 삼국대전 Samguk Taejŏn

266 오관참장기 Ogwan Ch'amjang ki

314 위왕별전 Wi Wang Pyŏlchŏn

378 장비마초실기 Chang Pi Ma Ch'o Silgi

391 적벽가 Chŏkpyŏk ka

412 제갈양전 Chegal Yang chŏn

424 조자룡전 Cho Charyong chŏn

514 화용도 Hwayongdo

521 황부인전 Hwang Puin chŏn

Several others are also referred to this work less confidently.

157. 삼대충효록 Samdae Ch'unghyo rok

Courant, 885: 삼뒤충효록 三代忠孝錄 Samdăe Ch'yunghyo rok, "The Loyalty and
Filial Piety of Three Generations" (title only). Kim T'aejun, 161, has the same
in a list of titles of this type which seems to be derived largely from Courant.
Kim Kidong, 598, lists it as a moral tale in Korean set in China, existing in
manuscript(s). He refers to Kim T'aejun.

158. 삼문규합록 Sammun Kyuhap nok

Courant, 912 삼문규합록 三門閨閤錄 Sammun Kyuhap nok, "Records of the
Women of the Three Families" (title only).

159. 삼문충효록 Sammun Ch'unghyo rok

Courant, 889: 삼문충효록 三門忠孝錄 Sammun Ch'yunghyo rok, "Record of the
Loyalty and Filial Piety of the Three Families" (title only). 삼 Sam is misprinted as 상 Sang. Kim T'aejun, 161, has the same in a list of titles of this
type which seems to be derived largely from Courant. Kim Kidong, 599, lists

the same as a moral tale in Korean set in China, existing in manuscript(s). He refers to Kim T'aejun.

삼사기 Samsa ki, etc.: see 162 삼설기 Samsŏlgi

160. 삼생기연   Samsaeng Kiyŏn

Kim Kidong, 596, lists 三生奇緣 Samsaeng Kiyŏn as a love story in Korean set in China, existing in paperback edition(s) (also page 32), but not made known before.

삼생유혜록 Samsaeng Yuhye rok: see 164 삼성유혜록 Samsŏng Yuhye rok

161. 삼선기 Samsŏn ki "Record of the Three Fairies"

Kim Kidong, 553-560, describes this satirical story of a *yangban* of strict morals being led into more easy-going ways by two *kisaeng*. 三仙記 Samsŏn ki in **Hyŏndae Munhak**, 54, 55, 58, 60, 61, June 1959—January 1960, is an edition by him of the text which he used for this description, a publication by Imundang, 1918, 90 pages. The story has several features in common with **354** 이충풍선 **Yi Ch'unp'ung chŏn**: the name of the hero, the setting in P'yŏngyang, the family name of one of the *kisaeng* and a generally satirical aim, though there are great differences between the two stories.

The following text was mistakenly placed under this heading. There is no connection at all between it and the story above, but the mistake was discovered too late to make a separate entry for it:

취미삼선녹 Ch'ywimi Samsyŏn nok, manuscript, 2 vols, 58, 45½ (+12½) leaves (11 or 12 columns, 15-20 syllables). Title on the cover 翠微三仙錄 Ch'wimi Samsŏn nok. **[Imanishi collection, Tenri]**
The catalogue describes this as "a lending library manuscript of about 1927". The *ch'wimi* of the title is a place name, and the story is set in China in the first century.

162. 삼설기 Samsŏlgi

Courant, 825 삼셜긔 三說記 Samsyŏlgŭi, "Books with Three Tales", Seoul block print, 3 vols, "newly engraved at 由洞 Yudong in 戊申 (1848?)", in Paris, etc. He gives outlines of the nine stories, as below, 1-3 in vol. 1, 4-6 in vol. 2, and 7-9 in vol. 3. He gives no titles for the stories.

Petrova, 210 and 211, gives a vol. 2, 26 leaves, containing stories 4, 5 and 6, the last two with titles, and a vol. 3, 26 leaves, 戊申十一月日由洞新板 "newly engraved at Yudong, eleventh month 1848", containing stories 7, 8 and 9, all without titles, in the Aston collection in Leningrad.

There is a copy of vol. 3 in the **British Museum,** 26 leaves, no colophon, stories 7, 8 and 9, with titles, as below.

Kim Ikhwan's copy, 3 vols, was shown in the **1947 exhibition,** as item 183.

Kim T'aejun, 136-141, gives no details of publication, but outlines of six stories, 1 and 2 as in vol. 1, 4 and 5 as in vol. 2, and 3 and 6 as in vol. 3. **Kim Kidong (1956),** 351-356, follows Kim T'aejun closely, but with fuller outlines of the stories, and **Pak Sŏngŭi,** 324-326, also follows Kim T'aejun, but not in full.

Kim Kidong, 104-110, gives a publication 別三說記 Pyŏl Samsŏlgi by Sin'gu Sŏrim, 1913, as having stories 1, 3, 4, 5 and 6, which he describes.

Sin Kihyŏng does not describe the whole work as such, but does describe separately story no. 1, 407-408, and story no. 6, 443.

Kim Tonguk, 385-386, gives the Seoul block print as 3 vols, with the colophon almost exactly as in Petrova, and notes that it is in Courant, but gives only the six stories (1, 2, 4, 5, 3 and 6) as in Kim T'aejun,

이회승　Yi Hŭisŭng, ed.: 국어대사전 **Kugŏ Taesajŏn,** 민중서관 Minjung Sŏgwan, Seoul, 1961, under 삼설기 Samsŏlgi, gives the same six stories as Kim T'aejun. and also a seventh, 知囊記 Chinang ki. This looks as if it might be the same as **79 담낭전 Tamnang chŏn,** but I have not seen any other reference to the title.

Thus there is some conflict of information in the sources, but is clear that this collection of short stories was a very early, perhaps the very first, publication of *kodae sosŏl* in Korean. The stories are as follows:

(1) This appears in both the Hoedong Sŏgwan (1915, 15 pages) and the Sech'ang Sŏgwan (currently available, 13 pages) editions of **42 금산사창업연몽유록 Kŭmsan-sa Ch'angŏbyŏn Mongyu rok.** The title appears as 三士橫入黃泉記 Samsa Hoengip Hwangch'ŏn ki, "How the Three Gentlemen Went to Hell by an Unfortunate Accident" (in Kim T'aejun, 136, and elsewhere); 三士誤入黃泉記 Samsa Oip Hwangch'ŏn ki, "How the Three Gentlemen Went to Hell by Mistake" (in Kim T'aejun, 137, and elsewhere); 洛陽三士記 Nagyang Samsa ki (in Kim Kidong, 105· he gives the setting as Korea, about 1750, in his text, in which case Nagyang could mean Seoul); 三士記 Samsa ki (also 삼사긔 Samsa Kŭi and 숨사긔

Sămsa kŭi) "The Three Gentlemen" (in the paperback editions). The first of these titles, Samsa Hoengip Hwangch'ŏn ki, is also given as one of the appendices to 忘老却愁記 Mango Kaksu ki, Yi Pyŏnggi's one volume manuscript of poetry which was shown in the 1947 exhibition as item 34. Neither of these titles is given as in the Karam collection, see also 42 금산사창업연몽유록 Kŭmsan-sa Ch'angŏbyŏn Mongyu rok and 36 규중칠우 Kyujung Ch'iru.

The story is that three gentlemen get drunk and are taken to hell as dead. The King of Hell accepts their protests and asks their wishes on return to earth.

(2) This appears also in both the Sech'ang Sŏgwan (currently available, 9 pages) and defective paperback editions of 514 화용도 Hwayongdo. The title is given as 五虎大將記 Oho Taejang ki, "The Five Great Generals" by all critics, and appears as 오호딕장긔 五虎將記 Oho Tăejang kŭi, Ohojang ki in the paperback editions. A general is compared by his fawning officers to five generals from San-kuo-chih Yen-i (see 156 삼국지연의 Samgukchi Yŏnŭi), but a common soldier disagrees, and argues his case so well that he is made a general.

(3) Kim Kidong, 105, gives the title as 黃州牧使記 Hwangju Moksa ki, "The Magistrate of Hwangju [or Huang-chou]". All other sources follow Kim T'aejun, 137 and 140: 黃州牧使戒 Hwangju Moksa Kye, "The Warning of . . . . . ". According to the critics, the magistrate tells the fortunes of his three sons correctly from their behaviour as young men.

(4) All critics give the title as 西楚霸王記 Sŏch'o P'aewang ki, "The Dictator of Western Ch'u", and the story as of a young scholar shaming 項羽 Hsiang Yü for having been with his mistress at a time of crisis. 453 초패왕전 Ch'o P'aewang chŏn may be the same, and both may be taken from Hsi-han Yen-i, see 174 서한연의 Sŏhan Yŏnŭi.

(5) Kim Kidong, 108, gives the title as 三子願從記 Samja Wŏnjong ki, "How the Three Disciples Had Their Wishes Followed". All other sources follow Kim T'aejun, 136 and 139: 三子遠從記 Samja Wŏnjong ki, "How the Three Disciples Followed Far Off". Apparently the three disciples of a Taoist teacher have their wishes fulfilled, and the story tells mainly of their reunion later in life.

(6) All sources give the title as 老處女歌 Noch'ŏnyŏ ka, "The Song of the Old Maid", and say that it is in metrical form and tells of a woman who is unattractive until she marries late in life. She is then transformed and produces a perfect son without any delay.

(7) Title in the British Museum text 황시결송 Hwangsăe Kyŏlsong, "The Stork Decides a Case". The story is told before a corrupt court of the bribing of a

stork who was judging which bird had the sweetest voice. 황셔젼 Hwangsǎe chyǒn, 3½ leaves, appendix to the Seattle manuscript, dated 1909, of 410 졍울션젼 Chǒng Ŭlsǒn chǒn, may be the same. The story is not mentioned by any critic.

(8) Title in the British Museum text 녹쳐ᄉ연회 Nok Ch'yǒsǎ Yǒnhoe, "Mr Stag's Party". The animals honour the stag on his birthday with poetical addresses.

(9) Title in the British Museum text 노셤샹좌괴 Nosyǒm Syangjwa kǔi, "How Old Toad Took the Seat of Honour". This is widely known as 95 두껍젼 Tukkǒp Chǒn.

163.　삼셩기 Samsǒng ki

Kim Kidong, 596, lists 三聖記 Samsǒng ki (presumably) "Record of the Three Saints" as an historical story in Korean set in China, existing in paperback edition(s), but not made known before. It has been advertised by Taech'ang Sǒwǒn (with various other publishers) several times since 1918.

164.　삼셩유혜록 Samsǒng Yuhye rok

Courant, 868: 삼셩유혜록 Samsyǒng Yuhye rok, 三生有惠錄 Samsaeng Yuhye rok, "Record of the Graces of the Three Existences" (title only).

삼자원죵기 Samja Wǒnjong ki: see 162 삼셜기 Samsǒlgi

165.　삼주기화 Samju Kihwa

1947 exhibition, 163: 三珠奇話 Samju Kihwa, manuscript, 1 vol. (Kim Sambul).

삼학사젼 Sam Haksa chǒn: see 133 병자록 Pyǒngja rok

상문충효록 Sangmun Ch'yunghyo rok: see 159 삼문충효록 Sammun Ch'unghyo rok

상번군사 Sangbǒn Kunsa: see 256 어우야담 Ǒu Yadam

166.　상은삼진록 Sangǔn Samjin nok

Courant, 928: 샹은삼진록 Syangǔn Samjin nok, "Record of Sangǔn and Samjin" (title only).

샤시 . . . . . Sya-si . . . . . : see 사씨 . . . . . Sa-ssi . . . . .

서궁록 **Sŏgung nok**, etc. : see 16 계축일기 **Kyech'uk Ilgi**

서대주전 **Sŏ Taeju chŏn**, and

서동지전 **Sŏ Tongji chŏn**: see 431 쥐전 **Chwi chŏn**

167. 서문충효록 Sŏ-mun Ch'unghyo rok

Courant, 881: 셔문충효록 徐門忠孝錄 <u>Syŏ-mun Ch'yunghyo rok</u>, "The Loyalty and Filial Piety of Sŏ [Chinese: Hsü]" (title only). **Kim T'aejun**, 161, has the same in a list of titles of this type which seems to be derived largely from Courant. **Kim Kidong**, 598, referring to Kim T'aejun, lists it as a moral tale in Korean set in China, existing in manuscript(s).

168. 서산대사전 Sŏsan Taesa chŏn "The Story of Sŏsan Taesa"

西山大師 Sŏsan Taesa was a master of Sŏn (Ch'an, Zen) Buddhism, 1520-1604, and he figures in *kodae sosŏl* usually because he was a leader of righteous armies in the wars of 1592-1597. **Kim Kidong** mentions this work several times (16, 209, 225, etc.), but other critics only seem to mention its hero as figuring in **366** 임진록 **Imjin nok**, e.g. **Kim T'aejun**, 69-70.

In a paperback by Taejo sa, 1959, there is 셔산대사젼 <u>Syŏsan Taesa chyŏn</u> (pages 1-14), 셔산대사부록 <u>Syŏsan Taesa Purok</u>, "Appended Record of Sŏsan Taesa" (15-30), and then **146** 사명당전 **Samyŏngdang chŏn** (31-70), in which Sŏsan Taesa also figures largely.

169. 서상기 Sŏsang ki "Records of the West Chamber"

西廂記 <u>Hsi-hsiang-chi</u> is a title which has been used by many Chinese writers for versions of the favourite Chinese story 鶯鶯傳 <u>Ying-ying-chuan</u>. (See, for instance, Lu Hsun: <u>A Brief History of Chinese Fiction</u>, Foreign Languages Press, Peking, 1959, pages 103, 104, 172, 193 and 411.)

Several Korean critics mention that <u>Hsi-hsiang-chi</u> had a great influence on Korean drama, and therefore on the *kodae sosŏl*.

서상긔 **Sŏsang Kŭi**, manuscript, 2 vols. Title on the cover 西廂記 <u>Sŏsang ki</u>. **[Seoul University]** Inside the back cover is 大韓隆熙三年 (1909) which might be the date of the text.

西廂記 <u>Sŏsang ki</u>, manuscript, 96 leaves, mixed script, given as in the **Ilsa collection.**

李玉 Yi Ok (Li Ogg, who is now in Paris) showed his 元曲西廂記譯解 Wŏn'gok Sŏsang ki Yŏkhae, "Explanatory Text of the Yüan Drama 'Record of the West Chamber'", in an exhibition held by Yŏnhŭi (now Yŏnse) University at Pusan in July 1952. The catalogue describes it as an astonishingly complete and accurate translation", which would seem to imply that it is old, but the quotations given from it are modern in style.

There are also modern Korean editions.

The only direct Korean imitation of Hsi-hsiang-chi appears to be 東廂記 Tongsang ki, "Record of the East Chamber", a novel in *hanmun* (see **Kim T'aejun, 165-166**, and **Sin Kihyŏng, 398-401**).

170. 서씨육렬기 Sŏ-ssi Yungnyŏl ki

Courant, 896: 셔시뉵녈긔 徐氏六烈記 **Syŏ-si Nyungnyŏl kŭi**, "The Six Heroes of the Sŏ [Chinese: Hsü] Family" (title only). Perhaps "Virtuous Wives", not "Heroes".

서옥기 **Sŏ ok ki**, etc., and
서옹전 **Sŏ Ong chŏn**, and
서용전 **Sŏ Yong chŏn**: see **431** 쥐전 **Chwi chŏn**

171.　서유기 Sŏyu ki "Record of a Trip to the West"

西遊記 **Hsi-yu-chi** is a famous Chinese novel (see W.T. de Bary, A.T. Embree, ed. : A Guide to Oriental Classics, Columbia University Press, New York and London, 1964, 161-163), and it seems to have been much enjoyed in Korea from about 1600 on (see **Kim T'aejun**, 95, **Kim Kidong**, 16, 21, etc.).

1947 exhibition, 171: 西遊記 **Sŏyu ki**, manuscript, 12 vols. (Yi Haech'ŏng).

Courant, 760: 셔유긔 西遊記 **Syŏyu kŭi**, Seoul block print, 2 vols, "newly engraved at 華山 Hwasan in the tenth month of 丙辰1856", in Paris, etc. He adds: "There exist some manuscripts in Korean in 60 vols and others in 25 vols." **Kim Tonguk**, 392, adds that the block print is of 31, 28 leaves.

172.　서정기 Sŏjŏng ki "Record of the Western Conquest"

西征記 (셔졍긔) **Syŏjyŏng kŭi**, Sin'gu Sŏrim and Pangmun Sŏgwan 1923, 59 pages and currently available from Sech'ang Sŏgwan, 56 pages.

This is a sequel to **185** 셜인귀전 **Sŏl In'gwi chŏn**, and gives as its sequel **186** 셜정산실기 **Sŏl Chŏngsan Silgi**.

서정록 Sŏjŏng nok: see 133 병자록 Pyŏngja rok

173. 서주연의 Sŏju Yŏnŭi "Romance of the Western Chou"

"Western Chou" is the first part, traditionally 1122-771 B.C., of the Chou Dynasty of China.

셔쥬연의 西周演義 Syŏjyu Yŏnŭi, manuscript, 25 vols. [Palace]

Courant, 750, gives the title, and **Kim T'aejun**, 99, gives a quotation in evidence for the existence of a translation into Korean about 1700.

　　서진기 Sŏjin ki, etc. : see 369 자치통감 Chach'i T'onggam

　　서천흥별전 Sŏ Ch'ŏnhŭng Pyŏlchŏn: see 240 쌍주기연 Ssangju Kiyŏn

　　서초패왕기 Sŏch'o P'aewang ki: see 162 삼설기 Samsŏlgi

174. 서한연의 Sŏhan Yŏnŭi "Romance of the Western Han"

"Western Han" is the first half, 206 B.C.—24 A.D., of the Han Dynasty of China.

1947 exhibition, 191: 西漢演義 Sŏhan Yŏnŭi, manuscript, 8 vols. (Kim Kyŏngch'un). The catalogue notes: "A precious book, with the seal of 暎嬪李氏 Yŏnghoe Yi-ssi", i.e. that it dates from the eighteenth century.

1961 exhibition, 73: 西漢演義 Sŏhan Yŏnŭi, manuscript, 10 vols. (Yi Nŭngu).

The title was advertised by Hansŏng Sŏgwan and Yuil Sŏgwan in 1915.

Kim T'aejun, 97 (see also pages 86, 92), states that this work, in Chinese Hsi-han Yen-i, made the deepest impression in Korea of all the Ming romances imported about 1600, and that from it are derived **454** 초한전 Ch'o-han chŏn, **453** 초패왕전 Ch'o P'aewang chŏn (see also 162 삼설기 Samsŏlgi, story 4) and **382** 장자방전 Chang Chabang Chŏn. See also 502 홍문연 Hongmun yŏn.

175. 서해무릉기 Sŏhae Murŭng ki "Record of Murŭng in the Western Sea".

셔히무룽긔 Syŏhăe Murŭng kŭi, manuscript, 53 leaves (11 columns, 18 syllables), dated 갑즈 (甲子 1924, etc.), reproduced in the **Ewha Series**, IV 171-275, with a note, 412-416, which gives the title as 西海武陵記 Sŏhae Murŭng ki. The story is that the hero, Yu Yŏn, has his bride-to-be stolen on their wedding day, becomes a priest, and journeys to an island called Sŏhae Murŭng, amongst other places, in search for her. The work does not seem to be known except for this text, which is not described or identified in this publication.

176. 서화담전 Sŏ Hwadam chŏn

Sŏ Hwadam is 花潭 Hwadam, 徐敬德 Sŏ Kyŏngdŏk (1489-1546), a scholar who seems to have given his attention largely to the practice of magic. **Kim T'aejun,** 87-89, wonders whether the similarity of this story to **500** 홍길동전 **Hong Kiltong chŏn** and **396** 전우치전 **Chŏn Uch'i chŏn,** added to the fact that Sŏ Kyŏngdŏk was a teacher of 許筠 Hŏ Kyun's father, does not suggest that this story was a creation of Hŏ Kyun's. **Kim Kidong** mentions it, 196, 209 and 588, adding that it exists in paperback edition(s). The only advertisement of the title which I have seen, by Kwangdong Sŏguk in 1926, lists it among the modern novels.

177. 석중옥 Sŏkchungok

1947 exhibition, 145: 石中玉 Sŏkchungok, manuscript, 1 vol. (Yi Haech'ŏng).

178. 석태룡전 Sŏk T'aeryong chŏn

Mibalp'yo Kodae Sosŏl ko describes 석틔룡젼 (石太龍傳) Syŏk T'ăeryong chyŏn, "The Story of Shih T'ai-lung", set in 15th century China (Ming, Ch'eng-hua), from a manuscript, 35½ leaves (13 columns, 30 syllables), in Korea University Library.

179. 석화룡전 Sŏk Hwaryong chŏn "The Story of Shih Hua-lung"

석화룡뎐 Syŏk Hwaryong tyŏn, manuscript, 1 vol. (described as a vol. 1, but probably complete), 63 leaves (12 columns, 25 syllables), dated 무술 (戊戌 1898). Title on the cover 石花龍傳 Sŏk Hwaryong chŏn [**Chŏng Pyŏnguk**]

The story in this text is set in Sung China. **Kim T'aejun,** 229, gives 石化龍傳 Sŏk Hwaryong chŏn as a story in 7 episodes based on the life of a Shih Hua-lung of 蘇州 Su-chou in a period which he calls 大明정관. Neither the person nor the period appears to be historical. **Kim Kidong,** 590, adds the information that it exists in paperback edition(s), and it was advertised by Taech'ang Sŏwŏn and Pogŭp Sŏgwan in 1920 and by Taesŏng Sŏrim in 1929.

180. 선악보은록 Sŏnak Poŭn nok

Courant, 865: 션악보은록 善惡報恩錄 Syŏnak Poŭn nok, "Record of Requiting Good and Evil" (title only).

선언편 Sŏnŏn p'yŏn: see **469** 파수록 **P'asu rok**

181.　선진일사 Sŏnjin Ilsa

션진일ᄉ 仙眞逸史 Syŏnjin Ilsă, two manuscripts, one of 14 vols (vols 1 and 3-15) and one of 21 vols. [Palace] Their titles suggest a Taoist content, but the title of the Chinese work which would be the same as this in Korean, 禪眞逸史 Ch'an-chen I-shih suggests rather a Buddhist content.

182.　설문충효록 Sŏl-mun Ch'unghyo rok

Kim T'aejun, 161, gives 薛門忠孝錄 Sŏl-mun Ch'unghyo rok (presumably) "Record of the Loyalty and Filial Piety of the Hsüeh Family" in a list of titles of this type. This list appears to be derived largely from **Courant,** who does not give this title, but does give **188 설하충효록 Sŏl Ha Ch'unghyo rok,** which Kim T'aejun does not give. **Kim Kidong,** 599, referring to Kim T'aejun, describes this work as a moral tale in Korean set in China, existing in manuscript(s).

183.　설씨내범서 Sŏl-ssi Naebŏmsŏ

1947 exhibition, 155: 薛氏內範書 Sŏl-ssi Naebŏmsŏ, manuscript, 6 vols. (Yi Haech'ŏng). This was shown as a *sosŏl,* though its title would appear to mean "Book of Rules for the Women of the Sŏl [or Hsüeh] Family". There is a defective text in Seoul University, which I did not examine closely, but which has a very similar title, 셜시너　셔 Syŏl-si Năe　Syŏ manuscript, 4 vols (vols 2, 4, 5, 6), 38, 38, 36, 37 leaves (12 columns, 21 syllables). Title at the end of vol. 6 셜시너　후셔 Syŏl-si Năe　Husyŏ, again with the unusual space in the title.

184.　설월매전 Sŏl Wŏl Mae chŏn

셜월미전 雪月梅傳 Syŏl Wól Măe chyŏn, manuscript, 20 vols. [Palace] This is known as the title of a Chinese novel. **Yi Nŭngu: Kukmunhak Kaeron,** page 6, gives a 10 volume manuscript of this title as in Tokyo University. **Kim Kidong,** 597, referring to Yi Nŭngu, states that it exists in paperback edition(s). **Sin Kihyŏng,** 478, describes it as a love story in Korean set in China.

185. 설인귀전 Sŏl In'gwi chŏn "The Story of Hsüeh Jen-kuei"

Hsüeh Jen-kuei (614-683) was a general of T'ang during the wars in which T'ang aided Silla against Koguryŏ. **11** 개소문전 **Kaesomun chŏn** concerns a Koguryŏ statesman of the time. **Kim T'aejun,** 106-107, describes the popularity of stories about Hsüeh Jen-kuei and his family in China and Korea, and wonders whether they were not the inspiration for all such tales about military heroes.

Courant, 787: 셜인귀젼 薛仁貴傳 Syŏl In'gwi chyŏn, block print, 30 leaves, in Paris, etc. **Petrova,** 202-204, same, three copies, one of 40 leaves and two of 20 leaves. **Kim Tonguk,** 391, gives the 30 leaf edition and a two volume edition (vol. 1 of 17 leaves) as Seoul block prints.

薛仁貴傳 셜인귀젼 Sŏl In'gwi chyŏn, currently available from Sech'ang Sŏgwan, 136 pages. The title was advertised by Tongmi Sósi in 1915, by Pangmun Sŏgwan and Sin'gu Sŏrim in 1919, 1923, 1925 and 1932, and by Yŏngch'ang Sŏgwan and Hanhŭng Sŏrim in 1925.

This paperback is not only itself very much longer than the block prints could possibly be, but it is also only the first of a series which continues with **172** 서정기 **Sŏjŏng ki,** **186** 설정산실기 **Sŏl Chŏngsan Silgi** and **127** 번이화정서전 **Pŏn Yihwa Chŏngsŏ chŏn.** All of these are well known in China.

186. 설정산실기 Sŏl Chŏngsan Silgi "The True Story of Hsüeh Ting-shan"

셜뎡산실긔 (薛丁山實記) Syŏl Tyŏngsan Silgŭi, currently available from Sech'ang Sŏgwan, 112 pages. The title was advertised by Sin'gu Sŏrim in 1925.

This is a sequel to **172** 서정기 **Sŏjŏng ki,** and the third in the series which begins with **185** 설인귀전 **Sŏl In'gwi chŏn.** **127** 번이화정서전 **Pŏn Yihwa Chŏngsŏ chŏn** is given as the sequel to this story.

187. 설제전 Sŏl Che chŏn

Kim Kidong, 598, lists 薛齊傳 Sŏl Che chŏn (presumably) "The Story of Hsüeh Ch'i" as in Korean, set in China, and existing in manuscript(s), but not made known before. **Sin Kihyŏng,** 478, describes it as a tale of the marvellous.

188.　설하충효록　Sŏl Ha Ch'unghyo rok

Courant, 890: 셜하츙효록 薛河忠孝錄 Syŏl Ha Ch'yunghyo rok, "The Loyalty and Filial Piety of Sŏl Ḥa [or Sŏl and Ha or Hsüeh (and) Ho ?]" (title only). See **182** 셜문충효록 Sŏl-mun Ch'unghyo rok.

189.　셜홍젼　Sŏl Hong chŏn

Kim Kidong, 591, lists 薛弘傳 Sŏl Hong chŏn (presumably) "The Story of Hsüeh Hung" as a biography of a hero set in China, existing in paperback edition(s), but not made known before.

　　　　섬동지전 **Sŏm Tongji chŏn,** and
　　　　섬처사전 **Sŏm Ch'ŏsa chŏn:** see **95** 두껍전 **Tukkŏp chŏn**
　　　　셩씨부인열녀록 **Sŏng-ssi Puin Yŏllyŏ rok:** see **460** 춘향젼 **Ch'unhyang chŏn**

190.　셩풍류　Sŏngp'ungnyu

셩풍뉴 醒風流 Syŏngp'ungnyu, manuscript, 7 vols. [**Palace**]
The title is known as that of a Chinese novel.

191.　셩현공슉렬긔　Sŏnghyŏn-gong Sungnyŏl ki

Courant, 898: 셩현공슉녈긔 聖賢公淑烈記 Syŏnghyŏn-gong Syungnyŏl kŭi, "Record of the Pure Virtue of Duke Sheng-hsien" (title only). **Kim T'aejun,** 161, gives the same in a list of titles of this type which seems to be derived largely from Courant. **Kim Kidong,** 599, referring to Kim T'aejun, lists the same as a moral tale in Korean set in China, existing in manuscript(s). Sheng-hsien would be a posthumous title.

　　　　셔..... **Syŏ** ..... : see 서..... **Sŏ** .....
　　　　셕..,,. **Syŏk** ..... : see 석..... **Sŏk** .....
　　　　션..,,. **Syŏn** ..... : see 선..... **Sŏn** .....
　　　　셜..... **Syŏl** ..... : see 설..... **Sŏl** ,....
　　　　셩..... **Syŏng** ..... : see 성..... **Sŏng** .....

192.   소군연전 So Kunyŏn chŏn

Petrova, 224, gives an untitled manuscript of 49 leaves (irregular) as in Leningrad. She quotes the opening passage as:

네쨰명시졀의활영산참총거경겟의사온지샹이이시리
셩은쇠오즈는군연이니송형셩의현손이라

I cannot identify this with any work of known title, and so follow her in calling it "The Story of So Kunyŏn", though he would appear to be Chinese. See the note following **195 소문록 So Mun nok.**

193.   소노천삼대록 So Noch'ŏn Samdae rok

Kim Kidong, 595, lists 蘇老泉三代錄 So Noch'ŏn Samdae rok (presumably) "Record of the Three Generations of Su Lao-ch'üan" as a love story in Korean set in China, existing in manuscript(s). He gives as his source "introduced by 李秉岐 Yi Pyŏnggi", but I have not been able to find any such published reference. The most obvious Su Lao-ch'üan is 蘇洵 Su Hsün (1008-1065), father of 東坡 Tung-p'o, 蘇軾 Su Shih. See also the note following **195 소문록 So Mun nok.**

194.   소대성전 So Taesŏng chŏn

This story, of a general who led armies against Tartars in fifteenth century China (Ming, Ch'eng-hua), seems to have been continuously popular in Korean for at least a hundred years. **Kim T'aejun,** 99, 102, 108, includes it among "the best of the war tales", in which, as a group, however, he "cannot recognize all that much literary interest or value", and all the other critics have followed him in giving it only bare mentions.

The title is quoted from Shōsho Kibun by Kim Tonguk, see **Introduction**, §7. 2. **Courant** and **Petrova**, as below, give the title as 蘇大擊傳 So Taesŏng chŏn, "The Story of Su Ta-sheng". Courant may have taken this from the *hanmun* manuscript which he also gives (778: 49 leaves, no further details), and it would be supported by the Korean texts, in which the hero's name is given to him after a description of his remarkable qualities as a baby, which ends: "his voice was magnificent, like the rolling of gongs and drums". However, all the critics, and such of the texts as give the title in characters, give 蘇大成傳 So Taesŏng chŏn, "The Story of Su Ta-ch'eng". I have not found any historical reference to him. **305 용문전 Yong Mun chŏn** is a companion story about the Tartar general who who fought against him in this story.

쇼듸셩젼 <u>Syo Tǎesyŏng chyŏn</u>, lending library manuscript, 2 vols, 32, 32 leaves (11 columns, 12 syllables), dated 신축 (辛丑 1901) in vol. 1, and 계축 (癸丑 1913) in vol. 2. Title on the cover 蘇大成傳 <u>So Taesŏng chŏn</u>. [**Tōyō Bunko**]

Petrova, 189, gives a manuscript of 67 leaves (10 or 11 columns), dated 丙辰, which she takes as 1796 or perhaps 1856, as in the Aston collection in Leningrad.

The Seoul block prints are all entitled 쇼대셩젼 <u>Syo Taesyŏng chyŏn</u> or 소듸셩젼 Syo Tǎesyŏng chyŏn, and none have colophons. Hardly any two copies seen or reported have the same number of leaves. 36 leaves [**British Museum**, and **Petrova**, 188, in Leningrad]; 24 leaves [**Courant**, 811 and 3349, in Paris, etc.]; 23 leaves [**British Museum**]; 21 leaves, story incomplete [**Imanishi collection, Tenri**]; 20 leaves [**Kim Tonguk**, 391, see a possible Ansŏng block print, below]; 15½ leaves [**Harvard**]. The last looks like a late printing, and a lithograph of the same number of leaves was published by 翰南書林 Hannam Sŏrim, Keijō, 191-.

The block print in the **Tōyō Bunko** of 20 leaves is boxed with Ansŏng block prints, but it has no colophon.

1947 exhibition, 103: 蘇大成傳 <u>So Taesŏng chŏn</u>, Chŏnju block print, 1 vol. (Cho Yunje, not shown). **Kim Tonguk**, 397, gives for the Chŏnju block print: "43 leaves, 戊申仲春完龜洞新刊 "newly engraved at Kwidong, Chŏnju, second month 1908 ?". The query presumably allows the possibility of the date being 1848.

The catalogue of the **Karam collection** gives a block print of 81 leaves which contains 쇼듸셩젼 <u>Syo Tǎesŏng chŏn</u> and 용문젼 <u>Yong Mun chyŏn</u>.

Kim Kidong, 31, gives a publication by Kwangmun Sŏsi, 1914, 84 pages, and the title was advertised by Tongmi Sŏsi in 1915, by Sin'gu Sŏrim in 1918, by Taech'ang Sŏwŏn and Pogŭp Sŏgwan in 1920, by Chosŏn Tosŏ Chusik Hoesa, Tongyang Sŏwŏn, and Yŏngch'ang Sŏgwan and Hanhŭng Sŏrim in 1925, and by Tŏkhŭng Sŏrim in 1935.

소대셩젼 <u>So Taesyŏng chŏn</u>, Sinmyŏng Sŏrim, 1918 (reprinted from 1916), 62 pages.

소대셩젼 <u>So Taesyŏng chŏn</u>, currently available from Sech'ang Sŏgwan (but text as composed before 1945), [36+] 28 pages.

Both the last two paperbacks have the titles on the cover 大成龍門傳 <u>Taesŏng Yong Mun chŏn</u>, "The Story of Ta-ch'eng and Lung Men". I have not compared the two directly, but only the Sech'ang edition seems to have **305 용분전 Yong Mun chŏn** (separately paginated), and the 28 page version of So Taesŏng chŏn in that edition seemed to be much the same as the 62 page version of the Sinmyŏng edition.

195. 소문록 So Mun nok

1947 exhibition, 210: 蘇門錄 So Mun nok (presumably) "Record of the So [Chinese: Su] Family", manuscript, 14 vols (Seoul University). I did not see this in Seoul University in 1962.

Note: There are in this index very many titles of the form "Record of (usually some virtues of) (a certain) Family", perhaps, one suspects, of a particular woman of that family, or of all the women of that family, on which little information is usually available. The So or Su families seem to have more than the average number. There is this title, from a text, but not mentioned in any source, and the equally enigmatic **201 소씨전 So-ssi chŏn** and **198 소부인전 So Puin chŏn**, each known only from a mention by one contemporary critic. There are texts of three works with titles including the name of a member of an unidentified So or Su family, **192 소군연전 So Kunyŏn chŏn, 204 소약란직금도 So Yangnan Chikkŭm to** and **210 소현성록 So Hyŏnsŏng nok**, the last probably also mentioned by a critic. Two works could well concern the family of the famous Chinese writer Su Shih, **193 소노천삼대록 So Noch'ŏn Samdae rok**, mentioned by one critic only, and **199 소소매전 So Somae chŏn**, in a text, but not mentioned by any critic (unless 소저기전 So Chŏgi chŏn is the same, see **494 형산백옥 Hyŏng-san Paegok**). **205 소위명행록 So Wi Myŏnghaeng nok**, mentioned by critics, could concern the Su family of the well known **208 소학사전 So Haksa chŏn**. Apart from these, and **194 소대성전 So Taesŏng chŏn**, which is also well known, there are seven very similar titles. Courant gives **196 소문명현충효록 So-mun Myŏnghyŏn Ch'unghyo rok, 200 소씨명행충의록 So-ssi Myŏnghaeng Ch'ungŭi rok, 202 소씨정충효봉 So-ssi Chŏng Ch'ung Hyo Pong**, and **211 소효문충의록 So Hyomun Ch'ungŭi rok**. Kim T'aejun, in his list, page 161, of titles of this type which seems to be derived largely from Courant, quotes **196** and **200** exactly, and also gives 소씨충효록 So-ssi Ch'unghyo rok, which is perhaps meant to be either **202** or **211** or both, but which is so similar to **197 소문충효록 So-mun Ch'unghyo rok**, which he also gives, that it is difficult to believe that the two represent different works. **Kim Kidong**, in his index, page 599, quotes only

196 and **197**, not **200** or 소세충효록 So-ssi Ch'unghyo rok from Kim T'aejun. He also gives, page 600, **203** 소씨청행록 So-ssi Ch'ŏnghaeng nok, the only one of these seven of which I have seen, or even seen mention of, any text.

196. 소문명현충효록 So-mun Myŏnghyŏn Ch'unghyo rok

Courant, 883: 소문명현충효록 蘇門明賢忠孝錄 So-mun Myŏnghyŏn Ch'yunghyo rok, "The Exemplary Wisdom, Loyalty and Filial Piety of So [Chinese: Su]" (title only). **Kim T'aejun**, 161, has the same in his list of titles of this type which seems to dervied largely from Courant. **Kim Kidong**, 599, referring to Kim T'aejun, has 蘇門名賢忠孝錄, same, but "Famous" for "Exemplary", as a moral tale in Korean set in China, and existing in manuscript(s). See the note following **195** 소문록 **So Mun nok**.

197. 소문충효록 So-mun Ch'unghyo rok

Kim T'aejun, 161, has 蘇門忠孝錄 So-mun Ch'unghyo rok and 蘇氏忠孝錄 So-ssi Ch'unghyo rok, both (presumably) "Record of the Loyalty and Filial Piety of the Su Family" in his list of titles of this type. **Kim Kidong**, 599, referring to Kim T'aejun, lists the first only as a moral tale in Korean set in China, existing in manuscript(s). See the note following **195** 소문록 **So Mun nok**.

198. 소부인전 So Puin chŏn

Kim Kidong, 32, gives 蘇夫人傳 So Puin chŏn (presumably) "The Story of the Lady So [or Su]" as a modern publication of a *kodae sosŏl*, and, page 36, the same as a title of a *kodae sosŏl* existing in manuscript(s). See the note following **195** 소문록 **So Mun nok**.

199. 소소매전 So Somae chŏn

소쇼미뎐 **So Syomǎe tyŏn**, manuscript, [58+] 9½ leaves (8 or 9 columns, 16 or 17 syllables), dated 을묘 (乙卯 1915). [**Chŏng Pyŏnguk**] The 58 leaves are 113 문창진군탕평록 **Munch'ang Chin'gun T'angp'yŏng nok**, and some poems.

The most famous "Miss Su" is 蘇小妹 Su Hsiao-mei, the younger sister of the famous Chinese writer 東坡 Tungp'o, 蘇軾 Su Shih (1036-1101), and story no. 17 in Chin-ku-ch'i-kuan, see **39** 금고기관 **Kŭmgo Kigwan**, seems to be the most famous Chinese story about her. See also **494** 형산백옥 **Hyŏng-san Paegok**, and the note following **195** 소문록 **So Mun nok**.

200. 소씨명행충의록 So-ssi Myŏnghaeng Ch'ungŭi rok

Courant, 884: 소시명힝츙의록 蘇氏明行忠義錄 (?) So-si Myŏnghǎeng Ch'yungŭi rok, "The Exemplary Acts, Loyalty and Righteousness of So [Chinese: Su]" (title only: the query is Courant's). **Kim T'aejun,** 161, has the same in a list of titles of this type which seems to be derived largely from Courant. See the note following 195 소문록 So Mun nok.

201. 소씨전 So-ssi chŏn

Sin Kihyŏng, 478, lists 소써전 (蘇氏傳) So-ssi chŏn as an anonymous moral tale in Korean, of unknown date, set in China. This is the only title in his list of over three hundred which I have not found mentioned elsewhere. See the note following 195 소문록 So Mun nok.

202. 소씨정충효봉 So-ssi Chŏng Ch'ung Hyo Pong

Courant, 880: 소시정츙효봉 蘇氏貞忠孝奉 So-si Chyŏng Ch'yung Hyo Pong, "The Chastity, Loyalty, Filial Piety and Service of the Su Family" (title only). See the note following 195 소문록 So Mun nok.

소씨직금도 So-ssi Chikkǔm to, etc.: see 204 소약란직금도 So Yangnan Chikkǔm to

203. 소씨청행록 So-ssi Ch'ŏnghaeng nok

1961 exhibition, 41: 소써청힝록 So-ssi Ch'yŏnghǎeng nok, manuscript, 1 vol. (National Library). The catalogue notes: "A moral work with the virtuous conduct of the wife of a Su as its contents". **Kim Kidong,** 600, lists 蘇氏清行錄 So-ssi Ch'ŏnghaeng nok as a moral tale in Korean set in China, existing in manuscript(s), but not made known before. See the note following 195 소문록 So-mun nok.

소씨충효록 So-ssi Ch'unghyo rok: see 197 소문충효록 So-mun Ch'unghyo rok

204. 소약란직금도 So Yangnan Chikkǔm to

소약논짐문녹 So Yangnǎn Chǎengmun nok, manuscript, 63 leaves (10 columns, 21 syllables). Title on the cover 蘇惹蘭織錦圖 So Yangnan Chikkǔm to. Date on the cover 己酉. [**Chŏng Pyŏnguk**]

소약난직금도 蘇惹蘭織錦圖 <u>So Yangnan Chikkŭm to</u>, manuscript, 37 leaves (17 columns, 30 syllables). [**Chŏng Pyŏnguk**]

Chŏng Pyŏnguk thought that the second of these was copied from the first. The first is written partly on the back of some tax computations which seem to indicate a date 1849 or 1909 for 己酉, and the second is written on the back of a calendar for 1833. The character 惹 is usually read 야 *ya*. At the time I saw these, I did not form the impression that they were texts of *sosŏl*, but the following two texts are classified in their catalogues as *sosŏl*:

소약난직금도 <u>So Yangnan Chikkŭm to</u>, manuscript, 1 vol. Title on the cover 蘇氏織綿圖 <u>So-ssi Chikkŭm to</u>. [**Seoul University**]

蘇氏織錦回文錄 <u>So-ssi Chikkŭm Hoemun nok</u>, manuscript, 58 leaves, dated 갑인 (甲寅), given as in the Ilsa collection. The catalogue dates it "1854?".

소운전 **So Un chŏn**: see 208 소학사전 **So Haksa chŏn**

205.　소위명행록 **So Wi Myŏnghaeng nok**

Kim T'aejun, 161, includes 蘇渭明行錄 <u>So Wi Myŏnghaeng nok</u> in his list of titles of this type. **Kim Kidong**, 599, adds that the story is set in China, and that the work exists in manuscript(s). The title presumably means "Record of the Exemplary Behaviour of Su Wei", and Su Wei could well be the brother of Su Yün, who figures in 208 소학사전 **So Haksa chŏn**. See also the note following 195　소문록 **So Mun nok**.

소저기전 **So Chŏgi chŏn**: see 494 형산백옥 **Hyŏng-san Paegok**

206.　소진장의전 **So Chin Chang Ŭi chŏn** "The Story of Su Ch'in and Chang Yi"

Su Ch'in and Chang Yi were statesmen who brought about the union of several Chinese kingdoms in the fourth century B.C. This story, as below, starts with them as pupils of the same Taoist master, and ends with their deaths. **Kim Kidong**, 209-210, includes it among the works which are partial or complete translations of Chinese works. For the Chinese works which cover this period in general see 261 열국지 **Yŏlgukchi**.

소진장의전 蘇秦張儀傳 <u>So Chin Chang Ŭi chŏn</u>, currently available from Sech'ang Sŏgwan, 56 pages. The title was advertised by Kwangdong Sŏguk in 1926.

207. 소하록 Soha rok

1947 exhibition, 245: 消夏錄 <u>Soha rok,</u> manuscript, 14 vols [**Palace**]. This did not appear to be in the Palace library in 1962, but I have been told that it is, or was, a collection of historical stories. The title presumably means "Stories for the Heat of Summer".

208. 소학사전 So Haksa chǒn "The Story of the Minister Su"

Kim T'aejun, 225-228, discusses the Chinese and Korean variations on the stories of a Su family (see also the note following **195** 소문록 **So Mun nok**), especially of the brothers 蘇渭 **Su Wei** (see also **205** 소위명행록 **So Wi Myǒnghaeng nok**) and 蘇雲 **Su Yün**. In this story, which has several different titles, and probably many variations of plot, Su Wei is killed by a pirate ·徐 Hsü, but his posthumously born son, who comes to be adopted by that pirate and called 雲敬 Yün-ching, attains high office, and in the end settles accounts for the family. This takes place in fifteenth century China (Ming, Ch'eng-hua) in the texts which I have seen, but Kim T'aejun gives the setting as seventeenth century China (Ming, Ch'ung-chen). In other stories, such as **279** 옥소전 **Okso chǒn** and, apparently, **137** 봉황금 **Ponghwang kǔm**, the names of the characters, the location, and, to varying extents, the plot are changed. **339** 음양옥지환 **Ǔmyang Okchihwan** and **53** 김상서재세록 **Kim Sangsǒ Chaese rok** may be in the same category. **Kim Kidong (1956)**, 278-281, **Pak Sǒngǔi**, 387-389, and **Sin Kihyǒng**, 434, etc., give fuller summaries of the plot than Kim T'aejun.

Kim Tonguk quotes 蘇雲傳 <u>So Un chǒn</u> "The Story of Su Yün" from <u>Shōsho Kibun</u>, see **Introduction**, §7.2.

월봉긔 **Wǒlbong kǔi**, "Record of Yüeh-feng", manuscript, 44 leaves (10 columns, 24 syllables), dated 갑자 (甲子 1924, etc.). [**Harvard**] This may be a vol.1 only.

비쇼긔 **Pisyo kǔi**, manuscript, 1 vol. (vol.2—of three—only), 43 leaves (12 columns, 21-22 syllables), stamped "K.Mayema Jan.7 1892". Title on the cover 悲笑記 **Piso ki**. [**Tōyō Bunko**]

The title as in Chinese would appear to mean "Record of Grief and Laughter", but it does not seem to be known otherwise. The story, as I read it, appeared to be part of the story of Yün-ching, as described above, and there is in any case little to be gained by listing this one defective text as a separate work.

1947 exhibition, 186: 月峯記 **Wǒlbong ki**, manuscript, 1 vol., and block print, 3 vols (both Kim Ikhwan).

Courant, 805: 월봉긔 月峯記 Wŏlbong kŭi, Seoul block print, 2 vols, "printed at 紅樹洞 Hongsudong, newly engraved at 山泉 Yuch'ŏn", in Paris, etc., and, 3358: 3 vols, "different edition at 泉 Ch'ŏn (? 由泉 Yuch'ŏn)", in Paris. **Kim Tonguk**, 387, gives three Seoul block prints: (1) 2 vols, at Hongsudong, 24, 23 leaves; (2) newly engraved at Yuch'ŏn; (3) 3 vols, at Yuch'ŏn?.

소학사젼 So Haksa chŏn, currently available from Sech'ang Sŏgwan, 63 pages. This has on the cover 蘇學士傳 So Haksa chŏn, 一名 *Ilmyŏng* ("also called") 소운뎐 So Un tyŏn [and] 텬도화 T'yŏndohwa. **Kim Kidong**, 34, gives 天桃花 Ch'ŏndohwa "The Heavenly Peach Blossom", a title which was advertised by Tŏkhŭng Sŏrim in 1935. Kim T'aejun, as above, also gives 月峯山記 Wŏlbong-san ki "Record of Yüeh-feng-shan", a title which was advertised by Pangmun Sŏgwan and Sin'gu Sŏrim in 1923, 1925 and 1932, by Yŏngch'ang Sŏgwan and Hanhŭng Sŏrim in 1925, and by Kwangdong Sŏguk in 1926. So Un chŏn was advertised by Taech'ang Sŏwŏn and Hanyang Sŏjŏgŏp Chohapso in 1918.

209. 소헌몽록 Sohŏn Mong nok

1947 exhibition, 150: 疎軒夢錄 Sohŏn Mong nok, manuscript, 1 vol. (Yi Haech'ŏng). The title appears to mean "Record of Sohŏn's [or Shu-hsüan's] Dream", but I have not been able to find the name elsewhere.

210. 소현성록 So Hyŏnsŏng nok

쇼현셩녹 Syo Hyŏnsyŏng nok, manuscript, 2 vols (vols 25 and 26), 37, 48 leaves (12 columns, 21 syllables). Title on the cover 蘇賢聖錄 So Hyŏnsŏng nok. [Seoul University] All 26 volumes were shown in the **1947 exhibition**, as item 211, according to the catalogue.

Kim Kidong, 598, lists 蘇玄聖傳 So Hyŏnsŏng chŏn as a story in Korean set in China, existing in manuscript(s), but not made known before. It seems unlikely to be different from the Seoul University text above. See also the note following **195** 소문록 So Mun nok.

211. 소효문충의록 So Hyomun Ch'ungŭi rok

Courant, 891: 쇼효문츈의록 蘇孝門忠義錄 Syo Hyomun Ch'un(g)ŭi rok, "Record of the Loyalty and Righteousness of the Filial Son Su" (title only). See the note following **195** 소문록 So Mun nok

속자경편 **Sok Chagyŏng p'yŏn**: see 247 야사속자경편 **Yasa Sok Chagyŏng p'yŏn**

속홍루몽 **Sok Hongnu mong**: see 501 홍루몽 **Hongnu mong**

212. 손방연의 **Son Pang Yŏnŭi** "Romance of Sun and P'ang"

손방연의 孫龐演義 <u>Son Pang Yŏnŭi</u>, manuscript, 5 vols. [**Palace**]

According to the librarian, a seal print on this text is that of "the wife of King Yŏngjo", i.e. the text may be eighteenth century. **Kim T'aejun**, 97, mentions it as a Chinese work translated in about the seventeenth century. The Chinese work of this title concerns 孫臏 Sun Pin and 龐涓 P'ang Chüan, opposing generals and bitter personal enemies in the wars of the fourth century B.C., see **261** 열국지 **Yŏlgukchi**. The title was advertised by Sinmyŏng Sŏrim in 1930.

손텬ᄉ녕이록 **Sont'yŏnsă Nyŏngirok**: see 265 영이록 **Yŏngirok**

213. 송부인전 **Song Puin chŏn** "The Story of the Lady Sung"

송부인젼 <u>Syong Puin chyŏn</u>, manuscript, 66 leaves (13 columns, 20 syllables). On the cover 宋송婦부人인傳젼丁졍巳ᄉ二이月월日일 "The Story of the Lady Sung, Year of the Red Snake". [**Harvard**]

If the date on the cover is the date of the text, 1857 would be the most likely date. The story begins in China in 1503

송장가 **Songjang ka**: see 1 가루지기타령 **Karujigi T'aryŏng**

214. 송파삼문금회보 **Songp'a Sammun Kŭmhŭibo**

Courant, 934: 송파삼문금회보 松坡三門金 ? ?, Syongp'a Sammun Kŭmhŭibo, "? ? of the Three Families of Songp'a" (title only: all the queries are Courant's).

쇼..... **Syo.....**: see 소 ..... **So.....**

속홍루몽 **Syok Hongnu mong**: see 501 홍루몽 **Hongnu mong**

숑..... **Syong.....**: see 송 ..... **Song.....**

수궁가 **Sugung ka**: see 468 토끼전 **T'okki chŏn**

215. 수당연의 Su Tang Yŏnŭi

Courant, 759: 슈당연의 隋唐演義 <u>Syu Tang Yŏnŭi</u>, "Romance of Sui and T'ang". He mentions no specific texts. **Kim T'aejun** mentions it, page 97 (see also pages 86, 92), as a Chinese work popular in Korea from the seventeenth century on. **217** 수사유문 **Susa Yumun** presumably covers a period also covered by this work, and **218** 수양제행락기 **Su Yang-je Haengnak ki** concerns one emperor of Sui.

216. 수매청심록 Sumae Ch'ŏngsim nok "Record of the Pure Heart of Sumae"

The only note I have on the contents of the following texts is the translation of the title as given above.

슈매쳥심녹 <u>Syumăe Ch'yŏngsim nok</u>, manuscript, 2 vols, 74, 80 leaves (10 columns, 23 syllables). Title on the cover 樹梅淸心錄 <u>Sumae Ch'ŏngsim nok</u>. [**Seoul University**]

슈매쳥심녹 <u>Syumăe Ch'yŏngsim nok</u>, manuscript, 2 vols, 43, 57 leaves (vol. 1: 13-15 columns, 24 syllables, vol. 2: 14-15 columns, 21 syllables), dated 갑인 (甲寅 1854, etc.). [**Chŏng Pyŏnguk**]

슈매쳥심녹 <u>Syumăe Ch'yŏngsim nok</u>, manuscript, 1 vol. (vol. 3), 43 (+4) leaves. On the title page 壽梅淸心錄 <u>Sumae Ch'ŏngsim nok</u>, 갑진甲辰 (1904). [**Chŏng Pyŏnguk**]

수매쳥심록 腴梅淸心錄 <u>Sumăe Ch'yŏngsim nok</u>, Pogŭp Sŏgwan, 1918, 101 pages. The title appears to have been advertised only in 1918, by Taech'ang Sŏwŏn and Hanyang Sŏjŏgŏp Chohapso, and in 1919, by Taech'ang Sŏwŏn and Pogŭp Sŏgwan.

217. 수사유문 Susa Yumun

Petrova, 219: 隋史遺聞 쉬수유문 <u>Swisă Yumun</u>, "Remaining Reports from the History of Sui", manuscript, 12 vols, 594 leaves (12 columns, 25 syllables) in all, in the Aston collection in Leningrad. The first page is reproduced in her table 3, with the title 슈수유문 <u>Syusă Yumun</u>. There is a Chinese work entitled 隋史遺文 <u>Sui-shih I-wen</u>. **215** 수당연의 **Su Tang Yŏnŭi** will presumably cover the same period of Chinese history. See also **218** 수양제행락기 **Su Yang-je Haengnak ki**.

218. 수양제행락기 Su Yang-je Haengnak ki "Record of the Pleasures of Emperor Yang of Sui"

隋煬帝行樂記 슈양뎨힝락긔 <u>Syu Yang-dye Hăengnak kŭi</u>, Sin'gu Sŏrim, 1918, 137 pages.

This gives the impression of being taken from an original in Chinese. Emperor Yang of Sui (580-618) was the ruler who ordered the invasion of Koguryŏ which was defeated in 612 by Ŭlchi Mundŏk (see **337** 울지문덕전 Ŭlchi **Mundŏk chŏn**), and his behaviour has figured in the titles of Chinese novels from the seventeenth century on at least. He will presumably also figure in **215** 수당연의 **Su Tang Yŏnŭi** and **217** 수사유문 **Susa Yumun**.

219. 수저옥란빙 Sujŏ Ongnan ping

슈져옥난빙 <u>Syujyŏ Ongnan ping</u>, lending library manuscript, 8 vols, 243 leaves (11 columns, 13-15 syllables) in all, dated 을사 (乙巳 1905) in vol.2 and 을묘 (乙卯 1915) in all other volumes. Title on the cover 水渚玉鸞 <u>Sujŏ Ongnan</u>. [**Tōyō Bunko**]

Unfortunately I made no note of the contents.

220. 수제옥환빙 Suje Okhwan ping

Courant, 937: 슈졔옥환빙 ? ? 玉環 ? <u>Syujye Okhwan ping</u> (doubtful title only: the queries are all Courant's).

221. 수제월암록 Suje Wŏram nok

Courant, 927: 슈졔월암록 <u>Syujye Wŏram nok</u>, "Record of Suje Wŏram" (title only).

222. 수호지 Suho chi "The Water Margin Story"

水滸傳 <u>Shui-hu-chuan</u> is one of the four great favourite novels in China (see W.T. de Bary, A.T. Embree, ed.: <u>A Guide to Oriental Classics</u>, Columbia University Press, New York and London, 1964, 157-160). It has been translated into Korean, as below, but Korean critics usually mention it only as the inspiration for **500** 홍길동전 **Hong Kiltong chŏn**, e.g. Kim T'aejun, 79 (also 93-94, see **504** 홍윤성전 **Hong Yunsŏng chŏn**), Kim Kidong, 176, etc.

1947 exhibition, 134: 水滸志 Suho chi, manuscript, 1 vol. (Yi Hŭisŭng). 최현배 Ch'oe Hyŏnbae: 한글갈 <u>Han'gŭl Kal</u> (정음사 Chŏngŭm sa, Seoul, 1961), page 79,

123

has a photograph of one page of Yi Hŭisŭng's "manuscript of the late nineteenth century". The page is the first of *kwŏn* 16, and has the title 통의슈호뎐
T'yungŭi Syuho tyŏn. These two may be the same.

Courant, 766, 767: 슈호지 水滸志 Syuho chi, Seoul block print, 2 vols, "engraved
in the year 庚申 (1860)", in Paris, etc., and an unidentified 충의슈호지
忠義水滸志 Ch'yungŭi Syuho chi of 23 vols. **Kim Tonguk**, 389, gives a Seoul
block print as Courant, adding that there may also be a three volume edition.
He also gives, page 396, an Ansŏng block print of 3 vols, 20, 20, 21 leaves, and
reproduces one page of this on page 402.

There are also many modern translations, and 후슈호젼 Hu Syuho chyŏn,
後水滸誌 Hu Suho Chi, manuscript, 12 vols, in the **Palace** library, is presumably
a translation of one of the Chinese sequels to this story. See also 296
왈짜타령 Waltcha T'aryŏng.

223. 숙녀지기 Sungnyŏ Chigi

숙녀지긔 Syungnyŏ Chigŭi, lending library manuscript, 5 vols, 34, 33, 33, 31,
30 leaves, dated 을사 or 을수 (乙巳 1905) in all vols except vol. 2, which may be
incomplete. Title on the cover 淑女知己 Sungnyŏ Chigi. [Tōyō Bunko]

숙녀지긔 Syungnyŏ Chigŭi, manuscript, 3 vols. Title on the cover 淑女志記
Sungnyŏ Chigi. [Seoul University]

The story appears to concern a family 녀 (呂?, Korean: Yŏ, Chinese: Lü) and
conclude with happy endings for several married women. See perhaps 260
여씨삼대록 Yŏ-ssi Samdae rok. The title in characters as on the Seoul University copy appears to give easier sense, but **Kim Kidong**, 593, lists the title
as on the Tōyō Bunko copy as of a moral tale in Korean set in China, existing
in paperback edition(s). He refers to Ku, Son and Kim: Kungmunhak Kaeron, in
which it is mentioned, page 256, as being similar to 229 심청전 Sim Ch'ŏng
chŏn. 숙여지긔 Sugyŏ Chigŭi was advertised by Hansŏng Sŏgwan and Yuil
Sŏgwan in 1915.

224. 숙영낭자전 Sugyŏng Nangja chŏn "The Story of the Maiden Sugyŏng"

The story, of a couple 白仙君 Paek Sŏn'gun and 淑英 Sugyŏng, the wife certainly
a fairy, and the husband also skilled in the magical arts, whose marriage survives a parting, the scheming of a jealous woman-servant, and even the death

of the wife, is summarised in many works on Korean literature. See **Kim T'aejun**, 218-219, **Kim Kidong**, 412-415 (**1956**: 206-209), **Pak Sŏngŭi**, 428-432, and **Sin Kihyŏng**, 299-301. Kim T'aejun suggests that a *hanmun* novel called 再生緣 <u>Chaesaeng yŏn</u> (see perhaps **390** 재생연전 **Chaesaeng yŏn chŏn**) was the original from which this was derived, and the others follow him almost verbatim. <u>Song Manjae ŭi Kwan-u-hŭi</u>, 114, and <u>P'ansori Palsaeng ko</u>, 278, see **Introduction**, §7.3, point out that this story appears to have taken the place of 3 가짜신선타령 **Katcha Sinsŏn T'aryŏng** in the repertoire of the *kwangdae*, and the second adds that the novel is such that it is unlikely to have been derived from a *p'ansori* story and likely that the reverse is true.

숙영낭ᄌ젼 <u>Syugyŏng Nangjă chyŏn</u>, Seoul block print, 28 leaves. [**British Museum**]

Courant, 823: same, "engraved at 紅樹洞 Hongsudong in the year 庚申 (1860)", and, 3366: same again, "engraved at Hongsudong", both in Paris, etc. **Petrova**, 187: 숙영낭ᄌ젼 淑英郎子傳 <u>Syugyŏng Nangjă chyŏn</u>, Seoul block print, 18 leaves, 庚申二月紅樹洞新刊 "newly engraved at Hongsudong, second month 1860", in the Aston collection in Leningrad.

숙영낭ᄌ젼 <u>Syugyŏng Nangjă chyŏn</u>, Seoul block print, 15½ leaves, reproduced in the **Ewha Series**, I 357-387, with a note 434, and also reproduced lithographically by 翰南書林 Hannam Sŏrim, Keijō, 1920, 16 single leaves.

Kim Tonguk, 385, lists the 28 leaf edition with the colophon as in Petrova, and the 18 and 16 leaf editions without colophons.

Kim Kidong, 412, reports publications by Hansŏng Sŏgwan, 63 pages, and Sin'gu Sŏrim, 43 pages, both 1915, and the title has been advertised by almost all publishers of paperbacks since that date.

淑英娘子傳 숙영낭자젼 <u>Sugyŏng Nangja chyŏn</u>, Chungang Ch'ulp'ansa, 1945, 28 pages.

淑英娘子傳 숙영낭ᄌ젼 <u>Sugyŏng Nangjă chyŏn</u>, currently available from Sech'ang Sŏgwan, 30 pages.

淑英娘子傳 <u>Sugyŏng Nangja chŏn</u> in the **Hŭimang Series**, V 211-235.

See also perhaps **77** 낭자전 **Nangja chŏn**.

225. 숙향전 Sukhyang chǒn "The Story of Shu-hsiang"

The tale is set in Sung China, and the heroine survives being abandoned as a baby during a war, imprisonment, attempts to thwart her lover's love for her, and many other trials. See **Kim T'aejun**, 214-218, **Kim Kidong**, 427-432 (1956: 234-236), **Pak Sŏngǔi**, 424-428, and **Sin Kihyǒng**, 296-299.

There is a reference to this story in the 1754 *hanmun* version of **460** 춘향전 Ch'unhyang chǒn, verse 10 (see **Kim Tonguk**, 168), and the title is given as in Shōsho Kibun (see **Introduction**, §7.2). All critics mention that there are *hanmun* versions of the story, and Kim Kidong, as above, states that these exist in manuscripts entitled 梨花亭記 Ihwa-jǒng ki (presumably) "Record of the Pear Blossom Pavilion", 梨花亭奇遇記 Ihwa-jǒng Kiu ki (presumably) "Record of the Miraculous Encounter at the Pear Blossom Pavilion", and 梨花亭奇跡 Ihwa-jǒng Kijǒk (presumably) "Miracle at the Pear Blossom Pavilion". He also states that a *hanmun* version was published by Hoedong Sǒgwan in 1916, 84 pages, and it is presumably this for which Pak Sǒngǔi gives the author as Yi Kyuyong.

숙향젼 Syukhyang chyǒn, manuscript, 4 vols, 42, 41, 55, 55 leaves, dated 신축辛丑 (1901). Title on the cover 淑香傳 Sukhyang chǒn. [**Harvard**]

The first three volumes of this text are embellished with pen and ink drawings of flowers and birds, and the writer, identified as 一波, may be a Japanese.

別淑香傳 Pyǒl Sukhyang chǒn, manuscript by Nakamura, 2 vols. [**Ogura collection, Tokyo**]

숙향젼 Syukhyang chyǒn, manuscript, 2 vols, 60, 54 leaves, reproduced in the **Ewha Series**, I 1-227, with a note 423-425. **Kim Tonguk**, 385, states that there is a manuscript in Ewha University, and it is presumably that which is reproduced.

Courant, 793: 숙향젼 熟香傳 Syukhyang chyǒn, Seoul block print, 2 vols, "engraved at 冶洞 Yadong in the year 戊午 (1858)", in Paris, etc.; 3353: 3 vols, same place and date. **Petrova**, 201: 숙향젼 熟香傳 Syukhyang chyǒn, Seoul block print, 20 leaves, 戊午十月冶洞新板 "newly engraved at Yadong, tenth month, 1858", with a note by Aston: "Another version of this.....story is found in a M.S. in my possession. Unfortunately it only contains the first part.....", in the Aston collection in Leningrad. **Kim Tonguk**, 384-385, gives two Seoul block prints:
(1) 2 vols, 戊午九月冶洞新刊 "newly engraved at Yadong, ninth month 1858";
(2) 2 vols bound as one, 23, 20 leaves, colophon as in Petrova.

Kim Kidong reports a publication by Tŏkhŭng Sŏrim, 1914, 91 pages, and the title was advertised by Pangmun Sŏgwan and Sin'gu Sŏrim in 1923, 1925 and 1932, by Chosŏn Tosŏ Chusik Hoesa, by Tongyang Sŏwŏn and by Yŏngch'ang Sŏgwan and Hanhŭng Sŏrim in 1925, and by Sech'ang Sŏgwan as currently available.

숙향전 (淑香傳) <u>Sukhyang chŏn</u>, Taejo sa, 1959, 104 pages.

淑香傳 <u>Sukhyang chŏn</u> in the Hŭimang Series, V 343-421.

쉬ᄉ유문 **Swisă Yumun**: see 217 수사유문 Susa Yumun

슈..... **Syu.....**: see 수 .... **Su.....**
숙..... **Syuk.....**: see 숙 .... **Suk.....**

226. 신계후전 Sin Kyehu chŏn

Kim Kidong, 592, lists 申桂厚傳 <u>Sin Kyehu chŏn</u> (presumably) "The Story of Sin Kyehu" as a moral tale in Korean set in Korea, existing in paperback edition(s), but not made known before. On page 394 he gives a publication by Sin'gu Sŏrim, 1926, 45 pages, and states that it is a rewriting of **62** 김학공전 **Kim Hakkong chŏn**, with the scene shifted to Korea. In the Sech'ang Sŏgwan's current list of publications it is classified as a "New Novel", but advertisements by Pangum Sŏgwan and Sin'gu Sŏrim in 1923, 1925 and 1932 classified it as a *kodae sosŏl*.

신류복전 **Sin Ryubok chyŏn**: see **228** 신유복전 **Sin Yubok chŏn**

227. 신미록 Sinmi rok "Record of the Year of the White Sheep [1811]"

The works listed below concern the revolt led by 洪景來 Hong Kyŏngnae, self-styled 平西大元帥 "Commander-in-chief for the Pacification of P'yŏngan Province". The whole revolt actually took place in 1812 by the solar calendar.

임신평난록 <u>Imsin P'yŏngnan nok</u>, "Record of the Settling of the Revolt in the Year of the Black Monkey [1812]", 平西錄 <u>P'yŏngsŏ rok</u>, "Record of Pacifying the West [i.e. P'yŏngan Province]", manuscript, 3 vols. [**Palace**]

Maema Kyōsaku: Kosen Sappu, II 1019, describes 壬申定亂錄 <u>Imsin Chŏngnan nok</u>, which is essentially the same title as that of this Palace text, as a contemporary account of the revolt in *hanmun*, manuscript, 1 vol., in his own possession.

신미록 辛未錄 <u>Sinmi rok</u>, manuscript, 1 vol. [**Palace**]
임신편란록 <u>Imsin P'yŏllan nok</u>, manuscript, 3 vols, with the title on the cover
安陵日記 <u>Allŭng Ilgi</u> (presumably) "Diary at Allŭng [=Anju]", given as in the

Karam collection. The catalogue dates it as twentieth century. This was shown in the **1947 exhibition**, item 236.

Courant, 818: 신미녹 辛未錄 <u>Sinmi nok</u>, Seoul block print, 32 leaves, "engraved at 紅樹洞 Hongsudong, second month of the year 辛酉 (1861)". **Petrova,** 21, gives the same as in the Aston collection in Leningrad. The same was re-printed lithographically by 翰南書林 Hannam Sŏrim, Keijō, 191-. **Kim Tonguk,** 391, gives the same information on the Seoul block print, and in <u>Hyangt'o Sŏul,</u> 8, **1960,** 43 and 44, he prints photographs of the first and last pages. In both these photographs and the lithograph, the title on the first page is 신미녹 <u>Sinmi nok</u> and on the last page 임신녹 <u>Imsin nok,</u> and the colophon is 辛酉二月日紅樹洞 新板 "newly engraved at Hongsudong, second month 1861."

Several modern novels on the subject exist, but the old works are barely mentioned by any critic.

<blockquote>

신방초일 **Sinbang Ch'oil:** see 139 부담 **Pudam**

신선타령 **Sinsŏn T'aryŏng:** see 3 가짜신선타령 **Katcha Sinsŏn T'aryŏng**

</blockquote>

228. 신유복전 Sin Yubok chŏn "The Story of Sin the Fatherless"

A Korean boy, late in the sixteenth century, loses his father before he is born, his mother at five, and his guardian at nine, and even after his fortunes mend suffers many reverses, but he rises to high military office and saves the Ming from defeat by the Manchu. See **Kim Kidong,** 415-420 (1956:212-215), **Sin Kihyŏng,** 325-328.

Kim Kidong, 32 and 415, gives publications by Kwangmun Sŏsi, 1917, 76 pages, and Yŏngch'ang Sŏgwan, 1928, 68 pages, and the title was advertised by Yŏngch'ang Sŏgwan and Hanhŭng Sŏrim in 1925, and by Tŏkhung Sŏrim in 1935.

신류복젼 申遺腸傳 <u>Sin Ryubok chyŏn,</u> currently available from Sech'ang Sŏgwan, 68 pages.

229. 심청전 Sim Ch'ŏng chŏn "The Story of Sim Ch'ŏng"

The story of the sacrifices made by the heroine for her blind father, and of the rewards which she was given for her piety, was perhaps the greatest favourite of all old stories in Korea. Some texts below make it clear that the scene is set in China, but this not usually so, and the Korean feeling seems to be very strong that the girl is Korean. The story is described and discussed in almost every work on Korean literature, see **Kim T'aejun**, 144-153, **Kim Kidong**, 370-381 (1956: 254-261), **Pak Sŏngŭi**, 318-324, and **Sin Kihyŏng**, 328-333. 방종현 (方鍾鉉) **Pang Chonghyŏn**: 심청전 (沈淸傳) Sim Ch'ŏng chŏn (Seoul, 한글학회 Han'gŭl Hakhoe: 한글 Han'gŭl, 119, October 1956, 59-61) is a short but very clear and authoritative summary of the story, assessment of its popularity and account of the texts.

Kim T'aejun, 150, suggests that it had a long oral tradition, but was not written down until the early eighteenth century. Kwan-u-hŭi, stanza 15, is evidence of its currency early in the nineteenth century, see the **Introduction**, §7.3, Song Manjae ŭi Kwan-u-hŭi, 106 and 118, and P'ansori Palsaeng ko, 264-266. This latter also gives the later nineteenth century references which are given by Kim T'aejun, 152-153. Sim Ch'ŏng ka is among the works of Sin Chaehyo, and part of it is quoted in **Yi and Paek: Kungmunhak Chŏnsa**, page 180. Kim T'aejun, 152, insists that 沈靑傳 Sim Ch'ŏng chŏn is a completely different story, a biography of a fifteenth century Chinese man.

심쳔갸 Sim Ch'yŏn kya, manuscript, 32 [+5] leaves, copy by Hashimoto dated 明治二十七 (1894) of a text dated 계사 (癸巳 1893, etc.). Title on the title page 심쳔젼 Sim Ch'yŏn chyŏn, etc.; title on the cover 沈氏傳 Sim-ssi chŏn, etc. [**Harvard**]

Although this text bears the earliest date which I have seen on any text, there are many other texts which are clearly of earlier date, and the many obvious mistakes in the first few pages of this text raise serious doubts as to its value. However, it is unlikely to be a deliberate rewriting itself and interesting in that the colophon states that it was copied in Pusan. The five leaves are 오륜갸 Oryun kya, a poem.

심쳥젼 Sim Ch'yŏng chyŏn, manuscript, 33 (+22) leaves (14 columns, 27 syllables), copy made by Hashimoto dated 丁酉 (1897) of a text dated 丙申 (1896, etc.). Title on the cover 沈淸傳 Sim Ch'ŏng chŏn. [**Harvard**] The 22 leaves are **468** 토끼전 **T'okki chŏn**.

沈淸錄 Sim Ch'ŏng nok, manuscript, 29 leaves, dated 무술 (戊戌 1898, etc.), given as in the **Karam collection**.

심쳥젼 Sim Ch'yŏng chyŏn, manuscript, 46 leaves, dated 辛亥 (1911, etc.), given as in the **Karam collection**.

1961 exhibition, 52: 심쳥젼 Sim Ch'yŏng chyŏn, manuscript, 1 vol. (National Library).

심쳥젼 <u>Sim Ch'yŏng chyŏn</u>, Seoul block print, 26 leaves. [**British Museum**]

심쳥젼 <u>Sim Ch'yŏng chyŏn</u>, Seoul block print, 24 leaves, defective.
[**British Museum**]

As far as leaf 24a, the 24 leaf edition is very similar to the first 18 leaves of
the 26 leaf edition. Leaf 24b is difficult to understand, and ends in mid-sentence.
The same, without the last part sentence, is reproduced in the **Ewha Series**,
I 229-276, with a note 425-428, and was also reprinted lithographically by
翰南書林 Hannam Sŏrim, Keijŏ, in 1917 according to Pang Chonghyŏn, in 1920
according to the only copy I have seen.

Courant, 809: 심쳥젼 沈青傳 <u>Sim Ch'yŏng chyŏn</u>, block print, 16 leaves, in Paris,
etc. (but he also describes the first British Museum block print as of 16
leaves). **Petrova**, 191, same, in Leningrad. **Kim Tonguk**, 388, gives three Seoul
block print editions: (1) 20 leaves, 宋洞新刊 "newly engraved at Songdong";
(2) 16 leaves; (3) 24 leaves.

심쳥젼 <u>Sim Ch'yŏng chyŏn</u>, block print, 21 leaves. Title on the cover 沈青傳
Sim Ch'ŏng chŏn. [**Tōyō Bunko**] This is boxed with several Ansŏng block
prints, but Kim Tonguk, 396, gives the only Ansŏng block print as of 20 leaves.

심쳥젼 <u>Sim Ch'yŏng chyŏn</u>, Chŏnju block print, 2 *kwŏn*, 30, 41 leaves, usually in
one volume.

Pang Chonghyŏn, in his article, given above, states that the copy in the National
Library has the colophon 大韓光武十年丙午孟春完西溪刊 "engraved at Sŏgye,
Chŏnju, first month 1906" and that it was sold by 西溪書舗 Sŏgye Sŏp'o in 1911.
One of the two copies in the **Ogura collection, Tokyo**, has an inscription on the
front cover 辛亥拾壹月日貿得 "sold in the eleventh month of 1911", and one of
the two copies given as in the **Karam collection** is also described as "Sŏgye
Sŏp'o, 1911". There are also copies owned by **Chŏng Pyŏnguk** and by 張德順
Chang Tŏksun.

A third copy in the **Karam collection** is described as of 30 + 40 leaves,
多佳書舗 Taga Sŏp'o, 1916, but Pang Chonghyŏn states that this publication, as
in the National Library, is identical with the 1906 edition.

Kim Tonguk, 397, also gives an edition in two volumes, 41, ?, leaves,
乙巳完山開刊 "engraved at Chŏnju in 1905 [etc.]".

沈清傳 심쳥젼 <u>Sim Ch'yŏng chyŏn</u>, Kwangdong Sŏguk, Pangmun Sŏgwan and
Hansŏng Sŏgwan, 1920 (reprinted from 1915), 64 (+25) pages. The 25 pages are

심부인젼 Sim Puin chyŏn. I made no note of the contents of this when I saw a copy of it, and I have not seen it mentioned elsewhere.

심쳥젼 Sim Ch'yŏng chyŏn, currently available from Sech'ang Sŏgwan, 50 pages. The title has been advertised by almost all publishers of paperbacks from 1915 to the present day.

심쳥젼 Sim Ch'ŏng chŏn, Yŏnghwa Ch'ulp'ansa, 1958, 53 pages.

심쳥젼 Sim Ch'ŏng chŏn, Taejo sa, 1959, 52 pages.

沈清傳 Sim Ch'ŏng chŏn in the Hŭimang Series, III 127-173.

I also have a note of a publication by Hoedong Sŏgwan, with no further details, and Pang Chonghyŏn, in his article, above, states that it was also published by Tŏkhŭng Sŏrim and Chungang Sŏrim.

沈清傳 Sim Ch'ŏng chŏn in: 張志暎 Chang Chiyŏng, ed.: 洪吉童傳·沈清傳 Hong Kiltong chŏn, Sim Ch'ŏng chŏn, 正音社 Chŏngŭm sa, Seoul, 1964, pages 83-252, with a note 253-260. A school text-book.

There are many modern rewritings. The one by 李海朝 Yi Haejo is 江上蓮 Kangsangnyŏn, "The Lotus on the River", but **Kim Kidong**, 29, gives it as 江山蓮 Kangsannyŏn, published by Sin'gu Sŏrim, 1912. 沈清王后傳 Sim Ch'ŏng Wanghu chŏn, "The Story of Queen Sim Ch'ŏng" by 呂奎亨 Yŏ Kyuhyŏng is also mentioned in several sources, but very imprecisely. (There is a version by him of **460 춘향젼 Ch'unhyang chŏn**.) There is also a version of the story in English, "Sim Chung", in H.N. Allen: Korean Tales, G.P. Putnam, New York and London 1889, 152-169. This should also be in his Korea, Fact and Fancy, 1904, which I have not seen.

230. 심향루기 Simhyang-nu ki

Kim Kidong, 597, lists 沈香樓記 Simhyang-nu ki (presumably) "Record of the Ch'en-hsiang Pavilion" as a love story in Korean set in China, existing in paperback edition(s), but not made known before.

231. 십리봉 Simnibong

Courant, 845: 심니봉 十里逢 Simnibong, "The Encounter of Ten Leagues" (title only).

소뎍남졍긔 **Să-tsăe Namjyŏng kŭi:** see **149 사씨남졍기 Sa-ssi Namjŏng ki**

232.　쌍두장군전 Ssangdu Changgun chŏn

Kim Kidong, 33, includes 雙頭將軍傳 <u>Ssangdu Changgun chŏn</u> (presumably, and intriguingly) "The Story of the Two-headed General" in a list of *kodae sosŏl* which have appeared in paperback editions, but which he was not able to discuss.

233.　쌍룡보은기 Ssangnyong Poŭn ki

Courant, 863: 쌍룡보은긔 雙龍報恩記 <u>Ssangnyong Poŭn kŭi</u>, "Record of the Two Dragons Returning a Favour" (title only).

234.　쌍면주기연 Ssangmyŏnju Kiyŏn

Courant, 945: 쌍면쥬긔연雙 ? 珠奇緣 (?) <u>Ssyangmyŏnjyu Kŭiyŏn</u> (doubtful title only: the queries are all Courant's).

235.　쌍문충효록 Ssangmun Ch'ungyo rok

Kim Kidong, 599, lists 雙門忠孝錄 <u>Ssangmun Ch'unghyo rok</u> (presumably) "Record of the Loyalty and Filial Piety of the Two Families" as a moral tale in Korean set in China, existing in paperback edition(s), but not made known before. The title was advertised by Pangmun Sŏgwan and Sin'gu Sŏrim in 1919.

236.　쌍선기 Ssangsŏn ki

쌍션긔 <u>Ssangsyŏn kŭi</u>, manuscript, 5 vols, 31, 31, 30, 23, 26 leaves (18 columns, 25 syllables). Title on the cover 雙仙記 <u>Ssangsŏn ki</u>. [Tōyō Bunko]

This text is not dated in the usual way, but the date 大正四年 (1915) inside the back cover of vol. 2 would not be unreasonable as a date for it. I have noted that it contains nineteen stories, but no further details. **Yi Nŭngu: Kungmunhak Kaeron** lists this text, page 6. **Kim Kidong**, 597, lists it as existing in paper- back edition(s), and refers to Yi Nŭngu. **Sin Kihyŏng**, 477, lists it as a love story in Korean set in China, but queries this.

237.　쌍성봉효록 Ssangsŏng Ponghyo rok

Courant, 877: 쌍성봉효록 雙星奉孝錄 <u>Ssangsyŏng Ponghyo rok</u>, "Record of the Filial Piety of Ssangsŏng". He gives the title only, but his note on **238** 쌍성효행록 <u>Ssangsŏng Hyohaeng nok</u> probably applies to this title also.

238. 쌍성효행록 Ssangsŏng Hyohaeng nok

Courant, 876: 쌍셩효힝록 雙星孝行錄 Ssangsyŏng Hyohăeng nok, "Record of Acts of Filial Piety of Ssangsŏng". He mentions no texts, but notes that Ssangsŏng may be "the two stars" ("the cowherd" and "the weaver"), or that it may be the name of a woman.

쌍션긔 Ssangsyŏn kŭi: see 236 쌍선기 Ssangsŏn ki

239. 쌍재자기연 Ssangjae Chagiyŏn

1947 exhibition, 149: 雙才自起緣 Ssangjae Chagiyŏn, manuscript, 1 vol. (Yi Haech'ŏng).

240. 쌍쥬기연 Ssangju Kiyŏn "The Miraculous Encounter of the Two Pearls"

쌍쥬긔젼 Ssangjyu Kŭijyŏn, manuscript, 40 leaves (14 columns, 30 syllables), dated 을묘 (乙卯 1915). Title on the cover 雙珠記 Ssangju ki. [**Chŏng Pyŏnguk**]

1947 exhibition, 117: 雙珠奇緣 Ssangju Kiyŏn, manuscript, 1 vol. (Cho Yunje, not shown).

Courant, 3363: 雙珠奇緣 Ssangju Kiyŏn, and, 3364: 雙珠記演 Ssangju Kiyŏn, both block prints, 32 leaves, in Paris. **Kim Tonguk**, 388, gives 雙珠好緣 Ssangju Hoyŏn, two Seoul block prints, one of 32 leaves and one of 22 leaves, 宋洞新刊 "newly engraved at Songdong".

쌍쥬긔연 Ssangjyu Kŭiyŏn, 남궁셜편집 "compiled by Namgung Sŏl", Hansŏng Sŏgwan and Yuil Sŏgwan, 1915, 100 pages.

The story in the two texts which I have seen concerns a 셔천흥 Syŏ Ch'yŏnhŭng (possibly 徐天興 Hsü T'ien-hsing, etc.), whose birth is announced by a fairy with a gift of a jewel bearing the character 雄 "male", and who is to marry a girl who has a jewel with the character 雌 "female".

Courant refers to this from **487** 항주기연 Hangju Kiyŏn. Chŏng Pyŏnguk's text gives as its sequel 셔천흥별젼 Syŏ Ch'yŏnhŭng Pyŏlchyŏn, which I have not seen mentioned elsewhere.

241. 쌍천기봉 Ssangch'ŏn Kibong

쌍천긔봉 雙釧奇逢 Psangch'yŏn Kŭibong, manuscript, 18 vols. [**Palace**]

Petrova, 217: same, manuscript, 22 vols, 1233 leaves in all, in the Aston collection in Leningrad. Vol. 1 of this, 59 leaves, is reproduced facsimile, with an introduction in and translation into Russian in N.I. Nikitina, A. Trotsevich, ed.: Ssangch'ŏn Kŭibong, Izdatel'stvo Vostochnoi Literaturui, Moscow, 1962.

The story opens in early fifteenth century China (Ming, Yung-lo), but apparently concerns the fortunes of a Li family for nearly two hundred years. I have not been able to identify any of the characters as historical or as figuring in other works.

Courant, 933: 쌍천긔봉 雙川奇逢 (?) Ssyangch'yŏn Kŭibong, "The Miraculous Encounter of the Two Rivers" (title only), is probably the same. Both texts above have 釧 "Bracelets" for 川 "Rivers". Kim T'aejun, 229, quotes Courant, and Kim Kidong, 594, referring to Kim T'aejun, describes it as a love story in Korean set in China, existing in paperback edition(s).

242. 쌍환호구성취후록 Ssanghwan Hogu Sŏngch'wi Hurok

Courant, 847: 쌍환호구성취후록 雙環狐裘成就後錄 Ssanghwan Hogu Syŏngch'ywi Hurok, "The Later Record of What Resulted from the Two Rings and the Skin of the Fox" (title only).

쌍 . . . . . Ssyang . . . . . : see 쌍 . . . . . Ssang . . . . .

243. 아녀영웅전 Anyŏ Yŏngung chŏn

Kim T'aejun, 159, mentions the Chinese novel 兒女英雄傳 Erh-nü Ying-hsiung chuan, in Korean Anyŏ Yŏngung chŏn, as having been translated into Korean late in the eighteenth century. A few other sources follow him in giving it a bare mention.

244. 안녹산전 An Noksan chŏn

Courant, 761: 안록산전 安祿山傳 An Noksan chyŏn. He mentions no texts, but describes it as a translation of a Chinese novel about An Lu-shan, a general who repeatedly defeated Tartar invaders between 736 and 752, but later revolted himself, and was killed by his son in 757. Among the generals who fought against him was Kuo Tzu-i, see 24 곽분양전 Kwak Punyang chŏn.

245. 안락국전 Allakkuk chŏn

Kim Kidong, 598, lists 安樂國傳 Allakkuk chŏn as a tale of the marvellous in Korean set in India, existing in manuscript(s), but not made known before.

However there is clearly a misprint here, and on page 37 he states that the work exists in *hanmun* manuscript(s) only.

안락국전 <u>Allakkuk chŏn</u>, "A Story of Paradise", in **Hyŏndae Munhak**, 50, February 1959, 327-336, is a "modern translation" by 李東林 Yi Tongnim, but from what is not made clear. The story in this is about the Buddha and his disciples.

안록산젼 **An Noksan chyŏn**: see 244 안녹산전 **An Noksan chŏn**

안룽일기 **Allŭng Ilgi**: see 227 신미록 **Sinmi rok**

246. 안승상전 **An Sŭngsang chŏn**

Kim Kidong, 591, lists 顏丞相傳 <u>An Sŭnsang chŏn</u> (presumably) "The Story of the Minister Yen" as a tale of a hero in Korean (?) set in China, existing in paperback edition(s), but not made known before.

247. 야사속자경편 **Yasa Sok Chagyŏng p'yon**

1947 exhibition, 177: 野史續自警編 <u>Yasa Sok Chagyŏng p'yŏn</u>, manuscript, 1 vol. (Kim Sambul).

續自警編 <u>Sok Chagyŏng p'yŏn</u>, "Sequel to the <u>Tzu-ching-pien</u>", compiled by 金昌集 Kim Ch'angjip (1648-1721) on the model of 自警編 <u>Tzu-ching-pien</u>, "Compilation for my Own Precaution", by 趙善璙 Chao Shan-liao of Sung, usually runs to five or six volumes of manuscript in *hanmun*, but does include 野史 *yasa*, "historical tales", see **Maema Kyōsaku: Kosen Sappu**, I 531-532.

248. 양기손전 **Yang Kison chŏn**

양기손젼 <u>Yang Kison chyŏn</u> (?), manuscript, 27 leaves, given as in the **Ilsa** collection.

249. 양문충의록 **Yang-mun Ch'ungŭi rok**

양문충의록 楊門忠義錄 <u>Yang-mun Ch'yungŭi rok</u>, manuscript, 32 vols. [**Palace**] **Courant**, 892: same (but 냥 Nyang for 양 Yang), "The Loyalty of the Yang Family" (title only).

양문충효록 <u>Yang-mun Ch'yunghyo rok</u>, 楊門忠義錄 <u>Yang-mun Ch'ungŭi rok</u>, manuscript, 43 vols. [**Palace**]

The title in Chinese on the cover of this text is the same as that of the text above, but the title in Korean inside is different, "Record of the Loyalty and Filial Piety of the Yang Family", and the contents of the two works appeared, on a cursory examination, to be completely different. Courant does not list this.

Kim T'aejun includes this, but not the other, in his list, page 161, of titles of this type, which seems to be derived largely from Courant. **Kim Kidong**, 599, quotes Kim T'aejun.

250.　양산백전 **Yang Sanbaek chŏn** "The Story of Liang Shan-po"

In fifteenth century China (Ming, Ch'eng-hua), two lovers are parted, die, and meet again in their next lives. **Kim T'aejun**, 220-223, gives the origin of the story in a Chinese legend, and points out the changes made for the novel. He states that the legend appeared under the title 梁山伯寶卷 <u>Liang Shan-po Pao-Chüan</u> "The Precious Book on Liang Shan-po", in Ming times, and under the title 訪友記 <u>Pang-yu-chi</u>, "Record of Searching out a Friend", in Ch'ing times, and that it is also known under the titles 楊山白 [傳] <u>Yang Shan-po chuan</u> or <u>Yang Sanbaek chŏn</u>, "The Story of Yang Shan-po", and 祝英臺 [傳] <u>Chu Ying-t'ai chuan</u> or <u>Ch'u Yŏngdae chŏn</u>, "The Story of Chu Ying-t'ai" (she is the heroine). See also **Kim Kidong** (1956), 237-241, for further discussion, and **Pak Sŏngŭi**, 436-442, and **Sin Kihyŏng**, 305-307, for fuller summaries of the story.

Courant, 806: 양산빅젼 楊山柏傳 <u>Yang Sanbǎek chyŏn</u>, and 3359: 량산빅젼 梁山伯傳 <u>Ryang Sanbǎek chyŏn</u>, both block prints, 24 leaves, in Paris, etc. **Petrova**, 212: 양산빅젼 楊山柏傳 <u>Yang Sanbǎek chyŏn</u>, Seoul block print, 24 leaves, in the Aston collection in Leningrad. **1947 exhibition**, 108: 梁山伯傳 <u>Yang Sanbaek chŏn</u>, Seoul block print, 1 vol. (Cho Yunje, not shown). **Kim Tonguk**, 388 梁山伯傳 <u>Yang Sanbaek chŏn</u>, Seoul block print, 24 leaves.

양산백전 <u>Yang Sanbaek chŏn</u>, currently available from Sech'ang Sŏgwan (but text as composed before 1945), 53 pages. The title has been advertised by nearly all publishers of paperbacks from 1915 on.

梁山伯傳 <u>Yang Sanbaek chŏn</u> in the **Hŭimang Series**, V 237-282.

251.　양주밀전 **Yang Chumil chŏn**

Courant, 930: 냥쥬밀젼 <u>Nyang Chyumil chyŏn</u>, "The Story of Yang Chumil" (title only).

252. 양주봉전 Yang Chubong chŏn

양쥬봉젼 <u>Yang Chyubyong chyŏn</u>, manuscript, 17 leaves (12 columns, 38 syllables). Title on the cover 梁周鳳傳 <u>Yang Chubong chŏn</u>. [**Harvard**]

This is in mixed script, probably very recent, and its general appearance does
not inspire confidence. The title on the cover would translate "The Story of
Liang Chou-feng". 趙潤濟 Cho Yunje: 國文學史 <u>Kungmunhak sa</u> (東國文化社
Tongguk Munhwasa, Seoul, 1954), page 318, includes a 楊朱鳳傳 <u>Yang Chubong</u>
<u>chŏn</u>, "The Story of Yang Chu-feng", in a list of war tales. **Kim Kidong**, 590,
quotes this from Cho Yunje as a tale of a hero set in China, existing in paper-
back edition(s). On page 32 he gives 梁朱鳳傳 <u>Yang Chubong chŏn</u>, "The Story of
Liang Chu-feng", as one of the *kodae sosŏl* existing in paperback editions which
he was not able to discuss. The title was advertised by Hansŏng Sŏgwan and
Yuil Sŏgwan in 1915, by Pangmun Sŏgwan and Sin'gu Sŏrim in 1919, by Sin'gu
Sŏrim and by Yŏngch'ang Sŏgwan and Hanhŭng Sŏrim in 1925, and by Tŏkhŭng
Sŏrim in 1935.

253. 양풍전 Yang P'ung chŏn

In Han China, the hero is one of the children dispossessed by a step-mother,
but he reaches high military rank and rights all wrongs.

양풍뎐 <u>Yang P'ung tyŏn</u>, Seoul block print, 24 leaves. [**British Museum**]

Courant, 781: 양풍전 梁豊傳 <u>Yang P'ung chyŏn</u>, block print, 24 leaves, in Paris.
Petrova, 199: same, but 25 leaves, in the Aston collection in Leningrad.

翰南書林 Hannam Sŏrim, Keijō, reprinted a 24 leaf Seoul block print lithograph-
ically in 1920, and the same is reproduced photographically in the **Ewha Series**,
III 179-226, with a note 420-423. **1947 exhibition**, 107: 양풍전 <u>Yang P'ung chyŏn</u>,
Seoul block print, 1 vol. (Cho Yunje, not shown).

양풍운젼 <u>Yang P'ungun chyŏn</u>, Ansŏng block print, 21 leaves. Title on the
cover 楊風雲傳 <u>Yang P'ungun chŏn</u>. [**Tōyō Bunko**]

양풍운젼 <u>Yang P'ungun chyŏn</u>, Ansŏng block print, 20 leaves. [**Harvard**]

梁風雲傳 <u>Yang P'ungun chŏn</u>, Hansŏng Sŏgwan, 1915, 50 pages, reported by **Kim
Kidong**, 31 and 347, and the title was advertised by Taech'ang Sŏwŏn and Pogŭp
Sŏgwan in 1920, by Pangmun Sŏgwan and Sin'gu Sŏrim in 1923, 1925 and 1932,
and by Chosŏn Tosŏ Chusik Hoesa, by Tongyang Sŏwŏn, and by Yŏngch'ang
Sŏgwan and Hanhŭng Sŏrim, all in 1925.

梁風雲傳 양풍운전 Yang P'ungun chyŏn, 남궁설편집 "Compiled by Namgung Sŏl", currently available from Sech'ang Sŏgwan, 32 pages, separately paginated from 385 장풍운전 Chang P'ungun chŏn.

This story has many similarities with 385 장풍운전 Chang P'ungun chŏn, as Kim T'aejun pointed out, 188, and this may have led to the change of the hero's personal name from P'ung to P'ungun, and so to the change of title. With the variations in the characters used for the surname, there are four versions of the title in translation: "The Story of Liang Feng"; "The Story of Yang Feng", "The Story of Liang Feng-yun", and "The Story of Yang Feng-yŭn", with further variations in the personal name which do not affect the translation. Kim Kidong gives a full description of the story 347-350, and also Pak Sŏngŭi, 378-381.

Kim Tonguk's account of the block prints seems to contain several inaccuracies. In particular, the first Seoul block print of this story which he gives on page 388 appears to be an exact description of one of the Seoul block prints of 385 장풍운전 Chang P'ungun chŏn, and the description of the Chŏnju block print which he gives on page 397 under 梁風雲傳 Yang P'ungun chŏn is also exactly a description of the Chŏnju block print of 385 장풍운전 Chang P'ungun chŏn. In Hyangt'o Sŏul, 8, page 48, in 1960, he gives only 梁風雲傳 Yang P'ungun chŏn as the title of a Seoul block print, and the print he gives is the same print of 385 장풍운전 Chang P'ungun chŏn as in the later version, but he gives the Chŏnju block print correctly under 張風雲傳 Chang P'ungun chŏn on page 61.

양현령경의혼고녀 Yang Hyŏllyŏng Kyŏngui Hon Konyŏ: see 116 박문수전 Pak Munsu chŏn

254. 양현문직절기 Yang Hyŏnmun Chikchŏl ki

양현문직결긔 楊賢門直節記 Yang Hyŏnmun Chikchyŏl kŭi, manuscript, 24 vols. [Palace]

A manuscript of the same title shown in the 1947 exhibition, as item 200, is described as belonging to Seoul University. I could not find it there in 1962, and suspect that it was in fact the above text which was shown. I have no note of the contents, nor have I found any other mention of the title.

어사박문수 Ŏsa Pak Munsu, etc. : see 116 박문수전 Pak Munsu chŏn

255. 어용전 Ŏ Yong chŏn "The Story of Yŭ Lung"

In Sung China, the hero is dispossessed by a step-mother, but finally reaches
high office, where his colleague turns out to be the husband of his missing
sister. See **Kim T'aejun,** 187, **Kim Kidong,** 344-347 (**1956:** 320-322), **Pak Sŏngŭi,**
373-376, and **Sin Kihyŏng,** 318.

Kim Kidong, 344, gives a publication by Kwangdong Sŏguk, 1923. The title was
advertised by them in 1926, and also by Taech'ang Sŏwŏn and Hanyang Sŏjŏgŏp
Chohapso in 1918, by Pangmun Sŏgwan and Sin'gu Sŏrim in 1923, 1925 and 1932,
by Chosŏn Tosŏ Chusik Hoesa in 1925, by Yŏngch'ang Sŏgwan and Hanhŭng
Sŏrim in 1925, and by Tŏkhŭng Sŏrim in 1935, and 魚龍傳 어룡전 Ŏ Ryong chyŏn
is currently available from Sech'ang Sŏgwan, 58 pages.

256. 어우야담 Ŏu Yadam "Ŏu's Historical Tales"

於于 Ŏu is 柳夢寅 Yu Mongin (1559-1623). *Hanmun* works 於于野談 Ŏu Yadam
are reported by many sources. It is not clear from the catalogue whether the
copy in the **Karam collection** is in *hanmun* or Korean. One of the copies in the
Ilsa collection is fairly clearly in *hanmun,* the other may be in Korean. This,
and the copy in the Karam collection are both single volumes, 48 leaves
(Karam) and 33 leaves (Ilsa), and so presumably contain only selections.

Several sources give 李秉岐 Yi Pyŏnggi, ed.: 於于野談 Ŏu Yadam, 國際文化舘
Kukche Munhwagwan, Seoul, 1949, but the standard bibliographies do not list it,
and I have not found a copy.

Two stories in Korean from Ŏu Yadam are included in 李秉岐 Yi Pyŏnggi, ed.:
要路院夜話記 Yorowŏn Yahwa ki (乙酉文化社 Ŭryu Munhwasa, Seoul, 1949, and
reprints), pages 57-67. These are 상번군사 (上番軍士) Sangbŏn Kunsa, "The
Duty Officer", and 포쇄별감 (曝曬別監) P'oswae Pyŏlgam, "The Airer of the
Archives." The second of these concerns 蔡壽 Ch'ae Su (1449-1515).

於于野談 Ŏu Yadam (國文學資料 Kungmunhak Charyo, 4). 通文舘 T'ongmun'gwan,
Seoul, 1960. 2 vols, 87, 77 pages, bound as one. Mimeographed.

The text for this publication is described as 舊皇室內殿秘藏本 but the librarian of
the Palace library was not able to find any such work in Korean for me in 1962.
This text does not give titles for individual stories.

257. 언봉쌍계록 Ŏn Pong Ssanggye rok

Courant, 899: 언봉쌍계록 彥逢雙季錄 Ŏn Pong Ssanggye rok, "The Record of Ŏn Meeting the Two Brothers" (title only). 彥 is not usual as a person's name either in China or Korea, but any translation of this title could only be a guess.

언삼국지 Ŏn Samgukchi: see 156 삼국지연의 Samgukchi Yŏnŭi

258. 엄씨효문청행록 Ŏm-ssi Hyomun Ch'ŏnghaeng nok

엄시효문청힝녹 嚴氏孝門淸行錄 Ŏm-si Hyomun Ch'yŏnghǎeng nok, manuscript, 30 vols. [**Palace**]

Courant, 813: 엄시효문졍힝록 嚴氏孝門正行錄 Ŏm-si Hyomun Ch'yŏnghǎeng nok, "Record of the Filial Piety and Rectitude of Ŏm". He mentions no specific texts, but suggests that it might concern 嚴興道 Ŏm Hǔngdo, who erected a tomb for King Tanjong (1453-55) against the wishes of his successor, King Sejo. He is, on the face of it, an unlikely subject for a work with such a title in the Palace library, but by the time this library was founded, in the reign of King Yŏngjo (1725-76) or later, he had been posthumously forgiven, and his descendants were holding high office. I have not seen any *kodae sosŏl* which touches at all on the subject of King Tanjong, but his story has caught on as a subject for modern popular novels.

259. 여선외사 Yŏsŏn Oesa

녀션외ᄉᆞ 女仙外史 Nyŏsyŏn Oesǎ, manuscript, 45 vols. [**Palace**]

The Chinese work of the same title, "The Unrecorded History of a Witch", is a work of 1711 by 呂熊 Lü Hsiung about a rebellion raised by a woman called 唐賽兒 T'ang Sai-erh early in the fifteenth century (Ming, Yung-lo).

260. 여씨삼대록 Yŏ-ssi Samdae rok

녀씨삼되록 Nyŏ-ssi Samdǎe rok, manuscript, 2 vols, 52, 36 (+10) leaves (12 or 13 columns, 20-22 syllables), dated 무자 (戊子 1888). Title on the cover 엿써삼되록 Yŏt-ssi Samdǎe rok. [**Chŏng Pyŏnguk**]

The title is presumably 呂氏三代錄 "Record of the Three Generations of the Yŏ [Chinese: Lü] Family". **223** 숙녀지기 **Sungnyŏ Chigi** also seems to concern several generations of a Yŏ or Lü family, but I was not able to confirm that the two stories have anything more in common. The last ten leaves in vol. 2 are a *kasa* entitled 춘풍감별곡 Ch'yunp'ung Kambyŏl kok.

여와전 Yŏwa chŏn, etc: see 113 문창진군탕평록 Munch'ang Chin'gun T'angp'yŏng nok

여자충효록 Yŏja Ch'unghyo rok: see 66 김희경전 Kim Hŭigyŏng chŏn

여장군전 Yŏ Changgun chŏn: see 403 정수정전 Chŏng Sujŏng chŏn

여중호걸 Yŏjung Hogŏl: see 66 김희경전 Kim Hŭigyŏng chŏn

연의각 Yŏn ŭi Kak: see 531 흥부전 Hŭngbu chŏn

연정구운몽 Yŏnjŏng Kuun mong: see 31 구운몽 Kuun mong

261. 열국지 Yŏlgukchi "Records of the Kingdoms"

춘츄녈국연의 Ch'yunch'yu Nyŏlguk Yŏnŭi (vols 2 and 3), 녈국지 Nyŏlgukchi 春秋列國誌 Ch'unch'u Yŏlgukchi (vol. 4), 춘츄열국지 Ch'yunch'yu Yŏlgukchi (vol. 5, with 春秋烈國誌 and 春秋列國志, both Ch'unch'u Yŏlgukchi, on the last leaf), 춘츄녈국지 Ch'yunch'yu Nyŏlgukchi (vols 7-34), lending library manuscript, 32 vols (vols 2-5 and 7-34). [**British Museum**]

Vols 2 and 3 are uniform with each other. Vol. 3 has its volume number deleted, and written in a different hand is 일 "one", altered in the same hand to 삼 "three". It also has a colophon with a date which could be read 긔묘 (己卯 1879). Vol. 4 is not uniform with any other, nor is vol. 5, which is dated 임오 (壬午 1882). Vols. 7 to 34 are roughly uniform, and vol. 34 is clearly the last of its text. As the texts exists now, it has no Korean covers and has 1025 leaves altogether. Several half leaves are certainly missing, several volumes end in mid-sentence, suggesting that some full leaves are also missing, and the general state of the text is not good.

녈국지 Nyŏlgukchi, lending library manuscript, 42 vols, most dated 계묘 (癸卯 1903). Title on the cover 列國誌 Yŏlgukchi. [**Tōyō Bunko**]

Courant, 752: 년국지 Nyŏngukchi, 列國誌 Yŏlgukchi, 7 vols, in the "Royal Library".

1947 exhibition, 175: 列國志 Yŏlgukchi, manuscript, 11 vols. (Yi Haech'ŏng).

These works are clearly romances set in the period of Chinese history variously known as the period of 東周 Tung-chou "Eastern Chou", 春秋 Ch'unch'iu "the Annals', 戰國 Chan-kuo 'the Warring Kingdoms", 六國 Liu-kuo "the Six Kingdoms", etc., that is the four or five hundred years preceding the establishment of the 秦 Ch'in dynasty in the third century B.C. They will almost certainly be derived from one or more Chinese works, but exactly which has not been established. **Kim T'aejun,** 97, suggested that 東周列國志 Tung-chou Lieh-kuo-chih "The Records of the Kingdoms of Eastern Chou" was the most popular. **Courant,** 751, suggests that the British Museum text is derived from the same, but this title does not appear anywhere in that text, and there is no obvious resemblance between it and any Chinese text of that title that I have seen. This Chinese work is of about 1750 or slightly earlier, but there have been many editions, and there are also several works with slightly different titles covering the same period of history, written from the fourteenth to the late nineteenth centuries.

Other stories in Korean are also set in the same period, including, of the works listed in this index:

206 소진장의전 So Chin Chang Ŭi chŏn
212 손방연의 Son Pang Yŏnŭi
269 오자서전 O Chasŏ chŏn
310 월왕전 Wŏl Wang chŏn
415 제환공전 Che Hwan-gong chŏn

262.   열녀전 Yŏllyŏ chŏn

Kim T'aejun, 64-65, quotes near contemporary evidence that 劉向列女傳 Liu Hsiang's "Tales of Women" was translated by order of King Chungjong in 1543, and that the translation, like the original, was illustrated, by 李上佐 Yi Sangjwa, the Royal Artist. **Pak Sŏngŭi,** 181-182, quotes this, and several other sources mention it as the first translation of a novel into Korean. All agree that it is now lost, except that 劉昌惇 Yu Ch'angdon: 古語辭典 Koŏ Sajŏn (東國文化社 Tongguk Munhwasa, Seoul, 1955, page 673) states that a block print of vol. 4 is extant in the possession of 翰南書林 Hannam Sŏrim. Since that bookshop itself no longer existed in 1955, it is difficult to know what this means.

1947 exhibition, 260: 列女傳 Yŏllyŏ chŏn, manuscript, 4 vols. (全鎣弼 Chŏn Hyŏngp'il). Note: "In the handwriting of Miss Hong of the Hyegyŏng Palace [1735-1815] and with a title page by [her husband] Prince Sado [1735-1762]". In the collection of Mr. Chŏn, this is perfectly credible, but this text was not shown as a *sosŏl*, and, from descriptions given of this work, it would appear to be a work of pure moral instruction. Liu Hsiang lived 77 B.C.-6 A.D., and Korean interest in the work appears to be due to the official recognition of its educative value by the Ming authorities. However it is included in many works on *kodae sosŏl,* some of which give it incorrectly as 烈女傳 Yŏllyŏ chŏn, "Tales of Faithful Women", and was advertised as a *kodae sosŏl* by Tae-ch'ang Sŏwŏn and Pogŭp Sŏgwan in 1919 and 1920, and by Sinmyŏng Sŏrim in 1930.

열녀춘향수절가 **Yŏllyŏ Ch'unhyang Sujŏl ka:** see 460 춘향전 Ch'unhyang chŏn

263. 열선전 **Yŏlsŏn chŏn**

1947 exhibition, 192: 列仙傳 **Yŏlsŏn chŏn,** manuscript, 3 vols (Kim Kyŏngch'un).

".... [of] six *hsiao-shuo* [小說] attributed to Han dynasty writers ..... only Liu Hsiang's [劉向] Account of the Saints [列仙傳] is genuine ..... when Liu Hsiang wrote, however, he was not aware that he was writing fiction, but thought he was recording facts. It is we who regard his work as fiction. The fragmentary legends in these books are still used as reading material for children today [i.e. in the 1920's]". (Lu Hsun: A Brief History of Chinese Fiction, Foreign Languages Press, Peking, 1959, page 399.) See **Kim T'aejun,** 93.

열여충향슈절가 **Yŏryŏ Ch'unhyang Syujyŏl ka:** see 460 춘향전 Ch'unhyang chŏn

엿씨삼듸록 **Yŏt-ssi Samdăe rok:** see 260 여씨삼대록 Yŏ-ssi Samdac rok

264. 영소전역대 **Yŏngsojŏn Yŏktae**

1947 exhibition, 182: 영소전역듸 **Yŏngsojŏn Yŏktăe,** manuscript, 1 vol. (T'ong-mun'gwan). See the **Introduction,** §6.4.2, for the peculiar characteristics of all the T'ongmun'gwan texts shown in this exhibition.

영양사난창의록 **Yŏngyang Sanan Ch'angŭi rok:** see 133 병자록 Pyŏngja rok

265. 영이록 **Yŏngirok** ·

손뎐ᄉ녕이록 **Sont'yŏnsă Nyŏngirok,** 靈异錄 **Yŏngirok,** manuscript, 3 vols. [**Palace**]

I have no note on the contents of this text. The title as in Chinese presumably means something like "Records of the Supernatural", but I have not been able to find any Chinese work of exactly this title, nor has reference to Chinese works of similar title suggested any explanation of the title in Korean on this text.

143

266.   오관참장기 Ogwan Ch'amjangki

오관참장긔 五關斬將記 <u>Ogwan Ch'amjang kŭi</u>, Taech'ang Sŏwŏn and Pogŭp
Sŏgwan, 1918, 56 pages.

The story concerns 關羽 Kuan Yü and other heroes of <u>San-kuo-chih Yen-i</u>, see
156 삼국지연의 **Samgukchi Yŏnŭi,** but I did not read beyond the first few pages.
The title was advertised by the same publishers also in 1919 and 1920.

   오대잔당연의 **Odae Chandang Yŏnŭi**: see **370** 잔당오대연의 **Chandang Odae
Yŏnŭi**

267.   오색석 Osaeksŏk

1947 exhibition, 190: 五色石 <u>Osaeksŏk</u>, manuscript, 8 vols. (Kim Kyŏngch'un).
The title is known as that of a Chinese novel.

268.   오선기봉 Osŏn Kibong

Kim Kidong, 32, includes 五仙奇逢 <u>Osŏn Kibong</u> (presumably) "The Miraculous
Encounter of the Five Fairies" in a list of *kodae sosŏl* which have been pub-
lished in paperback editions. The same title is mentioned in **Ku, Son and Kim:
Kungmunhak Kaeron,** 244.

269.   오자서전 O Chasŏ chŏn "The Story of Wu Tzu-hsü"

오ᄌᆞ셔젼 <u>O Chăsyŏ chyŏn</u>, manuscript, 46 leaves, dated 신축 (辛丑 1901) given as
in the **Ilsa collection.**

오ᄌᆞ셔실긔 <u>O Chăsyŏ Silgŭi</u>, Taech'ang Sŏwŏn and Hanyang Sŏjŏgŏp Chohapso,
1918, 108 pages. The title was also advertised by Taech'ang Sŏwŏn and Pogŭp
Sŏgwan in 1919 and 1920.

伍子胥 Wu Tzu-hsü is an historical figure from the period of Chinese history
covered by **261** 열국지 **Yŏlgukchi.**

   오호되장긔 **Oho Tăejang kŭi,** etc.: see **162** 삼설기 **Samsŏlgi**

270.   옥경기 Okkyŏng ki

Titles on the front cover, outside 옥경긔 <u>Okkyŏng kŭi</u>, inside 玉鏡記 <u>Okkyŏng ki</u>,
manuscript, 60 leaves (12 columns, 22 syllables). [**Chŏng Pyŏnguk**]

This is a very nice "palace style" manuscript, which Chŏng Pyŏnguk thought might be of the eighteenth century or earlier, but unfortunately the beginning of it is missing and at the time he showed it to me he had not been able to identify the work. He was not even sure how much of it might be missing. The title as in Chinese could be translated "Record of the Precious Mirror"

271. 옥교리전 Okkyori chŏn

Kim T'aejun quotes 玉嶠梨傳 Okkyori chŏn and Kim Tonguk quotes 玉橋 (梨) 傳 Okkyo(ri) chŏn from Shōsho Kibun, see **Introduction**, §7.2. This is almost certainly the Chinese work 玉嬌梨 (小傳) Yü-chiao-li (Hsiao-chuan), for which see Lu Hsun: A Brief History of Chinese Fiction, Foreign Languages Press, Peking, 1959, pages 246-248.

옥난긔봉 **Ongnan Kŭibong**, etc.: see **274** 옥란기연 **Ongnan Kiyŏn**

272. 옥낭자전 Ongnangja chŏn "The Story of the Girl Ongnang"

Ongnang changes places in prison with her fiancé in order to save him from punishment for a murder which he did not commit. See **Kim T'aejun,** 188-190, **Kim Kidong,** 386-389 (**1956:** 268-269), and **Pak Sŏngŭi,** 384-385. No other critic seems to have taken further Kim T'aejun's suggestion that the novel may be derived from a story in 北關誌 Pukkwan chi, "Chronicles of North Hamgyŏng". There is an account of the incident concerned in 李能和 Yi Nŭnghwa: 朝鮮女俗考 Chosŏn Yŏsokko, "Korean Women and Their Ways", 翰南書林 Hannam Sŏrim, and 東洋書院 Tongyang Sŏwŏn, Keijō, 1927, leaf 81.

옥낭자전 Ongnangja chŏn, currently available from Sech'ang Sŏgwan (but **text as** composed before 1945), 32 pages.

Kim Kidong clearly used a text identical with this, and the title was advertised by Taech'ang Sŏwŏn and Pogŭp Sŏgwan in 1926.

玉娘子傳 Ongnangja chŏn in the **Hŭimang Series,** V 115-137, appears to be slightly rewritten.

옥누몽 **Ongnu mong:** see **276** 옥루몽 **Ongnu mong**

옥닌몽 **Ongnin mong:** see **277** 옥린몽 **Ongnin mong**

옥단전 **Oktan chŏn:** see **297** 왕경룡전 **Wang Kyŏngnyong chŏn**

273. 옥단춘전 Oktanch'un chŏn "The Story of Oktanch'un"

Oktanch'un is a *kisaeng* who loves and saves the life of a *yangban*. See **Kim T'aejun**, 223-224, **Kim Kidong**, 472-478 (1956: 203-206), **Pak Sŏngŭi**, 432-435, and **Sin Kihyŏng**, 302-304. Kim T'aejun pointed to several similarities with **460** 춘향전 Ch'unhyang chŏn, and quoted evidence for the wide currency of the heroine's name as evidence for an early date for the story. The other critics follow him, only Kim Kidong adding significantly to the discussion.

옥단츈젼 <u>Oktanch'yun chyŏn</u>, manuscript by Hashimoto, 24 leaves (12 columns, 20 syllables), copy made in 庚子 (1900) of a text dated 丙申 (1896, etc.). It was copied at 南平 Namp'yŏng, in Chŏlla South Province. [**Harvard**]

Kim Kidong, 32 and 472, reports publications by Pangmun Sŏgwan, 1916, 38 pages, and by Ch'ŏngsongdang Sŏjŏm, 1916, 42 pages, and the title has been advertised by almost all publishers of paperbacks since 1915.

玉丹春傳 <u>Oktanch'un chŏn</u> in the **Hŭimang Series**, V 321-342.

274. 옥란기연 Ongnan Kiyŏn

옥난긔연 玉鸞奇綠 <u>Ongnan Kŭiyŏn</u>, manuscript, 14 vols (vols 6-19). [**Palace**]

Title on the cover 玉蘭奇綠 <u>Ongnan Kiyŏn</u>, manuscript, 7 vols. Vol. 7 is dated 룡희ᄉ년경술 (隆熙四年庚戌 1910). [**Harvard**]

The condition of this text was such that I did not like to open it further than it had been opened already. (Compare **439** 창란호연 Ch'angnan Hoyŏn.) The catalogue gives its title as 옥ᄂ긔연 <u>Ongnăn Kŭiyŏn</u>.

Courant, 840: 옥난긔봉 玉蘭奇逢 <u>Ongnan Kŭibong</u>, and 841: 옥란긔연 玉蘭奇綠 <u>Ongnan Kŭiyŏn</u>, "The Miraculous Encounter (840; 841: Destiny) of the Iris of Jade" (title only). **Kim Kidong**, 33, includes 玉蘭奇綠 <u>Ongnan Kiyŏn</u> in a list of *kodae sosŏl* which have been published in paperback editions. When 옥난긔연 <u>Ongnan Kŭiyŏn</u> was advertised by Hansŏng Sŏgwan and Yuil Sŏgwan in 1915, it was included amongst works translated from Chinese.

275. 옥력필담 Ongnyŏk P'iltam

Kim Kidong, 597, lists 玉力筆談 <u>Ongnyŏk P'iltam</u> as existing in paperback edition(s). He gives as his source **Yi Nŭngu: Kungmunhak Kaeron**. It may be a mistake for 玉少華談 Okso Hwadam, given by Yi Nŭngu, page 6, a manuscript collection of historical stories in *hanmun*, which Kim Kidong does not list. **Sin Kihyŏng**, 479, lists the same as Kim Kidong, with a query that it may be a love story in Korean set in China.

276. 옥루몽 Ongnu mong "The Dream of the Jade Pavilion"

The story opens in heaven at the White Jade Pavilion, and develops with a series of pre-ordained love affairs for a fallen star turned mortal. See **Kim T'aejun,** 120-122, **Kim Kidong,** 289-296 (**1956:** 117-120), **Pak Söngŭi,** 283-287, and **Sin Kihyŏng,** 356-359. Most general works on Korean literature also mention it.

It seems to be generally agreed that the work was first written in *hanmun* by 玉蓮子 Ongnyŏnja, and who he (or she ?) was is much discussed. The date too is much debated, some critics placing it as early as about 1700, others having reservations. 玉蓮夢 Ongnyŏn mong (presumably) "The Dream of Ongnyŏn[ja]" is apparently a shorter version of the story, and the critics debate which is the earlier. This appears to have existed only in *hanmun* until modern times, but there are old texts in Korean entitled Ongnu mong:

옥누몽 玉樓夢 Ongnu mong, manuscript, 15 vols. [**Palace**]

옥누몽 Ongnu mong, manuscript, 14 vols, dated 병오 (丙午 1906) in vols 13 and 14. [**Seoul University**] Chinese characters are added where appropriate.

옥누몽 Ongnu mong, lending library manuscript, 30 vols, 924 leaves in all (11 columns, 14 syllables), dated 무신 (戊申 1908), but 무술 in vol. 8. This may be 戊戌 1898, or it may be a mistake. Title on the cover 玉樓夢 Ongnu mong. [**Tōyō Bunko**]

1961 exhibition, 49: 玉樓夢 Ongnu mong, manuscript, 5 vols (National Library).

One modern publication which I have seen has the title 白玉樓 Paegongnu, "The White Jade Pavilion".

277. 옥린몽 Ongnin mong

See **Kim Kidong,** 307-313. No other critic gives this work more than a brief mention, and Kim Kidong points out that their comments seem to be mere assumptions from the title only. He finds this work very similar in fact to **149** 사씨남정기 **Sa-ssi Namjŏng ki,** and gives a summary of the plot, which seems to be a typically complicated story of domestic and political intrigue set in Sung

China. He bases his account on an unidentified manuscript in *hanmun*. I have seen, but not read in detail, two undated manuscripts in Korean with this title which seem to be fairly old:

옥닌뭉 **Ongnin mong**, manuscript, 13 vols. Title on the cover 玉麟夢 Ongnin mong. [**Seoul University**]

1961 exhibition, 40: 玉麟夢 Ongnin mong (National Library).

Kim Kidong, 307, also gives a publication in Korean by Hoedong Sŏgwan, 1918, 2 vols.

I have also seen the following text:

玉麟夢刪正 Ongnin mong, Sanjŏng (".....Revised"), manuscript, 2 vols, 57, 69 leaves (15 columns, up to 50 syllables), dated 丁卯. [**Chŏng Pyŏnguk**]

This is in ten *kwŏn*, written in mixed script by an old man in his seventies called 金栗溪 Kim Yulgye (Yulgye is presumably a *ho*). There is a preface describing the revision, but I had no other text with which to compare this one. Chŏng Pyŏnguk thought that 1927 was not impossible as the date of the text, yet it is tantalizingly similar to the following:

Courant, 774: 增刪玉麟夢 Chŭngsan Ongnin mong, manuscript, 8 vols, a translation into Chinese dated 丙寅 (1866, etc.) by 溪西 Kyesŏ of a work in Korean by 悔軒 Hoehŏn.

Yi and Paek: Kungmunhak Chŏnsa, 172, states that Ongnin mong was written by 悔軒 Hoehŏn, 李庭緯 Yi Chŏngjak, and that his work was so highly praised in China that he rewrote it in 80 instead of 15 *kwŏn*. The source for this information is given as 楊山趙彦林二四齋記門錄 Yangsan Cho Ŏllim Isajae Kimun nok. I cannot identify this work, and Kim Kidong, 307, also states that he had not found the reference. This does seem to indicate, however, that Hoehŏn wrote the work in *hanmun*. Other sources give Hoehŏn Yi Chŏngjak 晦軒李庭緯 (sometimes as 李延緯) as born in 1678, but I have not found any which confirm the suggestions quoted above.

There is a more famous 晦軒 Hoehŏn, 趙觀彬 Cho Kwanbin (1691-1757), who is of a 楊州 Yangju (Yangsan appears to be the same) Cho family which was much involved in court politics at the time, and seems to have produced several writers of talent. He is recorded as having been in China in the winter of 1745-1746, but I have not been able to find any more positive evidence to connect him with Ongnin mong.

As to the title, I cannot see from any account of the story what it might mean, nor have I access now to any text from which to discover this.

278. 옥백가전 Ok Paekka chŏn

Courant, 929: 옥빅가젼 Ok Păekka chyŏn, "The Story of Ok Paekka" (title only).

279. 옥소전 Okso chŏn "The Story of the Jade Flute"

Kim Tʻaejun, 225-228, describes this as differing from 208 소학사전 So Haksa chŏn essentially only in the names of the characters and the setting. He gives 玉簫奇逢 Okso Kibong, "The Miraculous Encounter of the Jade Flute", and 江陵秋月 Kangnŭng Chʻuwŏl, "The Autumn Moon at Kangnŭng", as alternative titles. Other critics follow him more briefly, but Sin Kihyŏng, 433-435, gives a fuller account of the story. Those texts which I have seen agree with Kim Tʻaejun's account in that the hero is 이선군 Yi Sŏn'gun, son of 이춘백 Yi Chʻunbaek, of Kangnŭng, in Silla. See also perhaps 347 이선군전 Yi Sŏn'gun chŏn.

강능츄월전 Kangnŭng Chʻyuwŏl chyŏn, manuscript, 53 leaves (14 columns, 33 syllables), dated 임ᄌ (壬子 1852, etc.). Title on the cover 秋月傳 Chʻuwŏl chŏn. [Tōyō Bunko]

秋月歌 Chʻuwŏl ka, manuscript, 20 leaves, dated 을ᄉ (乙巳 1905), given as in the Karam collection, is classified as a sosŏl and may therefore be related to this work.

1947 exhibition, 164: 玉簫奇緣 Okso Kiyŏn, manuscript, 1 vol. (Kim Sambul).

강능츄월옥쇼젼 江陵秋月玉簫傳 Kangnŭng Chʻyuwŏl Oksyo chyŏn, Kyŏngsŏng Sŏjŏgŏp Chohapso, 1920 (reprinted from 1915), 79 pages, and Tŏkhŭng Sŏrim, 1924 (reprinted from 1915), 74 pages.

江陵秋月 (강능추월) Kangnŭng Chʻuwŏl, currently available from Sechʻang Sŏgwan, 68 pages. Title on the last page 강능츄월옥소전 Kangnŭng Chʻyuwŏl Okso chyŏn. The title was also frequently advertised by the above publishers in the 1920's and 1930's, and by Chosŏn Tosŏ Chusik Hoesa, Pangmun Sŏgwan and Sin'gu Sŏrim.

280. 옥수기 Oksu ki

옥슈긔 Oksyu kŭi, manuscript, 9 vols, 372 leaves in all. Title on the cover
玉樹記 Oksu ki. [**Seoul University**]

The title does not seem to be mentioned elsewhere, but Ku, Son and Kim:
Kungmunhak Kaeron, 251, mention an 玉樹傳 Oksu chŏn as a biographical tale
set in Sung China.

281. 옥쌍환기봉 Okssanghwan Kibong

Kim T'aejun, 229, quotes 玉雙環奇逢 Okssanghwan Kibong (presumably) "The
Miraculous Encounter of the Jade Double Ring" from **Courant,** but Courant
does not seem to have it. **Kim Kidong,** 594, referring to Kim T'aejun, describes
it as a love story in Korean set in China, existing in paperback editions(s).

282. 옥연재합록 Ogyŏn Chaehap nok

Courant, 858: 옥연지합녹 玉緣再合錄 Ogyŏn Chăehap nok, "The Second Encounter
of a Miraculous Destiny" (title only: 녹 is misprinted 눅). **Kim T'aejun,** 229,
quotes this from Courant, and **Kim Kidong,** 595, quoting it from Kim T'aejun,
describes it as a love story in Korean set in China, existing in paperback edi-
tion(s). See 283 옥원재합기연 **Ogwŏn Chaehap Kiyŏn.**

　　　옥연즁회연 **Ogyŏn Chyunghŭiyŏn:** see 285 옥원즁회연 **Ogwŏn Chunghoeyŏn**

　　　옥원뎐히셔 **Ogwŏn Tyŏnhăesyŏ:** see 284 옥원전해서 **Ogwŏn Chŏnhaesŏ**

　　　옥원듕회연 **Ogwŏn Tyunghoeyŏn:** see 285 옥원즁회연 **Ogwŏn Chunghoeyŏn**

283. 옥원재합기연 Ogwŏn Chaehap Kiyŏn

옥원지합긔연 Ogwŏn Chăehap Kŭiyŏn, manuscript, 21 vols, dated 병오 (丙午
1906). Title on the cover 玉鴛再合 Ogwŏn Chaehap. [**Seoul University**]

I have no note of the contents of this work, and have seen no mention of it
elsewhere. 282 옥연재합록 **Ogyŏn Chaehap nok** may be a mistake for this (as
옥연즁회연 Ogyŏn Chyunghŭiyon may be a mistake for 285 옥원즁회원 **Ogwŏn
Chunghoeyŏn**). 玉鴛 "Jade-Drake" does not appear in any title of Chinese
novels which I have seen, but 玉燕 "Jade-Swallow", which would be 옥연 Ogyŏn
in Korean, is fairly common. 284 옥원전해서 **Ogwŏn Chŏnhaesŏ** is another work
of similar title on which I have little information.

284. 옥원전해서 Ogwŏn Chŏnhaesŏ

옥원뎐히셔 Ogwŏn Tyŏnhăesyŏ, manuscript, 5 vols, dated 경슐 (庚戌 1910). Title on the cover 玉鴛箋解 Ogwŏn Chŏnhae. [**Seoul University**]

1947 exhibition, 193: 玉鴛傳解書 Ogwŏn chŏn Haesŏ, manuscript, 6 vols. (Kim Kyŏngch'un). This is presumably the same work, but I have found no mention of any of these titles elsewhere, and have no note of the contents of the Seoul University text. See also **283** 옥원재합기연 **Ogwŏn Chaehap Kiyŏn.**

285. 옥원중회연 Ogwŏn Chunghoeyŏn

옥원듕회연 玉鴛重會緣 Ogwŏn Tyunghoeyŏn, manuscript, 16 vols. (vols 6-21). [**Palace**]

I have no note of the contents of this work, and have seen no mention of it elsewhere. **Courant,** 936: 옥연즁회연 Ogyŏn Chyunghŭiyŏn may be a mistake for this, see 283 옥원재합기연 **Ogwŏn Chaehap Kiyŏn.**

286. 옥인기 Ogin ki

Courant, 784 옥인긔 玉人記 Ogin kŭi, "Record of the Lady of Jade". He suggests that the lady is probably the lady 甘 Kan, wife of 劉備 Liu Pei, that is that the story may be derived from San-kuo-chih Yen-i (see **156** 삼국지연의 **Samgukchi Yŏnŭi**), but he mentions no texts, and I cannot see the grounds for his suggestion. **Kim T'aejun,** 92 and 106, includes the title among those of stories which are partial translations of San-kuo-chih Yen-i, but he may only have been quoting Courant.

287 옥전해남서 Okchŏnhaenamsŏ

Courant, 939: 옥젼히남셔玉?海南書(?) Okchyŏnhăenamsyŏ (doubtful title only: the queries are Courant's).

288. 옥조금천빙 Okchogŭmch'ŏnbing

Courant, 943: 옥조금천빙玉?金川?(?) Okchogŭmch'yŏnbing (doubtful title only: the queries are Courant's).

289. 옥쥬호연 Okchu Hoyŏn

Courant, 790: 옥쥬호연 玉珠好緣 Okchyu Hoyŏn, "The Good Union of the Jade and the Pearl", block print, 29 leaves "newly engraved at 武橋 Mugyo in 辛亥 (1851?)", in Paris, etc. **Petrova, 209:** same, Seoul block print, 20 leaves, 辛亥元月武橋新刊 "newly engraved at Mugyo, first month 1851", in the Aston collection in Leningrad. **Kim Tonguk,** 392, gives two Seoul block prints of 29 leaves both dated first month 1851.

From the notes in these three works, it appears that the story is set in tenth century China and tells of the three sons of a 蔡 Ts'ai family and the three daughters (posing first as boys) of a 劉 Liu family studying together and subsequently marrying.

　　　　옥중화　Okchunghwa: see 460 춘향전 Ch'unhyang chŏn

290. 옥호기연 Okho Kiyŏn

Kim Kidong, 596, lists 玉壺奇緣 Okho Kiyŏn as a love story in Korean set in China, existing in paperback edition(s), but not made known before.

291. 옥호빙심 Okho Pingsim

옥호빙심 玉壺氷心 Okho Pingsim, manuscript, 2 vols (vols 1 and 3). [**Palace**]

옥호빙심 Okho Pingsim, manuscript, 4 vols. 35, 34, 39, 30 (+7) leaves (11 columns 20 syllables). Title on the cover 玉壺氷心 Okho Pingsim. [**Seoul University**]

The only note which I have on the contents of these texts is that the last seven leaves of the Seoul University text are 한단몽긔 Handan mong kŭi and a Chinese poem in translation. This suggests that Handan mong kŭi is 邯鄲夢記, a translation of 湯顯祖 T'ang Hsien-tsu's Han-tan-meng-chi, and that Okho Pingsim is a version of one of the Chinese stories about a jade pillow (of pottery, like a jar) on which Han-tan-meng-chi was based. (See Lu Hsun: A Brief History of Chinese Fiction, Foreign Languages Press, Peking, 1959, pages 92, etc.) Otherwise there are several Chinese works, mostly collections of Buddhist or Taoist writings, with very similar titles. See **Kim T'aejun,** 93.

292. 옥환기봉 **Okhwan Kibong "The Miraculous Encounter of the Jade Rings"**

Courant, 782, describes the story: the man who subsequently became 光武 Kuang-wu, emperor 25-57 A.D., and founder of the Eastern or Later Han, was born after his mother had dreamt of a jade ring with the character 天 and that his destiny was to marry a girl with ring inscribed with the character 地. The girl turns out to belong to a family in a rival faction, and the story tells mainly of the acquisition of power by Kuang-wu. This seems to be the story in the British Museum text, below, at least. **94** 동한연의 **Tonghan Yŏnŭi** would presumably cover the same ground.

옥환긔봉 Okhwan Kŭibong, manuscript, 12 vols, 806 leaves in all. Title on the cover 玉環奇逢 Okhwan Kibong. [**British Museum**]. The last 46 leaves are brief biographies said to be translated from 후한서, i.e. 後漢書 Hou-han-shou.

This was purchased by the British Museum from "Stanley Steele, Esq." in 1913. It is in several different hands, all nicely written. The paper looks so new that it could not have been written very long before 1913.

옥환긔봉 Okhwan Kŭibong, manuscript, 5 vols, 40, 40, 45, 65, 40 leaves (11, 12 or 13 columns, 20 syllables), dated 뎡유 (丁酉 1897) in several volumes. [**Tōyō Bunko**]

This is a very untidy copy on used paper. The volumes are numbered as *kwŏn* in black and the chapters as *kwŏn* in red, as follows: vol. 1: chapters 1 and 2 (both numbered 1); vol. 2: chapters 3 and 4; vol. 3: chapter 5; vol. 4: chapters 6 and 7; no chapter 8; vol. 5: chapters 9 and 10.

옥환긔봉 Okhwan Kŭibong, manuscript, 15 vols, 2 chapters in each volume, 30 to 40 leaves per volume. Chapter 1 has the date 계묘 (癸卯 1903) and chapters 16, 20 and 30 the date 임ㅈ (壬子 1912). Title on the cover 玉環奇逢 Okhwan Kibong. [**Seoul University**]

This may be a lending library copy.

293. 옹고집전 **Ong Kojip chŏn, "The Story of Ong Kojip, the Stubborn Old Man"**

A heartless miser is punished by magic and converted to Buddhism. This one of the stories sung in *p'ansori*, see Song Manjae ŭi Kwan-u-hŭi, 106 (Kwan-u-hŭi, stanza 17), and P'ansori Palsaeng ko, 281-282, as described in the **Introduction, §7.3**. Kim Kidong, 549-553 (1956: 343-346), gives a summary of the story and comments on its nature, based on Kim Sambul's text:

雍固執傳 Ong Kojip chŏn in: 金三不 Kim Sambul, ed.: 裵裨將傳·雍固執傳 Pae Pijang chŏn, Ong Kojip chŏn, 國際文化舘 Kukche Munhwagwan, Seoul, 1950, pages 87-111.

The text for this is said to be taken from a manuscript of 42 years earlier (1907-1908) in the possession of 朴憲玉 Pak Hŏnok, with reference also to a manuscript in the possession of 李明善 Yi Myŏngsŏn. The spelling is modernised, and some characters are also given.

雍固執傳 Ong Kojip chŏn in the **Hŭimang Series**, I 399-412. The introductory note by 張德順 Chang Tŏksun is interesting. The text is close to that in Kim Sambul's text, but with constant variations of words used.

294. 와사옥안 Wasa Ogan

Kim T'aejun, 153, 191, mentions 蛙蛇獄案 Wasa Ogan (presumably) "The Prison Plea of the Frog and the Snake" as a satirical court case story written in *idu* (吏讀). This is the only mention I have seen of a *kodae sosŏl* written in *idu* (Korean written entirely with Chinese characters), and it is suprising that there appears to be no other mention of the fact. **Yi Nŭngu: Kungmunhak Kaeron** lists the title, page 6, as of a text owned by **Maema Kyōsaku**, but I cannot find it in **Kosen Sappu** or in the catalogue of the **Tōyō Bunko**.

295. 완월회맹연 **Wanwŏl Hoemaengyŏn**

완월회밍연 玩月會盟宴 Wanwŏl Hoemăengyŏn, manuscript, 180 vols. **[Palace]**

李明善 Yi Myŏngsŏn: 朝鮮文學史 Chosŏn Munhak Sa (朝鮮文學社 Chosŏn Munhak Sa, Seoul, 1948), page 132, states that there is a copy of it in Seoul University Library in 93 vols, 180 *kwŏn*.

This is the longest known novel in Korean. Two students of Seoul University took turns, I have been told, to read right through it aloud to each other some years ago, and there have been newspaper reports that it has been recently investigated again, but nothing has been published on it yet. **Courant**, 920, has 완월회밍 玩月會盟 Wanwŏl Hoemăeng, "Pact (of Love) under the Moon" (doubtful title only), and **Kim Kidong**, 597, lists the same as a love story in Korean set in China, existing in manuscript(s). He gives his source "李秉岐 Yi Pyŏnggi introduced", but I have not found any reference in any of Yi Pyŏnggi's published works.

296. 왈짜타령 Waltcha T'aryŏng

This is one of the stories sung in *p'ansori*, but all that is known of it now is in **Kwan-u-hŭi**, stanza 14, see **Song Manjae ŭi Kwan-u-hŭi**, 105-106, and **P'ansori Palsaeng ko**, 283-284, as described in the **Introduction**, §7.3. These articles explore several possibilities for further information, but with little success. *Waltcha* (曰者 in Kwan-u-hŭi, 曰字 in modern dictionaries) is a euphemism for a whoremonger. In P'ansori Palsaeng ko, Kim Tonguk prefers the title 武叔이打令 Musugi T'aryŏng for this story. Musugi is the name of one of a group of whoremongers in a quotation given in Song Manjae ŭi Kwan-u-hŭi. It must be this that **Kim Kidong, 44,** means by 武松打令 Musong T'aryŏng, and I have not found any support for his suggestion that this *p'ansori* story is based on 武松 Wu-sung, one of the characters in Shui-hu-chih (**222** 수호지 Suho chi).

297. 왕경룡전 **Wang Kyŏngnyong chŏn "The Story of Wang Ch'ing-lung"**

The story is set in 16th century China (Ming, Chia-ching), and tells of the love of 慶龍 Ch'ing-lung ("the Dragon") and 玉檀 Yü-tan ("the Jewel"). In his article on **458** 최충전 Ch'oe Ch'ung chŏn, Chŏng Pyŏnguk states that the manuscript in question contains, leaves 29-54, a 王慶龍傳 Wang Kyŏngnyong chŏn in *hanmun*. **Kim Kidong, 420-424,** describes this story from a manuscript in *hanmun* of the same title. He gives 玉檀傳 Oktan chŏn "The Story of Yü-tan" as an alternative title, and states that it was translated into Korean and published under the title 靑樓之烈女 Ch'ŏngnu chi Yŏllyŏ (presumably) "The Faithful Lady of the Green Pavilion [=*kisaeng*]" by Sin'gu Sŏrim, 1917, 112 pages. 王慶龍傳 Wang Kyŏngnyong chŏn, a one volume manuscript belonging to Cho Yunje, was announced for the **1947 exhibition,** as item 114. There is no indication in the catalogue of whether it was in *hanmun* or in Korean, and it was not shown.

I have seen only the following text in Korean: 王御史傳龍含玉 Wang Ŏsa chŏn, Yong-ham-ok, "The Story of the Government Inspector Wang: the Jewel Swallowed by the Dragon", manuscript, 40 leaves. In mixed script, in the style of *hanmun* with Korean suffixes added. The author is given on leaf 1 as 金華山人 Kŭmhwa Sanin. The colophon gives the date as 光武十年 (1906) and the title as 龍含玉傳 Yong-ham-ok chŏn. The cover has the title 王御史慶龍傳 Wang Ŏsa Kyŏngnyong chŏn and the date 己亥 (1899, etc.). [**Chŏng Pyŏnguk**]

　　왕교란백년장한 **Wang Kyoran Paengnyŏn Changhan:** see **39** 금고기관 Kŭmgo Kigwan and **443** 채봉감별곡 Ch'aebong Kambyŏl kok

298. 왕랑반혼전 **Wang-nang Panhon chŏn "The Story of Mr. Wang's Soul being Returned"**

This story of a widower who is warned by his wife in a dream of his imminent death in time to be reading the scriptures when he is called, and of his and his wife's return to life as a result, is printed as an appendix to a scripture, in *hanmun*, with interspersed translation. There have been several printings. The best known, and the only one I have seen, is that at Haein-sa in 1776, which has also been reprinted as 王郎返魂傳 Wang-nang Panhon chŏn (國語國文學研究資料 2-2) by 慶北大學校大學院 Kyŏngbuk University Graduate School, Taegu, 9 leaves. See **Kim T'aejun**, 42-43, **Kim Kidong**, 113-114 (1956: 347-348), **Pak Sŏngŭi**, 140-141, and **Sin Kihyŏng**, 404-407.

299. 왕비호전 Wang Piho chŏn

Kim Kidong, 591, lists 王飛虎傳 Wang Piho chŏn as a story of a hero (probably in Korean) set in China, existing in paperback edition(s) (also page 33). He gives as his source his own work of 1956, but I have not been able to find the reference. The title was advertised by Sech'ang Sŏgwan in 1933.

왕어사경룡전 **Wang Ŏsa Kyŏngnyong chŏn**, etc.: see **297** 왕경룡전 **Wang Kyŏngnyong chŏn**

300. 왕장군전 Wang Changgun chŏn

Kim T'aejun, 99, 102 and 108, mentions 王將軍 (傳) Wang Changgun (chŏn) (presumably) "(The Story of) General Wang" as amongst the best of the biographies of generals, in which, however, as a group, he finds little literary interest. **Kim Kidong**, 590, quoting Kim T'aejun, describes it as a story of a hero set in China, existing in paperback edition(s) (also page 33). The title was advertised by Taesan Sŏrim in 1926.

301. 요로원야화기 Yorowŏn Yahwa ki "Record of a Night's Talking at the Post Station"

要路院夜話記 Yorowŏn Yahwa ki in: 李秉岐 Yi Pyŏnggi, ed.: 要路院夜話記外十一篇 Yorowŏn Yahwa ki oe Sibil p'yŏn, "Yorowŏn Yahwa ki and Eleven Other Stories" (乙酉文化社 Ŭryu Munhwasa, Seoul, 1949 and reprints), pages 7-46.

The event takes place in a year 무오 (戊午), and, since the author is given in some texts as 朴斗世 Pak Tuse (late seventeenth century), this is taken to be a work of 1678. The source of the text here is presumably the manuscript of 32 leaves which is listed as in the **Karam collection**. This was shown in the **1947 exhibition**, under item 140, together with a manuscript in *hanmun* belonging to Yi Myŏngsŏn. Another manuscript, 1 vol., from the Palace Library was announced, but it was not shown, and I was not able to find it there in 1962.

302. 요화전 Yohwa chŏn

요화전 瑤華傳 <u>Yohwa chyŏn</u>, manuscript, 22 vols. [Palace]

This is presumably a translation of the Chinese novel of the early nineteenth century, which tells the story of 瑤華 Yao-hua, daughter of one 常洵 Ch'ang Hsün, in Ming times. A copy in 7 vols (14 *kwŏn*) is given as in the Kyujanggak Library, Seoul University.

303. 용매기연 Yongmae Kiyŏn

Kim Kidong, 596, lists 龍媒奇緣 <u>Yongmae Kiyŏn</u> as a love story in Korean set in China, existing in paperback edition(s) (also page 33), but not made known before.

304. 용문도총 Yongmun Toch'ong

Courant, 917: 용문도총 龍門都摠 <u>Yongmun Toch'yong</u>, "The General of Yongmun" (doubtful title only). This title bears a resemblance to that of **305** 용문전 **Yong Mun chŏn**, but *toch'ong* as such does not seem to be a generally used name of a military rank.

305. 용문전 Yong Mun chŏn "The Story of Lung Men"

龍門 Lung Men is the Chinese name for the Tartar general who fought against Su Ta-sheng (or -ch'eng) in the story **194** 소대성전 **So Taesŏng chŏn**. No critic gives this work more than a bare mention.

농문젼 <u>Nyong Mun chyŏn</u>, Seoul block print, 25 leaves, 己未石橋新刊 "newly engraved at Sŏkkyo in 1859". [British Museum]

There is also another copy which is virtually identical, but does not have the colophon.

Courant, 3362: 룡문젼 <u>Ryong Mun chyŏn</u>, block print 24 leaves, in Paris (also 826, the British Museum text); **Petrova**, 198, as the British Museum text without the colophon, in the Aston collection in Leningrad; **Kim Tonguk** also gives, page 393, another Seoul block print, of 40 leaves; in the **Karam collection**, a block print of 81 leaves is given, containing **194** 소대성전 **So Taesŏng chŏn** and <u>Yong Mun chŏn</u>.

Yi Nŭngu: Kungmunhak Kaeron, 10, gives a Chŏnju block print described as: 咸豐乙未石橋坊刻本 "at the local press at Sŏkkyo ín [an impossible date which could be a mistake for 1859]". This would appear to be a mistake, having the colophon from a Seoul block print as in a Chŏnju block print. **Kim Tonguk**, 397, gives a Chŏnju block print, 咸豊己未石榴坊刻本 "at the local press at Sŏngnyu, 1859", and he attaches some importance to the identity of the dates of the Seoul and Chŏnju block prints, but one wonders whether it is not simply a compounding of a mistake by Yi Nŭngu. I have not found any location or ownership given for a Chŏnju print.

龍門將軍傳 <u>Yong Mun Changgun chŏn</u>, "The Story of General Lung Men", Yŏngch'ang Sŏgwan and Hanhŭng Sŏrim, 1925, 40 pages.

룡문장군전 龍門將軍傳 <u>Ryong Mun Changgun chyŏn</u>, 朴健會繹述 "told by Pak Kŏnhoe", Chungang Ch'ulp'ansa, Seoul, 1945. 49 pages.

龍門將軍傳 <u>Yong Mun Changgun chŏn</u>, title at the head of each page 룡문장군전 <u>Ryong Mun Changgun chŏn</u>, title on the cover 大成龍門傳 대성용문전 <u>Tăesyŏng Yong Mun chyŏn</u>, "The Story of Ta-ch'eng and Lung Men", currently available from Sech'ang Sŏgwan (but text as composed before 1945), 36 (+28) pages. The 28 pages are **194** 소대셩전 **So Taesŏng chŏn**.

The title was advertised by Sin'gu Sŏrim in 1918, by Taech'ang Sŏwŏn and Pogŭp Sŏgwan in 1919 and 1920, by Pangmun Sŏgwan and Sin'gu Sŏrim in 1923, 1925 and 1932, and by Tŏkhŭng Sŏrim in 1935.

龍文傳 <u>Yong Mun chŏn</u>, "The Story of Lung Wen", given by **Kim Kidong**, page 32, is presumably a mistake for this, and **304** 용문도총 **Yongmun Toch'ong** may also be.

용함옥전 **Yong-ham-ok chŏn**: see **297** 왕경룡전 **Wang Kyŏngnyong chŏn**

306. 운영전 Unyŏng chŏn "The Story of Unyŏng"

This work is well known as a novel in *hanmun*. **Kim Kidong**, 400-405, is an important study of it. See also **Kim T'aejun**, 71, **Kim Kidong** (1956), 194-197, and **Pak Sŏngŭi**, 232-234. The story as described is unusual in that it ends unhappily with suicide of Unyŏng and her lover. There have been many modern versions in Korean, but the only version in traditional form in Korean which I have seen is:

운영젼 <u>Unyŏng chyŏn</u>, manuscript, 47 leaves (12 columns, 25 syllables), dated 大韓光武八年甲辰 (1904). Title on the cover and in the colophon 雲英傳 <u>Unyŏng chŏn</u>. [**Tōyō Bunko**]

307.　울지경덕전 Ulchi Kyŏngdŏk chŏn "The Story of Yü-ch'ih Ching-te"

尉遲恭 Yu-ch'ih Kung (Tzu: 敬德 Ching-te) is a warrior who helps T'ai-tsung of T'ang in the early years of the dynasty. The story as in the texts below is clearly taken from Chinese.

울지경덕전 Ulchi Kyŏngdŏk chyŏn, Seoul block print, 26 leaves, 甲子季秋銅峴新刊 "newly engraved at Tonghyŏn in the ninth month of 1864". [British Museum]

Courant, 758 and 3347, gives the same as also in Paris. **Kim Tonguk**, 389, gives two Seoul block prints:

(1) 35 leaves, 同治甲子銅峴 "at Tonghyŏn, 1864", and

(2) 26 leaves, no date or place.

울지경덕실긔 蔚遲敬德實記 Ulchi Kyŏngdŏk Silgŭi, currently available from Sech'ang Sŏgwan, 72 (+2) pages.

The title was also advertised under this form of the hero's name by Taech'ang Sŏwŏn and Pogŭp Sŏgwan, and by Chosŏn Tosŏ Chusik Hoesa in 1925.

　　웅치전 Ungch'i chŏn: see 375 장끼전 Changkki chŏn

　　원곡서상기역해 Wŏn'gok Sŏsang ki Yŏkhae: see 169 서상기 Sŏsang ki

　　원본열녀춘향수절가 Wŏnbon Yŏllyŏ Ch'unhyang Sujŏl ka, etc.: see 460 춘향전 Ch'unhyang chŏn

308.　원촉지 Wŏnch'ŏkchi

1947 exhibition, 174: 原蜀誌 Wŏnch'okchi, manuscript (Yi Haech'ŏng, not shown). **Courant**, 803: 원촉지 元蜀誌 Wŏnch'yukchi, "History of the Yüan at 四川 Szu-ch'uan" (?), title only.

　　월봉기 Wŏlbong ki, etc.: see 208 소학사전 So Haksa chŏn

309.　월영낭자전 Wŏryŏng Nangja chŏn

Kim T'aejun, 224: " 月英娘子傳 Wŏryŏng Nangja chŏn tells of the love of 崔喜星 Ch'oe Hŭisŏng [Chinese: Ts'ui Hsi-hsing] and 胡月英 Ho Wŏryŏng [Chinese: Hu Yüeh-ying]". **Kim Kidong**, 592, gives the same as the title of a family story in Korean set in China, existing in paperback edition(s). On page 30 he gives a publication by Hansŏng Sŏgwan, 1917, 81 pages. The same publishers, with Yuil Sŏgwan, advertised the title in 1915, and it was also advertised by Chosŏn Tosŏ Chusik Hoesa in 1925 and by Sinmyŏng Sŏrim in 1930.

Ku, Son and Kim: Kungmunhak Kaeron, 254, and Sin Kihyŏng, 480, give the same, but 影 for 英.

310. 월왕전 Wŏl Wang chŏn

월왕전 Wŏl Wang chyŏn, lending library manuscript, 5 vols, 31, 30, 29, 30, 29 leaves (11 columns, 14 syllables), dated 임ㅈ (壬子 1912) in vols 2-5. Title on the cover 越王傳 Wŏl Wang chŏn. [Tōyō Bunko]

Courant, 780: same title, no texts, suggests that it concerns 勾踐 Chü Chien, King of Yüeh, in the fifth century B.C.; 3350: same title, block print, 3 vols, "engraved at 由洞 Yudong", in Paris, with a note that the action takes place in Sung China. Kim Tonguk, 393, also gives a Seoul block print of 3 vols, 20, 24, 19 leaves, "newly engraved at Yudong" and the story as about the rise and fall of Chü Chien, taken from Tung-chou Lieh-kuo-chih, see 261 열국지 Yŏlgukchi. Kim Kidong, 210, states that it is based on the life of 夫差 Fu Ch'a, King of Yüeh, but he is usually given as a king of 吳 Wu, who first (in 494) defeated, and subsequently (in 473) was defeated by Chü Chien.

311. 월하선전 Wŏrhasŏn chŏn "The Story of Wŏrhasŏn"

월하선견 Wŏrhasyŏn chyŏn, manuscript, 24 leaves (11 columns, 28 syllables), dated 乙卯 (1915, etc.). Title on the cover 月下仙傳 Wŏrhasŏn chŏn. [Chŏng Pyŏnguk]

The hero is 황진경 Hwang Chin'gyŏng, son of a governor of Ch'ungch'ŏng Province, and Wŏrhasŏn is the daughter of a kisaeng. Chŏng Pyŏnguk thought that it appeared to be imitative of 460 춘향전 Ch'unhyang chŏn.

312. 월황전 Wŏrhwang chŏn

Courant, 829: 월황전 月黃傳 (?) Wŏrhwang chyŏn, "The Story of Wŏrhwang", 2 vols, in the collection of von der Gabelentz. His query is on the Chinese version of the title.

313. 위씨오세삼난현행록　Wi-ssi Ose Samnan Hyŏnhaeng nok

위시오세삼난현힝녹　魏氏五世三難賢行錄 Wi-si Osye Samnan Hyŏnhăeng nok, manuscript, 27 vols. [Palace]

위시셰딕록 Wi-si syedăe rok, 衛氏賢行錄 Wi-ssi Hyŏnhăeng nok, manuscript, 27 vols. [Palace]

The only note I have on these two texts is that they seem to be the same apart from their titles. **Courant,** 869:'위시오세삼난현힝긔 魏氏五世三難賢行記 Wi-si Osye Samnan Hyŏnhăeng kŭi,"Record of the Wisdom of the Wi [Chinese: Wei] family for Five Generations in Triple Adversity" (title only).

314. 위왕별전　Wi Wang Pyŏlchŏn

Courant, 785: 위왕별전 魏王別傳 Wi Wang Pyŏlchyŏn,"The Special Story of the King of Wei". He mentions no texts, but suggests that it concerns 曹操 Tsao Ts'ao, one of the leading characters of San-kuo-chih Yen-i, see 156　삼국지연의 **Samgukchi Yŏnŭi.** Kim T'aejun, 92 and 106, and **Kim Kidong,** 210, mention the same title in much the same terms.

315. 유경옥　Yugyŏngok

Courant, 941: 유경옥 Yugyŏngok (doubtful title only).

316. 유금필전　Yu Kŭmp'il chŏn

Kim Kidong, 589, lists 庾黔弼傳 Yu Kŭmp'il chŏn (presumably) "The Story of Yu Kŭmp'il" as an historical story in Korean set in Korea, existing in paperback edition(s) (also page 33), but not made known before. The title was advertised by Taech'ang Sŏwŏn and Hanyang Sŏjŏgŏp Chohapso in 1918, and by Taech'ang Sŏwŏn and Pogŭp Sŏgwan in 1919. Yu Kŭmp'il (died 941) was a military man who assisted the establishment of the Koryŏ dynasty.

유리국심청전　Yuri-guk Sim Ch'ŏng chŏn: see 229 심청전 Sim Ch'ŏng chŏn

317. 유문성전　Yu Munsŏng chŏn "The Story of Liu Wen-ch'eng"

The story is of the triumph of love over the improper commands of the emperor and other difficulties. See **Kim Kidong,** 248-252 (1956: 163-166), who gives a publication by Kwangmun Sŏsi, 1918, 78 pages. The title was advertised by Sin'gu Sŏrim in 1925, by Tongyang Sŏwŏn in 1925, and by Tŏkhŭng Sŏrim in 1935.

류문셩젼(柳文成傳) <u>Ryu Munsyŏng chyŏn,</u> currently available from Sech'ang Sŏgwan, 73 pages.

유백아솔금사지옴 <u>Yu Paega Solgŭm Sajiŭm:</u> see 39 금고기관 <u>Kŭmgo Kigwan</u>

318. 유소제전 **Yu Soje chŏn**

유소제젼 <u>Yu Sojye chyŏn,</u> manuscript, 69 leaves (8 columns, 13 syllables), dated on the first leaf 을묘 (乙卯 1915) and in the colophon 무오 (戊午 1918) [**Harvard**]

This was a recent acquisition when I saw it, in April 1965, and had not been catalogued, but I thought that its date could well be 1915 or 1918. I found it difficult to read, and have only noted that the story is set in twelfth century China (Sung, Cheng-ho).

319. 유승상전 **Yu Sŭngsang chŏn**

Mibalp'yo Kodae Sosŏl ko describes 유승상전 (劉丞相傳) <u>Yu Sŭngsang chyŏn</u> (presumably) "The Story of the Minister Liu" from a manuscript in Korea University, 3 vols, 56½, 48, 39½ leaves (12 columns, 24-28 syllables in vol. 1, 13 columns, 30-34 syllables in vols 2 and 3), as a family story set in Ming China.

320. 유씨삼대록 **Yu-ssi Samdae rok**

뉴시삼디록 劉氏三代錄 <u>Nyu-si Samdăe rok,</u> manuscript, 20 vols. [**Palace**]
뉴시삼디록 劉氏三代錄 <u>Nyu-si Samdăe rok,</u> manuscript, 8 vols (vols 4, 7, 10, 12, 13, 16, 17 and 18 out of 22). [**Palace**]

뉴쎠삼디록 <u>Nyu-ssi Samdăe rok,</u> manuscript, 73 (+7) leaves (10, occasionally 13 columns, 26 syllables). Title on the cover 劉氏三代錄 <u>Yu-ssi Samdae rok.</u> [**Harvard**] The seven leaves are of the same title as **329** 유효공선행록 Yu Hyogong **Sŏnhaeng nok.**

1947 exhibition, 189: 劉氏三代錄 <u>Yu-ssi Samdae rok,</u> manuscript, 18 vols. (Kim Kyŏngch'un). The catalogue notes: "Describes the three generations of 劉禹性 Liu Yü-hsing of Ming; a record of discord with an ethical content".

Courant, 905: 뉴시삼디록 劉氏三代錄 <u>Nyu-si Samdăe rok,</u> "Record of Three Generations of the Liu Family" (title only). **Kim Kidong** mentions the titles 柳氏三代錄 page 37 and 劉氏三代錄 page 38, both <u>Yu-ssi Samdae rok.</u>

321. 유씨양문록 Yu-ssi Yangmun nok

Courant, 908: 뉴시냥문록 劉氏兩門錄 Nyu-si Nyangmun nok, "Record of the Two Branches of the Yu [Chinese: Liu] Faimly" (title only). **Kim T'aejun**, 160, gives the same, implying that it is imitative of a Chinese work. **Kim Kidong**, 594, quoting Kim T'aejun, lists it as a love story in Korean set in China, existing in paperback edition(s). Recent press reports mention a 劉李兩門錄 Yu Yi Yangmun nok, "Record of the Two Families Yu and Yi [Chinese: Liu and Li]" as being in the **Palace** library. I did not see this in 1962, but, if the reports are correct, this may be the original for Courant's title as above.

322. 유씨충효록 Yu-ssi Ch'unghyo rok

Courant, 888: 뉴시충효록 劉氏忠孝錄 Nyu-si Ch'yunghyo rok, "Record of the Loyalty and Filial Piety of the Yu [Chinese: Liu] Family" (title only). **Kim T'aejun**, 161, gives the same in a list of titles which seems to be derived largely from Courant. **Kim Kidong**, 599, quoting Kim T'aejun, lists the same as a moral tale in Korean set in China, existing in manuscript(s).

유이양문록 Yu Yi Yangmun nok: see 321 유씨양문록 Yu-ssi Yangmun nok

323. 유충렬전 Yu Ch'ungnyŏl chŏn "The Story of Liu Chung-lieh"

The hero, in China about 1500 (Ming, Hung-chih), becomes a loyal and victorious general and rights the wrongs done to his family. **Kim T'aejun**, 92 mentions it as one of the partial translations of San-kuo-chih Yen-i (**156** 삼국지연의 **Samgukchi Yŏnŭi**), but I have not seen any support for this suggestion. See **Kim Kidong**, 238-243 (1956: 152-155), and **Pak Sŏngŭi**, 210-213.

유충열 Yu Ch'ungyŏl, manuscript, 2 vols, 20, 52 leaves (16 columns, 16 syllables). Volume 1 has *kwŏn* 1, leaves 1-20, and volume 2 *kwŏn* 1, leaves 23-31, and *kwŏn* 2, 43 leaves. There is a date 壬寅 on the reverse of the last leaf. The copy could be dated 1902. [**Chŏng Pyŏnguk**]

뉴충열젼 Nyu Ch'yungyŏl chyŏn, lending library manuscript, 7 vols, about 30 leaves per volume (11 columns, 15 syllables), dated 임인 (壬寅 1902) in vols 2, 3, 5 and 7, and 졍미 (丁未 1907) in vols 1, 4 and 6. Title on the cover 劉忠烈傳 Yu Ch'ungnyŏl chŏn. [**Tōyō Bunko**]

1961 exhibition, 46: 劉忠烈傳 Yu Ch'ungnyŏl chŏn, manuscript, 1 vol. (National Library).

유충렬전 劉忠烈傳 Yu Ch'ungnyŏl chŏn, manuscript, 2 vols, dated 경술 (庚戌 1910, etc.), given as the **Karam collection**.

유충열전 Yu Ch'ungyŏl chyŏn in the **Ewha Series**, II 169-340, with a note 438-441, is a reproduction of a Chŏnju block print of two *kwŏn*, 39, 47 leaves. The same block print is given as in the **Karam collection**, and Cho Yunje's Chŏnju block print was announced for the **1947 exhibition**, as item 121, but was not shown. **Kim Tonguk**, 397, on the Chŏnju Block prints, as also **Yi Nŭngu: Kungmunhak Kaeron**, 11, adds 豊雨重印 "reprinted at P'ungu".

Kim Kidong, 238, gives publications by Tŏkhŭng Sŏrim, 1913, 112 pages, and by Taech'ang Sŏwŏn, 1919, 86 pages, and the title has been advertised by almost all publishers of paperbacks since that date.

劉忠烈傳 류충렬젼 Ryu Ch'yungnyŏl chyŏn, Kwandong Sŏguk, Hoedong Sŏgwan, Taech'ang Sŏwŏn and Pangmun Sŏgwan, 1921 (reprinted from 1913), 99 pages.

劉忠烈傳 류충렬젼 Ryu Ch'yungnyŏl chŏn, no publisher, not dated [probably about 1945], 76 pages.

류충렬젼 Ryu Ch'yungnyŏl chyŏn, currently available from Sech'ang Sŏgwan, 72 pages.

劉忠烈傳 Yu Ch'ungnyŏl chŏn in the **Hŭimang Series**, II 337-445.

324. 유치요람 Yuch'i Yoram

1947 exhibition, 176: 幼穉要覽 Yuch'i Yoram, manuscript, 1 vol. (Yi Pyŏnggi). This title would presumably mean something like "Children's Encyclopaedia", but it was shown as a *sosŏl*. The nearest title in the catalogue of the **Karam collection** is 유취요람 Yuch'wi Yoram, manuscript, 72 leaves, dated 신히 (辛亥 1911, etc.). This could mean "Classified Encyclopaedia", but it is given the decimal number for didactic poetry.

325. 유한당사씨언행록 Yuhandang Sa-ssi Ŏnhaeng nok "Record of the Words and Actions of Yuhandang, Miss Sa"

유한당ᄉᆞ시언ᄒᆡᆼ녹 Yuhandang Să-si Ŏnhăeng nok, manuscript, 2 vols, 89, 70 (+11) leaves (10-11 columns, 18-21 syllables), dated 계묘 (癸卯 1903), from the royal household at Maenghyŏn (孟峴). [**Chŏng Pyŏnguk**]

The 11 leaves are two short works of advice from mothers to daughters.

幽閑堂言行錄 Yuhandang Ŏnhaeng nok, manuscript, 75 leaves, is given as in the **Ilsa collection**. It is catalogued with the decimal number for biographies of women, and when a manuscript of the same title belonging to Pang Chonghyŏn, but of three volumes, was shown in the **1947 exhibition**, as item 247, it was shown under the "miscellaneous" category. Chŏng Pyŏnguk's text is certainly a biography, and it may not be fictional, but I have included it here at least until I can find some evidence that it is historical. **150** 사씨행록 **Sa-ssi Haengnok** may be the same work.

326. 유화기몽 Yuhwa Kimong

Kim Kidong, 596, lists 柳花奇夢 Yuhwa Kimong (presumably) "The Miraculous Dream of the Willow Flower" as a love story in Korean set in China, existing in paperback edition(s). It is listed immediately after **327** 유화기연 **Yuhwa Kiyŏn,** but it is difficult to believe that the two are different. **Kim T'aejun,** 247, quotes Yuhwa Kimong first in a short list of distinctive titles of "New Novels", but the title was advertised amongst those of *kodae sosŏl* by T'aech'ang Sŏwŏn and Pogŭp Sŏgwan in 1919 and 1920.

327. 유화기연 Yuhwa Kiyŏn

뉴화긔연 Nyuhwa Kŭiyŏn, lending library manuscript, 7 vols, 227 leaves in all (11 columns, 14 syllables), dated 을사 or 을ᄉ (乙巳 1905) in all vols except vol. 5, which is dated 긔유 (己酉 1909). Title on the cover 柳花奇緣 Yuhwa Kiyŏn. [Tōyō Bunko]

The title presumably means "The Miraculous Destiny of the Willow Flower". **Yi Nŭngu: Kungmunhak Kaeron,** 5, mentions this manuscript, and **Kim Kidong,** 596, quoting Yi Nŭngu, lists the title as of a love story in Korean, set in China, and existing in paperback edition(s). Immediately after this he lists **326** 유화기몽 **Yuhwa Kimong.**

328. 유황후전 Yu Hwanghu chŏn "The Story of the Empress Liu"

The story is set in 16th century China, opening in Ming, Cheng-te.

류황후 Ryu Hwanghu, Taech'ang Sŏgwan, 1926, 72 pages.

Kim Kidong, 33, includes 劉皇后傳 Yu Hwanghu chŏn in a list of *kodae sosŏl* published in paperback editions.

329. 유효공선행록　Yu Hyogong Sŏnhaeng nok

劉孝公善行錄 Yu Hyogong Sŏnhaeng nok, manuscript, 6 vols (5 *kwŏn*), given as in the **Karam collection**. There is also a 뉴효공션힝녹 Nyu Hyogong Syŏnhăeng nok, 7 leaves, as an appendix to the Harvard manuscript of **320** 유씨삼대록 **Yu-ssi Samdae rok**.

Courant, 871: 뉴효공션힝긔 劉孝公善行記 Nyu Hyogong Syŏnhăeng kŭi, "The Good Behaviour of Yu, Hyogong [Chinese: Liu, Hsiao-kung]" (title only). **Kim T'aejun**, 161, has 劉孝公善行錄 Yu Hyogong Sŏnhaeng nok in a list of titles of this type which seems to be derived largely from Courant. **Kim Kidong**, 599, quoting Kim T'aejun, lists 劉孝公美行錄 Yu Hyogong Mihaeng nok as a moral tale in Korean set in China, existing in manuscript(s). **Sin Kihyŏng**, 481, gives the title the same form.

330. 육선기　Yuksŏn ki

뉵션긔 Nyuksyŏn kŭi, manuscript, 33 leaves (12 columns, 15 syllables), dated 갑오 (甲午 1894). Title on the cover 六仙記 Yuksŏn ki. [**Imanishi collection, Tenri**]

The catalogue describes this as a lending library copy. The title as in Chinese presumably means "Record of the Six Magicians".

331. 육염기　Yugyŏm ki

1947 exhibition, 142: 六艶記 Yugyŏm ki (presumably) "Records of the Six Beauties", manuscript, 2 vols (Yi Haech'ŏng), and same, manuscript (Pang Chonghyŏn). No such title is given as in the **Ilsa collection**.

332. 육인기봉조구연　Yugin Kibong Choguyŏn

Courant, 856: 뉵인긔봉조구연 六人奇逢遭舊緣 Nyugin Kŭibong Choguyŏn, "The Miraculous Way in which the Six Men Met their Destiny" (title only).

333. 육효자전　Yuk Hyoja chŏn "Stories of Six Filial Sons"

륙효ᄌ전 六孝子傳 Ryuk Hyojă chyŏn, "compiled by 박건회 Pak Kŏnhoe", currently available from Sech'ang Sŏgwan, 78 pages.

This has the pre-title 고딕소셜 *kodăe sosyŏl*, and at least two of the stories occur separately as *kodae sosŏl*, but as a whole it is very like the collections of short moral tales (五倫行實 Oryun Haengsil, etc.), which are excluded from this survey.

The first story concerns one 김효징 Kim Hyojing, and is very probably the same as **65 김효증전 Kim Hyojŭng chŏn**. The second story is virtually identical in text with the Seoul block print of **358 이해룡전 Yi Haeryong chŏn**. The filial sons in the remaining four are 오준 O Chun, 양보 Yang Po, 밍계샹 Măeng Kyesyang (he is Chinese) and 양일 Yang Il. I have not been able to identify any of these as historical or as occurring in other stories.

The title was advertised by Pangmun Sŏgwan and Sin'gu Sŏrim in 1919, by Sin'gu Sŏrim in 1925, and by Yŏngch'ang Sŏgwan and Hanhŭng Sŏrim in 1925.

334. 윤지경전 Yun Chigyŏng chŏn "The Story of Yun Chigyŏng"

The story, in the first text below, opens early in the sixteenth century. Such information as I have on it indicates that it may concern the historical Yun Chigyŏng (尹知敬, 1584-1634), who was concerned in the restoration of 1623 (see **17 계해반정록 Kyehae Panjŏng nok**), but does not confirm this.

윤지경젼 Yun Chigyŏng chyŏn, manuscript, 69 leaves (7 columns, 20-21 syllables). **[Harvard]**

This is written on the back of a printed almanack for a 甲申 year, probably 1884.

윤디경젼 Yun Tigyŏng chyŏn, manuscript, 51 leaves, given as in the **Ilsa collection**.

335. 윤하정삼문취록 Yun Ha Chŏng Sammun Ch'wirok

윤하뎡삼문취록 尹河鄭三門聚錄 Yun Ha Tyŏng Sammun Ch'ywirok, 105 vols. **[Palace]**

Recent newspaper reports of work done on the Palace collection describe this as a story of a family in 102 volumes, and as a sequel to **102 명주보월빙 Myŏngju Powŏl ping**.

Courant, 914: Same, "Collected Records of the Three Families Yun, Ha and Chŏng [Chinese: Yin, Ho and Cheng]" (title only). 河 is not usually a surname in either Korea or China, but I have not been able to confirm any other possible translation of the title. **Kim T'aejun**, 160, includes the same in a list of works which are imitative of Chinese works. **Kim Kidong**, 594, quoting Kim T'aejun, lists it as a love story in Korean set in China, existing in paperback edition(s), and also mentions it on page 33.

336. 율병연 Ŭlbyŏngyŏn

Courant, 857: 율병연 乙丙緣 Ŭlbyŏngyŏn, "The Second and Third Destinies" (title only).

337. 을지문덕전 Ŭlchi Mundŏk chŏn "The Story of Ŭlchi Mundŏk"

乙支文德 Ŭlchi Mundŏk—the original form of his name is a matter of conjecture—is an historical figure, a general of Koguryŏ, who is particularly noted for his cunning in defeating a Chinese (Sui) invasion in 612. **218** 수양제행락기 **Su Yang-je Haengnak ki** concerns the emperor who ordered this invasion, and works like **215** 수당연의 **Su Tang Yŏnŭi** and **217** 수사유문 **Susa Yumun** may cover these invasions also.

을지문덕전 (乙支文德傳) Ŭlchi Mundŏk chŏn, currently available from Sech'ang Sŏgwan, 38 pages. The title was also advertised by Pangmun Sŏgwan and Sin'gu Sŏrim in 1923, 1925 and 1932.

The style of this publication is a curious mixture of old-time story telling and straightforward history. One might perhaps regard it as a modern derivation of a traditional type of story from an historical work (see also **Kim Kidong**, 33 and 209). There are completely modern novels about the same person which antedate this publication, and, from earlier than those, historical works with more than a touch of romance.

338. 음양삼태성 Ŭmyang Samt'aesŏng

Kim Kidong, 596, lists 陰陽三台星 Ŭmyang Samt'aesŏng as a love story in Korean set in China, existing in paperback edition(s), but not made known before.

339. 음양옥지환 Ŭmyang Okchihwan

Kim Kidong, 595, lists 陰陽玉指環 Ŭmyang Okchihwan (presumably) "The Love Token of a Jewelled Ring" as a love story in Korean set in China, existing in paperback edition(s). He refers to **Ku, Son and Kim: Kungmunhak Kaeron,** in which the title is mentioned, page 254. **Kim Kidong (1956), 11,** suggests that it was inspired by **208** 소학사전 **So Haksa chŏn.** Rings figure in many stories as talismans and love tokens.

음혈록 **Ŭphyŏl lok:** see **485** 한중록 **Hanjung nok**

340. 의열왕비충효록 **Ŭiyŏl Wangbi Ch'unghyo rok**

의렬왕비충효록 <u>Ŭiryŏl Wangbi Ch'yunghyo rok</u>, manuscript, 67 leaves (10 columns, 18 syllables), dated 신축 (辛丑 1901). Title on the cover 忠孝 [錄] Ch'unghyo [rok]. [**Chŏng Pyŏnguk**]

The first six leaves are well written, but the rest are done by a thirteen year old.

의녈비충효록 <u>Ŭinyŏl Pi Ch'yunghyo rok</u>, manuscript, 69 leaves, title on the cover 義烈妣忠孝錄 <u>Ŭiyŏl Pi Ch'unghyo rok</u>, given as in the **Karam collection.**

의열비퉁효록 <u>Ŭiyŏl Pi T'yunghyo rok</u>, manuscript, 73 leaves, dated 癸巳 (1893), given as in the **Karam collection.** The title on the title leaf appears to be given as 壺峯公家狀 Hobong-gong Kajang, "Family Record of Hobong [Chinese: Hu-feng]".

Several explanations of the title are possible, but reference to the texts, which might not, in any case, all tell the same story, would be necessary to produce a reliable translation.

341. 이대봉전 **Yi Taebong chŏn "The Story of Li Ta-feng"**

The hero, in fifteenth century China (Ming, Ch'eng-hua), and his fiancée both reach high military rank and avenge wrongs done to their families. See **Kim Kidong, 246-248 (1956: 160-162),** and **Sin Kihyŏng, 364-367.**

이듸봉젼 <u>Yi Tăebong chyŏn</u>, manuscript, 75 leaves (10 columns, 24 syllables), dated 임슐 (壬戌 1862, etc.). [**Harvard**]

The catalogue dates this 1802, and I certainly did not think it as late as 1922.

이듸봉젼 <u>Yi Tăebong chyŏn</u> (in vol. 1), 니듸봉젼 <u>Ni Tăebong chyŏn</u> (in vols. 2-4), lending library manuscript, 4 vols, 34, 29, 31, 33 leaves (11 columns, 13 syllables), dated 을사 or 을ᄉ (乙巳 1905). Title on the cover 李大鳳傳 <u>Yi Taebong chŏn.</u> [**Tōyō Bunko**]

니듸봉젼 <u>Ni Tăebong chyŏn</u>, manuscript, 64 leaves (12 columns, 23 syllables), dated 긔유 (己酉 1909, etc.), reproduced in the **Ewha Series,** IV 277-403, with a note 416-419.

리듸봉젼 <u>Ri Tăebong chyŏn</u>, manuscript, 55 leaves (11 columns, 30 syllables), dated 癸丑 (1913, etc.). [**Chŏng Pyŏnguk**]

듸봉젼 <u>Tăebong chyŏn</u>, manuscript 64½ leaves (11 columns, 24 syllables). Title on the cover 리대봉젼 <u>Ri Taebong chyŏn</u> [**Chŏng Pyŏnguk**]

Chŏng Pyŏnguk thought that this was "almost certainly early twentieth century"

1947 exhibition, 120: 李大鳳傳 Yi Taebong chŏn, Chŏnju block print, 1 vol. (Cho Yunje, not shown). **Yi Nŭngu: Kungmunhak Kaeron,** 11, lists this as the title of a Chŏnju block print, and **Kim Tonguk,** 397, states that it is of two vols, 45 and 38 leaves.

Kim Kidong, 30, gives a paperback publication by Tŏkhŭng Sŏrim, 1914, 122 pages, and on page 246 he gives publication by Pangmun Sŏgwan, 1916, 70 pages, and by Hoedong Sŏgwan, 1916, 67 pages.

리대봉전 Ri Taebong chyŏn, Tongyang Sŏwŏn, 1925, 52 pages.

Kim T'aejun, 230, mentions an alternative title 鳳凰臺 Ponghwang-dae (presumably) "The Phoenix Terrace". **Kim Kidong,** 246, gives this as the title of a rewritten version. He also gives, page 29, 鳳皇臺 , also Ponghwang-dae, and presumably a mistake, as the title of a rewritten version published by Yuil Sŏgwan in 1912. Yi Taebong chŏn was also advertised by Sin'gu Sŏrim in 1925, and by Yŏngch'ang Sŏgwan and Hanhŭng Sŏrim in 1925, and Ponghwang-dae was advertised by Chosŏn Tosŏ Chusik Hoesa in 1925, and by Taesan Sŏrim in 1926.

이대장전 Yi Taejang chŏn: see 355 이태경전 Yi T'aegyŏng chŏn

342. 이도령전 Yi Toryŏng chŏn

Kim Kidong, 596, lists 李進令傳 Yi Toryŏng chŏn (presumably) "The Story of Master Yi" as a love story in Korean set in Korea, existing in paperback edition(s) (also page 33), but not made known before. There is one "Master Yi", the hero of **460** 춘향전 Ch'unhyang chŏn, but this is so obvious that Kim Kidong could not possible have listed this story separately if there had been any connection. However, the nature of the title is such that it could well be of a story which is also known by another title. This title was advertised by Taech'ang Sŏwŏn and Hanyang Sŏjŏgŏp Chohapso in 1918, and by Taech'ang Sŏwŏn and Pogŭp Sŏgwan in 1919 and 1920.

343. 이백경전 Yi Paekkyŏng chŏn

李白慶傳 Yi Paekkyŏng chŏn (presumably) "The Story of Li Po-ch'ing" is given as in Shōsho Kibun by both Kim T'aejun and Kim Tonguk, see **Introduction,** §7.2. **Kim Kidong,** 594, referring to Kim T'aejun, lists it as a love story in Korean set in China, existing in paperback edition(s).

344. 이봉빈전 Yi Pongbin chŏn

리봉빈젼 Ri Pongbin chyŏn, title on the cover 李鳳彬傳 Yi Pongbin chŏn, Sech'ang Sŏgwan, 1933, 71 pages.

A biographical story set in fifteenth century China (Ming, Ch'eng-hua). **Kim Kidong** lists it, page 591, and refers to his own work of **1956**. I can only find a bare mention there, page 57, of a title 李鳳濱傳 Yi Pongbin chŏn.

345. 이봉황연 Yi Ponghwang yŏn

Courant, 940: 니봉황연 李 ？ ？ 緣 Ni Ponghwang yŏn (doubtful title only: the queries are Courant's).

346. 이상서전 Yi Sangsŏ chŏn

Courant, 897: 니샹셔젼 李尙書傳 Ni Syangsyŏ chyŏn, "The Story of the Minister Yi [Chinese: Li]" (title only).

347. 이선군전 Yi Sŏn'gun chŏn

Kim Kidong, 601, lists 李仙君傳 Yi Sŏn'gun chŏn (presumably) "The Story of Li Hsien-chün" as in Korean, set in China, and existing in paperback edition(s). The characters given for the hero's name are exactly those given by **Kim T'aejun**, 227, for the name of the hero of **279** 옥소전 Okso chŏn, but that story is set in Silla.

348. 이순신전 Yi Sunsin chŏn

Kim Kidong mentions 李舜臣傳 Yi Sunsin chŏn several times (16, 38, 209, 225, 589) as an embellished biography of the hero of the wars of 1592-1597 (see **366** 임진록 Imjin nok). He states that it exists in manuscript(s), and he does not appear to regard it very highly. See also **Kim T'aejun**, 69-70, and advertisements of the title by Pangmun Sŏgwan and Sin'gu Sŏrim in 1923, 1925, 1928 and 1932, and by Sech'ang Sŏgwan in 1933.

349. 이씨세대록 Yi-ssi Sedae rok

니시셰디록 李氏世代錄 Ni-si Syedăe rok, manuscript, 26 vols. [**Palace**]

Courant, 902, gives exactly the same title, "Record of the Several Generations of the Yi [Chinese: Li] Family" (title only).

350. 이씨효문록 Yi-ssi Hyomun nok

Courant, 878: 니시효문록 李氏孝門錄 <u>Ni-si Hyomun nok</u>, "The Filial Piety of Yi [Chinese: Li]" (title only). **Kim T'aejun**, 161, includes the same in a list of titles of this type which seems to be derived largely from Courant. **Kim Kidong**, 599, referring to Kim T'aejun, lists it as a moral work in Korean set in China, existing in manuscript(s).

351. 이언총림 Iŏn Ch'ongnim

Title on the cover 俚諺叢林 <u>Iŏn Ch'ongnim</u>, manuscript, 1 vol. [**Palace**]

This title presumably means "Forest of Sayings", and the work is probably a collection of historical stories. The title which I have noted as on leaf 1, 명일남뎐 <u>Tyŏng Illam tyŏn</u>, is presumably only the title of the first story in it. I have not found any information on either title.

352. 이윤구전 Yi Yun'gu chŏn

Kim Kidong, 564-569, describes 李允九傳 <u>Yi Yun'gu chŏn</u>, "The Story of Yi Yun'gu", from a manuscript of 50 pages (12 columns, 30 syllables), "apparently late Yi", as one of virtue triumphing over a most remarkable collection of adversities from wicked step-mothers to Japanese pirates.

이적선취초혁만서 **Yi Chŏksŏn Ch'wich'o Hyŏngmansŏ**: see **39** 금고기관 **Kŭmgo Kigwan** and **356** 이태백실기 **Yi T'aebaek Silgi**

353. 이진사전 Yi Chinsa chŏn

Kim Kidong, 478-481, describes 李進士傳 <u>Yi Chinsa chŏn</u>, "The Story of the Top Class Graduate Yi" from a publication by Hoedong Sŏgwan, 1925, 54 pages, as a love story with an uncommon plot set in eighteenth century Korea, but undistinguished as a novel. The story which he gives is completely different from the <u>Yi Chinsa chŏn</u> which is one text of **355** 이태경전 **Yi T'aegyŏng chŏn**. The title was advertised by Pangmun Sŏgwan and Sin'gu Sŏrim in 1919 and 1925, and by Yŏngch'ang Sŏgwan and Hanhŭng Sŏrim in 1925.

354. 이춘풍전 Yi Ch'unp'ung chŏn "The Story of Yi Ch'unp'ung"

The story is satirical of the *yangban* at the end of the Yi dynasty, though the setting is about 1700. See 張德順 Chang Tŏksun: 李春風傳研究 <u>Yi Ch'unp'ung chŏn Yŏn'gu</u> "A Study of The Story of Yi Ch'unp'ung" (**Kugŏ Kungmunhak** 5, June 1953, 1-5), **Kim Kidong**, 529-533 (1956: 219-222), **Sin Kihyŏng**, 439-440.

Chang Tŏksun, ed.: 李春風傳 <u>Yi Ch'unp'ung chŏn</u> (in **Hyŏndae Munhak**, 46, 47, 48 and 50, October 1958—February 1959) is taken from a manuscript in his possession of 28 leaves, dated 乙巳, 1905, which I saw briefly in the 1961 **exhibition**, as item 54. See also 李春風傳 <u>Yi Ch'unp'ung chŏn</u> in the **Hŭimang Series**, IV 223-240, and the prefatory note there by Chang Tŏksun.

李春風傳 <u>Yi Ch'unp'ung chŏn</u>, manuscript, 28 leaves, dated 壬子 (1912, etc.), given as in the **Karam collection**. Chang Tŏksun, in his article of 1953 above, states that 林和 Yim Hwa was intending to publish this (it was advertised by Pangmun Ch'ulp'ansa in 1947), but that it was never published.

金永錫 Kim Yŏngsŏk, ed.: 李春風傳 <u>Yi Ch'unp'ung chŏn</u>. 朝鮮金融組合聯合會 Chosŏn Kŭmyong Chohap Yŏnhap hoe, Seoul, 1947. 109 pages, plus a two page note which includes the information that this is modern derivation from an unidentified manuscript.

Kim Kidong, 529, states that he used a manuscript of 46 pages (12 columns, 20 syllables), which he does not identify further.

161 삼선기 **Samsŏn ki** has several features in common with this story.

355. 이태경전 **Yi T'aegyŏng chŏn** "The Story of Yi T'aegyŏng"

The action takes place in the fifteenth century, and the plot is a very involved one of personal relationships and obligations, further complicated by the scene shifting from Korea to China and then to Manchuria. See **Kim Kidong**, 575-581.

이진사전 <u>Yi Chinsa chyŏn</u>, "The Story of the Top Class Graduate Yi", manuscript by Hashimoto, 42 (+33) leaves (12 columns, 21 syllables), copy made in 庚寅 (1910) of a text dated 庚子 (1900, etc.). Title on the cover 李進士傳 <u>Yi Chinsa chŏn</u>. [**Harvard**]

In this version, the action takes place about 1700, but otherwise it appears to be essentially the same story as in the following texts. It is not the same story as that which Kim Kidong describes under the same title, see **353** 이진사전 **Yi Chinsa chŏn**. The 33 leaves in this text are **432** 진대방전 **Chin Taebang chŏn**.

Kim Kidong, 32, gives a publication by Tonga Sŏgwan, 1917 (on page 575: 1916), 48 pages.

삼국리대장젼 <u>Samguk Ri Taejang chyŏn</u>, "The Story of Yi, General of Three Countries", 李泰景傳 <u>Yi T'aegyŏng chŏn</u>, Kyŏngsŏng Sŏjŏgŏp Chohap, 1926, 51 pages.

Kim Kidong does not list <u>Yi T'aegyŏng chŏn</u> in his table, though he does describe it fully, as above. 李大將傳 <u>Yi Taejang chŏn</u>, which he lists, page 591, with rather uncertain details, seems best taken as a title of this story. The same title was advertised by Taech'ang Sŏwŏn and Hanyang Sŏjŏgŏp Chohapso in 1918 and by Pangmun Sŏgwan and Sin'gu Sŏrim in 1923, 1925 and 1932.

356. 이태백실기　Yi T'aebaek Silgi

Kim T'aejun, 96, gives 酒中奇仙李太白實記 <u>Chujung Kisŏn Yi T'aebaek Silgi</u>, "The True Record of Li T'ai-po [Li Po], The Drunken Genius" as a Korean story derived from the Chinese collection Chin-ku-ch'i-kuan, story no. 6, see **39** 금고기관 **Kŭmgo Kigwan. Kim Kidong**, 210, mentions 李太白實記 <u>Yi T'aebaek Silgi</u> as one of the partial or complete translations of Chinese novels based on Chinese historical persons which he does not discuss, and the same has been advertised by Taech'ang Sŏwŏn and Hanyang Sŏjŏgŏp Chohapso several times since 1918.

357. 이학사전　Yi Haksa chŏn

Kim T'aejun, 229, describes 李學士傳 <u>Yi Haksa chŏn</u> (presumably) "The Story of the Minister Li" as a novel in 12 episodes based on the life of 李賢慶 Li Hsien-ch'ing of 靑州 Ch'ing-chou in sixteenth century China (Ming, Chia-ching). I have not been able to identify him as an historical person. **Kim Kidong**, 590, referring to Kim T'aejun, lists the same, adding that it exists in paperback edition(s). **Ku, Son and Kim: Kungmunhak Kaeron**, 257, gives the same title as of a story of the love of a *yangban* for a *kisaeng* in Korea.

358. 이해룡전　Yi Haeryong chŏn "The Story of Yi Haeryong"

A story of a filial son set in eighteenth century Korea.

니히룡젼 Ni Hăeryong chyŏn, Seoul block print, 20 leaves. [**Harvard**]

There is also a Seoul block print in the **Ogura collection, Tokyo**, but I did not note the number of leaves. The text is reprinted faithfully as the second story in the paperback publication of **333** 육효자전 **Yuk Hyoja chŏn**.

Kim Kidong, 598, lists 李海龍傳 <u>Yi Haeryong chŏn</u>, but only as existing in paperback edition(s) and not made known before. The work does not appear to have been described by any critic, and the usual sources do not even give it in lists of Seoul block prints.

359. 이화몽 **Yihwa mong**

Kim Kidong, 597, lists 梨花夢 <u>Yihwa mong</u> as a love story in Korean, set in China, existing in paperback edition(s) (also page 33), but not made known before. The title was advertised by Pangmun Sŏgwan and Sin'gu Sŏrim in 1918, 1919 and 1928.

360. 이화전 **Yi Hwa chŏn**

Kim Kidong, 110-113, describes 李華傳 <u>Yi Hwa chŏn</u>, "The Story of Yi Hwa", from a manuscript of 40 pages (13 columns, 18 syllables), as a tale of battles against evil spirits, set in Korea, and later in China also, about 1600.

이화정기 **Yihwa-jŏng ki**, etc.: see 225 숙향전 **Sukhyang chŏn**

이화정서전 **Yihwa Chŏngsŏ chŏn**: see 127 번이화정서전 **Pŏn Yihwa Chŏngsŏ chŏn**

361. 인봉소 **Inbongso**

인봉쇼 麟鳳韶 <u>Inbongsyo</u>, manuscript, 3 vols. [Palace]
This would be <u>Lin-feng-shao</u> in Chinese. 引鳳簫 <u>Yin-fen-hsiao</u> in Chinese, but also <u>Inbongso</u> in Korean, is known as the title of a Chinese novel but only from Japanese sources.

Kim Kidong, 595, lists 麟鳳韶 <u>Inbongso</u> as a love story in Korean set in China, existing in manuscript(s). He gives as his source "introduced by 李秉岐 Yi Pyŏnggi", but I have not been able to find any mention of it in any published work by Yi Pyŏnggi. On page 37, Kim Kidong states that it exists in manuscript(s) in *hanmun*.

인향전 **Inhyang chyŏn**: see 58 김인향전 **Kim Inhyang chŏn**

362. 인현왕후전 **Inhyŏn Wanghu chŏn "The Story of Queen Inhyŏn"**

The historical records about this queen are full and clear. She became the second wife of King Sukchong in 1681 at the age of fourteen, was displaced by another wife eight years later, restored after five years, and died, childless, in 1701 at the age of thirty five. Her treatment in 1689-1694 is said to have been the object of allegorical criticism in **149** 사씨남정기 **Sa-ssi Namjŏng ki. 118** 박태보실기 **Pak T'aebo Silgi** is a biography of one courtier who opposed the king over her banishment. For descriptions and discussion of *kodae sosŏl* versions of the story of her life, see **Kim Kidong**, 361-363 (1956: 140-142), **Pak Sŏngŭi**, 398-399, and **Sin Kihyŏng**, 412-416. All these appear to rely on:

李秉岐 **Yi Pyŏnggi**, ed.: 仁顯王后傳 **Inhyŏn Wanghu chŏn.** 博文出版社 **Pangmun Ch'ulp'ansa. 86 pages.**

The only copy of this which I have to refer to is not dated. Some bibliographies date it 1946, other 1947. The place of publication was probably Seoul.

仁顯王后傳 **Inhyŏn Wanghu chŏn** in the **Hŭimang Series**, III 9-55, appears to follow this closely, but with considerable variation in the actual words used.

金用淑 **Kim Yongsuk**: 仁顯王后傳作者考 **Inhyŏn Wanghu chŏn Chakcha ko**, "A Consideration of the Authorship of The Story of Queen Inhyŏn" (**Kugŏ Kungmunhak**, 21, August 1959, 158-173) compares the story with the historical records and concludes that the authorship of the story cannot be determined on the evidence of the extant texts, but that it dates from at least a hundred years or so later than the time of the action.

Kim Yongsuk states that she worked from two versions, and quotes 金東旭 **Kim Tonguk**: 仁顯王后傳異本攷 **Inhyŏn Wanghu chŏn Ibon ko**, "A Study of the Variant Texts of the Story of Queen Inhyŏn" ("文理師大學報創刊號"), which I have not seen, for the opinion that a text belonging to 方鍾鉉 **Pang Chonghyŏn** is closer to the original than a text belonging to Yi Pyŏnggi.

In the **1947 exhibition**, item 87 was 仁顯王后傳 **Inhyŏn Wanghu chŏn**, manuscript, 1 vol. (Yi Pyŏnggi) and item 88 was 仁顯王后德行錄 **Inhyŏn Wanghu Tŏkhaeng nok**, "Record of the Virtuous Conduct of Queen Inhyŏn", manuscript, 1 vol. (Pang Chonghyŏn).

Yi Pyŏnggi's text was presumably the basis for his edition of 1946 or 1947, given above, but I have not found any subsequent mention of it. The only text which might be of this story in the **Karam collection** is:

인현성모민사덕힝녹 **Inhyŏn Syŏngmo Min-sa Tŏkhăeng nok**, manuscript, 63 leaves, title on the cover 仁顯聖母德行錄 **Inhyŏn Sŏngmo Tŏkhaeng nok**.

The Queen was of the 閔 Min family of 驪興 Yŏhŭng, and Sŏngmo is a title given fairly regularly to queen mothers.

On Pang Chonghyŏn's text also I have not seen any subsequent clear information. In an exhibition held by Yŏnhŭi (now Yŏnse) University in Pusan in 1952, item 41 was 인현왕후성덕실기 **Inhyŏn Wanghu Sŏngdŏk Silgi**, "The True Record of the Good Virtue of Queen Inhyŏn", manuscript, 31 leaves, belonging to Pang

Chonghyŏn. Kim Yongsuk, in her article of 1959, states that she found the title 閔聖王后德行錄 **Min Sŏngwanghu Tŏkhaeng nok** in the catalogue of Seoul University Library, but could not find the text itself. She wonders whether it may not be the same as Yi Pyŏnggi's text, but in her bibliography at the end of the article she gives this as the title of Pang Chonghyŏn's text. (For Yi Pyŏnggi's text there she gives his edition of 1946 or 1947, above.) No such title appears in the catalogue of the **Ilsa collection** and the **Karam collection**, nor does there seem to be in that catalogue any text in the Ilsa collection which might be of this story. I have seen only one old text of it:

인현왕후덕힝녹 <u>Inhyŏn Wanghu Tŏkhăeng nok</u>, manuscript, 36 leaves (10 or 11 columns, 22 syllables), dated 임즈 (壬子). [**Seattle**]

This is nicely written in a woman's hand. Written beside the date in pen and ink was " 서기 1912", but Dr. Doo Soo Suh was sure that the date should be taken as 1852.

Ku, Son and Kim: Kungmunhak Kaeron, 246, has a short quotation from an 인현왕후성덕성힝녹 <u>Inhyŏn Wanghu Syŏngdŏk Syŏnghăeng nok</u>.

363. 임경업전 Yim Kyŏngŏp chŏn "The Story of Yim Kyŏngŏp"

林慶業 **Yim Kyŏngŏp** (1594-1646) is a famous general from the time of the Manchu invasions (see **133** 병자록 **Pyŏngja rok**). Many interesting and colourful, but basically factual accounts of his actions and attitudes can be found by reference to the standard historical works, and I list here only the works which I have seen, with a few obviously similar ones which I have seen mentioned, which are in *kodae sosŏl* form in Korean. See **Kim T'aejun,** 107-108, **Kim Kidong,** 232-236 (**1956:** 134-139), and **Pak Sŏngǔi,** 221-223. Kim T'aejun quotes 林慶業傳 <u>Yim Kyŏngŏp chŏn</u>, and Kim Tonguk quotes 林將軍忠烈傳 <u>Yim Changgun Ch'ungnyŏl chŏn</u>, "The Story of the Loyal Ardour of General Yim", from <u>Shōsho Kibun</u>, see **Introduction,** §7.2. The second of these is similar to some of the titles of the more factual accounts of his life.

님장군전 <u>Nim Changgun chŏn</u>, "The Story of General Yim", lending library manuscript, 2 vols, 31, 37 leaves (11 columns, 12 syllables), dated 경자 (庚子 1900). Title on the cover 林將軍傳 <u>Yim Changgun chŏn</u>. [**Tōyō Bunko**]

림장군전 林將軍傳 <u>Rim Changgun chyŏn</u>, manuscript, 2 vols, 25, 28 leaves (10 columns, 15-18 syllables). [**Kaai Bunko, Kyoto**]

This is obviously fairly recent, on nice paper, with Chinese characters added in explanation, but it is thought to be by a Korean, not a Japanese.

林慶業傳 Yim Kyŏngŏp chŏn. 外務省 Gaimushō (Foreign Office), Tokyo, 1881. 2, 56 leaves (10 columns, 21 syllables). [Imanishi collection, Tenri, and Ogura collection, Tokyo]

The two leaves describe the conventions used in this reprint in movable type of a Korean text.

님쟝군젼 Nim Chyanggun chyŏn, Seoul block print, 27 leaves. [British Museum, two copies]

Petrova, 193, gives the same as also in the Aston collection in Leningrad, and Courant, 815, gives the same, but "newly engraved at 華泉 Hwach'ŏn", as also in Paris. Kim Tonguk, 385, adds that it is 華泉新刊　重刊 "newly engraved and re-engraved at Hwach'ŏn"

님쟝군젼 Nim Chyanggun chyŏn, block print, 21 leaves, dated 丁亥孟冬 (tenth month 1887). Title on the cover 林將軍傳 Yim Changgun chŏn. [Tōyō Bunko and Ogura collection, Tokyo]

The Tōyō Bunko copy is boxed with Ansŏng block prints. I have noted the date as above independently on the two copies, and feel confident that it is correct, but Maema Kyōsaku: Kosen Sappu, III 1942, gives it as 乙亥孟冬, tenth month 1875. Kim Tonguk, 385, also gives this date and describes it as a Seoul block print, but in the 1960 version of his article, page 46, he comments: "one wonders whether the 1875 text is not an Ansŏng block print, but it is impossible to prove it."

림경업젼 Rim Kyŏngŏp chyŏn, 남궁셜역술 "told by Namgung Sŏl", Chosŏn Tosŏ Chusik Hoesa, 1923 (reprinted from 1915), 56 pages.

림경업젼 Rim Kyŏngŏp chyŏn, currently available from Sech'ang Sŏgwan, 46 pages.

The texts of these two appear to be identical.

Kim Kidong, 233, gives a publication by Kongdong Munhwasa, 1954, 43 pages, and the title has been frequently advertised in paperbacks between 1915 and the present.

林慶業傳 Yim Kyŏngŏp chŏn in the Hŭimang Series, I 185-214.

Several hanmun versions are probably also fictionalised to some extent at least. Of those which I have seen, 林將軍傳 Yim Changgun chŏn, dated 1711 and attributed (by the Tōyō Bunko catalogue) to 宋時烈 Song Siyŏl (1607-1689), seems to be particularly close to the fictional versions in Korean.

임신록 **Imsin nok**, etc.: see 227 신미록 **Sinmi rok**

364. 임씨삼대록 **Yim-ssi Samdae rok**

임시삼딕록 林氏三代錄 Yim-si Samdae rok, two manuscripts, one of 40 and one of 39 vols. [**Palace**]

Courant, 903: same (but 님 Nim for 임 Yim), "Record of the Three Generations of the Yim [Chinese: Lin] Family" (title only)

임씨정연삼문취록 **Yim-ssi Chŏng Yŏn Sammun Ch'wirok**: see 368 임화정연 **Yim Hwa Chŏng Yŏn**

365. 임씨현행쌍린기 **Yim-ssi Hyŏnhaeng Ssangnin ki**

Courant, 906: 님씨현힝쌍닌긔 林氏賢行雙麟記 Nim-ssi Hyŏnhaeng Ssangnin kŭi, "Record of the Two Wise Sons of the Yim [Chinese: Lin] Family" (title only).

임장군전 **Yim Changgun chŏn**, etc.: see 363 임경업전 **Yim Kyŏngŏp chŏn**

366. 임진록 **Imjin nok** "Record of the Year of the Black Dragon"

There are very many works dealing with the Japanese invasions of 1592-1597 to be found in the standard historical reference works, but they are very difficult to assess as to their proportions of fact to fiction without a much more detailed study than I have been able to make. Those listed below are all that I have seen or found clear descriptions of, which seem to be clearly fictionalised accounts in Korean in pre-modern forms. See **Kim T'aejun**, 69-70, **Kim Kidong**, 210-225 (**1956**: 126-128), and **Pak Sŏngŭi**, 209-210 (and his introductory remarks to the chapter). All critics assume that works about these wars date from near that period, but none give any proof of this, and one feels that more distinctions of types of works might usefully be made.

Title on the cover 壬辰錄 Imjin nok, manuscript, 30 leaves (16 columns, 30 syllables). [**School of Oriental and African Studies, University of London**]

This is nicely written and bound. The story ends with the sort of exhortation to remember this period of Korean history which is found in the paperback editions of other stories set in these wars, and from its wording I would suggest dating this text between 1880 and 1910.

Yi Myŏngsŏn's 1948 edition, below, was based partly on a manuscript in Korean entitled 黑龍錄 Hŭngnyong nok, "Record of the Black Dragon [Year]", which does not seem to have been very highly regarded.

金根洙 Kim Kŭnsu: 小說資料集成 Sosŏl Charyo Chipsŏng (no publisher, no date, but there is a preface of 1962 and the compiler is described as a professor of Tongguk University, Seoul), includes, pages 37-116, a mimeographed copy of a 흑농일긔 (黑龍日記) Hŭngnyong Ilgŭi, manuscript, 40 leaves (16 colums, 25-30 syllables).

Kim Kidong, 211, states that the text which he used was a manuscript of 85 pages (12 columns, 24 syllables), which was nearer to the original than Yi Myŏngsŏn's, above, "perhaps even the original itself".

임진녹 Imjin nok, Seoul block print, 3 vols, 25, 23, 23 leaves, the second volume 武橋新刊 "newly engraved at Mugyo". [British Museum]

Courant, 814, gives this as also in Paris, etc. Kim Tonguk, 386, gives the same but no place or date, and also a two volume edition bound as one volume.

W. G. Aston: On Corean Popular Literature (Transactions of the Asiatic Society of Japan, XVIII, Tokyo, 1890, 108-113) gives a version in English of a story about Samyŏngdang (see 146 사명당전 Samyŏngdang chŏn), which is probably taken from the block print of 84 leaves (5 kwŏn) of Imjin nok described as in the Aston collection in Leningrad by Petrova, 37.

李明善 Yi Myŏngsŏn, ed.: 壬辰錄 Imjin nok. 國際文化舘 Kukche Munhwagwan, Seoul, 1948. 160 pages. This is in modern Korean, but is said to be based partly on his manuscript in Korean, above, and partly on a version in hanmun.

壬辰錄 Imjin nok in: 李慶善 Yi Kyŏngsŏn, ed.: 壬辰錄 朴氏傳 Imjin nok, Pak-ssi chŏn, 正音社 Chongŭmsa, Seoul, 1962, 9-100, seems to follow the kodae sosŏl versions fairly closely, but the source of the text is not given. It is annotated for school use.

The following stories which are included in this list of kodae sosŏl are set in the same wars, but in almost every case it has been difficult to find evidence that they existed as works of fiction in Korean in pre-modern times:

26 곽재우전 Kwak Chae'u chŏn
34 권율장군전 Kwŏn Yul Changgun chŏn
52 김덕령전 Kim Tŏngnyŏng chŏn
74 남윤전 Nam Yun chŏn

367. 임호은전 **Yim Hoŭn chŏn** "**The Story of Lin Hu-yin**"

The story is set in Sung China. **Kim T'aejun**, 118, describes it briefly, and suggests that it may have been a precursor of **31** 구운몽 **Kuun mong**, perhaps by the same author. **Kim Kidong**, 296-301, describes it more fully, and argues that it is rather a pale imitation of that work.

1961 exhibition, 47: 林虎隱傳 Yim Hoŭn chŏn, manuscript, 1 vol. (National Library).

林虎隱傳 림호운전 Rim Hoŭn chŏn, Hoedong Sŏgwan, Sammunsa Sŏjŏm, and Sinmyŏng Sŏrim, 1932, 126 pages, and, with almost identical text, currently available from Sech'ang Sŏgwan, 124 pages. Kim Kidong, 296, gives a text apparently identical with this second one, but published 1953, as the text which he used, and the title was advertised by Hansŏng Sŏgwan and Yuil Sŏgwan in 1915, by Pangmun Sŏgwan and Sin'gu Sŏrim in 1923, 1925 and 1932, by Tongyang Sŏwŏn in 1925, and by Yŏngch'ang Sŏgwan and Hanhŭng Sŏrim in 1925.

368. 임화정연 **Yim Hwa Chŏng Yŏn** "**Lin, Hua, Cheng and Yen**"

This appears to be a love story set in fourteenth century China (Ming, Hungwu), but I have not seen enough texts to be at all sure about it.

林花鄭延 림화정연 Rim Hwa Chyŏng Yŏn, Chosŏn Tosŏ Chusik Hoesa, 1928 (reprinted from 1925), 5 vols. (The only copy of this which I have seen was missing volume 1.)

The critics give it only bare mentions. **Kim T'aejun**, 160 and 229, calls it "a translation", and an advertisement of the title by Hansŏng Sŏgwan and Yuil Sŏgwan in 1915 classifies it with several Chinese works. **Kim Kidong**, 33 and 276, seems to suggest that this is an alternative title for **147** 사성기봉 **Sasŏng Kibong**. The four volumes above all have 四姓奇逢 Sasŏng Kibong as a subtitle.

Courant, 900: 임화정연긔 林華鄭延記 Yim Hwa Chyŏng Yŏn kŭi, "Record of Yim Hwa and Chŏng Yŏn" (title only), and 913: 림화정연삼문츄록 林華鄭延三門聚錄 Rim Hwa Chyŏng Yŏn Sammun Ch'yurok [Ch'wirok], "Collected Records of the Three Families, of Yim Hwa and of Chŏng Yŏn" (title only) may both be taken as versions of this title. **Kim T'aejun**, 160, 林氏鄭延三門聚錄 <u>Yim-ssi Chŏng Yŏn Sammun Ch'wirok</u> looks like a version of Courant's second title, but **Kim Kidong**, 594, quotes it in the form given by Kim T'aejun.

자치가   **Chach'i ka**: see 375 장끼전 **Changkki chŏn**

369. 자치통감 **Chach'i T'onggam** "The Everlasting Mirror as a Guide to Government"

ᄌ티통감셔진긔 <u>Chăt'i T'onggam Syŏjin kŭi</u>, "The Everlasting Mirror as a Guide to Government, Annals of Western Chin" (volumes 1-3), ᄌ티통감동진긔 <u>Chăt'i T'onggam Tongjin kŭi</u> "The Everlasting Mirror as a Guide to Government, Annals of Eastern Chin" (volumes 4-11), manuscript, 11 vols. Titles on the covers 西晉演義 <u>Sŏjin Yŏnŭi</u>, "Romance of Western Chin" (volumes 1-3), 東晉演義 <u>Tongjin Yŏnŭi</u>, "Romance of Eastern Chin" (volumes 4-11). [**Seoul University**]

The titles on the covers are known as titles of Chinese novels, but those do not seem to claim the derivation from 資治通鑑 <u>Tzu-chih-t'ung-chien</u>, compiled by 司馬光 Szu-ma Kuang between 1065 and 1084, which the titles inside these Korean volumes appear to claim.

370. 잔당오대연의 **Chandang Odae Yŏnŭi**

잔당오디연의 殘唐五代演義 <u>Chandang Odăe Yŏnŭi</u>, manuscript, 6 vols. [**Palace**]

This is presumably a translation of the Chinese work "Romance of the Expiring T'ang and the Five Dynasties", which covers the period from about 900 to 960, but I did not examine its contents at all. See **Kim T'aejun**, pages 86, 92.

371. 장경부전 **Chang Kyŏngbu chŏn**

Sin Kihyŏng, 482, lists 장경부전 (章敬夫傳) <u>Chang Kyŏngbu chŏn</u> (presumably) "The Story of Chang Ching-fu" as a love story in Korean set in China. He gives no source for the information, but it may be **Kim Kidong**, who lists the same title, page 597, with no information at all, only a reference to 李明善 Yi Myŏngsŏn: 朝鮮文學史 <u>Chosŏn Munhak sa</u> (朝鮮文學社 Chosŏn Munhaksa, Seoul, 1948). The nearest to this title which I can find in that work is 章敬天傳 <u>Chang Kyŏngch'ŏn chŏn</u> which is listed, page 135, as a novel in *hanmun* by 權韠 Kwŏn P'il (1569-1612).

372. 장경전 Chang Kyŏng chŏn "The Story of Chang Ching"

The story is set in 11th century China and seems to be a fairly conventional biography. **Kim Kidong** mentions it, 238, 590, etc., but does not include it among those of its type which "have value". Others give it similarly brief mentions, including 趙潤濟 Cho Yunje: 國文學史 Kungmunhak sa (東國文化社 Tongguk Munhwasa, Seoul, 1954), who gives the title, page 318, as 張敬傳 Chang Kyŏng chŏn. It is, however, well represented by texts.

장경젼 Chang Kyŏng chyŏn, lending library manuscript, 1 vol. (vol. 1 only), 34 leaves (11 columns, 15 syllables), dated 임인 (王寅 1902). Title on the cover 張景傳 Chang Kyŏng chŏn. [**Imanishi collection, Tenri**]

댱경젼 Tyang Kyŏng chyŏn, lending library manuscript, 2 vols, 33, 34 leaves (11 columns, 12-13 syllables), dated 병오 (丙午 1906) in vol. 1 and 을ᄉ (乙巳 1905) in vol. 2. Title on the cover 張景傳 Chang Kyŏng chŏn. [**Tōyō Bunko**]

댱경젼 Tyang Kyŏng chyŏn, Seoul block print, 25 leaves. [**British Museum**]

Courant, 795, gives a summary of the story from a Seoul block print, 38 leaves, "newly engraved at 美洞 Midong in the ninth month of the year 王子 (1852?)", in Paris, etc. He gives the title as 張慶傳 Chang Kyŏng chŏn, which would translate as "The Story of Chang Ch'ing". **Kim Tonguk**, 392, gives three Seoul block prints: (1) 35 leaves, 咸豊壬子七月美洞 "at Midong, seventh month, 1852"; (2) 26 leaves; (3) 38 leaves, 王子九月美洞新刊 "newly engraved at Midong, ninth month, 1852".

댱경젼 Tyang Kyŏng chyŏn, block print, 16 leaves. [**Imanishi collection, Tenri**]

At the time when I saw this, I thought that it was more likely to be an Ansŏng than a Seoul block print, but it was in very poor condition, and I certainly could not be sure on the point now. There is also a (lithographic?) reprint of a block print of 16 leaves at Harvard, which does not have the details of publication such as are usually given in such reprints of Seoul block prints.

장경젼 張景傳 Chyang Kyŏng chyŏn, currently available from Sech'ang Sŏgwan, two *kwŏn*, 70 pages.

373. 장국정전 Chang Kukchŏng chŏn

장국증젼 Chang Kukchŭng chŏn, manuscript, 56 leaves (10 columns, 27 syllables), dated 丙辰 (1916). Title on the cover 張局正傳 Chang Kukchŏng chŏn. [**Chŏng Pyŏnguk**]

Unfortunately I made no note of the contents of this text, and the title does not seem to be mentioned elsewhere.

374. 장국진전　Chang Kukchin chŏn "The Story of Chang Kuo-chen"

The hero acquires a full harem incidentally to reaching high military rank and thereby, in the end, doing his duty to his parents, whom he lost in wartime. **Kim T'aejun** mentions the title, 99, 102, 108 and 229. On pages 118-119 he suggests that it was a precursor of **31** 구운몽 **Kunm mong.** There are summaries of the story in **Kim Kidong,** 243-246 (**1956: 156-159**) and **Pak Sŏngŭi,** 215-221, which appear to have been taken from the second paperback edition given below.

모란졍긔 (牧丹亭記) Moran-jyŏng kŭi, "Record of the Peony Pavilion", currently available from Sech'ang Sŏgwan, 68 pages. This is clearly taken from a text in Chinese. The hero's name is given as 張國鎭, and the setting is in fourteenth century China (Ming, Hung-wu). There are works of similar title known in China, but I have not found one with the same story.

장국진젼 Chang Kukchin chyŏn, currently available from Sech'ang Sŏgwan (but text as composed before 1945), 44 pages. The story is the same as in the last, but told in a completely different way, with the setting in fifteenth century China (Ming, Cheng-hua) and the hero's name on the cover as 張國振

張國振傳 Chang Kukchin chŏn in the **Hŭimang Series,** II 267-308. The text is close to that of the last, but is modernised in spelling, wording and expression in general.

Both titles have been advertised in paperbacks, Moran-jŏng ki by Hansŏng Sŏgwan and Yuil Sŏgwan in 1915 and by Sinmyŏng Sŏrim in 1930, and Chang Kukchin chŏn by Taech'ang Sŏwŏn and Hanyang Sŏjŏgŏp Chohapso in 1918, by Taech'ang Sŏwŏn and Pogŭp Sŏgwan in 1919 and 1920, by Chosŏn Tosŏ Chusik Hoesa, by Tongyang Sŏwŏn and by Yŏngch'ang Sŏgwan and Hanhŭng Sŏrim in 1925, and by Taesan Sŏrim in 1926.

375. 장끼전　Changkki chŏn "The Story of the Cock Pheasant"

A moral tale of a cock pheasant who died because he ignored his mate's advice, and the subsequent refusal of his mate to remarry within the mourning period. It is one of the stories which were sung in p'ansori, see Song Manjae ŭi Kwan-u-hŭi, 107 and 118 (Kwan-u-hŭi stanza 20), and P'ansori Palsaeng ko, 284, as described in the Introduction §7.3. Most of the versions listed below are in the rythmic style used by *kwangdae*. The story, and its implications, are discussed in **Kim T'aejun**, 125-126, **Kim Kidong**, 152-156, (1956: 358-360), **Pak Sŏngŭi**, 295-299, **Sin Kihyŏng**, 382-385, and many other works on Korean literature, folk-lore, etc.

1961 exhibition, 84: 자치가 (雌雉歌) Chach'i ka, "The Song of the Hen Pheasant", manuscript, 1 vol. (National Library).

1947 exhibition, 85: 장끼傳 (華蟲歌) Changkki chŏn (Hwach'ung ka), manuscript, 1 vol. (Yi Pyŏnggi). Neither of these titles appears in the catalogue of the **Karam collection**.

화충선성전 Hwach'yung Syŏnsăeng chyŏn, lending library manuscript, 2 vols, 32, 32 leaves (10 columns, 12 syllables), dated 임진 (壬辰 1892). Title on the cover 華虫傳 Hwach'ung chŏn. [**Seoul University**]

I have no note on the contents of this text, and list it here only because the title means the same as Changkki chŏn and is not given as the title of a separate story elsewhere.

崔常壽 Ch'oe Sangsu, ed.: 장끼전 (雌雉傳) Changkki chŏn (Ungch'i chŏn), in **Hyŏndae Munhak**, 8, August 1955, 34-46, and 9, September 1955, 206-220. Annotated.

장끼傳 Changkki chŏn in the **Hŭimang Series**, IV 307-316.

장끼전 Changkki chŏn, Sammun sa, 1953, 12 pages.

장끼전 Changkki chyŏn, Yŏnghwa Ch'ulp'ansa, probably not earlier than 1951, 24 pages.

장써전 Changkki chŏn, currently available from Sech'ang Sŏgwan, 32 pages.

The title was advertised by Tŏkhŭng Sŏrim in 1923 and 1924, and by Yŏngch'ang Sŏgwan and Hanhŭng Sŏrim in 1925, and I also have a note of an edition by "Chungang Insŏgwan", but no note of having seen it.

장문충효록 Chang-mun Ch'unghyo rok: see 494   형산백옥   Hyŏng-san Paegok

376. 장박전 **Chang Pak chŏn**

Kim Tonguk quotes 張朴傳 Chang Pak chŏn from Shōsho Kibun, as described in the **Introduction**, §7.2.

377. 장백전 **Chang Paek chŏn "The Story of Chang Po"**

The hero loses his family, reaches high military rank, and is involved in the struggle between Yüan and Ming. See **Kim Kidong**, 254-257.

댱빅젼 Tyang Păek chyŏn, Seoul block print, 28 leaves. [**British Museum and Asami collection, Berkeley**]

The Asami collection copy has written inside the back cover a great deal, including the information that it was in use as a lending library copy in 戊子 무ᄌ (1888). **Courant**, 802, gives the British Museum copy, with the characters 張甴傳 Chang Paek chŏn, and, 3357, an apparently identical block print as in Paris. Korean sources usually give the characters 張伯傳, but **Kim Tonguk**, 392, gives 張白(伯)傳

장백젼 張伯傳 Chyang Paek chyŏn, Tŏkhŭng Sŏrim, 1923 (reprinted from 1915), 61 pages. (Kim Kidong gives a publication by Tŏkhŭng Sŏrim, 1915, 110 pages.)

장빅젼 張伯傳 Chyang Păek chyŏn, Kyŏngsŏng Sŏgwan, 1925, 61 pages.

These two appear to have identical texts, and the title has been advertised in paperbacks also by Taesan Sŏrim in 1926, Tongyang Sŏwŏn in 1925, and Yŏng-ch'ang Sŏgwan and Hanhŭng Sŏrim in 1925.

378. 장비마초실기 **Chang Pi Ma Ch'o Silgi "The True Story of Chang Fei and Ma Ch'ao"**

張飛馬超實記 Chang Pi Ma Ch'o Silgi, Kwangdong Sŏguk, 1919 (reprinted from 1917).

This work does not appear to be mentioned elsewhere, and I read only enough of it to confirm that it concerns the leading characters of San-kuo-chih Yen-i, see **156** 삼국지연의 **Samgukchi Yŏnŭi**, but it was subsequently advertised by Chosŏn Tosŏ Chusik Hoesa in 1925, by Yŏngch'ang Sŏgwan and Hanhŭng Sŏrim in 1925, and by Kwangdong Sŏguk in 1926.

　　장셔전 **Changkki chŏn**: see **375** 장끼전 **Changkki chŏn**

379. 장운수전 **Chang Unsu chŏn**

Kim Kidong, 601, lists 張雲水傳 Chang Unsu chŏn (presumably) "The Story of Chang Yün-shui" as a story in Korean set in China, existing in paperback edition(s) (also page 33), but not made known before.

380. 장익성전 **Chang Iksŏng chŏn "The Story of Chang I-hsing"**

A conventional biographical tale, in which the hero reaches high military rank, set in China about 1000 ("Northern" Sung, Ch'un-hua).

장익셩젼 (張翼星傳) Chyang Iksyŏng chyŏn, currently available from Sech'ang Sŏgwan, 58 pages. The title was advertised by Yŏngch'ang Sŏgwan and Hanhŭng Sŏrim in 1925.

Kim Kidong, 30, gives a publication by Kwangmun Sŏsi, 1922, 65 pages. He also mentions the work, on page 238, implying that it does not have any value, and lists it, page 590, giving as his source **Kim T'aejun**, who only seems to mention the title, page 107.

381. 장인설전 **Chang In'gŏl chŏn**

장인걸젼 Chang In'gŏl chyŏn, manuscript, 2 vols, dated 辛丑 (1901, etc.), given as in the **Karam collection**. This was shown in the **1947 exhibition**, as item 86, and it is presumably from this text that 張人傑傳 Chang In'gŏl chŏn "The Story of Chang In'gŏl", is described in **Yi and Paek: Kungmunhak Chŏnsa**, pages 173-174, as a tale of a master magician of late Koryŏ, who serves the Chinese emperor as well as the Korean king. Other sources give the characters as 張仁傑傳.

382. 장자방전 **Chang Chabang chŏn "The Story of Chang Tzu-fang"**

張良 Chang Liang (tzu: 子房 Tzu-fang) played a major part in the establishment of the Han dynasty and died in 168 B.C. This story is said by **Kim T'aejun**, 97, **Kim Kidong**, 210, etc., to be taken from Hsi-han Yen-i, see **174** 서한연의 Sŏhan Yŏnŭi, but there are also separate Chinese novels about the same man.

댱자방젼 Tyang Chabang chyŏn, lending library manuscript, 2 vols, 31, 34 leaves (11 columns, 12-13 syllables), dated 을ᄉ and 을사 (乙巳 1905). Title on the cover 張子房傳 Chang Chabang chŏn. [**Tōyō Bunko**]

쟝자방실긔 張子房實記 Chyang Chabang Silgŭi 快齋朴健會述 "told by K'waejae, Pak Kŏnhoe", currently available from Sech'ang Sŏgwan, 125 pages. The title was advertised by Hansŏng Sŏgwan and Yuil Sŏgwan in 1915 and by Yŏngch'ang Sŏgwan and Hanhŭng Sŏrim in 1925.

장자휴고분성대도 **Changja Hyu Kobun Sŏng Taedo:** see **39** 금고기관 **Kŭmgo Kigwan**

383. 장장군전 **Chang Changgun chŏn**

Kim Kidong, 591, lists 張將軍傳 Chang Changgun chŏn (presumably) "The Story of General Chang" as a biographical tale in Korean set in China, extisting in paperback edition(s) (also page 32), but not made known before.

384. 장장백전 **Chang Changbaek chŏn**

Kim Kidong, 601, lists 張長白傳 Chang Changbaek chŏn (presumably) "The Story of Chang Ch'ang-po" as a story in Korean set in China, existing in paperback edition(s), but not made known before.

385. 장풍운전 **Chang P'ungun chŏn** "The Story of Chang Feng-yün"

The story of a filial son in Sung China. It has many similarities with **253** 양풍전 **Yang P'ung chŏn**. See **Kim T'aejun**, 187-188, **Pak Sŏngŭi**, 376-378, and **Sin Kihyŏng**, 317-318. Kim Tonguk quotes 張豊雲傳 Chang P'ungun chŏn from Shōsho Kibun, as described in the **Introduction**, §7.2.

장풍운전 Chyang P'ungun chyŏn, Seoul block print, 31 leaves. [**British Museum**]

Petrova, 195, gives the same as in the Aston collection in Leningrad.

장풍운뎐 Chang P'ungun tyŏn, Seoul block print, 29 leaves, 戊午紅樹洞新刊 "newly engraved at Hongsudong in 1858". [**British Museum**]

Courant, 794 and 3354, gives the same as also in Paris, etc., with the characters 張風雲傳 Chang P'ungun chŏn. The texts of the two block prints in the British Museum appear to be essentially the same.

Kim Tonguk, 388, gives essentially the same details for the 29 leaf block print, but under the title 梁豊傳 Yang P'ung chŏn, together with two block print editions of that story and a summary of it. In Hyangt'o Sŏul, 8, in **1960**, page 48, he gave the same 29 leaf block print under the title 梁風雲傳 Yang P'ungun chŏn.

1947 exhibition, 105: 장풍운전 Chang P'ungun chyŏn, Chŏnju block print, 1 vol. (Cho Yunje, not shown). **Yi Nŭngu: Kungmunhak Kaeron**, 10, gives for the Chŏnju block print ○○仲春完西溪新刊 "newly engraved at Sŏgye, Chŏnju, in the second month of -----". **Kim Tonguk**, 397, gives the same, but under the title 梁風雲傳 Yang P'ungun chŏn, but in Hyangt'o Sŏul 8, in **1960**, page 61, he gave it under 張風雲傳 Chang P'ungun chŏn

張豊雲傳 (장풍운전) Chang P'ungun chyŏn, currently available from Sech'ang Sŏgwan, 32 pages, in the same volume as, but separately paginated from 253 양풍전 Yang P'ung chŏn.

Kim Kidong, 30 gives a publication by Hansŏng Sŏgwan, 1916, 43 pages, and the title was advertised by Taech'ang Sŏwŏn and Pogŭp Sŏgwan in 1920, by Tongyang Sŏwŏn in 1925, and by Yŏngch'ang Sŏgwan and Hanhŭng Sŏrim in 1925.

386. 장하연정기 Chang Ha Yŏnjŏng ki

Kim Kidong, 595, lists 張河演征記 Chang Ha Yŏnjŏng ki (?) as a love story in Korean set in China existing in paperback edition(s). He refers to Ku, Son and Kim: Kungmunhak Kaeron, where the title is mentioned, page 255.

387. 장학사전 Chang Haksa chŏn "The Story of the Minister Chang"

A story of domestic troubles set in Korea about 1400. Kim Kidong, 313, states that it is a revision of 418 조생원전 Cho Saengwon chŏn, with the scene changed to Korea and the characters altered, and the paperback editions of the two stories are certainly remarkably similar.

댱학ᄉ젼 Tyang Haksă chyŏn, manuscript, 45 leaves (12 columns, 25 syllables), dated 디졍사연음을피연 (大正四年陰乙卯年 1915). Title on the cover 張學士傳 장학ᄉ젼 Chang Haksă chyŏn. [Seattle]

장학[사]젼 Chang Hak[sa] chyŏn, (lending library?) manuscript, 24 leaves. [Harvard] This is in extremely poor condition, and is certainly not complete.

張學士傳 장학사젼 Chang Haksa chyŏn, 永昌書舘版 "published by Yŏngch'ang Sŏgwan", currently available from Sech'ang Sŏgwan, 56 pages. The title was advertised by Sin'gu Sŏrim in 1918 and by Yŏngch'ang Sŏgwan and Hanhŭng Sŏrim in 1925.

388. 장한절효기 Chang Han Chŏrhyo ki

Courant, 799: 장한절효긔 張韓節孝記 Chang Han Chyŏrhyo kŭi, "Record of the Virtue and Filial Piety of Han, Wife of Chang", Seoul block print, 29 leaves, "newly engraved at 紅樹洞 Hongsudong", in Paris, etc. He also gives a summary of the story. Kim Tonguk, 390, gives essentially the same information (and in Hyangt'o Sŏul in 1960, page 51, but there 19 leaves, not 29). From these summaries, and from longer ones in Kim Kidong (1956), 275-277, and Sin Kihyŏng, 335-337, it would appear that the title might perhaps be better translated "Record of the Faithful Wife Han and her Filial Son Chang". The story is set in China in the thirteenth century, opening in the first years of the Yüan dynasty.

The Seoul blockprint as above, was also reproduced lithographically and published by 翰南書林 Hannam Sŏrim, Keijō, 1920.

Yi Nŭngu: Kungmunhak Kaeron, 11, and **Kim Tonguk**, 397, give a Chŏnju block print, with no details.

The title was advertised by Chosŏn Tosŏ Chusik Hoesa in 1925.

389. 장화홍련전 **Changhwa Hongnyŏn chŏn "The Story of Changhwa and Hongnyŏn"**

The death of the two heroines is accomplished by their wicked step-mother, but they are avenged, and reborn to the same father. See **Kim T'aejun**, 180-186, **Kim Kidong**, 321-326 (1956: 299-304), **Pak Sŏngŭi**, 364-370, **Sin Kihyŏng**, 308-312, and the relevant passage in most survey histories of Korean literature. It is generally agreed that the novel in Korean is very close to an account given in *hanmun* by 全東屹 Chŏn Tonghŭl in his collected works, 嘉齋集 Kajae chip, of a case with which he dealt while he was magistrate of 鐵山 Ch'ŏlsan (P'yŏngan Province) about 1660. No precise reference is given, and I have not been able to locate any copy of Kajae chip. (Some sources give Chŏn Tonghŭl's *ho* as 佳齋 Kajae.) All the above also give a 薔花紅蓮傳 Changhwa Hongnyŏn chŏn in *hanmun* by 朴慶壽 Pak Kyŏngsu, dated 戊寅, either 1698 or 1758, but I have not been able to trace any copy of this either, and **Kim T'aejun**, 186, gives a 長花紅蓮傳 Changhwa Hongnyŏn chŏn in *hanmun* in 文獻備考 Munhŏn Pigo.

장화홍연뎐 Changhwa Hongyŏn chyŏn, manuscript, 33 leaves, given as in the **Karam collection**. (Yi Pyŏnggi's 薔花紅蓮傳 Changhwa Hongnyŏn chŏn, manuscript, 1 vol., was announced for the 1947 exhibition, as item 136, but it was not shown.)

Courant, 819, 쟝화홍년뎐 壯花紅蓮傳 Chyanghwa Hongnyŏn chyŏn, block print, 28 leaves, in Paris, etc. **Petrova**, 205: same, with a derogatory note by Aston dated 1887, in the Aston collection in Leningrad. **Kim Tonguk**, 387, gives two Seoul block prints, one of 28 leaves, and the other as "18 leaves, 紫岩新刊 newly engraved at Chaam".

장화홍련전 (薔花紅蓮傳) Changhwa Hongnyŏn chŏn, Sammun sa, 1953, 26 pages.

장화홍련전 Changhwa Hongnyŏn chŏn, Taejo sa, 1959, 24 pages.

薔花紅蓮傳 Changhwa Hongnyŏn chŏn in the **Hŭimang Series**, III 243-260.

Kim Kidong, 31 and 321, gives publications by Sech'ang Sŏgwan, 1915, 50 pages, Tongmyŏng Sŏgwan, 1915, 50 pages, Pangmun Sŏgwan, 1917, 40 pages, and Taech'ang Sŏwŏn, 1923, 40 pages, and the title has been advertised in paper-**backs** consistently since 1915.

There is a summary of the plot in English in W.G. Aston: On Corean Popular Literature (Transactions of the Asiatic Society of Japan, XVIII, Tokyo, 1890, page 107), and a fuller version of the story in English in Zong In-sob: Folk Tales from Korea (Routledge and Kegan Paul, London, 1952), pages 201-207.

　　　장화효절 Changhwa Hyojyŏl: see 528 효열지 Hyoyŏl chi

390. 재생연전 **Chaesaengyŏn chŏn**

지성연전 再生緣傳 Chăesăengyŏn chyŏn, manuscript, 52 vols. [**Palace**]

The title would appear to mean something like 'The Story of Rebirth and Fate', but I have no note of the contents. I have not seen any mention of this exact title elsewhere, and although it is very similar to 再生緣 Chaesaeng yŏn, the *hanmun* novel which is widely reported to be the source for **224** 숙영낭자전 **Sugyŏng Nangja chŏn**, I have no means of knowing whether there is any connection.

　　　쟁끼전 **Chaengkki chŏn**: see 375 장끼전 **Changkki chŏn**

　　　쟝 . . . . . **Chyang** . . . . . : see 쟝 . . . . . **Chang** . . . . .

　　　저마무전 **Chŏ Mamu chŏn**: see 413 제마무전 **Che Mamu chŏn**

391. 적벽가 **Chŏkpyŏk ka "The Song of the Red Wall"**

赤壁 Ch'ih-pi (in Korean Chŏkpyŏk), "The Red Wall", is the name of the cliff below which was fought in 208 A.D. perhaps the greatest and most decisive battle of the wars in third century China, which form the subject of San-kuo-chih Yen-i, see 156 삼국지연의 **Samgukchi Yŏnŭi**. 赤壁歌 Chŏkpyŏk ka appears as the title of several works in Korean which tell of this and other battles of the period, and which appear to be taken from several chapters around chapter 50 of San-kuo-chih Yen-i.

This was one of the stories sung in *p'ansori*, which Sin Chaehyo rewrote, see **Introduction**, §7. 3, and Song Manjae ŭi Kwan-u-hŭi, 103 and 118 (Kwan-u-hŭi stanza 10), and P'ansori Palsaeng ko, 285-287. It is probably Sin Chaehyo's version which was published by 姜漢永 Kang Hanyŏng in **Hyŏndae Munhak**, 9, 11, 13, and 16, September 1955—April 1956.

적벽가전 Chŏkpyŏk ka chŏn, 24 pages, following and separately paginated from 521 황부인전 **Hwang Puin chŏn** in 黃夫人傳 Hwang Puin chŏn, currently available from Sech'ang Sŏgwan (but text of this story as composed before 1945). This would appear to be a translation of a work in Chinese. **Kim T'aejun**, 92 and 106, mentions 赤壁大戰 Chŏkpyŏk Taejŏn (presumably) "The Great Battle of the Red Wall", and **Kim Kidong**, 210, mentions 赤壁大戰記 Chŏkpyŏk Taejŏn ki, "Record of ....."

The titles Chŏkpyŏk ka and Chŏkpyŏk Taejŏn have been frequently advertised in paperbacks since 1920, usually both separately in the same advertisement.

392. 적성의전　Chŏk Sŏngŭi chŏn

This story is of a filial younger son, and has a strongly Buddhist flavour. The opening and ending of the story are set in a place called 안평국 Anp'yŏng-guk in 강남 Kangnam, usually explained as 安平國, which would be in Chinese "the country of An-p'ing", in 江南 i.e. southern China. However, the time of the action is not clear. Part of it takes place in Annam, part in China proper, and part in India. The hero may well have been non-Chinese, and this might explain the variations in the characters given for the title, which make it impossible to give a reliable transcription of his name as Chinese. He is frequently referred to as Chŏk Sŏng only, see perhaps **393** 적성호연 **Chŏk Sŏng Hoyŏn**. See **Kim T'aejun**, 141-143, **Kim Kidong**, 381-384 (1956: 282-283), **Pak Sŏngŭi**, 326-327, and **Sin Kihyŏng**, 334-335.

뎍셩의젼 狄城義傳 Tyŏk Syŏngŭi chyŏn, manuscript, 1 vol. [**Palace**]

젹셩의젼 Chyŏk Syŏngŭi chyŏn, lending library manuscript, 2 vols, 30, 30 leaves (11 columns, 14 syllables), dated 을묘 (乙卯 1915, etc.). Title on the cover 狄成義傳 Chŏk Sŏngŭi chŏn. [**Tōyō Bunko**]

젹셩의젼 Chyŏk Syŏngŭi chyŏn, Seoul block print, 23 leaves. [**British Museum**]

Courant, 822, gives the same as in Paris, etc., and **Petrova**, 194, gives the same as in the Aston collection in Leningrad. Both give the characters 赤聖義傳 Chŏk Sŏngŭi chŏn. The same block print is reproduced in the **Ewha Series**, III 227-

272, with a note 423-424. Various Korean sources mention it with varying amounts of detail, but **Kim Tonguk**, 388, gives a 30 leaf, as well as the 23 leaf, Seoul block print.

적성의전 Chyŏk Syŏngǔi chyŏn, Ansŏng block print, 19 leaves. [**Tōyō Bunko** and **Ogura collection, Tokyo**] The Tōyō Bunko copy has the title on the cover 赤聖義傳 Chŏk Sŏngǔi chŏn, with 狄成 written in smaller characters beside 赤聖

1947 exhibition, 104: 狄成義傳 Chŏk Sŏngǔi chŏn, Chŏnju block print, 1 vol. (Cho Yunje, not shown).

The usual sources list this by title as a Chŏnju block print, but give no further details.

적성의전 Chyŏk Syŏngǔi chyŏn, Taesan Sŏrim, 1926, and currently available from Sech'ang Sŏgwan, both 32 pages, with identical texts. The title was also advertised by Yŏngch'ang Sŏgwan and Hanhǔng Sŏrim in 1925, and by Taech'ang Sŏwŏn and Pogǔp Sŏgwan in 1926.

Various sources also give the title in characters as 積成義傳 and 翟成義傳, both Chŏk Sŏngǔi chŏn, and sometimes 霍 Kwak is given for 翟 Chŏk.

393. 적성호연 Chŏk Sŏng Hoyŏn

1947 exhibition, 178: 赤城好緣 Chŏk Sŏng Hoyŏn, manuscript, 8 vols. (T'ongmun-gwan). See the **Introduction**, §6.4.2, for the peculiar characteristics of all the T'ongmun'gwan texts shown in this exhibition. Since the name of the hero of **392** 적성의전 Chŏk Sŏngǔi chŏn sometimes occurs as 적성 Chŏk Sŏng, there may possibly be some connection between this work and that.

394. 전등신화 Chŏndǔng Sinhwa "New Anecdotes for which one Trims the Lamp-light"

剪燈新話 Chien-teng Hsin-hua by the early Ming writer 瞿佑 Ch'ü Yu was significant in the development of the writing of fiction in China (see Lu Hsun: A Brief History of Chinese-Fiction, Foreign Languages Press, Peking, 1959, page 269). It is said to have become known quickly in Korea, and may even have been translated into Korean at a very early date (see **Kim T'aejun**, 53-56, and **Pak Sŏngǔi**, 151-156). However, I have not seen any suggestion that any story in Korean was derived directly from any story in it, and the only text of it in Korean which I have seen is certainly very late.

1961 exhibition, 37: 剪燈新話 Chŏndŭng Sinhwa, manuscript, 5 vols. This belongs to 李謙魯 Mr. Yi Kyŏmno, see **Introduction**, §6.4.2.

1947 exhibition, 173 剪燈新話 Chŏndŭng Sinhwa, manuscript. (Pang Chonghyŏn). No such work appears in the catalogue of the **Ilsa collection**.

395. 전수재전　Chŏn Sujae chŏn

Kim Kidong, 596, lists 錢秀才傳 Chŏn Sujae chŏn (presumably) "The Story of Mr. Ch'ien" as a love story in Korean set in China, existing in paperback edition(s) (also page 32), but not made known before. As far as this information goes, it could well be a version of story no. 27 in Chin-ku-ch'i-kuan, see **39** 금고기관 Kŭmgo Kigwan.

396. 전우치전 Chŏn Uch'i chŏn "The Story of Chŏn Uch'i"

The hero is a master of magic, and there is a great deal of social commentary in the story, which is set in Korea about 1400. (However in some versions at least a Sŏ Hwadam appears, see **176** 서화담전 Sŏ Hwadam chŏn.)

There may be some historical basis for the story. This is investigated by all critics, see **Kim T'aejun**, 87-89, **Kim Kidong**, 189-196 (**1956**: 336-342), **Pak Sŏngŭi**, 248-253, and **Sin Kihyŏng**, 349-350, but no firm conclusion has been presented. Neither the earlier form of the title Chŏn Uch'i chŏn, nor Courant's variant Chŏn Ulch'i chŏn, lead to any historical figure either.

던운치젼 Tyŏn Unch'i chyŏn, manuscript, 73 leaves, given as in the **Ilsa collection**.

Courant, 3365: 젼운치견 田雲致傳 Chyŏn Unch'i chyŏn, block print, 22 leaves, in Paris. He refers from this to his entry 924: 젼울치젼 Chyŏn Ulch'i chyŏn (title only).

Kim Kidong, 191, reports a publication under the title 全雲致傳 Chŏn Unch'i chŏn by Haedong Sŏgwan, 1918, and one under the title 田禹治傳 Chŏn Uch'i chŏn by Yŏngch'ang Sŏgwan, 1917, 37 pages.

田禹治傳 던우치젼 Tyŏn Uch'i chŏn, currently available from Sech'ang Sŏgwan, 32 pages.

田禹治傳 Chŏn Uch'i chŏn in the **Hŭimang Series**, II 309-336, text virtually identical with the last.

194

There is a version in English of the story as "recently reprinted by Bagmun Sŏgwan; Seoul" in Zong In-sob: <u>Folk Tales from Korea</u> (Routledge and Kegan Paul, London, 1952, pages 224-234).

397. 절화기담 Chŏrhwa Kidam

Sin Kihyŏng, 483, lists 절화기담 (折花奇談) <u>Chŏrhwa Kidam</u> as a love story in Korean set in China. He gives no source for the information in this table, but it may be the similar table in **Kim Kidong**, which includes this title, page 597, as existing in paperback edition(s). He refers to **Yi Nŭngu: Kungmunhak Kaeron**, which only appears to mention, page 6, the **Tōyō Bunko** manuscript of this title, which is in *hanmun*. (折話奇緣 <u>Chŏrhwa Kiyŏn</u>, printed in 1814, according to **Kim Tonguk**, 383, may also be the same.)

398. 정도령전 Chŏng Toryŏng chŏn "The Story of Master Chŏng"

鄭道令傳 정도령전 <u>Chyŏng Toryŏng chyŏn</u>, 永昌書籍版 "published by Yŏngch'ang Sŏgwan", currently available from Sech'ang Sŏgwan, 60 (+3) pages.

The story begins as a sort of romance involving several families and pranks by boys with identical twin sisters which end in marriage. It is the same story as that described in **Kim Kidong**, 316-320, and **Sin Kihyŏng**, 319-322, under the title 鄭進士傳 <u>Chŏng Chinsa chŏn,</u> "The Story of the Top Class Graduate Chŏng." On page 316, Kim Kidong states: "There is a variant text of this story entitled <u>Chŏng Toryŏng chŏn</u>, but I have taken as my text the publication by Tongmun Sŏrim, 65 pages, 10.10.1918". However, on page 31 he gives "<u>Chŏng Toryŏng chŏn</u>, Tongmun Sŏrim, 10.10.1918, 65 pages", and the quotation which he gives, page 320, from his text is to be found verbatim in my text, above, page 14.

정명록 **Chŏng Myŏng nok**: see 410 정을선전 Chŏng Ŭlsŏn chŏn

399. 정목란전 Chŏng Mongnan chŏn

Kim Kidong, 597, lists 鄭木蘭傳 <u>Chŏng Mongnan chŏn</u> (presumably) "The Story of Cheng Mu-lan" as a love story in Korean set in China, existing in paperback edition(s), but not made known before. He lists it next to **409 정옥란전 Chŏng Ongnan chŏn**, which is identical in all the details which he gives. **Kim T'aejun**, 250, describes <u>Chŏng Mongnan chŏn</u> as a work written after 1910 by Namgung Chun, and this title was advertised by Chosŏn Tosŏ Chusik Hoesa and by Tongyang Sŏwŏn in 1925. One is also reminded of Mu-lan, the woman general famous in Chinese fiction.

정묘양호거의록 Chŏngmyo Yanghogŏ Ŭirok: see 133 병자록 Pyŏngja rok

400. 정백문 Chŏngbaengmun

Courant, 938: 정빅문鄭 ? ? Chyŏngbăengmun (doubtful title only: the queries are Courant's).

정본삼국지 Chŏngbon Samgukchi: see 156 삼국지연의 Samgukchi Yŏnŭi

401. 정비전 Chŏng Pi chŏn

뎡비전 Tyŏng Pi chyŏn, lending library manuscript, 4 vols, 30, 30, 30, 33 leaves (11 columns, 15 syllables), dated 갑인 (甲寅 1914, etc.). Title on the cover 鄭妃傳 Chŏng Pi chŏn. [Tōyō Bunko]

1961 exhibition, 45: 정비젼, Chyŏng Pi chyŏn, manuscript, 1 vol. (vol. 1 only) (National Library). A note in the catalogue states: "Tells of the extreme loyal courage and devotion of 雪梅 Sŏlmae, young wife of 정윤 Chŏng Yun". This is supported by the characters of the cover title of the Tōyō Bunko copy.

Yi Nŭngu: Kungmunhak Kaeron, 6, has the title of the Tōyō Bunko copy misprinted as 鄭始傳 Chŏng Si chŏn, and Kim Kidong, 597, and Sin Kihyŏng, 483, both list this.

402. 정수경전 Chŏng Sugyŏng chŏn "The Story of Chŏng Sugyŏng"

Set in Korea, tells of three murder incidents in which the hero is involved. See Kim Kidong, 562-564, and Mibalp'yo Kodae Sosŏl ko.

정수경전 Chyŏng Sugyŏng chyŏn, manuscript, 51 leaves (10 columns, 23 syllables), dated 계축 (癸丑 1853). [Harvard]

This text dates the action of the story as in the reign of King Sŏnjo, i.e. about 1600. No other text seems to date the action at all, which is rather suprising in view of the fact that all other texts are later than this one, but I had little doubt when I saw this text that it could not be as late as 1913.

뎡슈경젼 Tyŏng Syugyŏng chyŏn, manuscript, 28 leaves (10 columns, 22 syllables), dated 디한광무오년신축 (大韓光武五年辛丑 1901), and: 뎡슈경젼 Tyŏng Syugyŏng chyŏn, manuscript, 31 leaves (irregular), dated 大正拾貳年 (1923), both reported in Mibalp'yo Kodae Sosŏl ko as in Korea University Library.

1961 exhibition, 61: 鄭壽景傳 Chŏng Sugyŏng chŏn, manuscript, 1 vol. (Chang Tŏksun).

196

Kim Kidong, 28, states that there was a Seoul block print, but this is a mistake, due to a misreading of 정수정전, see **403** 정수정전 **Chŏng Sujŏng chŏn**, in **Yi Nŭngu: Kungmunhak Kaeron**, page 10. The same mistake results in the Seoul block print of that story being described as a block print of this story in the **Ewha Series**, I 434-435.

鄭壽景傳 **Chŏng Sugyŏng chŏn**, Yŏngch'ang Sŏgwan, 1918, 38 pages, is reported by **Kim Kidong**, 562, and in **Mibalp'yo Kodae Sosŏl ko**, and the title was advertised by Hansŏng Sŏgwan and Yuil Sŏgwan in 1915, by Taech'ang Sŏwŏn and Pogŭp Sŏgwan in 1920, by Pangmun Sŏgwan and Sin'gu Sŏrim in 1923, 1925 and 1932, and by Tongyang Sŏwŏn in 1925.

鄭壽景傳 뎡슈경젼 <u>Tyŏng Syugyŏng chyŏn</u>, Kyŏngsŏng Sŏjŏgŏp Chohap, 1924 (reprinted from 1915), and currently available from Sech'ang Sŏgwan, both 49 pages, and so alike that they might have been printed from the same plates. They have explanatory characters to the right of the columns of text, sometimes even when the words explained are not Sino-Korean.

정수경전 <u>Chŏng Sugyŏng chŏn</u>, Taejo sa, 1959, 25 pages.

403.　정수정전 **Chŏng Sujŏng chŏn** "The Story of Cheng Shui-ching"

The heroine becomes a commander-in-chief, and her husband her second-in-command, against the invading Khitan in early Sung China. See **Kim T'aejun**, 102, **Kim Kidong**, 271-274 (**1956**: 175-179), all under the title <u>Yŏ Changgun chŏn</u>, see below.

뎡슈졍젼 鄭水晶傳 <u>Tyŏng Syujyŏng chyŏn</u>, manuscript, 1 vol. [**Palace**]

뎡슈졍젼 <u>Tyŏng Syujyŏng chyŏn</u>, Seoul block print, 17 leaves. [**Ogura collection, Tokyo**]

On the front cover is written the date 병오 (丙午 1906).

뎡슈졍젼 <u>Tyŏng Syujyŏng chŏn</u>, Seoul block print, 16 leaves, reproduced in the **Ewha Series**, I 389-420, with a note in II 445-448 (the note in I 434-435 refers to **402** 정수경전 **Chŏng Sugyŏng chŏn** by mistake), and reprinted lithographically by 翰南書林 Hannam Sŏrim, Keijō, 191-.

女將軍傳 녀쟝군젼 <u>Nyŏ Changgun chyŏn</u>, currently available from Sech'ang Sŏgwan, 64 pages. This title was advertised by Taech'ang Sŏwŏn and Hanyang Sŏjŏgŏp Chohapso in 1918, by Pangmun Sŏgwan and Sin'gu Sŏrim in 1923, 1925 and 1932, and by Yŏngch'ang Sŏgwan and Hanhŭng Sŏrim in 1925, and Kim Kidong, 271, reports an edition by Sech'ang Sŏgwan in 1915, 100 pages.

姜漢永 Kang Hanyŏng, ed.: 鄭水品傳 <u>Chŏng Sujŏng chŏn</u> in **Hyŏndae Munhak**, 58, 59, 61 and 62, October 1959—February 1960. This is in modern spelling, without notes, and I cannot identify it with any other text.

Various sources give 鄭壽貞傳 and 鄭秀貞傳, both <u>Chŏng Sujŏng chŏn</u>, but giving Cheng Shou-chen and Cheng Hsiu-chen respectively for the heroine's name in Chinese.

　　　정시전 Chŏng Si chŏn: see 401 정비전 Chŏng Pi chŏn

404. 정씨복선록 Chŏng-ssi Poksŏn nok

1961 exhibition, 42: 정셔복션록 <u>Chyŏng-ssi Poksyŏn nok,</u> manuscript, 2 vols. (National Library). The catalogue notes: "A moralistic work, telling of the virtues as a wife of a Chŏng [Chinese: Cheng]". **Kim Kidong,** 600, lists 鄭氏福善錄 <u>Chŏng-ssi Poksŏn nok,</u> a moral tale in Korean set in China, existing in manuscript(s) (also page 37), but not made known before.

405. 정씨청행록 Chŏng-ssi Ch'ŏnghaeng nok

Kim Kidong, 37, includes 鄭氏清行錄 <u>Chŏng-ssi Ch'ŏnghaeng nok</u> (presumably) "Record of the Pure Actions of (the) Chŏng(s) [Chinese: Cheng(s)]" in a list of works which exist in manuscripts, but which he was not able to discuss. Since he does not include this in his table, this one mention of it may be a mistake for one of the other similar titles.

406. 정씨충효보은록 Chŏng-ssi Ch'unghyo Poŭn nok

Courant, 886: 뎡셔충효보은록 鄭氏忠孝報恩錄 <u>Tyŏng-ssi Ch'yunghyo Poŭn nok,</u> "The Loyalty, Filial Piety and Gratitude of the Family Chŏng [Chinese: Cheng]" (title only).

407. 정씨팔룡 Chŏng-ssi P'allyong

Courant, 832: 정셔팔룡 鄭氏八龍 <u>Chyŏng-ssi P'allyong,</u> "The Eight Dragons of the Chŏng [Chinese: Cheng] Family" (title only).

408. 정열사전 Chŏng Yŏlsa chŏn

Kim Kidong, 601, lists 程烈士傳 <u>Chŏng Yŏlsa chŏn</u> (presumably) "The Story of the Hero(es) Ch'eng" as a story in Korean set in China, existing in paperback edition(s), but not made known before.

409. 정옥란전 **Chŏng Ongnan chŏn**

Kim Kidong, 597, lists 鄭玉蘭傳 Chŏng Ongnan chŏn (presumably) "The Story of Cheng Yü-lan" as a love story in Korean set in China, existing in paperback edition(s), but not made known before. He lists it immediately next to **399** 정목란전 **Chŏng Mongnan chŏn,** which is identical with this in all the details which he gives. This title was advertised by Hansŏng Sŏgwan and Yuil Sŏgwan in 1915.

410. 정을선전 **Chŏng Ŭlsŏn chŏn "The Story of Chŏng Ŭlsŏn"**

The hero is tricked into abandoning his fiancée by her wicked step-mother. The girl commits suicide, but all is uncovered, and she is reborn to become the hero's second wife. The setting is sixteenth century Korea. See **Kim T'aejun,** 186-187, **Kim Kidong,** 330-333 (1956: 309-312), **Pak Sŏngŭi,** 370-373, and **Sin Kihyŏng,** 314-317.

뎡을션젼 Tyŏng Ŭlsyŏn chyŏn, lending library manuscript, 3 vols, 33, 33, 32 leaves (11 columns, 13-14 syllables), dated 임진 (壬辰 1892). Title on the cover 鄭乙善傳 Chŏng Ŭlsŏn chŏn. [**Seoul University**]

뎡을션젼 Tyŏng Ŭlsyŏn chyŏn, lending library manuscript, 3 vols, 31, 31, 30 leaves (11-12 columns, 13 syllables), dated 을ᄉ (乙巳 1905). Title on the cover 鄭乙善傳 Chŏng Ŭlsŏn chŏn [**Tōyō Bunko**]

뎡을션젼 Tyŏng Ŭlsyŏn chyŏn, manuscript, 48 (+3½) leaves (12 columns, 20 syllables), dated 긔유 (己酉 1909). [**Seattle**]

The 3½ leaves are 황싀젼 Hwangsăe chyŏn, see perhaps story no. 7 in **162** 삼셜기 **Samsŏlgi.**

鄭乙善傳 Chŏng Ŭlsŏn chŏn, manuscript, 1 vol., dated 隆熙四年 (1910), according to the catalogue of the **Karam collection.**

즁을션젼 Chŭng Ŭlsyŏn chyŏn, manuscript, 62 leaves (irregular), dated 정사. Title on the title page 鄭乙先傳 즁을션전 Chŭng Ŭlsŏn chŏn, and date on the title page 丁巳 정사 (1917, etc.). [**Harvard**] The spelling, as well as the lay out, is very irregular.

즁을션젼 Chŭng Ŭlsyŏn chyŏn, manuscript, 2 vols, 31½ leaves (10 columns, 21 syllables) in vol. 1, 71 leaves (10 columns, 14 syllables) in vol. 2. Title on the cover 졍을션젼 Chyŏng Ŭlsyŏn chyŏn. [**Harvard**]

The two volumes appear to be in different hands as well as different formats, and it seems highly likely that they did not originally belong together.

1961 exhibition, 44: 즁을선젼 Chŭng Ŭlsyŏn chyŏn, manuscript, 1 vol. Title on the cover 鄭明錄 Chŏng Myŏng nok. (National Library).

Kim Kidong, 600, lists the title as on the cover of this text as that of a work separate from Chŏng Ŭlsŏn chŏn, which he lists on page 593. He describes Chŏng Myŏng nok as a moralistic tale in Korean set in China, existing in manuscript(s), but not made known before. I have not found any other notice that such a story exists, but, on the other hand, I saw the text above only briefly, and have no reason for including it here other than the title, as given above, on the first leaf, and cannot see why the story Chŏng Ŭlsŏn chŏn should also be called Chŏng Myŏng nok.

정을선전 Chyŏng Ŭlsŏn chyŏn, Sech'ang Sŏgwan, 1935, 43 pages. In another cover, this is also currently available from Sech'ang Sŏgwan, and the title was advertised by Taech'ang Sŏwŏn and Pogŭp Sŏgwan in 1920, by Chosŏn Tosŏ Chusik Hoesa in 1925, by Tongyang Sŏwŏn in 1925, and by Yŏngch'ang Sŏgwan and Hanhŭng Sŏrim in 1925, and by Tŏkhŭng Sŏrim in 1935.

Kim Kidong, 31 and 330, gives a publication by Pangmun Sŏgwan, 1917, 43 pages.

정일남전 **Chŏng Illam chŏn**: see 351 이언총림 **Iŏn Ch'ongnim**

정진사전 **Chŏng Chinsa chŏn**: see 398 정도령전 **Chŏng Toryŏng chŏn**

411. 정현무전 Chŏng Hyŏnmu chon

Kim Kidong, 591, lists 鄭賢武傳 Chŏng Hyŏnmu chŏn (presumably) "The Story of Cheng Hsien-wu" as a story of a hero in Korean set in China, existing in paperback edition(s) (also page 32), but not made known before.

412. 제갈양전 Chegal Yang chŏn

Kim Kidong, 210, includes 諸葛亮傳 Chegal Yang chŏn (presumably) "The Story of Chu-ko Liang" in a list of stories about the wars in third century China which are partial or complete translations of Chinese works. Chu-ko Liang is a leading character in San-kuo-chih Yen-i, see 156 삼국지연의 **Samgukchi Yŏnŭi**. The title was advertised by Sinmyŏng Sŏrim in 1930.

413. 제마무전 **Che Mamu chŏn**

The story is in the form of a dream in which the evils of the period at the end of the Han dynasty are moralised over and compared with the glory of the establishment of the dynasty. **Sin Kihyŏng,** 350-354, has a full description of the story, but even with the help of this I found it unusually difficult to follow. **Kim T'aejun,** 91-92 (see also page 105), discusses the relationship between this story and Chinese works, especially 全相平話三國志 Ch'üan-hsiang P'ing-hua San-kuo-chih, but it is difficult to see the relationship by comparing actual texts.

In every text of this story which I have seen, this story is followed by a poem called 회심곡 Hoesim kok,"Song of Repentance", which is always virtually a Buddhist prayer, but varies considerably from text to text.

졔마무젼 Chye Mamu chyŏn, Seoul block print, 16 (+7) leaves. [**British Museum**]

졔마무젼 Chye Mamu chyŏn, block print, 16 (+4) leaves. [**Tōyō Bunko**] This is boxed with Ansŏng Llock prints.

Courant, 783: Seoul block print, 26 (+6) leaves, "newly engraved at 紅樹洞 Hongsudong", in Paris, etc. **Kim Tonguk,** 390, gives two Seoul block prints, one of 26 leaves, (including?) 4 leaves of Hoesim kok, 紅樹洞重刊 "re-engraved at at Hongsudong", and the other of 32 leaves, (including?) 6 leaves of Hoesim kok. On page 396, he gives an Ansŏng block print of 16 (+4) leaves, as the Tōyō Bunko text above, but with an identifying colophon. In Hyangt'o Sŏul, 8, **1960,** page 51, he gave under the Seoul block prints one of 16 (+4) leaves, "at Hongsudong", "and one other edition", and under the Ansŏng block prints, on page 57, one of 20 leaves, the last leaf of which is reproduced on page 59. The page of an Ansŏng block print reproduced on page 58 appears to be from the same text.

夢決楚漢頌 (몽결초한숑) Monggyŏl Ch'ohan syong, Chosŏn Tosŏ Chusik Hoesa, 1925, and the same, Taesan Sŏrim, 1925, both 51 (+10) pages. These follow the Seoul block print text given above, but the wording is rather different.

제마무젼 (一名夢決楚漢訟) Che Mamu chyŏn (Ilmyŏng Monggyŏl Ch'ohan song), currently available from Sech'ang Sŏzwan, 56 pages. The story in this differs considerably in detail from that in the last.

I would hazard a guess at the title Monggyŏl Ch'ohan song: "Settling in a Dream the Case of Ch'u versus Han", but this is based on a very imperfect under-standing of the story. I cannot identify Che Mamu as either historical or as occurring in any other Korean or Chinese work. The Tōyō Bunko block print, above, has on the cover 齊馬無傳 "The Story of Ch'i Ma-wu", the same as is given by Courant, but the catalogue gives 齊馬武傳, also "The Story of Ch'i Ma-wu". Most Korean sources give 諸馬武傳, "The Story of Chu Ma-wu", and some put this into Korean as 저마무전 Chŏ Mamu chŏn. **Ku, Son and Kim: Kungmunhak Kaeron**, 252, gives this with the characters 褚馬武傳 Chŏ Mamu chŏn, "The Story of Ch'u Ma-wu".

414. 제호연록 Che-hoyŏn nok

Courant, 861: 제호연록 諸好緣錄 Chye-hoyŏn nok, "Record of the Good Destinies" (title only).

415. 제환공전 Che Hwan-gong chŏn

Kim Kidong, 210, includes 齊恒公傳 Che Hang-gong chŏn in a list of partial or complete translations from Chinese which he would not discuss, and this title was advertised by Taech'ang Sŏwŏn in association with other publishers in 1918, 1919 and 1920. However, 恒 Hang is almost certainly a mistake for 桓 (Hwan in Korean), Huan, the fifteenth king of Ch'i, and this story will probably derive from a Chinese work which is related to **261** 열국지 Yŏlgukchi.

> 적..... Chyŏk.....: see 적 ..... Chŏk.....
>
> 전..... Chyŏn.....: see 전 ..... Chŏn.....
>
> 정.... Chyŏng.....: see 정 ..... Chŏng.....
>
> 제.... Chye.....: see 제 ..... Che.....

416. 조대가전 Chodaega chŏn

1947 exhibition, 168: 조대가전 Chodaega chŏn, manuscript, 1 vol. (Ewha University). I have not found any other mention of the title, nor any information to support any guess which I could make at the meaning, or even the romanisation, of the title.

417. 조맹행 Cho Maeng Haeng

Courant, 901: 됴밍힝 趙孟行 Tyo Măeng Hăeng, "The Deeds of Cho Maeng" (title only). It is not even impossible that this is a corruption of **88** 도앵행 To-aeng-haeng.

418. 조생원전 Cho Saengwŏn chŏn "The Story of Mr Chao"

In fifteenth century China (Ming, Ch'eng-hua), Mr Chao's son marries secretly, and there is consequent trouble when he is ordered to marry a grand-daughter of the emperor. See **Kim Kidong**, 313-316 (1956: 295-298), and **Sin Kihyŏng**, 322-324. Compare also **387** 장학사전 **Chang Haksa chŏn**.

趙生員傳 조생원전 Cho Saengwŏn chŏn, currently available from Sech'ang Sŏgwan, 49 pages.

Kim Kidong gives a publication by Sin'gu Sŏrim, 1917, 62 pages (on page 31) or 60 pages (on page 313), and the title was advertised by Tŏkhŭng Sŏrim in 1935.

419. 조씨삼대록 Cho-ssi Samdae rok

Courant, 904: 조시삼디록 曹氏三代錄 Cho-si Samdăe rok, "Record of the Three Generations of the Cho [Chinese: Ts'ao] Family". He describes it as "44 vols, in Korean", but does not give the location of any text.

420. 조야기문 Choya Kimun "Reports from Court and Country"

됴야긔문 朝野記聞 Tyoya Kŭimun, manuscript, 23 vols. [**Palace**]

This is a collection of historical tales. **Maema Kyōsaku: Kosen Sappu**, III 1374, gives a number of quotations describing it and attributing its authorship (presumably in *hanmun*) to 徐文重 Sŏ Munjung (1634-1709). This is presumably what **Courant**, 923, meant by 조야긔문 朝野奇文 Choya Kŭimun, "Remarkable Compositions in Korean (?)" (doubtful title only).

421. 조야첨재 Choya Ch'ŏmjae "Composite Records from Court and Country"

조야첨지 朝野僉載 Choya Ch'yŏmjăe, manuscript, 53 vols. [**Palace**]

됴야첨지 朝野僉載 Tyoya Ch'yŏmjăe, manuscript, 16 vols. [**Palace**]

These are collections of historical stories. There is a Chinese, T'ang, work of the same title (in Chinese: Ch'ao-yeh Ch'ien-tsai, see Lu Hsun: A Brief History of Chinese Fiction, Foreign Languages Press, Peking, 1959, page 204), and also a Korean work in *hanmun*, probably from early in the eighteenth century (see **Maema Kyōsaku: Kosen Sappu**, III 1375, and Korean historical reference works, for various attributions). It is presumably this that **Courant** meant by 942: 조야첨의 朝野 ?? Choya Ch'yŏmŭi (doubtful title only: the queries are his).

422. 조야회통 **Choya Hoet'ong "The Court and Country Compendium"**

됴야회통 朝野會通 Tyoya Hoet'ong, two manuscripts, 47 vols and 54 vols, the second incomplete. [**Palace**]

This is a collection of historical stories. There are at least two works in *hanmun* of this title, both probably eighteenth century (see **Maema Kyōsaku: Kosen Sappu**, III 1373, and the standard Korean historical reference works).

423. 조웅전 **Cho Ung chŏn "The Story of Chao Hsiung"**

In fifth century China, the hero defeats a usurper and restores the imperial family by his military and magical arts.

See **Kim Kidong**, 252-254 (**1956:** 167-169), and **Pak Sŏngŭi**, 213-215. The story does not yet seem to have received the attention it deserves.

조웅전 Cho Ung chyŏn, manuscript, 2 vols (vol. 3 is missing), 55, 51 leaves, dated 甲辰 (1904) in vol. 1 and 乙巳 (1905) in vol. 2. Title on the cover 趙雄傳 Cho Ung chŏn. [**Harvard**]

됴웅전 Tyo Ung chyŏn, Seoul block print, 21 leaves. [**British Museum**, two copies]

됴웅전 Tyo Ung chyŏn, Seoul block print, 20 leaves. [**British Museum**, two copies, and **Ogura collection, Tokyo**]

These two editions vary very slightly in text.

Courant, 801, gives a Seoul block print of 20 leaves, "newly engraved at 紅樹洞 Hongsudong", as in Paris, etc. **Petrova**, 190, gives a Seoul block print of 21 leaves as in the Aston collection in Leningrad. **Kim Tonguk**, 392, gives four Seoul block prints, two of 30 leaves, one of these "at Hongsudong", and two of 20 leaves. In Hyangt'o Sŏul, 8, **1960**, page 53, he gave only one 20 leaf edition, "at Hongsudong".

됴웅전 Tyo Ung chyŏn, Ansŏng block print, 20 leaves. Title on the cover 趙雄傳 Cho Ung chŏn. [**Tōyō Bunko**]

됴웅전 Tyo Ung chyŏn (vol. 1), 됴웅전 Tyo Ung chŏn (vol. 2) 조웅전 Cho Ung chyŏn (vol. 3), Chŏnju block print, 3 vols, 33, 33, 31 leaves, 完山新刊壬辰 (vol. 1), 임진완산신판 (vol. 3) both "newly engraved at Chŏnju in 1892". Title on the cover 趙雄傳 Cho Ung chŏn. [**Ogura collection, Tokyo**]

됴웅뎐 <u>Tyo Ung chyŏn</u> (vols. 1 and 2), 조웅뎐 <u>Cho Ung chyŏn</u> (vol. 3), Chŏnju block print, 3 vols, 30, 30, 32 leaves, bound as one volume. [**Ogura collection, Tokyo**]

What appears to be the same is reproduced in the **Ewha Series**, III 1-177, with a note 417-420.

1961 exhibition, 57: 됴웅뎐 <u>Tyo Ung chyŏn</u>, Chŏnju block print, bound as one volume (Kang Hanyŏng). The catalogue describes it as "as re-engraving of 1903".

Kim Tonguk, 397-398, gives the Chŏnju block prints as follows (without the numbers, which I have added):

(1) 丙午孟春完山開刊 "first engraved at Chŏnju in the first month of 1848 [sic]", 2 editions, one of 3 vols, 30, 30, 29 leaves, and one of two vols, 30, 32 leaves. 丙午 is 1846, 1906, etc., and to give it as 1848 is an extraordinary mistake for Kim Tonguk to make, especially in view of the importance which he attaches to the date of this text.

(2) 癸卯孟秋完山重刊 "re-engraved at Chŏnju in the seventh month of 1903".

(3) 무술중춘완산판 "engraved at Chŏnju in the second month of 1898".

(4) 完山新刊壬辰 "newly engraved at Chŏnju in 1892".

(5) 完府新刊 "newly engraved at Chŏnju".

(6) 光武七年癸卯夏完山北門內重刊 "re-engraved at Chŏnju, within the North Gate, Summer [i.e. fourth-sixth months], 1903".

(7) 3 vols, vol. 1, 33 leaves, 刻手박이력서봉운丁巳秋開板 "first engraved in the autumn [i.e. seventh-ninth months] of 1857 by engravers Pak Iryŏk and Sŏ Pongun"; vol. 2, 33 leaves; vol. 3, 38 leaves, 同治五年完西杏洞 "at Sŏ'aeng-dong, Chŏnju, 1866". The last page of vol. 1 is reproduced, page 402.

The layout of this is actually a little confusing. What is given above as (6) looks like two separate entries, but it is given as one in **Yi Nŭngu: Kungmunhak Kaeron**, page 10. What I have taken to be two editions of his (1) may in fact refer to (1) and (2) respectively. His (7) is listed below (4), (5) and (6), and may in fact be a further description of (5).

The first six are also given in the **1960** version of this article, page 61, with slightly less detail in some cases, and (2), (3), (4) and (6) are given by Yi Nŭngu, as above.

There is very little agreement between what Kim Tonguk lists and what I have seen. The first Chŏnju block print which I list above has, in the first volume, the same colophon as Kim Tonguk gives under (4), and the last one which I list, Kang Hanyŏng's, could be either his (2) or his (6).

Kim Kidong reports publications, on page 252, by Tŏkhŭng Sŏrim, 1914, 122 pages, and, on page 30, by Pangmun Sŏgwan, 1916, 114 pages, and the title has been advertised consistently by almost all publishers of paperbacks since.

됴웅젼 Tyo Ung chyŏn, Yŏnghwa Ch'ulp'ansa, probably not earlier than 1951, 93 pages.

趙雄傳 조웅전 Cho Ung chŏn, currently available from Sech'ang Sŏgwan, 75 pages.

조웅전 Cho Ung chŏn, Taejo sa, 1959, 90 pages.

趙雄傳 Cho Ung chŏn in the **Hŭimang Series**, II 173-266.

424. 조자룡전 Cho Charyong chŏn "The Story of Chao Tzu-lung"

The story clearly concerns the same characters and events as appear in San-kuo-chih Yen-i (see 156 삼국지연의 **Samgukchi Yŏnŭi**), the hero being 趙雲 Chao Yün (tzu: 子龍 Tzu-lung). **Kim Kidong**, 210, must be mistaken in referring it to the period of the establishment of the Han dynasty.

趙子龍傳 조자룡전 Cho Charyong chŏn, currently available from Sech'ang Sŏgwan (but text as composed before 1945), 32 pages. The title was advertised by Taech'ang Sŏwŏn and Pogŭp Sŏgwan in 1920, by Chosŏn Tosŏ Chusik Hoesa in 1925, and by Yŏngch'ang Sŏgwan and Hanhŭng Sŏrim in 1925.

425. 조충의전 Cho Ch'ungŭi chŏn

See 송신용 [宋申用] Song Sinyong: 조충의전 (趙忠毅傳) Cho Ch'ungŭi chŏn (Seoul, 조선어학회 Chosŏn Ŏhakhoe [now 한글학회 Han'gŭl Hakhoe]: 한글 Han'gŭl, 107 [originally numbered 14-1], July 1949, 17-30). The text is reprinted in full, with notes, and is described as having been taken from a manuscript of 54 leaves entitled 복션화음녹 Poksyŏn Hwaŭmnok, dated 긔히 (己亥 1899), owned by 金孝植 Kim Hyosik. This story is 18 leaves of that manuscript, entitled 됴츙의젼 Tyo Ch'yungŭi chyŏn. The hero is a minor official from Kyŏngsang Province (Song Sinyong explains ch'ungŭi as the title of a minor provincial official), who makes the acquaintance of the prince who later becomes King Hyojong. The action is said to cover the years 1637-1649.

426. 존주기략 Chonju Kiryak

존쥬긔략 Chonjyu Kŭiryak, lending library manuscript, 35 (+18) leaves (11 columns, 20 syllables), dated 무인 (戊寅 1878). Title on the cover 尊周記略 Chonju Kiryak. [Chŏng Pyŏnguk]

Chŏng Pyŏnguk describes this as "a sort of unofficial history", and it appears to be instructive in nature. It opens with letters from the Ming Wan-li Emperor, Shen-tsung (1573-1619). It is probably taken from a work in *hanmun*, possibly from 尊周彙編 Chonju Hwip'yŏn, a work of 1800 (see **Maema Kyōsaku: Kosen Sappu**, II 1227, etc.). The other 18 leaves in the text above are 한시부훈셔 Han-si Puhun syŏ, a *kasa* of instructions for women.

427. 종옥전 Chongok chŏn

Sin Kihyŏng, 483, lists 종옥전 (鍾玉傳) Chongok chŏn as a love story in Korean, set in China, but with a query. The source for this may be **Kim Kidong**, who lists the same, page 597. The only information he gives is that it exists in paperback edition(s), and he refers to **Yi Nŭngu: Kungmunhak Kaeron**. There it is listed, page 6, among works in *hanmun* as a one volume manuscript in the possession of Maema Kyōsaku. **Maema Kyōsaku: Kosen Sappu** does not appear to list it, nor could I find it in the **Tōyō Bunko**.

428. 주선전 Chu Sŏn chŏn "The Story of the Magican Chu"

The magician, whose name is Chu Chŏn in Korean, impresses T'ai-tsu of Ming with his powers.

쥬션뎐 朱仙傳 Chyu Syŏn tyŏn, manuscript, 1 vol. [**Palace**]

姜漢永 Kang Hanyŏng, ed.: 朱仙傳 Chu Sŏn chŏn, in **Hyŏndae Munhak**, 65, (318-323) and 67 (315-318), May and July, 1960.

The spelling is modernised in some respects, but there is an overall impression of faithfulness to an old text.

429. 주원장전 Chu Wŏnjang chŏn "The Story of Chu Yüan-chang"

The text below opens with Chu Yüan-chang, the founder of the Ming Dynasty, in Korea and being called from there to deal with the confused state of China. **Kim Kidong**, 210, includes 朱元璋傳 Chu Wŏnjang chŏn in a list of works which are partial or complete translations of Chinese works.

주원쟝창업실긔 (title on the cover 朱元璋刱業實記) Chyu Wŏnjyang Ch'angŏp Silgŭi, "The True Record of the Great Works of Chu Yüan-chang", Pangmun Sŏgwan and Sin'gu Sŏrim, 1919, 86 pages. The title was also advertised by Taech'ang Sŏwŏn and Hanyang Sŏjŏgŏp Chohapso in 1918, and by Taech'ang Sŏwŏn and Pogŭp Sŏgwan in 1919 and 1920.

주중기선이태백실기 Chujung Kisŏn Yi T'aebaek Silgi: see 356 이태백실기 Yi T'aebaek Silgi

430. 주해선전 Chu Haesŏn chŏn

Sin Kihyŏng, 432-433, describes 朱海仙傳 Chu Haesŏn chŏn, "The Story of Chu Hai-hsien", as one of a family being broken up and re-united in seventh century China. He describes the text as a manuscript of his dated 哲宗二年 (1851).

중산망월전 Chung-san Mangwŏl chŏn: see 468 토끼전 T'okki chŏn.

431. 쥐전 Chwi chŏn "The Story of the Rat"

The climax of all the satirical stories below is the dismissal of the squirrel's false indictment of a rat, who has kept him in idle luxury for some time, but eventually decides to do so no longer. See Kim T'aejun, 129-130, Kim Kidong, 165-175 (1956: 371-375), Pak Sŏngŭi, 310-311, and Sin Kihyŏng, 388-389.

다람의쇼지 Taram ŭi Syoji, "The Squirrel's Memorial", manuscript, 16 leaves (10 columns, 14 syllables), dated 계유 (癸酉 1873). [Chŏng Pyŏnguk]

Chŏng Pyŏnguk thought this realistic and sophisticated in style, and probably a composition of about the date given.

Kim Kidong, 30, gives a publication of 쥐傳 Chwi chŏn by Yŏngch'ang Sŏgwan, 1918, and, page 165, 1919, and the titles below have been fairly regularly advertised in paperbacks since those dates.

셔동지젼 鼠同知傳 Syŏ Tongji chyŏn, "The Story of Mr Rat", "compiled by 姜義永 Kang Ŭiyŏng". Yŏngch'ang Sŏgwan and Hanhŭng Sŏrim, 1924 (reprinted from 1922), 51 pages. Characters are given to the right of each column of text as appropriate.

鼠同知傳 Sŏ Tongji chŏn in the Hŭimang Series, I 321-346.

The critics also give as titles for the same story 鼠勇傳 Sŏ Yong chŏn (the significance of the yong here escapes me) and 鼠翁傳 Sŏ Ong chŏn, "The Story of Old Rat", and they also all at least mention (**Kim Kidong**, 169-175, gives a full description of) stories in *hanmun* with similar titles but very different plots: 鼠大州傳 Sŏ Taeju chŏn, "The Story of Sŏ Taeju [= Rat Great-rat]" and 鼠獄記 Sŏ Ok ki (or..... 說..... sŏl, or ..... 傳.....chŏn) "Record (Tale, Story) of the Rat's Case".

쥬..... **Chyu.....**: see 주..... **Chu.....**

즁산망월젼 **Chyung-san Mangwŏl chyŏn**: see **468** 토끼젼 **T'okki chŏn**

증산옥린몽 **Chŭngsan Ongnin mong**: see **277** 옥린몽 **Ongnin mong**

증을션젼 **Chŭng Ŭlsyŏn chyŏn**: see **410** 졍을션젼 **Chŏng Ŭlsŏn chŏn**

지낭기 **Chinang ki**: see **162** 삼셜기 **Samsŏlgi**

432. 진대방젼 Chin Taebang chŏn "The Story of Ch'en Ta-feng"

In Sung China, a most unfilial son is lectured by the magistrate and becomes a model of filial piety. See **Kim T'aejun**, 190-191, **Kim Kidong**, 384-386, **Pak Sŏngŭi**, 382-384, and **Sin Kihyŏng**, 325.

진大方젼 Chin Taebang chyŏn, manuscript by Hashimoto in mixed script, 57 leaves (8 columns, 21-22 syllables), copy made in 戊戌 (1898) of a text dated 丙申 (1896, etc.). Title on the cover 陳大方傳 Chin Taebang chŏn. [**Harvard**] This text was copied at 南平 Namp'yŏng, in Chŏlla South Province.

진딕방젼 Chin Tăebang chyŏn, manuscript by Hashimoto, 33 (+42) leaves (12 columns, 21 syllables), copy made in 庚寅 (1910) of a text dated 庚子 (1900, etc.). Title on the cover 陳大邦傳 Chin Taebang chŏn, "The Story of Ch'en Ta-pang". [**Harvard**] The 42 leaves are **355** 이태경젼 **Yi T'aegyŏng chŏn**.

진딕방젼 Chin Tăebang chyŏn, manuscript, 21 leaves (12 columns, 30 syllables), dated 을사乙巳 (1905, etc.). Title on the cover 陳大芳傳 Chin Taebang chŏn. [**Chŏng Pyŏnguk**]

陳大房傳 Chin Taebang chŏn, manuscript in mixed script, 59 leaves (8 columns, 16 syllables), date on the cover 大正四年 (1915). [**Chŏng Pyŏnguk**]

1947 exhibition, 116: 진딕방젼 Chin Tăebang chyŏn, manuscript, 1 vol. (Cho Yunje, not shown).

진대방젼 Chin Taebang chyŏn, Seoul block print, 16 (+11) leaves. [**British Museum**]

진대방젼 Chin Taebang chyŏn, Seoul block print, 18 (+10) leaves. [**British Museum**]

진대방젼 Chin Taebang chyŏn, block print, 16 (+6) leaves. [**Imanishi collection, Tenri**] In manuscript following the title is 陳大傍 Chin Taebang, in Chinese Ch'en Ta-pang or -p'ang.

All these block prints have sections at the end entitled 너훈졔슈 Nǎehun Chyesǎ "Words to Counsel Women", but no two of the three which I have seen appear to be the same.

Petrova, 131, gives a separate copy of this, 11 leaves, and, 197, Chin Tǎebang chyŏn, 18 leaves, both in the Aston collection in Leningrad. **Courant**, 792, gives a block print of 18 (+2) leaves as in Paris, etc. **Kim Tonguk**, 388, gives a Seoul block print of 18 leaves, perhaps + 18, 由洞新刊 "newly engraved at Yudong". In Hyangt'o Sŏul, 8, 1960, page 49, he gave "18 (+2) leaves". No source mentions an Ansŏng block print, and it therefore seems likely that the Imanishi text, above, is also a Seoul block print.

진듸방젼 陳大方傳 Chin Tǎebang chyŏn, Sin'gu Sŏrim, 1922 (reprinted from 1917), 30 (+32) pages.

Characters are given to the right of the columns of text as appropriate. **Kim Kidong** gives the same, but, page 384, 1915, and, page 32, 1915, 85 pages, and the title was also advertised by Tongyang Sŏwŏn, Pangmun Sŏgwan, Yŏngch'ang Sŏgwan and Hanhŭng Sŏrim, all in 1925.

진대방젼 陳大方傳 Chin Taebang chŏn, currently available from Sech'ang Sŏgwan, (but text as composed before 1945), 19 (+16) pages.

These two editions have virtually identical texts of this story, and also collections of short stories which are modern in style.

433. 진성운전 Chin Sŏngun chŏn

Kim Kidong, 36, includes 陳聖雲傳 Chin Sŏngun chŏn in a list of works existing in manuscripts in Korean which he was not able to discuss.

434. 진시황전 Chin Sihwang chŏn

Kim Kidong, 209, includes 秦始皇傳 Chin Sihwang chŏn, modelled on the life of the First Emperor, of Ch'in", among works which are partial or complete translations of Chinese works. The title was advertised by Chosŏn Tosŏ Chusik Hoesa in 1925.

435. 진장군전 **Chin Changgun chŏn**

Kim Kidong, 591, lists 陳將軍傳 Chin Changgun chŏn (presumably) "The Story of General Ch'en" as a story of a hero (in Korean, probably) set in China, existing in paperback edition(s), but not made known before.

436. 진주삼재합록 **Chinju Samjaehap nok**

Kim Kidong, 595, lists 眞珠三合再錄 Chinju Samhapchae rok as a love story in Korea, set in China, which exists in paperback edition(s). He refers to **Kim T'aejun**, who only seems to mention, in a list, page 229, of works of what he calls "the miraculous encounter type" in Courant, 眞珠三再合錄 Chinju Samjaehap nok. **Courant** does not have either title.

437. 진주탑 **Chinju-t'ap**

진쥬탑 珍珠塔 Chinjyu-t'ap, manuscript, 10 vols. **[Palace]**

I have no note on the content of this work. When this text was shown in the **1947 exhibition**, as item 199, the title was given as 眞珠塔 Chinju-t'ap. 眞珠 *chinju* seems to be used in Korean for "pearl", rather than 珍珠, which seems to be more usual in Chinese, *chen-chu*.

침홍전 **Chim Hǔng chyŏn: see 64** 김홍전 **Kim Hong chŏn**

438. 징세비태록 **Chingse Pit'ae rok**

징셰비틔록 懲世否泰錄 Chingsye Pit'ǎe rok, manuscript, 1 vol. **[Palace]**

Courant, 812, gives exactly the same title, "Record to Show the Distinction between Right and Wrong (?)" (the query is his own), as of a block print of 32 leaves, in Paris, etc. He notes that the story concerns one 安相文 An Hsiangwen in eighteenth century China (Ch'ing, Ch'ien-lung), who raised a rebellion in the name of loyalty to the Ming dynasty. No such person appears to be given in the standard Chinese reference works. **Kim T'aejun**, 222, mentions the work in much the same terms as Courant. **Kim Tonguk**, 389, gives two Seoul block prints, one of 32 leaves and one of 22 leaves, with a short note to much the same effect as Courant's.

The title would appear to be modelled on that of the Ming historical work 否泰錄 P'i-t'ai-lu, "Record of Fortune and Misfortune".

211

Other Korean sources give a title which is the same in Korean spelling, but with different characters and perhaps indications of a work of a different nature. **Kim Kidong**, 599, lists 懲世鄙熊錄 Chingse Pit'ae rok as a moral tale in Korea set in China (**Sin Kihyŏng**, 484, the same), which exists in manuscript(s). He refers to **Ku, Son** and **Kim: Kungmunhak Kaeron**, which summarizes it very briefly, page, 260, as a tale satirizing loose sexual morals. This suggests a translation of this title as "Record of Punishing the Mean Behaviour of the Age".

Since no one source lists both these titles as of separate works, I list them here as of one work only.

439.　창란호연 Ch'angnan Hoyŏn

창난호연 Ch'angnan Hoyŏn, manuscript, 10 vols. Title on the cover 昌蘭好緣 Ch'angnan Hoyŏn. [**Harvard**]

The condition of this text was such that I did not like to open it any further than it had been opened, but it appeared to be undated. It is very similar in appearance and condition to the Harvard text of **274** 옥란기연 **Ongnan Kiyŏn**.

Courant, 860, gives exactly the title as on the text above, "The Good Destiny of Ch'angnan". He suggests that Ch'angnan is the name of a woman, but mentions no texts. The title was advertised by Hansŏng Sŏgwan and Yuil Sŏgwan in 1915 among translations of Chinese works.

440.　창삼전 Ch'angsam chŏn

Title on the cover 창삼전 Ch'angsam chyŏn, manuscript, 49½ leaves (10-11 columns, 18 syllables). Date on the cover 壬辰 (1892). [**Chŏng Pyŏnguk**]

The story opens in the last years of the Ming dynasty, about 1630, but this text is so hastily written that it would require a great deal of close study to unravel it further. Even the title as given above is not certain, and the text may well be incomplete.

441.　창선감의록 Ch'angsŏn Kamŭi rok

A story set in sixteenth century China (Ming, Chia-ching) of the problems of households in which there is more than one wife. See **Kim T'aejun**, 160, 162, **Kim Kidong**, 350-355 (**1956**: 317-319), **Pak Sŏngŭi**, 340-341, and **Sin Kihyŏng**, 197-198. The first of these discusses the authorship, and this discussion is recapitulated in the other works. This is, in brief, that there are also versions

of this story in *hanmun,* which are thought to be the source of the story in
Korean, that there is a record that 趙聖期 Cho Sŏnggi (1638-1689) wrote a work
entitled 創善感義錄 Ch'angsŏn Kamŭi rok, and that it may be more than coincidence that **149** 사씨남정기 **Sa-ssi Namjŏng ki** dealt with a similar problem at
about the same time, but that internal evidence dates the work as no earlier
than the eighteenth century, supporting the theory, which is otherwise not so
well based, that the author was one 金道洙 Kim Tosu. The two copies of the
hanmun version in the Kyujanggak Library, Seoul University, are ascribed to
him, but no source gives any dates for his life or works. Another theory that
the author was one 鄭淚東 Chŏng Chundong is only mentioned, with no specific
details. **Courant**, 895, lists it as a story in Korean, by title only, and I have not
seen any date for a text in Korean earlier than that of Courant's mention of it,
though there are many undated manuscripts.

창선감의록 Ch'angsyŏn Kamŭi rok, manuscript, possibly a lending library copy,
1 vol. (vol. 1 only), 60 leaves (11 columns, 28 syllables), dated 뎌한광무사연경ㅈ
大韓光武四年庚子 (1900). Title on the title page 彰善感義錄 Ch'angsŏn Kamŭi rok.
[**School of Oriental and African Studies, University of London**]

창선감의록 Ch'angsyŏn Kamŭi rok, lending library manuscript, 10 vols, about
30 leaves (11 columns, 14 syllables) per volume, dated 신축 (辛丑 1901) in vol.
4, 을ᄉ (乙巳 1905) in vols 1 and 2, and 임자 (壬子 1912) in vols 5-10 which
are uniform. Title on the cover 彰善感義錄 Ch'angsŏn Kamŭi rok. [**Tōyō Bunko**]

창선감의록 Ch'angsŏn Kamŭi rok, manuscript, 3 vols, 54, 46, 42 leaves (12 columns, 27 syllables). Title on the cover 倡善感義錄 Ch'angsŏn Kamŭi rok.
[**Seoul University**]

This is in poor condition, but I could not see any other reason to date it as
earlier than any of the other manuscripts which I have seen.

챵션감의록 Ch'yangsyŏn Kamŭi rok, manuscript, 4 vols. [**Ogura collection, Tokyo**]

I have a note on this "c. 1900", but no indication of the source of this information.

1961 exhibition, 39: 챵션감의록 (倡善感義錄) Ch'yangsyŏn Kamŭi rok, manuscript, 3 vols (National Library).

倡善感義錄 Ch'angsŏn Kamŭi rok, manuscript, 5 vols, "in Korean", given as in
the **Ilsa collection**.

창선감의록 Ch'angsyŏn Kamŭi rok, manuscript, 1 vol. (vol. 2 only), given as in
the **Karam collection**.

창선감의록 Ch'angsŏn Kamŭi rok, manuscript, 83 leaves, given as in the **Karam collection.**

彰善感義錄 Ch'angsŏn Kamŭi rok, manuscript, 86 leaves, given as in the **Karam collection.** This may be in *hanmun*.

倡善感義錄 Ch'angsŏn Kamŭi rok, manuscript, 40 leaves, "in Korean", given as in the **Karam collection.**

Kim Kidong, 351, gives two publications in Korean, 倡善感義錄 Ch'angsŏn Kamŭi rok, by Chosŏn Sŏgwan, 1914, 113 pages, and 彰善感義錄 Ch'angsŏn Kamŭi rok, by Sin'gu Sŏrim, 1917, 140 pages, as well as one in *hanmun* by Hannam Sŏrim, 1916.

彰善感義錄 Ch'angsŏn Kamŭi rok, Hannam Sŏrim, 1924 (reprinted from 1917). 109 pages. There is a preface dated 1904, and the authors are given on page 1 as 池雲英 Chi Unyŏng and 白斗鏞 Paek Tuyong.

창선감의록 (彰善感義錄) Ch'angsŏn Kamŭi rok, currently available from Sech'ang Sŏgwan, 169 pages.

彰善感義錄 Ch'angsŏn Kamŭi rok in the **Hŭimang Series**, IV 317-423.

In addition to the forms given to the title in the texts above, there is 唱善感義錄 Ch'angsŏn Kamŭi rok in the **Tōyō Bunko** catalogue and 昌善感義錄 Ch'angsŏn Kamŭi rok in **Courant**, 895. The translation of the title will vary considerably according to the characters given to it, but until it can be determined which is the best attested or the most suitable to the contents, a rough translation such as "A Record of Good and Justice" will serve.

442. 채련전 Ch'aeryŏn chŏn

Kim Kidong, 596, lists 採蓮傳 Ch'aeryŏn chŏn as a love story in Korean set in China, existing in paperback edition(s) (also page 33), but not made known before.

The only text which I have seen of 18 계화몽 **Kyehwa mong** has two covers. The outside one seems unlikely to have belonged to it originally, and inside that is a damaged cover, which could be original. This bears the title ○蓮○○련○ ? ryŏn ?, and has a picture of some ladies picking lotus flowers out of a pond. Since the little information which Kim Kidong gives on these two stories, pages 596 and 597, is absolutely identical, there is a possibility that these two are titles for the same story. However, I cannot find anything in the text of Kyehwa mong to indicate why it should also be called "The Story of Picking Lotus".

443. 채봉감별곡 Ch'aebong Kambyŏl kok "Ch'aebong's Song of Lament of Being Parted"

In P'yŏngyang, at some time late in the Yi dynasty, the heroine is separated from her lover in order to be married to another, but she runs away, becomes a *kisaeng,* and finds her lover again through her long poem "Lament on Being Parted, to the Autumn Wind", which gives the title to some of the texts below. See **Kim T'aejun,** 230-231, **Kim Kidong,** 482-487 (**1956:** 198-203), **Pak Sŏngŭi,** 449-452, and **Sin Kihyŏng,** 440-443. Kim T'aejun, 96, also states that "one version of Ch'aebong Kambyŏl kok is a revised translation of" story no. 35 in Chin-ku-ch'i-kuan, see **39** 금고기관 **Kŭmgo Kigwan.** Kim Kidong doubts this, and the evidence for it does seem to be slight, especially in view of the comparative lengths of the Chinese and Korean stories and the wholly Korean air of the Korean story, but one would like to know exactly what Kim T'aejun meant by "one version of ..... ".

There is a manuscript (by Hashimoto) at **Harvard** entitled 秋風感別曲 **Ch'up'ung Kambyŏl kok,** "Lament on Being Parted, to the Autumn Wind", dated 1898. This is a long poem, and I have not been able to discover what connection, if any, this has with this story. However, it may be worth noting that a text of a poem of this title antedates considerably any text of the novel which I have been able to find.

1947 exhibition, 221: 彩鳳感別曲 **Ch'aebong Kambyŏl kok,** manuscript, 6 vols (Seoul University). I could not find this in 1962.

秋風感別曲 (츄풍감별곡) **Ch'yup'ung Kambyŏl kok,** currently available from Sech'ang Sŏgwan, 64 pages. I have also seen a copy with the same text, published by Yŏngch'ang Sŏgwan according to the front cover, and obviously dating from before 1945, but missing the back cover.

Advertisements in paperbacks sometimes give both titles separately in the same list.

金起東 **Kim Kidong, ed.:** 彩鳳感別曲 **Ch'aebong Kambyŏl kok** is given in the index in **Hyŏndae Munhak,** 100, April 1963, as having been carried in issue 95, November 1962, but I have not seen it.

彩鳳感別曲 **Ch'aebong Kambyŏl kok** in the **Hŭimang Series,** V 161-210.

챵선감의록 **Ch'yangsyŏn Kamŭi rok,** etc.: see **441** 챵선감의록 **Ch'angsŏn Kamŭi rok**

444. 천고은설 Ch'ŏn'go Ŭnsŏl

1947 exhibition, 148: 千古隱說 Ch'ŏn'go Ŭnsŏl, manuscript, 1 vol. (Yi Haech'ŏng).

445. 천궁몽유록 Ch'ŏn'gung Mongyu rok

See **Mongyu rok Sogo,** 137-138 and 144. Chang Tŏksun's manuscript, 1 vol., 天宮夢遊鍒 Ch'ŏn'gung Mongyu rok, "Record of a Dream Journey to the Heavenly Palace", was shown in the **1961 exhibition,** as item 53.

천도화 Ch'ŏndohwa: see 208 소학사전 So Haksa chŏn

446. 천리춘색 Ch'ŏlli Ch'unsaek

千里春色 천리춘색 Ch'yŏlli Ch'yunsaek, Taesŏng Sŏrim, 1925, 54 pages. The title was advertised by the same publishers in 1929.

The story concerns a family called 안 An in Korean, that is probably either An or Yen in Chinese, in fifteenth century China (Ming, Ch'eng-hua), and is in traditional form, but I have not read enough of it to summarise it with confidence, or to see the relevance of the title, presumably something like "The Beauty of Spring a Thousand Leagues Away", to the story.

447. 천수석 Ch'ŏnsusŏk

텬슈셕 泉水石 T'yŏnsyusyŏk, manuscript, 9 vols. **[Palace]**

Courant, 916: 텬슈셕 天授錫 T'yŏnsyusyŏk, "The Staff Bestowed by Heaven" (title only). The characters given by Courant do not agree with those on the text above, which appear to mean "The Stone in the Spring Water".

448. 청구야담 Ch'ŏnggu Yadam

청구야담 Ch'yŏnggu Yadam, manuscript, 19 vols, title on the cover 靑邱野談 Ch'ŏnggu Yadam, is catalogued as in the Kyujanggak Library at **Seoul University.**

Five stories from this, 귀매 (鬼魅) Kwimae, "The Spirit", 그안해 Kŭ Anhae, "His Wife", 배정승 (拜政丞) Pae-jŏngsŭng, "His Excellency the Minister", 한무변 (한武弁) Han Mubyŏn, "A Military Officer", and 축관장 (逐官長) Ch'yuk Kwanjang, "Chasing out the Magistrate", are quoted in 李秉岐 Yi Pyŏnggi, ed.: 要路院夜話記 Yorowŏn Yahwa ki (乙酉文化社 Ŭryu Munhwasa, Seoul, 1949, and reprints), pages 99-175. Yi Pyŏnggi praises the literary quality of the work, and notes that volume 20 is missing from the text above.

216

There is what appears to be a copy made from that text given as in the **Karam collection**, and another manuscript in three volumes containing *kwŏn* 1-5 (there is one *kwŏn* to each volume of the above texts), which is not described as being in Korean. There are also two manuscripts of the same work given as in the **Ilsa collection**, one of 64 leaves and one of 67 leaves, neither of which is described as being in Korean. The catalogue appears to suggest that the work was compiled in the twentieth century. A manuscript in *hanmun* belonging to Pang Chonghyŏn was shown in the **1947 exhibition**, as item 94, together with the Kyujanggak copy, above. The unidentified manuscript of 58 leaves mentioned by **Courant**, 775, appears also to be in *hanmun*.

Kim T'aejun, 52, couples with this work one called 靑邱笑叢 Ch'ŏnggu Soch'ong (presumably) "Amusing Stories from Korea", which I have not seen mentioned elsewhere. He dates them both as later than 1600.

449. 청년회심곡 Ch'ŏngnyŏn Hoesim kok "The Young Man's Song of Repentance"

In seventeenth century Korea, the young man is beguiled by a pretty face into losing his money and neglecting his sweetheart. His poem, and a reply to it, take up about half the text and lead quickly to a happy ending. See **Kim Kidong**, 487-492.

Kim Kidong, 32 and 487, gives a publication by Sin'gu Sŏrim, 1914, 99 pages, and the title was advertised by the same publishers in 1918 and, together with Pangmun Sŏgwan, in 1923, 1925 and 1932, and also by Yŏngch'ang Sŏgwan and Hanhŭng Sŏrim in 1925, by Kwangdong Sŏguk in 1926, and by Tŏkhŭng Sŏrim in 1935.

靑年悔心曲 청년회심곡 Ch'ŏngnyŏn Hoesim kok, currently available from Sech'ang Sŏgwan, 64 pages.

450. 청루기연 Ch'ŏngnu Kiyŏn

Kim Kidong, 596, lists 靑樓奇緣 Ch'ŏngnu Kiyŏn (presumably) "The Miraculous Destiny of the Green Pavilion [= *Kisaeng* House]" as a love story in Korean, set in China, and existing in paperback edition(s), but not made known before. The title was advertised by Tŏkhŭng Sŏrim in 1923, 1924 and 1935.

청루지열녀 Ch'ŏngnu chi Yŏllyŏ: see **297** 왕경룡전 **Wang Kyŏngnyong chŏn**

451.　청백운 Ch'ŏngbaegun

청빅운 靑白雲 Ch'yŏngbǎegun, manuscript, 10 vols. [Palace]
The title in characters has an obvious meaning, but I have no other information
on the work.

452.　청야만집 Ch'ŏngya Manjip

1947 exhibition, 248: 靑野漫集 Ch'ŏngya Manjip, manuscript, 1 vol. (Yi
Haech'ŏng). There is a much longer work in *hanmun* with the virtually identical title 靑野漫輯 Ch'ŏngya Manjip, compiled in the eighteenth century (according to **Maema Kyōsaku: Kosen Sappu,** II 1104-1105). Both titles presumably
mean something like "A Full Collection of Stories from Korean History", but
I have no means of knowing whether there is any connection between the two.

There is also 靑野談藪 Ch'ŏngya Tamsu, manuscript, 6 vols (vols 1-6), given as
in the **Karam collection**, and not described as being in Korean.

천리춘색 Ch'yŏlli Ch'yunsaek: see **446** 천리춘색 Ch'ŏlli Ch'unsaek

청..... Ch'yŏng....: see 청..... Ch'ŏng.....

453.　초패왕전 Ch'o P'aewang chŏn

Kim T'aejun, 97, gives 楚覇王實記 Ch'o P'aewang Silgi (presumably) "The
Story of the Dictator of Ch'u" as one of the translated selections from Hsi-han
Yen-i (see **174** 서한연의 **Sŏhan Yŏnŭi**). **Kim Kidong**, 210, includes 楚覇王傳 Ch'o
P'aewang chŏn (presumably) "The Story of the Dictator of Ch'u", "which tells
of the wars of the Ch'u-Han period", in a list of works which are partial or
complete translations of Chinese works. Such titles presumably refer to 項羽
Hsiang Yu, who also figures in story no. 4 in **162** 삼설기 **Samsŏlgi**, and in **454**
초한전 Ch'o-Han chŏn.

454.　초한전 Ch'o-Han chŏn "The Ch'u-Han Story"

This tells of the wars of the third century B.C. in China, and is clearly a translation of a Chinese work, perhaps part of Hsi-han Yen-i (see **174** 서한연의
Sŏhan Yŏnŭi), as suggested by **Kim T'aejun**, 97, and **Kim Kidong**, 210.

1947 exhibition, 102: 楚漢傳 Ch'o-Han chŏn, Chŏnju block print, 1 vol. (Cho
Yunje, not shown). **Kim Tonguk** gives the Chŏnju block print, on page 398, as
2 vols, 44, 44 leaves, 丁未孟夏完南龜石里新刊 "newly engraved at Kwisŏngni,
Chŏnju South, in the fourth month of 1907".

楚漢傳 <u>Ch'o-Han chŏn</u>, Hansŏng Sŏgwan, 1918 (reprinted from 1915), 79 pages.

초한전 <u>Ch'o-Han chyŏn</u>, Taesŏng Sŏrim, 1929, 79 pages.

초한전 <u>Ch'o-Han chyŏn</u>, Yŏnghwa Ch'ulp'ansa, probably not earlier than 1951, 79 pages.

초한전 (楚漢傳) <u>Ch'o-Han chŏn</u>, currently available from Sech'ang Sŏgwan, 72 pages.

초한전 <u>Ch'o-Han chŏn</u>, Taejo sa, 1959, 71 pages.

The title has also been advertised by Taech'ang Sŏwŏn and Pogŭp Sŏgwan in 1920, by Chosŏn Tosŏ Chusik Hoesa in 1925, by Tongyang Sŏwŏn in 1925, by Yŏngch'ang Sŏgwan and Hanhŭng Sŏrim in 1925, and by Taesan Sŏrim in 1926.

최고운전 **Ch'oe Koun chŏn**, and

최문헌전 **Ch'oe Munhŏn chŏn**: see 458 최충전 **Ch'oe Ch'ung chŏn**

455. 최보운전 Ch'oe Poun chŏn

최보운전 <u>Ch'oe Poun chyŏn</u>, manuscript, 2 vols, 61, 30 leaves (8 columns, 17 syllables), dated 긔희 (己亥 1899, etc.). Title on the cover 崔保雲傳 <u>Ch'oe Poun chŏn</u> [**Seoul University**]

Kim Kidong, 36, gives 崔寶雲傳 <u>Ch'oe Poun chŏn</u> among the stories existing in manuscript(s) which he was not able to describe, and, page 598, lists 崔報雲傳 <u>Ch'oe Poun chŏn</u> as a story in Korean set in China, existing in manuscript(s) but not make known before. It this is correct, all the versions of the title given above would translate as "The Story of Ts'ui Pao-yun".

456. 최장군전 Ch'oe Changgun chŏn

Kim Kidong, 591, lists 崔將軍傳 <u>Ch'oe Changgun chŏn</u> (presumably) "The Story of General Ts'ui" as a story of a hero, probably in Korean, set in China, which exists in paperback edition(s). He refers to **Yi Nŭngu: Kungmunhak Kaeron**, which only seems to mention it, page 14, also as a paperback publication.

The title was advertised by Taech'ang Sŏwŏn with other publishers in 1918, 1919, and 1920 and 1926.

457. 최척전 Ch'oe Ch'ŏk chŏn

Sin Kihyŏng, 484, lists 최척전 (崔陟傳) Ch'oe Ch'ŏk chŏn (presumably) "The
story of Ts'ui Chih" as (with a query) a love story in Korean set in China. His
source for this information may be **Kim Kidong**, who lists the same, page 597,
but gives no information at all. He does, however, give as the source of his
mention of the title 李明善 Yi Myŏngsŏn: 朝鮮文學史 Chosŏn Munhak sa
(朝鮮文學社 Chosŏn Munhak sa, Seoul, 1948). That work lists it, page 135, as
the title of a novel in *hanmun* by 趙緯韓 Cho Wihan (died 1649), and this information is based probably, on Yi Myŏngsŏn's manuscript in *hanmun*, 1 vol.,
which was shown in the **1947 exhibition** as item 139. There is also a manuscript of 14 leaves in *hanmun*, dated 1621, given as in the **Ilsa collection**. The
catalogue ascribes it to 趙韓·Cho Han, a name which I cannot find elsewhere.

458. 최충전 Ch'oe Ch'ung chŏn

This appears to be the earliest established title of any completely fictionalised
work in Korean about 崔致遠 Ch'oe Ch'iwŏn, the famous scholar-politician of
the late ninth century. Accounts of his life of all degrees of factual accuracy
can be found through the standard works of historical reference, and any complete investigation of the stories below will almost certainly involve considerable purely historical research.

Both Kim T'aejun and Kim Tonguk quote 崔忠傳 Ch'oe Ch'ung chŏn from
Shōsho Kibun, see **Introduction**, §7. 2.

崔忠傳 Ch'oe Ch'ung chŏn, manuscript, 50 leaves (10 columns, 16 syllables),
dated 明治六年癸酉 (1873). [**Ogura collection, Tokyo**]

This copy was made by a student at the Japanese Foriegn Office language
school, from a text owned by his teacher, and has characters added by way of
explanation where necessary.

Petrova, 215: 최충전 崔忠傳 Ch'oe Ch'yung chyŏn, manuscript, 43 leaves (9 columns), in the Aston collection in Leningrad. It is presumably this manuscript
which is "rendered freely" into English in W. G. Aston: Chhoi-chhung, a Corean
Märchen (Transactions of the Asiatic Society of Japan, XXVIII, Tokyo, 1900,
pages 1-31).

1947 exhibition, 179: 崔忠傳 Ch'oe Ch'ung chŏn, movable type, 1 vol.
(T'ongmun'gwan).

See the **Introduction**, §6. 4. 2, for the rather peculiar characteristics of all the T'ongmun'gwan texts shown in this exhibition.

鄭炳昱 Chǒng Pyǒnguk: 崔文獻傳紹介 Ch'oe Munhǒn chǒn Sogae, "Introducing The Story of Ch'oe Munhǒn" (庸齊白樂濬博士還甲記念論文集刊行會 Yongjae Paek Nakchun Paksa Hwan'gap Kinyǒm Nonmun chip Kanhaeng hoe, ed.: 國學論叢 Kukhak Nonch'ong, 思想界社 Sasanggye sa, Seoul, 1955, pages 807-833) reprints, with an introductory description, the text of his manuscript, "probably from early in the seventeenth century", of one story in *hanmun* about Ch'oe Ch'iwǒn. It appears to resemble the story as translated by Aston only in a very general way.

All the texts which I have seen give the name of Ch'oe Ch'iwǒn's father as Ch'ung. In the titles of the texts in Korean this is always written 忠 but Chǒng Pyǒnguk's text gives 冲. Furthermore, 崔冲 Ch'oe Ch'ung, who lived 984-1068, and does not seem to be related in any way to Ch'oe Ch'iwǒn, had the postumous title 文憲 Munhǒn, and Kim Kidong, 196, etc., gives the title of Chǒng Pyǒnguk's text as 崔文憲傳 Ch'oe Munhǒn chǒn, that is "The Story of [this unrelated] Ch'oe Ch'ung". **Kim T'aejun**, 171, gives "崔致遠傳 Ch'oe Ch'iwǒn chǒn, also known as 崔忠傳 Ch'oe Ch'ung chǒn, and incorrectly reported as 崔冲傳 Ch'oe Ch'ung chǒn".

Chǒng Pyǒnguk, in his article, states that he had compared his text with a 崔孤雲傳 Ch'oe Koun chǒn (Koun is the most commonly used *cha* of Ch'oe Cn'iwǒn) "recently published by Sech'ang Sǒgwan", and he finds that "it may perhaps be a publication of a translation into Korean, which has perhaps been handed down, of Ch'oe Munhǒn chǒn", though he does point out two or three differences in the story between the two versions. The title was not available from Sech'ang Sǒgwan in 1962, but it was included in their list of titles published, and also in another put out by Sinmyǒng Sǒrim in 1930.

Kim Kidong, 196-207, describes a 崔孤雲傳 Ch'oe Koun chǒn from a *hanmun* manuscript in his own possession. It seems that the story is very much as in Chǒng Pyǒnguk's text, but that the expression is very different. He mentions a paperback edition in Korean, without identifying it, and quotes the opening words from it, which are one of the conventional openings to *kodae sosǒl*, a formal description of spring, and therefore not very informative.

崔孤雲傳 Ch'oe Koun chǒn in the **Hŭimang Series**, I 161-184, could be a translation of Kim Kidong's manuscript in *hanmun*.

459. 최현전 Ch'oe Hyŏn chŏn

1947 exhibition, 99: 崔玄伊 Ch'oe Hyŏn chŏn, manuscript, 1 vol. (Pang Chonghyŏn). No such title is given as in the **Ilsa collection**. Kim Tonguk quotes 崔賢傳 Ch'oe Hyŏn chŏn from Shōsho Kibun, see **Introduction**, §7. 2. **Kim Kidong**, 598, lists this as a story in Korean set in China, which exists in manuscript(s) (also page 36), but had not been made known before. **Sin Kihyŏng**, 484, suggests that it might be a tale of marvels.

추영대전 **Ch'u Yŏngdae chŏn**: see **250** 양산백전 **Yang Sanbaek chŏn**

추월전 **Ch'uwŏl chŏn**, etc.: see **279** 옥소전 **Okso chŏn**

추풍감별곡 **Ch'up'ung Kambyŏl kok**: see **443** 채봉감별곡 **Ch'aebong Kambyŏl kok**

축관장 **Ch'uk Kwanjang**: see **448** 청구야담 **Ch'ŏnggu Yadam**

춘추열국지 **Ch'unch'u Yŏlgukchi**: see **261** 열국지 **Yŏlgukchi**

460. 춘향전 Ch'unhyang chŏn "The Story of Ch'unhyang"

The story of the faithfulness of Ch'unhyang to her husband is the most widely read today, the most written about, and the most frequently rewritten of all *kodae sosŏl*. Every work on Korean literature, almost every scholarly journal, and most general works on Korea will yield some information on this story, and practically every library contains a text of at least one version of it. Fortunately there are so many good editions of old texts, and it has been so thoroughly studied by **Kim Tonguk** (in his work listed in the Index of Brief References which follows the Introduction) and so well translated by Gale (see below, under **(2) The Sin Chaehyo version**) that it is necessary to list here only the old texts and the most vital references.

(1) Texts in *hanmun* and early references:

春香歌 Ch'unhyang ka, "The Song of Ch'unhyang", a *hanmun* poem of 200 couplets of seven character lines, written by 柳振漢 Yu Chinhan in 1754, is thought to have been taken from a version told by *kwangdae*. Kim Tonguk, 74-81, describes this fully from a text in Seoul University, said to have been taken from a copy of Yu Chinhan's complete works in the possession of his family. I have not seen this text, and cannot find any mention of it in any catalogue, but it is reprinted with notes in Kim Tonguk, 165-193.

Kwan-u-hŭi, stanza 9, refers to this story, see Song Manjae ŭi Kwan-u-hŭi, 103 and 118, as described in the **Introduction**, §7.3.

廣寒樓記 Kwanghallu ki, "Record of the Kwanghan Pavilion", by 水山 Susan (pseudonym), in *hanmun* prose, 8 episodes, texts dated 1874 (or 1934) and 1927, is thought to be a composition of the 1840's, according to **Kim Tonguk**, 81-89. Rather different information is given on a text of the same title in the catalogue of the Kyujanggak Library.

廣寒樓樂府 Kwanghallu Akpu, "Song of the Kwanghan Pavilion", by 尹達善 Yun Talsŏn, a *hanmun* poem of 108 stanzas (4 line stanzas, 7 character lines), written in 1852. There are three manuscripts of it given as in the **Karam collection**, and the full text of it is reprinted in Kim T'aejun's 1939 edition of the Chŏnju block print, see **(6)**, below. One of the copies in the Karam collection has the title on the cover 春娘詞 Hyang-nang sa, "Song of the Maiden Hyang", and another 湖南樂府 Honam Akpu, "Song of Chŏlla", and the third is entitled 湖南廣寒樓樂府 Honam Kwanghallu Akpu, "Song of the Kwanghan Pavilion in Chŏlla". See also **Kim Tonguk**, 102-106.

呂圭亨 Yŏ Kyuhyŏng: 春香傳 Ch'unhyang chŏn, mimeograph, 35 leaves, is given in the catalogue of the Kyujangguk Library, Seoul University, and elsewhere. **Kim Tonguk**, 72, dates it 1915 and describes it as in *hanmun*. (See also **229** 심청전 **Sim Ch'ŏng chŏn.**)

Kim Tonguk, 163, reports that 朴憲鳳 Pak Hŏnbong has a version in *hanmun* manuscript which he is keeping to himself until he can publish it, and quotes, pages 12-15, several less certain or less informative references for the history of the story other than as seen in the texts in Korean. Amongst these the name of the heroine appears as 春陽 Ch'unyang in 1855 and perhaps as 春娘 Ch'un-nang "the maiden Ch'un" before 1801.

(2) The Sin Chaehyo version and derived editions:

See the **Introduction**, §7.3, and P'ansori Palsaeng ko, as described there, pages 250-264.

春香歌 Ch'unhyang ka is given as the first volume of Sin Chaehyo's collected works in the Karam collection. **Yi Pyŏnggi: Kungmunhak Kaeron**, 154-168, contrasts five passages from this with the parallel passages from Oga Chŏnjip (see **Introduction**, §7.3.15).

Kim Tonguk, 162, describes very briefly a manuscript belonging to Pang Chonghyŏn of 40 leaves or more, called 사설春香歌 (申在孝本) Sasŏl Ch'unhyang ka

(Sin Chaehyo pon), as being a copy of Sin Chaehyo's version for male voice, and the first written version in rhythmic style. No such title is given in the **Ilsa collection**, though there are two manuscripts, listed below, under **(3)**, both of which fit the description only partially.

姜漢永 Kang Hanyŏng: 春香歌 Ch'unhyang ka (**Kugŏ Kungmunhak,** 5, June 1953, 15-18, 6, July 1953, 14-19, 7, August 1953, 16-21, and said to be completed in 8 and 9, which I have not seen), reproduces the version for male voice, with some explanatory characters added to the text, and gives an account of the history of the text as taken from a copy made in 1907 by Yu Nongsŏk, see **Introduction,** §7. 3. 14.

Kang Hanyŏng, ed.: 春香歌 Ch'unhyang ka. 新古典社 Sin'gojŏn sa, Seoul, 1959 and 1960, and 民協出版社 Minhyŏp Ch'ulp'ansa, Seoul, 1962. 316 pages. This has the version for male voice with very full notes, and the version for boy's voice without notes of any sort. (**Yi Pyŏnggi: Kungmunhak Kaeron,** 154, states that there was third version for woman's voice, but that this is now lost.)

春香傳 춘향전 Ch'unhyang chŏn, currently available from Sech'ang Sŏgwan, 62 pages, is a fairly faithful reproduction of the Sin Chaehyo male voice version in modernised spelling, and I suspect that, in spite of the given date of publication (1952), it is probably a pirate copy of Kang Hanyŏng's publication.

James S. Gale, translated: Choon Yang (Korea Magazine, vol. I, no. 9 - vol. II, no. 7, September 1917—July 1918) reads as a remarkably faithful translation of the same version. The preface states that the translations was made "a year or more" after a performance of this story had been given "at the Chosen Hotel" by "three Korean singers", but he does not state where he got his text from. Several Korean authorities have assured me that this is a translation of Yi Haejo's modern version, see (7), below, but I have not been able to check this.

(3) Other manuscripts:

Courant, 817: 남원고ᄉ 南原古詞 **Namwŏn Kosă**, "An Old Song of Namwŏn", manuscript, 5 vols, dated 甲子 (1864) in vol. 1, and 己巳 (1869) in vol. 5, in Paris.

This appears to be the oldest extant text in Korean of this story (Courant: "with further developments"), and it is a great pity that no more information on it is available. Its size, the widely differing dates of the first and last volumes, and Courant's comment all suggest that it may be a lending library copy.

별춘향전 Pyŏl Ch'yunhyang chyŏn, manuscript by Hashimoto, 95 leaves, dated
丁酉 (1897). Titles on the cover 別春香傳 Pyŏl Ch'yunhyang chŏn and
成氏婦人烈女錄 Sŏng-ssi Puin Yŏllyŏ rok, "Record of the Faithful Wife, Miss
Sŏng". [**Harvard**]

A glance showed that this was not in the tradition of the Seoul and Ansŏng block
prints, but it has not yet been investigated.

1947 exhibition, 132: 春香傳 Ch'unhyang chŏn, manuscript, 1 vol. (Yi Myŏngsŏn).

Although this appears to be lost now, and was apparently in any case undated, I
place it here because of Kim Tonguk's comment on the next text. In describing
this text, **Kim Tonguk**, 121-131, reports that it was of 93 leaves, that it was reprinted in 文章 Munjang (a literary journal published by 文章社 Munjang sa,
Keijō), vol. 2, no. 10, 1941, and that it was an unadorned transmission of the
story.

春香傳 Ch'unhyang chŏn, manuscript, 40 leaves, dated 己亥 (1899), given as in
the **Ilsa collection**.

Kim Tonguk, 131-133, describing this, gives its date as 己酉 (1909), and is
almost categorical that it is a copy of the last text.

춘향전 Ch'yunhyang chyŏn, lending library manuscript, 10 vols, about 30 leaves
(11 columns, 14 syllables) per volume, dated 경주 (庚子 1900) in vol. 8, 갑지
(?甲辰 1904) in vol. 6, 괴유 (己酉 1909) in vols 1-4, and 신히 (辛亥 1911) in
vols 5, 7, 9 and 10. Title on the cover 春香傳 Ch'unhyang chŏn. [**Tōyō Bunko**]

This has not yet been investigated, and it is about four times as long as any
other text which I have seen.

Kim Tonguk, 151-157, describes a manuscript which he calls 中 (學均)
本別春香歌 "The Sin (Hakkyun) text Pyŏl Ch'unhyang ka", giving the date as
己酉 (1909), but no other bibliographical information.

別春香傳 Pyŏl Ch'unhyang chŏn, manuscript, 105 leaves (12 columns, 17-23 syllables), reported as owned by Cho Yunje in his study of the variant texts (see
his edition of the Chŏnju block print, **(6)**, below, and also **Kim Tonguk**, 147-150).
Cho Yunje suggests that it may have been a draft for a publication which never
appeared.

別春香歌 Pyŏl Ch'unhyang ka, manuscript, 80 leaves (10 columns, 26 syllables),
dated 丁巳 (1917). A *p'ansori* version in mixed script. [**Chŏng Pyŏnguk**]

Kim Tonguk describes this briefly, pages 150-151. His information differs from that in the notes which I made on it in several details. He also describes very fully, pages 195-210, the contents of another manuscript owned by Chŏng Pyŏnguk, which I have no record of having seen, but which is apparently relatively recent.

具滋均 Ku Chagyun: 高大本춘향전 Kodae pon Ch'yunhyang chyŏn, "The Korea University Text of Ch'unhyang chŏn" (Seoul, 高麗大學校 Koryŏ Taehakkyo, Korea University, 文理科大學 Mullikwa Taehak, Liberal Arts College: 文理論集 Mulli Nonjip, The Humanities, 3, December 1958, 417-444) reprints, with an introductory note, 춘향전 Ch'yunhyang chyŏn, manuscript in mixed script, 54 leaves (10-11 columns, 25-26 syllables). He also reports that is was reprinted, but not very accurately, in Munjang (see above), April 1941. See also **Kim Tonguk**, 133-140.

春香傳 Ch'unhyang chŏn, manuscript, 41 leaves, given as in the **Ilsa collection**.

Kim Tonguk, 159-162, describes the contents of a manuscript which he owns himself. He gives the title as 春香歌 Ch'unhyang ka, but no other bibliographical information, apart from a comment that "it seems that it is not so old". He also comments that looks like a copy of a (Chŏnju) block print, and this is confirmed by his reproduction of the first page.

Kim Tonguk, 71, listing 古本春香傳 Kobon Ch'unhyang chŏn [=(고본) 춘향전 (Kobon) Ch'yunhyang chyŏn, "The Story of Ch'unhyang (an old Text)", 新文舘 Sinmun'gwan, 1913, 2, 240 pages, author 崔昌善 Ch'oe Ch'angsŏn preface by 南岳主人 Namak Chuin (= 崔南善 Ch'oe Namsŏn)], notes that 李熙昇 Yi Hŭisŭng told him that Ch'oe Namsŏn recollected that he had only added a preface to the text of an old manuscript in producing this edition. The text has characters added.

(4) Seoul block prints and derived editions:

춘향전 Ch'unhyang chyŏn, 30 leaves, 孝橋新刊 "newly engraved at Hyogyo". **[Harvard]**

Courant, 816, gives the same, but no colophon, as in Paris, etc., and **Petrova**, 207, gives the same (no colophon) as in the Aston collection in Leningrad.

춘향전 Ch'yunhyang chyŏn. 翰南書林 Hannam Sŏrim, Keijō, 1917 and 1920. 16 leaves. A lithograph of a Seoul block print, apparently.

Kim Tonguk, 393, also gives a 23 leaf Seoul block print. Of the Seoul block prints, only the 16 leaf edition, and perhaps only a lithograph of that, seems to have been studied (see **Kim Tonguk**, 91-98). It was reprinted in **Kugŏ Kungmun-hak**, 2-5, December 1952—June 1953, and again, this time with notes and an introduction by Ku Chagyun in Mulli Nonjip (see **(3)** above), 3, December 1958, pages 319-416, and there is also a mimeographed copy of it in 金根洙 Kim Kŭnsu, compiled: 小説資料集成 Sosŏl Charyo Chipsŏng, no publisher, no date, pages 3-34.

(5) Ansŏng block print:

춘향전 Ch'yunhyang chyŏn, 20 leaves. Title on the cover 杶乔傳 Ch'unhyang chŏn. [Tōyō **Bunko**]

This appears to follow the Seoul block print very closely, and is reported to have been reissued in 1912 by 北村書舖 Pukch'on Sŏp'o, Ansŏng. See **Kim Tonguk**, 98-102 and 396.

(6) Chŏnju block print and derived editions:

李秉岐 Yi Pyŏnggi's copy of a Chŏnju block print entitled 別春香傳 Pyŏl Ch'unhyang chŏn was lost during the Korean War. It was at one time thought to have been the oldest text of the story in Korean, and it was on the basis of reports of this text that Ch'unhyang chŏn came to be regarded as "an eighteenth century novel". No precise description of it was published while it was still in existence, and all that is known for certain about it now is that no complete copy of it has been seen by literary historians who are writing today. See **Kim Tonguk**, 89-91. Two defective block prints are given as in the **Karam collection**, but they would appear to be Seoul block prints.

열여춘향슈절가 Yŏryo Ch'unhyang Syujyŏl ka, "The Song of the Chastity of the Faithful Wife Ch'unhyang", two vols, 45, 39 leaves.

This is the only Chŏnju block print known now. Many copies exist, and one is reproduced in the **Ewha Series**, II 1-168, with a note 433-438. See **Kim Tonguk**, 140-147. He suggests that the first volume is a re-engraving and later than the second volume, and reports that printings were made from these blocks continuously until they were destroyed in the Korean War. The earliest date that has been suggested for them is 1870, but it is not clear what evidence there is for this. Some copies have the colophon 完酉溪書舖 "Sŏgye Sŏp'o, Chŏnju", and some do not, and some copies printed after 1910 are dated (for instance, Kim Tonguk, 142, gives one by 興社書舖 Hŭngsa Sŏp'o, 1912, and the copy in the **Karam collection** is given as by 多佳書舖 Taga Sŏp'o, 1916).

The story in this text is clearly derived from a *p'ansori* version, and there seems to be no reason at all to date this version of the story as earlier than Sin Chaehyo's. There has been an unusually high number of good scholarly editions of this text:

金台俊 Kim T'aejun, ed.: 原本春香傳 Wŏnbon Ch'unhyang chŏn, "The Original Text of the Story of Ch'unhyang". 學藝社 Hagye sa, Keijō, 1939. 165 pages.

This also prints the *hanmun* text of Kwanghallu Akpu, see (1) above.

原本烈女春香守節歌 Wŏnbon Yŏllyŏ Ch'unhyang Sujŏl ka. 乙酉文化社 Ŭryu Munhwa sa, Seoul, 1947. 96 pages. With illustrations.

板本烈女春香守節歌 P'anbon Yŏllyŏ Ch'unhyang Sujŏl ka. 珍書刊行會 Chinsŏ Kanhaeng hoe, Seoul, 1949. 45, 39 leaves, 6 pages. The 6 pages are an explanatory essay by 金三不 Kim Sambul, which I have not yet been able to study in detail. The main text is reprinted from blocks which the editor found in Chŏnju after 1945, but which seem to have been lost in the Korean War.

金思燁 Kim Sayŏp, ed.: 原本春香傳 Wŏnbon Ch'unhyang chŏn. 大洋出版社 Tae-yang Ch'ulp'ansa, Seoul, 1952 and reprints. 229 pages.

李家原 Yi Kawŏn, ed.: 春香傳 Ch'unhyang chŏn. 正音社 Chŏngŭm sa, Seoul, 1957. 320 pages.

趙潤濟 Cho Yunje, ed.: 春香傳 Ch'unhyang chŏn. 乙酉文化社 Ŭryu Munhwasa, Seoul, 1957 and reprints. 274 pages.

This also reprints his article 春香傳異本考 Ch'unhyang chŏn Ibon ko, "A Study of the Variant Texts of The Story of Ch'unhyang" from 震檀學報 Chindan Hakpo, journal of the 震檀學會 Chindan Hakhoe, Keijō (now Seoul), 11, December 1939, 94-134, and 12 (reported to be 1940, but I have not seen that issue). **Kim Tonguk,** 73, gives the first edition of this text as published by 博文文庫 Pangmun Mun'go, 1939, and the preface in the edition of 1957 is dated 1938.

(7) Miscellaneous:
The Chŏnju block print seems to be the basis for many modern reprints of the story, but with so many good editions available, there seems to be no point in listing the paperbacks here. There have also been very many rewritings, including some by Korea's best known modern writers, such as 李海朝 Yi Haejo and 李光洙 Yi Kwangsu. Yi Haejo's version (the earliest edition I have seen of it is by Hoedong Sŏgwan, 1911) is entitled 獄中花 춘향가 Okchunghwa, Ch'yunhyang ka, "The Flower in Prison", "The Song of Ch'unhyang" and the first of these is used in other paperback editions of this story also.

Apart from Gale's translation, given above, under (2), I have only seen para-phrases of the story in English, for instance by H. N. Allen in his "Korean Tales", and "The Waiting Wife" by Chai Hong Sim (沈載弘 Sim Chaehong).

Ch'unhyang chŏn is mentioned in relation to many other stories, but one often has the impression that the reasoning is that it is such a great story that any-thing resembling it must be inspired by it. This is, of course, a reasonable supposition or hypothesis, but few concrete examples are given to prove it.

461. 충렬소오의 Ch'ungnyŏl So-o-ŭi "The Five Younger Gallants"

충렬쇼오의 忠烈小五義 Ch'yungnyŏl Syo-o-ŭi, manuscript, 31 vols. [Palace]
The Chinese novel of this title, Chung-lieh Hsiao-wu-i, is a work of 1890.

462. 충렬협의전 Ch'ungnyŏl Hyŏbŭi chŏn "The Loyal and Gallant Men"

츙렬협의젼 忠烈俠義傳 Ch'yungnyŏl Hyŏbŭi chyŏn, manuscript, 40 vols. [Palace]
The Chinese work of this title, Chung-lieh Hsia-i-chuan, is a work of 1879.

충의수호지 Ch'ungŭi Suho chi: see 222 수호지 Suho chi

취미삼선록 Ch'wimi Samsŏn nok: see 161 삼선기 Samsŏn ki

463. 취승루 Ch'wisŭng nu

취승누 取勝樓 Ch'ywisŭng nu, manuscript, 30 vols. [Palace]
Kim Kidong, 595, lists 取勝樓記 Ch'wisŭng nu ki as a love story in Korea set in in China, existing in manuscript(s). He gives his source "李秉岐 Yi Pyŏnggi introduced". I have not found any published reference to it by Yi Pyŏnggi.

츄풍감별곡 Ch'yup'ung Kambyŏl kok: see 443 채봉감별곡 Ch'aebong Kambyŏl kok

축관장 Ch'yuk Kwanjang: see 448 청구야담 Ch'ŏnggu Yadam

츈츄녈국지 Ch'yunch'yu Nyŏlgukchi, etc.: see 261 열국지 Yŏlgukchi

츈향전 Ch'yunhyang chyŏn: see 460 춘향전 Ch'unhyang chŏn

충 렬..... Ch'yungnyŏl.....: see 충렬..... Ch'ungnyŏl.....

츙의슈호지 Ch'yungŭi Syuho chi: see 222 수호지 Suho chi

취미삼션녹 Ch'ywimi Samsyŏn nok: see 161 삼선기 Samsŏn ki

취승누 Ch'ywisŭng nu: see 463 취승루 Ch'wisŭng nu

464. 칠선기봉전 **Ch'ilsŏn Kibong chŏn**

1947 exhibition, 166: 七仙奇逢傳 Ch'ilsŏn Kibong chŏn (presumably) "The Mira-culous Encounter of the Seven Fairies", manuscript, 4 vols. (Kim Sambul).

465. 콩쥐팥쥐 **K'ongjwi P'atchwi** "K'ongjwi and P'atchwi"

K'ongjwi is the daughter of a first wife and P'atchwi the daughter of a second wife, and the story is of several incidents in which K'ongjwi is unfairly treated by her step-mother, of the killing of K'ongjwi by P'atchwi and her mother, and all of being made known to the father by magic. See **Kim T'aejun**, 127-129, **Kim Kidong**, 326-330 (1956: 305-308), **Pak Sŏngŭi**, 299-301, and **Sin Kihyŏng**, 313-314. All describe it as a typical Korean folk tale, mention a similar story from T'ang China, and comment on the similarity of one episode to the "Cinde-rella" story.

This last aspect is studied in 張德順 Chang Tŏksun: "Cinderella" 와 "콩쥐팥쥐", " 'Cinderella' and K'ongjwi P'atchwi" (**Kugŏ Kungmunhak**, 16, May 1957, 123-130), and Chang Tŏksun also introduces 콩쥐팥쥐 K'ongjwi P'atchwi in the **Hŭimang Series**, III 261-278.

Kim Kidong, 31 and 326, gives a publication by Taech'ang Sŏwŏn, 1919, 36 pages.

466. 쾌심편 **K'waesim p'yŏn**

쾌심편 快心篇 K'waesim p'yŏn, manuscript, 32 vols. [**Palace**] The title presum-ably means "Composition to Gladden the Heart".

태상감응편 T'aesang Kamŭng p'yŏn: see 126 백학선전 Paekhaksŏn chŏn

467. 태원지 **T'aewŏn chi**

태원지 太原誌 T'aewŏn chi, manuscript, 4 vols. [**Palace**] Recent press reports of work done on the Palace collection also classify this as a *sosŏl*.

태종전 T'aejong chŏn: see 83 당태종전 Tang T'aejong chŏn

텬도화 T'yŏndohwa: see 208 소학사전 So Haksa chŏn

텬슈셕 T'yŏnsyusyŏk: see 447 천수석 Ch'ŏnsusŏk

468. 토끼전 T'okki chŏn "The Story of the Hare"

The hare is enticed to the palace of the Dragon King by a turtle in order that his liver might be used to cure the king's illness. The hare persuades them that he has left his liver on dry land for safety, goes back for it, and so makes his escape. See Kim T'aejun, 131-134, **Kim Kidong**, 156-161 (1956: 361-365), **Pak Sŏngŭi**, 301-307, and **Sin Kihyŏng**, 367-376. All call it Korea's most popular folk tale, and mention similar stories from India and from elsewhere in the Far East. In the versions which I have read closely, the satire appears to be gentle and general, rather than pointed.

Kwan-u-hŭi, stanza 19, is evidence of the currency of the story in the repertoire of the *kwangdae* early in the nineteenth century, see Song Manjae ŭi Kwan-u-hŭi, 107 and 118, and also P'ansori Palsaeng ko, 282-283, as described in the **Introduction**, §7.3. This was one of the *p'ansori* stories rewritten by Sin Chaehyo, and 兎鱉歌 T'obyŏl ka, "Song of the Hare and the Turtle", is given as in vol. 5 of his works, also described in the Introduction, §7.3. **Yi Pyŏnggi**: **Kungmunhak Kaeron**, 149, also gives 토끼타령 T'okki T'aryŏng, "Ballad of the Hare", and 水宮歌 Sugung ka, "Song of the Water Palace", as alternative titles for the story.

中山望月傳 즁산망월젼 Chyung-san Mangwŏl chyŏn, "The Story of the Moon-viewing on Chung-san" [Chung-san is where the turtle is told that the hare lives], 兎碩士傳 T'o Sŏksa chŏn, "The Story of Mr Hare", 톡거젼 T'okkŭi chyŏn (all these titles are on the title leaf), manuscript, 41 leaves, copy made by Hashimoto in 明治廿八 (1895) of a text dated 임진 (壬辰 1892, etc.). Title on the cover 듕산망월젼 Tyung-san Mangwŏl chyŏn. [**Harvard**]

별쥬부젼 Pyŏl Chyubu chyŏn, "The Story of the Turtle-in-waiting", manuscript by Hashimoto, 22 (+33) leaves (14 columns, 27 syllables). The 33 leaves are a copy of **229** 심청젼 Sim Ch'ŏng chŏn made in 1897. [Harvard]

토긔젼 T'ogŭi chyŏn, manuscript, 42 leaves, dated 癸卯(1903), given as in the **Karam collection**.

Title on the cover 鱉主簿傳 Pyŏl Chubu chŏn, manuscript in several hands, 29 leaves (irregular), dated 을ㅅ (乙巳 1905). Date on the cover 庚戌 (1910). [**Chŏng Pyŏnguk**]

톳기젼 T'otki chyŏn, manuscript, 23 leaves (12-14 columns, 18-19 syllables). Title on the cover 툇기젼 T'oetki chyŏn, date on the cover 신히 (辛亥 1911, etc.). [**Chŏng Pyŏnguk**] Chŏng Pyŏnguk thought that the paper might just allow dating the text 1851.

1961 exhibition, 81: 별쥬부젼 Pyŏl Chyubu chyŏn, manuscript, 1 vol. (National Library). The catalogue noted: "Regarded as a *p'ansori* text of the *kwangdae*".

繁兎歌 Pyŏlt'o ka, manuscript, 44 leaves, given as in the **Karam collection**.

1947 exhibition, 77: 兎鼈歌 T'obyŏl ka, manuscript, 1 vol. (Song Sŏkha), and, 101: 鼈主傳 Pyŏl Chu chŏn, manuscript, 1 vol. (Cho Yunje, not shown), manuscript (Yi Myŏngsŏn), and manuscript in mixed script (Pang Chonghyŏn). The last is not given as in the **Ilsa collection**.

불로초 Pulloch'o, "The Herb of Eternal Youth", Yuil Sŏgwan, 1912, 56 pages.

토끼傳 T'okki chŏn, Sin'gu Sŏrim, 1913, 93 pages, reported by **Kim Kidong**, 30 and 156.

별쥬부젼 繁主簿傳 Pyŏl Chyubu chyŏn, no publisher, not dated (probably about 1920), 109 pages.

繁主簿傳 별쥬부젼 Pyŏl Chyubu chyŏn, 兎의肝 T'o ŭi Kan, "The Hare's Liver", Tŏkhŭng Sŏrim, 1925.

繁主簿傳 별쥬부젼 Pyŏl Chyubu chyŏn, 66 pages, and 불로초 Pulloch'o, 34 pages, both currently available from Sech'ang Sŏgwan. I also have a note that there was an edition by Chungang Insŏgwan, but no note of the source of the information.

토끼傳 T'okki chŏn in the **Hŭimang Series**, I 281-320.

Kim T'aejun, 131 and 134, gives 兎生員傳 T'o Saengwŏn chŏn, "The Story of Mr. Hare", as an alternative title, and also 兎鼈山水錄 토별산수록 T'obyŏl Sansu rok, "The Record of the Hare and the Turtle on the Mountain and in the Sea", as a title for a version "current everywhere". **Kim Kidong**, 156, gives the latter as of a *hanmun* text, and 鼈兎傳 Pyŏlt'o chŏn as the title of another *hanmun* text. Courant, 925: 토긔젼 T'o Kŭi chyŏn, "The Story of T'o Ki" (title only) is presumably this story.

퉁의슈호뎐 T'yungŭi Syuho tyŏn: see 222 수호지 Suho chi

469. 파수록 **P'asu rok**

劉昌惇 Yu Ch'angdon: 古語辭典 Koŏ Sajŏn (東國文化社 Tongguk Munhwasa, Seoul, 1955, page 675) and 최현배 Ch'oe Hyŏnbae: 한글갈 Han'gŭl Kal (정음사 Chŏngŭm sa, Seoul, 1961, page 78) give 罷睡錄 P'asu rok (presumably) "Record to Drive away Sleep" as the title of a *sosŏl*, and inclusion in these works would seem to imply that it exists in Korean. However, all the texts, e.g. in the **Karam collec-tion, Yi Nŭngu: Kungmunhak Kaeron, 6,Maema Kyōsaku: Kosen Sappu, III 1638,** etc., appear to be in *hanmun*. The source for the above mentions may be **Kim T'aejun,** 160. The other work mentioned there, 選諺篇 Sŏnŏn p'yŏn, also appears to exist only in *hanmun*.

470. 팔장사전 P'al Changsa chŏn

Kim Kidong, 601, lists 八將士傳 P'al Changsa chŏn (presumably) "The Story of the Eight Military Men" as a story in Korean set in China, existing in paperback edition(s), but not made known before. It is mentioned by **Kim T'aejun,** page 245, and the title was advertised by Yŏngch'ang Sŏgwan and Hanhŭng Sŏrim in 1925.

471. 평등관 P'yŏng-dŭng-gwan

1947 exhibition, 181: 平等觀 P'yŏng-dŭng-gwan, manuscript, 1 vol. (T'ong-mun'gwan). See the **Introduction,** §6.4.2, for the peculiar characteristics of the T'ongmun'gwan texts shown in this exhibition.

472. 평산냉연 P'yŏng San Naeng Yŏn

평산닝연 平山冷燕 P'yŏng San Naeng Yŏn, manuscript, 10 vols. [Palace]

This is presumably a translation of the Chinese novel P'ing Shan Leng Yen, a story of two talented girls, Shan and Leng, and the two talented men, P'ing and Yen, whom they marry. See Lu Hsun: A Brief History of Chinese Fiction, Foreign Languages Press, Peking, 1959, pages 248-251, and **Kim T'aejun,** 96.

평서록 P'yŏngsŏ rok: see 227 신미록 Sinmi rok

473. 평요기 P'yŏngyo ki

평요긔 平妖記 P'yŏngyo kŭi, manuscript, 9 vols. [**Palace**]

I have no note on the contents of this text, but the title appears to mean "Re-cord of the Suppression of Sorcery". Lu Hsun: A Brief History of Chinese Fiction, Foreign Languages Press, Peking, 1959, pages 198, ff., etc., refers to a type of story which arose in Ming, and which he calls "on the struggle between gods and devils" (this could include 113 문창진군탕평록 Munch'ang Chin'gun T'angp'yŏng nok), but which often seem to tell the stories of religious risings. Several of these have titles very similar to this one.

474. 포공연의 **P'o-gong Yŏnŭi**

포공연의 包公演義 <u>P'o-gong Yŏnŭi</u>, manuscript, 9 vols. [**Palace**]

This is presumably a translation of a Chinese work about 包拯 Pao Cheng, the magistrate-detective of the eleventh century who is famed in Chinese fiction, but I did not examine its contents.

포쇄별감 **P'oswae Pyŏlgam**: see 256 어우야담 **Ŏu Yadam**

475. 하씨선행후대록 **Ha-ssi Sŏnhaeng Hudae rok**

하시션힝후딕록 河氏善行後代錄 <u>Ha-ssi Syŏnhăeng Hudăe rok</u>, manuscript, 33 vols. [**Palace**]

Courant, 872: 하시션힝록 河氏善行錄 <u>Ha-si Syŏnhăeng nok</u>, "Record of the Good Acts of Ha" (title only). **Kim T'aejun**, 161, has the same in a list of titles of this type which seems to be taken largely from Courant. 河 is not usual as a surname in either China or Korea.

476. 하진양문록 **Ha Chin Yangmun nok** "Record of the Two Families Ho and Ch'en"

Set in tenth century China (Sung, T'ai-tsung), a long story of the fortunes of the two families, centred mainly on the love of a girl of the Ho family and a boy of the Ch'en family who are separated, both reach high military office, and are reunited. See **Kim Kidong**, 440-445, who admires it greatly and clearly regards it as a major Korean work. On the other hand **Kim T'aejun**, 159-160 and 229, appears to have regarded it as imitative.

하진냥문녹 河陳兩門錄 <u>Ha Chin Nyangmun nok</u>, manuscript, 25 vols. [**Palace**]

Petrova, 221 (also illustration 5), gives exactly the same, total 801 leaves (10 columns, 19 syllables), as in the Aston collection in Leningrad. **Courant**, 911, gives the title only.

하진양문녹 <u>Ha Chin Yangmun nok</u>, lending library manuscript, 29 vols, 915 leaves (11 columns, 15 syllables) in all, dated 무신 (戊申 1908) in vols 1-19 and 21-28 and 긔유 (己酉 1909) in vol. 20. Vol. 29 is undated. Title on the cover 河陳兩門錄 <u>Ha Chin Yangmun nok</u>. [**Tōyō Bunko**]

河陳兩門錄 하진양문록 <u>Ha Chin Yangmun nok</u>, 快齋編 "compiled by K'waejae [Pak Kŏnhoe]", Tongmi Sŏsi, 1915, 3 vols, 213, 167, 117 pages. (Kim Kidong seems to have used this or a very similar edition for his description, as above.)

477. 한강현전 Han Kanghyŏn chŏn

韓江玄傳 한강현젼 <u>Han Kanghyŏn chyŏn</u>, manuscript, 51 leaves (12 columns, 23 syllables), dated 긔히 (己亥 1899). [**Seoul University**]

The title presumably contains the name of the hero, but I have no note of the contents, have not found any mention of the work elsewhere, and cannot even say whether the hero is to be taken as Korean or Chinese. At least it seems that he is not historical.

> 한냥본긔 **Hannyang Pon'gŭi**: see **483** 한양본기 **Hanyang Pon'gi**
>
> 한당몽긔 **Handang mong kŭi**: see **291** 옥호빙심 **Okho Pingsim**
>
> 한듕록 **Handyung nok**, etc.: see **485** 한즁록 **Hanjung nok**

478. 한몽룡전 Han Mongnyong chŏn

Kim Kidong, 598, lists 韓夢龍傳 <u>Han Mongnyong chŏn</u> as a story which exists in paperback edition(s) (also page 32), but had not been made known before. **Sin Kihyŏng**, 485, describes it as a love story set in China. If this is true, the title may be translated "The Story of Han Meng-lung".

> 한무변 **Han Mubyŏn**: see **448** 청구야담 **Ch'ŏnggu Yadam**

479. 한문충의록 Han-mun Ch'ungŭi rok

Courant, 893: 한문충의록 韓門忠義錄 <u>Han-mun Ch'yungŭi rok</u>, "The Loyalty of the Han Family" (title only). **Kim T'aejun**, 161, in his list of titles of this type which seems to be taken largely from Courant, has 韓門忠孝錄 <u>Han-mun Ch'ung-hyo rok</u>, "Record of the Loyalty and Filial Piety of the Han Family". **Kim Kidong**, 599, quotes this from Kim T'aejun, describing it as a moral tale set in China, existing in manuscript(s).

> 한시..... **Han-si.....**: see 한씨..... **Han-ssi.....**

480. 한씨보응록 Han-ssi Poŭng nok

Kim Kidong. 598, lists 韓氏報應錄 <u>Han-ssi Poŭng nok</u> as a story existing in paperback edition(s) which had not been made known before. **Sin Kihyŏng**, 485, describes it (with a query) as a love story in Korean, set in China. **Kim T'aejun**, 248, describes it as a "New Novel" by 李海朝 Yi Haejo. Chosŏn Tosŏ Chusik Hoesa advertised a 韓氏報恩錄 <u>Han-ssi Poŭn nok</u> in 1925.

481. 한씨수연쌍룡기봉 Han-ssi Suyŏn Ssangnyong Kibong

Kim Kidong, 595, lists 韓氏壽筵雙龍奇逢 Han-ssi Suyŏn Ssangnyong Kibong (pre-sumably) "The Miraculous Encounter of the Two Dragons at the Party for Old Han" as a love story in Korean set in China, existing in manuscript(s). He gives as his source " 李秉岐 Yi Pyŏnggi introduced". I have not been able to find any published reference to it by Yi Pyŏnggi, but **Courant**, 836, gives a title which is so close that there is nothing to be gained by listing it separately: 한시슈현쌍룡긔봉 韓氏秀賢雙龍奇逢 Han-si Syuhyŏn Ssangnyong Kŭibong, "The Miraculous Encounter of the Sage Han and the Two Dragons".

482. 한씨팔룡 Han-ssi P'allyong

Courant, 833: 한시팔룡 韓氏八龍 Han-si P'allyong, "The Eight Dragons of the Han Family" (title only).

483. 한양본기 Hanyang Pon'gi

1947 exhibition, 157: 한냥본긔 Hannyang Pon'gŭi, manuscript, 1 vol. (Yi Hae-ch'ŏng). The best sense seems to be given by taking 한냥 as 한양 (= 漢陽 Hanyang, a Chinese place name which is also used for Seoul).

484. 한조삼성기봉 Hanjo Samsŏng Kibong

한조삼성긔봉 Hanjo Samsyŏng Kŭibong, 漢朝三姓 Hanjo Samsŏng, manuscript, 14 vols. [**Palace**]

The title appears to mean "(The Miraculous Encounter of the) Three Families of the Han Dynasty"

485. 한중록 Hanjung nok

The present works derive from the autobiography begun in 1795, the year of her sixtieth birthday, and completed in four stages over ten years by 惠慶宮洪氏 Miss Hong of the Hyegyŏng Palace, wife of 思悼世子 Crown Prince Sado. The work its writer, her husband, and his tragic death in 1762 are all described fully in the standard historical works. There is an excellent annotated edition by Kim Tonguk, listed below, and the work is also discussed and described in **Kim Kidong**, 364-368 (1956:143-145), **Pak Sŏngŭi**, 390-398, and **Sin Kihyŏng**, 417-421.

236

한둥만뇩 Handyung Mannok (usually taken as 만록 Mallok), manuscript, 3 vols, dated 高宗五年 (1901), according to the catalogue of the **Ilsa collection**. I saw this briefly in the **1961 exhibition**, as item 76.

한중록 Hanjung nok, manuscript, 6 vols, title on the cover 恨中錄 Hanjung nok, given as in the **Karam collection**.

李秉岐 Yi Pyŏnggi, ed.: 恨中錄 Hanjung nok, 白楊堂 Paegyang tang, Seoul, 1947, 165 pages, is given in many bibliographies. I have not seen it, but it is said to be based on the manuscript last listed above. It is also said by several sources that part of that same manuscript was reproduced in 閔丙燾 Min Pyŏngdo, ed.: 朝鮮歷代女流文集 Chosŏn Yŏktae Yŏryu Munjip "Collected Writings of Women through the Ages in Korea" (乙酉文化社 Ŭryu Munhwasa, Seoul, 1950), but I have not seen that either.

1961 exhibition, 75: 한듕녹 Hanjyung nok, manuscript, 6 vols (Kim Tonguk).

金東旭 Kim Tonguk and 李秉岐 Yi Pyŏnggi, ed.: 한듕록 Handyung nok (閑中漫錄 Hanjung Mallok). 民衆書館 Minjung Sŏgwan, Seoul, 1961. 25, 595 pages.

This is the finest edition of any *kodae sosŏl* that I have seen. The main text is that of Pang Chonghyŏn's manuscript, above, variant readings in Yi Pyŏnggi's and Kim Tonguk's manuscripts, above, are noted, a translation into modern Korean is given on facing pages, and there are also notes on the interpretation. There is an introduction and a description of the variant texts by 金用淑 Kim Yongsuk. She gives the date of Kim Tonguk's manuscript as 1919, and states that Yi Pyŏnggi's manuscript is not nearer to the original than Pang Chonghyŏn's. She also relates the *kwŏn* of each of these three texts to the four stages of the original composition, and mentions two versions in *hanmun*, 閑中漫錄 Hanjung Mallok in the National Library and 泣血錄 Uphyŏl lok, "Record of Weeping Blood" (manuscript, 55 leaves) in the Kyujanggak Library, Seoul University, the latter a translation of about one third of the original work.

1947 exhibition, 89: 恨中錄 Hanjung nok, manuscript (Kim Kyŏngch'un, not shown). I have not seen any other reference to this. Yi Pyŏnggi's manuscript, above, was shown at the same number in this exhibition.

한듕만일록 Hanjyung Manillok, manuscript, from the 孟峴 Maenghyŏn royal household, 6 vols, 42, 40, 37, 38, 36, 36 leaves (12 columns, 22 syllables), dated 신유 (辛酉 1921). [**Chŏng Pyŏnguk**]

Each two successive volumes seem to form one *kwŏn*. This text was not known when the annotated editions above were produced.

閑中錄 <u>Hanjung nok</u> in the **Hŭimang Series**, III 279-429.

(A 閑中隨錄 <u>Hanjung Surok</u>, manuscript, 84 leaves, "of the mid-nineteenth century" is also given as in the **Ilsa collection**, but separately from the above works.)

As to the title 閑 is indicated for *han*, and this would mean translating 한중록 (閑中錄) <u>Hanjung nok</u> as "Record Written at Leisure", 한중만록 (閑中漫錄) <u>Hanjung Mallok</u> as "Discourses at Leisure" and 한중만일록 (閑中漫日錄) <u>Hanjung Manillok</u> as "Memoires written at Leisure", but Yi Pyŏnggi thinks that the *han* should be 恨 "resentment", and many writers on the subject prefer not to disagree with him.

486. 한후룡전 Han Huryong chŏn

한후룡전 <u>Han Huryong chyŏn</u>, lending library manuscript, 2 vols, 32, 34 leaves (11 columns, 14 syllables), dated 임진 (壬辰 1892). Title on the cover 韓厚龍傳 <u>Han Huryong chŏn</u> [**Seoul University**]

Ku, Son and Kim: Kungmunhak Kaeron, 262, describes the plot briefly as the healing of a cripple by the power of the Buddha. The title was advertised by Taech'ang Sŏwŏn and Pogŭp Sŏgwan in 1920.

487. 항주기연 Hangju Kiyŏn

Courant, 828: 항쥬긔연 ? 珠奇緣 <u>Hangjyu Kŭiyon</u>, "The Miraculous Destiny of of Hangju", 1 vol., in the von der Gabelentz collection. He gives no further description of either the text or the collection, but he does give a reference to this entry from his entry 3363, see **240** 쌍주기연 **Ssangju Kiyŏn** and also perhap **524** 황주기연 Hwangjư Kiyŏn.

해서긔문 **Haesŏ Kŭimun**: see **139** 부담 **Pudam**

488. 행실록 Haengsil lok

행실록 <u>Haengsil lok</u>, manuscript, 26 leaves, given as in the **Karam collection**, and classified as a *sosŏl*, has a title in Korean, and therefore presumably also a text in Korean. One might guess that the title means "Records of Actions".

향낭사 **Hyang-nang sa**: see **460** 춘향전 **Ch'unhyang chŏn**

489. 현몽쌍룡기 **Hyŏnmong Ssangnyong ki**

현몽쌍농긔 現夢雙龍記 Hyŏnmong Psangnyong kŭi, manuscript, 18 vols. [**Palace**]

There is also a copy of *kwŏn* 13 and 14, bound as one volume, manuscript, 67 leaves (10 columns, 19 syllables), in the **Tōyō Bunko**. **Courant**, 834, lists the title and translates it "Record of the Two Dragons Seen in a Dream".

490. 현몽쌍의록 **Hyŏnmong Ssangŭi rok**

Courant, 854: 현몽쌍의록 現夢雙意錄 Hyŏnmong Ssangŭi rok, "The Two Thoughts in a Dream" (title only). It is difficult to believe that this is not the same as **491** 현봉쌍의록 **Hyŏnbong Ssangŭi rok**.

491. 현봉쌍의록 **Hyŏngbong Ssangŭi rok**

Kim Kidong, 600, lists 顯封雙意錄 Hyŏnbong Ssangŭi rok as a moral tale in Korean set in China, existing in manuscript(s) (also page 37), but not made known before. I find this title if anything more difficult to understand than 490 현몽쌍의록 **Hyŏnmong Ssangŭi rok**, which is so similar that both may have come from the same source.

492. 현수문전 **Hyŏn Sumun chŏn "The Story of Hsüan Shou-wen"**

The hero reaches high military rank in China about 1200. It is a long story, packed with all the favourite ingredients. See **Kim Kidong**, 258-261.

현슈문젼 Hyŏn Syumun chyŏn, lending library manuscript, 2 vols (vols 3 and 10), 26, 31 leaves, dated 긔히 (己亥 1899). [**Harvard**] This text is in very poor condition.

현슈문젼 Hyŏn Syumun chyŏn, lending library manuscript, 8 vols, 246 leaves (11 columns, 14 syllables) in all, dated 을사 (乙巳 1905; 을히 in vol. 6 must be a mistake). Title on the cover 女壽文傳 Hyŏn Sumun chŏn. [**Tōyō Bunko**]

Courant, 798: 현슈문젼 Hyŏn Syumun chyŏn, Seoul block print, 2 vols, "newly engraved at 由洞 Yudong", in Paris, etc., and, 3355: same, 3 vols, "engraved at Yudong", also in Paris. **Kim Tonguk**, 387, gives two Seoul block prints, one of 2 vols, 32, 32 leaves, "at Yudong", and one of 3 vols. **1947 exhibition**, 187: 현수문젼 Hyŏn Sumun chŏn, block print, 1 vol. (Kim Ikhwan).

Kim Kidong, 30 and 258, reports a publication by Chosŏn Sŏgwan, 1915, 124 pages.

현수문전 玄謏文傳 Hyŏn Sumun chyŏn, currently available from Sech'ang Sŏgwan, 110 pages, has the appearance of a translation from Chinese. See also 101 명주기봉 Myŏngju Kibong and 493 현씨양웅쌍린기 Hyŏn-ssi Yangung Ssangnin ki.

493. 현씨양웅쌍린기 Hyŏn-ssi Yangung Ssangnin ki

현시냥웅짱린긔 玄氏兩熊雙麟記 Hyŏn-si Nyangung Psyangnin kŭi, manuscript, 10 vols. [Palace]

Petrova, 222, and illustration 6: 현시양웅짱닌긔 Hyŏn-si Yangung Psangnin kŭi, manuscript, 6 vols, 351 leaves (13 columns, 18 syllables) in all, dated 경오 (庚午 1870, etc., given by Petrova as 1811 or 1871), in the Aston collection in Leningrad. The characters given are 玄氏兩雄雙麟記 Hyŏn-ssi Yangung Ssangnin ki, and the setting is given as in Korea.

현시양웅짱닌긔 Hyŏn-si Yangung Psangnin kŭi, manuscript, 6 vols, 277 leaves (12 columns, 23 syllables) in all, dated 임진 (壬辰 1892, etc.). Title on the cover 玄氏兩雄雙麟記 Hyŏn-ssi Yangung Ssangnin ki. [Seoul University]

玄氏兩雄錄 Hyŏn-ssi Yangung nok, manuscript, 56 leaves, date on the cover 大正五年 (1916), given as in the **Karam collection**, with no indication, however, that it is in Korean.

玄氏兩雄錄 Hyŏn-ssi Yangung nok, manuscript, 78 leaves, dated 정수 (丁巳 1917, etc.), given as in the **Karam collection**.

The last two texts are very much shorter than the others listed above, and their titles are also shorter, but there seems to be nothing to be gained by listing them separately.

1961 exhibition, 74: 현시냥웅짱닌긔 Hyŏn-si Nyangung Psangnin kŭi, manuscript, 1 vol. (Yi Nŭngu). This has the longer title, but the shorter text.

Courant, 907, translates the title "The Story of the Two Brave Sons of the Hyŏn Family", and **Kim Kidong**, 596, lists it as a love story in Korean set in China. The first few pages of such of the above texts as I have looked at indicate that they are stories concerning the same Hsüan Shou-wen who is the hero of 492 현수문전 Hyŏn Sumun chŏn, but I have not read enough to know how many, if any, of them are the same story as that.

494. 형산백옥 Hyŏng-san Paegok "The White Jewel of Ching-Shan"

The title is a phrase frequently used in *kodae sosŏl* to refer to a well loved child. This story concerns primarily the fortunes of 張禮善 Chang Chi-shan,

240

born, in the story, in 1375. It would appear to be a translation from Chinese.

荊山自玉 (형산빅옥) Hyŏng-san Păegok, Pangmun Sŏgwan, 1923 (reprinted from 1915), and same, currently available from Sech'ang Sŏgwan, both on page 1: 朴健會輯 "compiled by Pak Kŏnhoe", both 86 pages.

Kim Kidong has, in a list of paperback publications of *kodae sosŏl* on page 33: 荊山白玉蘇姐己傳 Hyŏng-san Paegok So Chŏgi chŏn, "The Story of Miss Su, the White Jewel of Ching-shan", but this might be two separate titles misprinted as one. I have not seen So Chŏgi chŏn as a separate title elsewhere (though **199** 소소매전 **So Somae chŏn** means the same), and the hero's mother in this story is a Su, but she does not figure largely in the story. At the end of the story in the texts above a sequel is announced 쟝문츙효록 Chyang-mun Ch'yunghyo rok (presumably) "Record of the Loyalty and Filial Piety of the Chang Family". This also does not appear to be mentioned elsewhere.

495. 형세언 Hyŏng-se-ŏn

형세언 型世言 Hyŏng-sye-ŏn, manuscript, 4 vols (vols 3-6 only, apparently of 6). [**Palace**]

I have no note of the contents, and have not seen the title even mentioned elsewhere.

496. 호독각씨전 Hodok Kak-ssi chŏn

Kim Kidong, 32, includes 狐獨閣氏傳 Hodok Kak-ssi chŏn in a list of paperback publications of *kodae sosŏl*. The title is very difficult. If 狐獨 *hodok* could be taken as 孤獨 *kodok*, Kodok Kakssi chŏn may be yet another variation on **67** 꼭두각시전 **Kkoktu Kaksi chŏn**.

497. 호백화 Ho Paekhwa

Courant, 915: 호빅화 胡白花 Ho Păekhwa, "(The Story of) Ho Paekhwa" (title only).

498. 호씨명행록 Ho-ssi Myŏnghaeng nok

Kim Kidong, 600, lists 胡氏名行錄 Ho-ssi Myŏnghaeng nok as a moral story in Korean set in China, existing in manuscript(s), but not made known before. On page 37 he gives 胡氏明行錄 Ho-ssi Myŏnghaeng nok: "Record of the Exemplary Behaviour of Hu".

홍경래실기 **Hong Kyŏngnae Silgi**: see **227** 신미록 **Sinmi rok**

499. 홍계월전 **Hong Kyewŏl chŏn** "The Story of Hung Kuei-yüeh"

In fifteenth century China (Ming, Ch'eng-hua), the heroine wins greater military glory than her husband, corrects his misbehaviour, restores her parents, saves the state, etc. See **Kim Kidong**, 268-271.

Title on the cover 홍계월전 洪桂月傳 **Hong Kewŏl chyŏn**, manuscript, 74 leaves (12 columns, 20 syllables). Date on the cover 光武二年 (1898). [**Seattle**]

홍계월전 **Hong Kyewŏl chyŏn**, manuscript, 2 vols bound as one, 37, 30 leaves (13 columns, 27 syllables), dated 갑인 (甲寅 1914). [**Chŏng Pyŏnguk**]

No title, manuscript, 49 leaves (11 columns, 24 syllables), defective in several places near the beginning. [**Chŏng Pyŏnguk**]

Kim Kidong, 31 and 268, reports a publication by Sin'gu Sŏrim, 1913, 56 pages, and the title was advertised by Pangmun Sŏgwan and Sin'gu Sŏrim in 1923, 1925 and 1932, and by Yŏngch'ang Sŏgwan and Hanhŭng Sŏrim in 1925.

홍계월전 洪桂月傳 **Hong Kyewŏl chyŏn**, currently available from Sech'ang Sŏgwan, 44 pages.

500. 홍길동전 **Hong Kiltong chŏn** "The Story of Hong Kiltong"

In early fifteenth century Korea, the son of a concubine is so ill-treated that he runs away from home, becomes a master of magic, forms a Robin Hood band and eventually leaves Korea to become king of his own Eutopia. The story is always attributed to 許筠 Hŏ Kyun (1569-1618) in the basis of a quotation from 李植 Yi Sik (1584-1647): 澤堂雜著 **T'aektang Chapchŏ**, which I have not found, but which is always given as 許筠作洪吉童傳以擬水滸 "Hŏ Kyun wrote The Story of Hong Kiltong in imitation of Shui-hu[-chuan]" (see **222** 수호지 **Suho chi**). On the basis of this attribution it is invariably described as the first novel in Korean, see **Kim T'aejun**, 78-87, **Kim Kidong**, 177-189 (**1956:** 327-335), **Pak Sŏngŭi**, 237-248, and **Sin Kihyŏng**, 158-170, and the appropriate passage in almost any work on Korean literature. It is unfortunate that no text can be dated as significantly earlier than the version in English by Allen, given below.

홍길동전 **Hong Kiltong chyŏn**, lending library manuscript, 3 vols, 31, 31, 33 leaves (11 columns, 12 syllables), dated 신축 (辛丑 1901). Title on the cover 洪吉童傳 **Hong Kiltong chŏn**. [**Tōyō Bunko**]

1961 exhibition, 48: 홍길동전 Hong Kiltong chyŏn, manuscript, 1 vol. (National Library).

All Seoul block prints are entitled 홍길동전 Hong Kiltong chyŏn. In descending order of size, these are: 30 leaves, "newly engraved at 冶洞 Yadong", in Paris, etc., according to **Courant**, 821, and **Kim Tonguk**, 384; 24 leaves, given as in the **Karam collection**, reproduced in the **Ewha Series**, I 277-324, with a note 428-432, and republished lithographically by 翰南書林 Hannam Sŏrim, Keijō, 1920; 23 leaves [**British Museum**]; 21 leaves, 宋洞新刊 "newly engraved at Songdong". [**Harvard**] There is also a Seoul block print in the **Ogura collection, Tokyo**, but I omitted to note the number of leaves.

홍길동전 Hong Kiltong chyŏn, Ansŏng block print, 23 leaves. Title on the cover 洪吉同傳 Hong Kiltong chŏn. [**Tōyō Bunko**]

Kim Tonguk, 395, gives an Ansŏng block print of 33 leaves.

홍길동전 Hong Kiltong chŏn, Chŏnju block print, 36 leaves, 多佳書鋪 Taga Sŏp'o, 大正五 (1916), given as in the **Karam collection**. This was shown in the **1947 exhibition** as item 73. The first page of a Chŏnju block print is reproduced by **Kim Tonguk**, page 402.

홍길동전 (洪吉童傳) Hong Kiltong chyŏn, Tŏkhŭng Sŏrim, 1925 (reprinted from 1915), 37 pages. Kim Kidong used what might have been the first edition, 70 pages, and the same publishers also advertised it in 1923 and 1935. Several other publishers listed it in 1925 and 1926, but it is rather surprising in view of opinions now held concerning it, how few of such lists issued by publishers of paperbacks it appears in.

홍길동전 (洪吉童傳) Hong Kiltong chyŏn, currently available from Sech'ang Sŏgwan, 36 pages.

홍길동전 Hong Kiltong chŏn, Taejo sa, 1958 and 1959, 34 pages.

洪吉童傳 Hong Kiltong chŏn in the **Hŭimang Series**, IV 195-222.

鄭鉒東 Chŏng Chudong: 洪吉童傳研究 Hong Kiltong chŏn Yŏn'gu, "A Study of 'The Story of Hong Kiltong'." 文豪社 Munho sa, Taegu, 1961. 321 pages.

This work includes an annotated text. It was reviewed at length by 金東旭 Kim Tonguk (Seoul, 高麗大學校亞細亞問題研究所 Koryŏ Taehakkyo Asea Munje Yŏn-guso, Asiatic Research Center, Korea University. 亞細亞研究 Asea Yŏn'gu, **The Journal of Asiatic Studies**, 9, May 1962, 205-209), who raises questions which I have not seen raised elsewhere, but which seem obvious. Was the inspiration for this story the 洪吉童 Hong Kiltong of the early fifteenth century whose family records note that "because of his magical powers there is a story about him", or was it the 洪吉同 Hong Kiltong of the early sixteenth century, an historical brigand? Or was it both of them, or neither? Did Hŏ Kyun write this story in Korean or *hanmun*? Why, indeed, it there no corroborating evidence that he wrote it at all? In addition, Kim Tonguk is critical of Chŏng Chudong's use of texts, but it should be stressed that he also finds much to commend in the work.

洪吉童傳 Hong Kiltong chŏn in 張志暎 Chang Chiyŏng, ed.: 洪吉童傳・沈淸傳 Hong Kiltong chŏn, Sim Ch'ŏng chŏn, 正音社 Chŏngŭm sa, Seoul, 1964, pages 7-79, is an annotated text for school use.

There are also many rewritten versions, including two in English, one in H.N. Allen: Korean Tales (G. P. Putnam, New York and London, 1889, 170-193, and presumably also in his Korea, Fact and Fancy, 1904, which I have not seen), and the other in Zong In-sob: Folk Tales from Korea (Routledge and Kegan Paul, London, 1952, 207-223). In addition **51** 김길동전 **Kim Kiltong chŏn** is said to be essentially the same story.

501. 홍루몽 Hongnu mong "The Dream of the Red Chamber"

The famous Chinese novel 紅樓夢 Hung-lou-meng (see Lu Hsun: A Brief History of Chinese Fiction, Foreign Languages Press, Peking, 1959, 298-315, etc.) is famous in Korea too, but the only old text of a translation of it which I have seen, or seen mentioned, is:

홍루몽 紅樓夢 Hongnu mong, manuscript, 117 vols (three volumes are missing). [**Palace**]

When this was shown in the **1961 exhibition**, as item 66, the catalogue noted: "may be a translation by 李鍾泰 Yi Chongt'ae in the reign of Kojong [1864-1906]".

There are also the following translations of Chinese sequels to this story in the Palace library (all in manuscript):

보홍루몽 補紅樓夢 Po Hongnu mong, 24 vols

쇽홍루몽 續紅樓夢 Syok Hongnu mong, 24 vols

홍루몽보 紅樓夢補 Hongnu mong po, 24 vols

홍루부몽 紅樓復夢 <u>Hongnu Pumong</u>, 50 vols

후홍루몽 後紅樓夢 <u>Hu Hongnu mong</u>, 20 vols

502. 홍문연 Hongmun yŏn

See **Sin Kihyŏng**, 401-404, who describes the story as one of intrigue and mur-
der in the third century B.C., derived from <u>Hsi-han Yen-i</u> (see **174** 서한연의
Sŏhan Yŏnŭi). 鴻門宴 *Hongmun yŏn* is a banquet in <u>Hsi-han Yen-i</u> (see **Kim
T'aejun**, 97) at which the action of this starts. The title was advertised by
Chosŏn Tosŏ Chusik Hoesa in 1925.

503. 홍백화전 Hongbaekhwa chŏn

The story is apparently one of thwarted, but eventually consummated love in
fifteenth century China (Ming, Ch'eng-hua). The heroine lives as a man for
most of the story. It is generally described as having been written first in
hanmun. See **Kim T'aejun**, 71-72, who indicates that there is a translation by
Kim Tongjin, (that is to say, in paperback edition: the title was advertised by
Yŏngch'ang Sŏgwan and Hanhŭng Sŏrim in 1925, and by Tŏkhŭng Sŏrim in 1935),
Pak Sŏngŭi, 236-237, who adds little to this, and **Kim Kidong**, 424-427, who gives
a very full description from his own manuscript in *hanmun*. The title presumably means "The Story of the Red and White Flower(s)", but I cannot see why
from the above descriptions, and was not able to examine closely either of the
texts which I have seen:

홍빅화뎐 紅白花傳 <u>Hongbăekhwa tyŏn</u>, manuscript, 3 vols. [**Palace**]

홍빅화젼 <u>Hongbăekhwa chyŏn</u>, manuscript, 3 vols, 53, 49, 38 leaves (9 columns,
13 syllables), dated 계묘 (癸卯 1903, etc.). Title on the cover 紅白花傳
<u>Hongbaekhwa chŏn</u>. [**Asami collection, Berkeley**]
This is a very nice manuscript in Palace style script. The catalogue dates it
1783, but there was apparently no sound reason for choosing that date.

홍원빈입궐초일긔 Hong Wŏnbin Ipkwŏl Ch'o Ilgŭi: see **17** 계해반정록 **Kyehae
Panjŏng nok**

504. 홍윤성전 Hong Yunsŏng chŏn

Kim T'aejun, 94, describes 洪允成傳 <u>Hong Yunsŏng chŏn</u>, "The Story of Hong
Yunsŏng" (he was a military official, 1425-1475) as a biography embellished
by the addition of several episodes from <u>Shui-hu-chuan</u> (see **222** 수호지| **Suho**

chi). **Kim Kidong** mentions it in much the same terms, pages 209 and 589, adding that it exists in manuscript(s), and referring to Kim T'aejun.

505. 홍장군전 Hong Changgun chŏn

Kim Kidong, 591, lists 洪將軍傳 Hong Changgun chŏn (presumably) "The Story of General Hung" as a story of a hero in Korean set in China, existing in paperback edition(s) (also page 33), but not made known before. **Kim T'aejun**, 248, gives the same as the title of a "New Novel" by 李海朝 Yi Haejo.

화뎡션힝녹 Hwa Tyŏng Syŏnhăeng nok: see 516 화정선행록 Hwa Chŏng **Sŏnhaeng nok**

화룡도 **Hwaryongdo**: see 514 화용도 **Hwayongdo**

506. 화문록 Hwamun nok

화문녹 花門錄 Hwamun nok, manuscript, 7 vols. [**Palace**]

I have no note on the contents of this, and have not found any reference to it elsewhere, but, if I may hazard a guess at the meaning of the title, this might be a convenient point to note that I have no precise information on three "Records of the ..... Hwa (or Hua) Family", 507 화문충의록 Hwa-mun Ch'ungŭi rok, 508 화문효감록 Hwa-mun Hyogam nok and 509 화문효행록 Hwa-mun Hyohaeng nok.

507. 화문충의록 Hwa-mun Ch'ungŭi rok

Courant, 894: 화문충의록 花門忠義錄 Hwa-mun Ch'yungŭi rok, "The Loyalty of the Hwa [Chinese: Hua] Family" (title only). **Kim T'aejun**, 161, includes 花門忠孝錄 Hwa-mun Ch'unghyo rok (presumably) "Record of the Loyalty and Filial Piety of the Hua Family" in a list of titles of this type which seems to be derived largely from Courant. In this case Courant has only the title above and 512 화씨충효록 Hwa-ssi Ch'unghyo rok, which Kim T'aejun quotes in the same list. **Kim Kidong**, 599, quotes Kim T'aejun, adding that it is a moral tale in Korean set in China, existing in manuscript(s). See **506** 화문록 **Hwamun nok**.

508. 화문효감록 Hwa-mun Hyogam nok

1947 exhibition, 146: 화문효감녹 Hwa-mun Hyogam nok, manuscript, 1 vol. (Yi Haech'ŏng). The title could mean "Record of the Filial Piety of the Hwa (or Hua) Family". See **506** 화문록 **Hwamun nok**.

509. 화문효행록 Hwa-mun Hyohaeng nok

화문효힝녹 Hwa-mun Hyohăeng nok, manuscript, 1 vol. (last vol. only), 44 leaves. [**Harvard**]

The title could mean "Record of the Filial Piety of the Hwa (or Hua) Family". See **506** 화문록 **Hwamun nok.**

510. 화산기봉 Hwa-san Kibong "The Miraculous Encounter at Hua-shan"

화산긔봉 華山奇逢 Hwa-san Kŭibong, manuscript, 13 vols. [**Palace**]

華山奇逢 Hwa-san Kibong, Tonga Sŏgwan, 1916, 112 pages.

The story is set in seventh century China, and the title is mentioned by **Courant**, 844, **Kim Kidong**, 596, etc.

511. 화산선계록 Hwa-san Sŏn'gye rok

화산션계록 華山仙界錄 Hwa-san Syŏn'gye rok, manuscript, 80 vols. [**Palace**]

Courant, 831, translates the title "Record of the Kingdom of the Saint of Hua-shan".

512. 화씨충효록 Hwa-ssi Ch'unghyo rok

화시튱효록 花氏忠孝錄 Hwa-si T'yunghyo rok, manuscript, 37 vols. [**Palace**]

Courant, 882: 화시츙효록 華氏忠孝錄 Hwa-si Ch'yunghyo rok, "The Loyalty and Filial Piety of Hwa [Chinese: Hua]" (title only). **Kim T'aejun**, 161, gives this in a list of titles of this type which seems to be derived largely from Courant. **Kim Kidong**, 598, quoting Kim T'aejun, describes it as a moral tale in Korean set in China, existing in manuscript(s). Compare **507** 화문충의록 **Hwa-mun Ch'ungŭi rok.**

513. 화옥쌍기 Hwa-ok-ssang-gi

Kim Kidong, 596, lists 花玉雙奇 Hwa-ok-ssang-gi as a love story in Korean set in China, which exists in paperback editions (also page 32), but had not been made known before.

514. 화용도 **Hwayongdo** "Hua-yung-tao"

This appears to be essentially the title given by various Chŏnju publishers to a version of San-kuo-chih Yen-i (**156** 삼국지연의 **Samgukchi Yŏnŭi**). It concerns chiefly 諸葛亮 Chuko Liang and his wife 黃 Huang (see **412** 제갈양전 **Chegal Yang chŏn** and **521** 황부인전 **Hwang Puin chŏn**), and has some connection with the story from about chapter 36 on of San-kuo-chih Yen-i. 華容道 Hua-yung-tao is the scene of the action after the battle of the Red Cliff (see **391** 적벽가 **Chŏkpyŏk ka**), around chapter 50 of San-kuo-chih Yen-i, and towards the end of this story. See **Sin Kihyŏng**, 390-396.

1947 exhibition, 78: 華容道 Hwayongdo, manuscript, 1 vol. (Song Sŏkha).

화룡도 華容道 Hwaryongdo. 多佳書舖 Taga Sŏp'o, Chŏnju, 1916, 2 vols, 1+34, 48 leaves. Author 梁珍泰 Yang Chint'ae (see next). This is a reissue of a Chŏnju block print, complete with the colophon 丁未孟秋龜洞新刊 "newly engraved at Kwidong, seventh month, 1907". I have seen two copies of this reissue as just described [**Chŏng Pyŏnguk** and **Harvard**], but **Kim Tonguk**, 398, gives the original as of 34, 50 leaves. The last page of it is reproduced in Hyangt'o Sŏul, 8, **1960**, page 63.

화룡도 Hwaryongdo, Chŏnju block print, 2 vols, 40, 44 leaves, 양칙방 戊申八月完山梁冊房開刊 "engraved at Yang's bookshop [see previous text], Chŏnju, eighth month, 1908". This is reproduced in the **Ewha Series**, IV 1-170, with a note 407-412. **Kim Tonguk** does not give this, but he does give, page 398, 戊申春完西溪新刊 "newly engraved at Sŏgye, Chŏnju, Spring [i.e. first-third months], 1908", and he gives as his source for this information "Kim Sambul's Chinsŏ Kan[haeng] hoe text", presumably of **460** 춘향전 **Ch'unhyang chŏn**.

1961 exhibition, 65: 화룡도 Hwaryongdo, block print, 2 vols, bound as one. (Kang Hanyŏng). This is presumably one of the two Chŏnju block prints above.

華容道實記 화용도실긔 Hwayongdo Silgŭi, currently available from Sech'ang Sŏgwan, 3, 170 pages. There is a three page index, then this story, 160 pages, then a 赤壁歌 적벽가 Chŏkpyŏk ka which is too short to be **391** 적벽가 Chŏkpyŏk ka, and an 오호디장긔 Oho Tǎejang kŭi, see **162** 삼셜기 Samsŏlgi, story no. 2. At the beginning of the index is: "compiled by Pak Kŏnhoe", and on page 160 the reader is requested to read other related stories "published by Chosŏn Sŏgwan". I have also seen (at **Harvard**) an earlier paperback edition identical with this except that the main story is of 207 pages, and the last page and the cover, including the details of publication, are missing. The title was regularly advertised in paperbacks in the 1920's and 1930's.

515. 화윤별취록 Hwa Yun Pyŏl-ch'wirok

Courant, 909: 화윤별취록 華尹別聚錄 Hwa Yun Pyŏl-ch'ywirok, "Collected Records of Hwa and Yun [Chinese: Hua and Yin]" (title only).

516. 화정선행록 Hwa Chŏng Sŏnhaeng nok

화뎡션힝녹 花鄭善行錄 Hwa Tyŏng Syŏnhăeng nok, manuscript, 15 vols. [**Palace**]

화뎡션힝녹 和靜善行錄 Hwa Tyŏng Syŏnhăeng nok, manuscript, 1 vol. (vol. 7 only, of 15). [**Palace**]

Petrova, 223: title as last, 15 vols, 770 leaves (15 columns, 19 syllables) in all, in the Aston collection in Leningrad. She translates the title as "Record of the Good Behaviour of Ho Ching". The first page is reproduced in illustration 7, and shows the story to be set in eleventh century China (Sung, T'ien-hsi).

Courant, 873: 화정션힝록 華鄭善行錄 Hwa Chyŏng Syŏnhăeng nok, "Record of the Good Acts of Hua and Cheng" (title only). It seems a reasonable assumption that this and the other titles given above are all of the same work, but I have not seen enough of the work to know which might be the best. **Kim T'aejun**, 161, quotes the title from Courant, and **Kim Kidong**, 599, quoting it from Kim T'aejun, gives 華鄭美行錄 Hwa Chŏng Mihaeng nok. **Sin Kihyŏng**, 486, repeats this last, with an appropriate Korean spelling also.

517. 화진전 Hwajin chŏn

Title on the cover 화진젼 Hwajin chyŏn, manuscript, 2 vols, 70, 56 leaves (10 columns, 27 syllables), dated 丙申 (1896) in vol. 1 and 을미 and 乙未 (1895) in vol. 2. [**Harvard**]

I have not found mention of any such title elsewhere.

화충가 Hwach'ung ka, etc.: see 375 장끼전 Changkki chŏn

518. 화향전 Hwahyang chŏn

Kim Kidong, 592, lists 花香傳 Hwahyang chŏn (presumably) "The Story of Hua-hsiang" as a domestic story in Korean set in China, existing in paperback edition(s) (also page 32), but not made known before. The title was advertised by Taech'ang Sŏwŏn with other publishers in 1918 and 1919.

519. 황경기대록 **Hwang Kyŏng Ki Tae rok**

Courant, 931: 황경긔디록 <u>Hwang Kyŏng Kŭi Tăe rok</u>, "Record of Hwang Kyŏng and Ki Tae" (title only).

520. 황명배신전 **Hwangmyŏng Paesin chŏn**

1947 exhibition, 180: 황명비신뎐 <u>Hwangmyŏng Păesin tyŏn</u>, manuscript, 1 vol. (T'ongmun'gwan). See the **Introduction**, §6.4.2, for the peculiar characteristics of the T'ongmun'gwan texts shown in this exhibition.

皇明陪臣傳 "The Story of the Ministers of the Ming" would seem to be a reasonable guess at the meaning of this title, but it is no more than a guess, and if it is not correct, even the romanisation given above may not be correct.

521. 황부인전 **Hwang Puin chŏn "The Story of the Lady Huang"**

The Lady Huang is the wife of 諸葛亮 Chuko Liang, one of the leading characters of <u>San-kuo-chih Yen-i</u> (see **156** 삼국지연의 **Samguchi Yŏnŭi**). The story may also be regarded as a condensed version of **514** 화용도 **Hwayongdo**. The title is mentioned by **Kim Kidong**, 210, etc.

황부인젼 黃夫人傳 <u>Hwang Puin chyŏn</u>, currently available from Sech'ăng Sŏgwan, 35 [+24] pages. (The 24 pages are **391** 적벽가 **Chŏkpyŏk ka**.) The title was advertised by Yŏngch'ang Sŏgwan and Hanhŭng Sŏri.n in 1925.

황시결송 **Hwangsăe Kyŏlsong**, etc.: see **162** 삼설기 **Samsŏlgi**

522. 황운전 **Hwang Un chŏn "The Story of Huang Yün"**

In fifth century China (Sung, Wen-tsung), the hero and his fiancee perform mighty military deeds. This title is given only brief mentions by the critics, but it appears to be the earliest title of the story described by **Kim Kidong**, 261-264, under the title <u>Hwang Changgun chŏn</u>, as below.

황운전 <u>Hwang Un chyŏn</u>, manuscript, 2 vols, 53, 54 leaves (10 columns, 20 syllables), dated 광셔이십갑오 (光緒二十甲午 1894). Title on the cover 黃雲傳 Hwang Un chŏn. [**Chŏng Pyŏnguk**]

황운뎐 <u>Hwang Un tyŏn</u>, manuscript, 2 vols, dated 갑오 (甲午 1894). [**Ogura collection, Tokyo**]

250

Courant, 800: 황운전 黃雲傳 Hwang Un chyŏn, block print, 2 vols, in Paris, etc., and, 3356: block print, 3 vols, in Paris. **Kim Tonguk**, 390, gives a 2 vol. Seoul block print, 30, 29 leaves, and a 3 vol. Seoul block print, 22, 19, 18 leaves.

黃將軍傳 황장군전 Hwang Changgun chyŏn, currently available from Sech'ang Sŏgwan, 113 pages.

Kim Kidong, 261, reports a publication of the same title as the last by Sin'gu Sŏrim (page 30: Chosŏn Sŏgwan), 1916, 128 pages, and the title advertised by Pangmun Sŏgwan and Sin'gu Sŏrim in 1923, 1925 and 1932, by Yŏngch'ang Sŏgwan and Hanhŭng Sŏrim in 1925, and by Kwangdong Sŏguk in 1926.

523. 황월선전 Hwang Wŏlsŏn chŏn

See **Kim Kidong**, 336-339. 黃月仙 Hwang Wŏlsŏn, the heroine, is apparently driven from home by her stepmother during her father's absence, but makes a good marriage, and is re-united with her father and brother at the end. He reports a publication, pages 336 and 338, by Tŏkhŭng Sŏrim, 1931, 38 pages.

황장군전 **Hwang Changgun chŏn**: see 522 · 황운전 **Hwang Un chŏn**

524. 황주기연 Hwangju Kiyŏn

Kim T'aejun, 229, has 黃珠奇緣 Hwangju Kiyŏn in a list of similar titles quoted from **Courant**. This title is not given by Courant, and it may have been intended as a version of **487** 항주기연 **Hangju Kiyŏn**. **Kim Kidong**, 595, quotes Kim T'aejun's title, adding that it is a love story in Korean set in China, which exists in paperback edition(s).

황주목사기 **Hwangju Moksa ki**, etc.: see 162 삼설기 **Samsŏlgi**

525. 황처사전 Hwang Ch'ŏsa chŏn

Kim Kidong, 598, lists 黃處士傳 Hwang Ch'ŏsa chŏn (presumably) "The Story of the Country Gentleman Huang" as a story in Korean set in China, which exists in manuscript(s) (also page 36), but had not been made known before. **Sin Kihyŏng**, 486, adds that it is a tale of marvels.

526. 황한기봉 Hwang Han Kibong

Courant, 852: 황한긔봉 黃韓奇逢 Hwang Han Kŭibong, "The Miraculous Encounter of Hwang [Chinese: Huang] and Han" (title only). **Kim T'aejun**, 229, quotes this from Courant, and **Kim Kidong**, 594, quotes it from Kim T'aejun, adding that it is a love story in Korean set in China, which exists in paperback edition(s).

527. 회문전 Hoemun chŏn

1947 exhibition, 147: 回文傳 Hoemun chŏn, manuscript, 1 vol. (Yi Haech'ŏng).

횡부가 **Hoengbu ka**: see 1 가루지기타령 **Karujigi T'aryŏng**

528. 효열지 Hyoyŏl chi

효열지 Hyoyŏl chi, manuscript, 113 leaves (10 columns, 24 syllables), dated 병오 (丙午 1906). [**Seoul University**]

The title on the cover may be the same as the title on leaf 1, given above. On leaf 1, that title has actually been crossed out, and beneath it is written 장화효절 Changhwa Hyojyŏl. I could not discover what this meant. The most obvious meaning for the title is "Chronicle of Filial Piety and Virtue", and **Kim Kidong** lists just such title, 孝烈志 Hyoyŏl chi, on page 600, as a moral tale, but in *hanmun*, set in China, and existing in manuscript(s) (also page 37), which had not been made known before.

1947 exhibition, 165: 孝烈錄 Hyoyŏl lok, manuscript, 1 vol. (Kim Sambul), is such a similar title that there seems to be nothing to be gained by listing it separately.

529. 효의정충예행록 Hyo Ŭi Chŏng Ch'ung Ye Haengnok

효의뎡튱예힝녹 孝義貞忠禮行錄 Hyo Ŭi Tyŏng T'yung Ye Hǎengnok, two manuscripts, one of 56 vols (vols. 1-28 and 30-57) and one of 29 vols. [**Palace**]

Courant, 870: 효의졍츙녜힝록 孝誼貞忠禮行錄 Hyo Ŭi Chyŏng Ch'yung Nye Hǎengnok, "Acts of Filial Piety, Justice, Devotion, Loyalty and Manners" (title only).

530. 후속루몽 Hu-song-nu-mong

Courant, 944: 후쇽누몽 後續樓夢 Hu-syong-nu-mong (doubtful title only: Courant queries the whole form and offers no translation).

후슈호전 **Hu Syuho chyŏn**: see **222** 수호지 **Suho chi**

후홍루몽 **Hu Hongnu mong**: see **501** 홍루몽 **Hongnu mong**

흑룡록 **Hŭngnyong nok**, etc.: see **366** 임진록 **Imjin nok**

531. 흥부전 Hŭngbu chŏn "The Story of Hŭngbu"

The story of the younger brother, Hŭngbu, whose kindness and virtue is re-warded by the swallows through the gift of a magic gourd seed, and his elder brother, Nolbu, whose cruelty and greed leads to his ruin in the same way, is an old favourite in Korea, and is related to similar stories throughout the Far East. See **Kim T'aejun**, 134-136, **Kim Kidong**, 542-549 **(1956: 262-267)**, **Pak Sŏngŭi**, 312-318, and **Sin Kihyŏng**, 337-343. All give 놀부傳 Nolbu chŏn as an alternative title.

This is one of the stories sung in *p'ansori*, see Song Manjae ŭi Kwan-u-hŭi, 103 and 118 (Kwan-u-hŭi stanza 11), and P'ansori Palsaeng ko, 280-281, as described in the **Introduction**, §7.3. Sin Chaehyo rewrote it about 1880, and 박타령 Pak T'aryŏng is given as in vol. 6 of his works in the **Karam collection**.

According to 姜漢永 Kang Hanyŏng: 春香歌 Ch'unhyang ka (**Kugŏ Kungmunhak**, 5, June 1953, 15-18) 柳寵錫 Yu Nongsŏk made a copy of a text of this work owned by Sin Chaehyo's son in 1903, and it would seem that it is this copy which is reprinted in: Kang Hanyŏng, ed.: 朴興甫歌 Pak Hŭngbo ka (**Hyŏndae Munhak**, 35-42, November 1957—June 1958).

In this version the family name of the brothers is Pak - in all others that I have seen it is 연 Yŏn - and this adds a complication to the translation of some of the titles. Pak T'aryong, above, for instance, might mean "The Ballad of the Paks" or "The Ballad of the Gourd". It might be noted also that the personal names of the brothers are sometimes 흥보 Hŭngbo and 놀보 Nolbo (and Nolbo often looks like 늘보 Nŭlbo, too) in the older texts.

흥보전 Hŭngbo chyŏn, manuscript, 51 leaves, dated 丁酉 (1897). Title on the cover 興甫傳 Hŭngbo chŏn. [**Harvard**] Perhaps a copy made by a Japanese.

흥부젼 Hŭngbu chyŏn, Seoul block print, 25 leaves. [**British Museum**]

The same is given by **Courant**, 820, as in Paris, etc., and by **Petrova**, 206, as in the Aston collection in Leningrad.

Title on the cover 興夫傳 Hŭngbu chŏn, Seoul block print, 20 leaves 宋洞新板 "newly engraved at Songdong". [**Tōyō Bunko**] This copy is missing leaves 1, 2 and 6.

There is also a Seoul block print in the **Ogura collection in Tokyo**, but I did not note any details. **Kim Tonguk**, 391, states that it is the 25 leaf, not the 20 leaf edition, which has the colophon given above, but in Hyangt'o Sŏul, 8, 1960, page 52, he gave only the 20 leaf edition with the colophon.

Kim Kidong, 543, gives a publication by Sinmun'gwan, 1913, 46 pages.

흥부젼 Hŭngbu chyŏn, Pangmun Sŏgwan, 1919 (reprinted from 1917), 89 pages, and 1924 (reprinted from 1917), 60 pages.

흥보젼 Hŭngbu chyŏn, currently available from Sech'ang Sŏgwan, 56 pages.

흥부젼 (興夫傳) Hŭngbu chŏn, Sammun sa, 1953, 64 pages.

The title was advertised by Sin'gu Sŏrim, by Tongyang Sŏwŏn, and by Yŏngch'ang Sŏgwan and Hanhŭng Sŏrim, all in 1925. I have also a note of a publication by Chungang Insŏgwan, but no note of the source of the information.

孫洛範 Son Nakpŏm, ed.: 興夫傳 Hŭngbu chŏn. 文獻社 Munhŏn sa, Seoul, 1957. 191 pages. This is annotated, and the text is said to be taken from one in the **Ilsa collection** (no such is given in the catalogue) and from an edition by 申明均 Sin Myŏnggyun (i.e. about 1940).

興夫傳 Hŭngbu chŏn in the **Hŭimang Series**, I 347-397.

There are many rewritings, including one entitled 鷰의脚 연의각 Yŏn ŭi Kak, "The Swallow's Leg", by 李海朝 Yi Haejo, made from a version told to him by a *kwangdae* of Chŏlla Province (1920 edition, 1923 reprint, seen). There is a version of the story in English entitled Hyung Bo and Nahl Bo in H. N. Allen: Korean Tales (G. P. Putnam, New York and London, 1889, 89-115). This should also be in his Korea, Fact and Fancy, 1904, but I have not seen that.

Index of Titles in Chinese Characters in Radical-Stroke Order

Reference is to entry numbers in the list of titles in Korean alphabetical order.

For Product Safety Concerns and Information please contact our EU
representative GPSR@taylorandfrancis.com
Taylor & Francis Verlag GmbH, Kaufingerstraße 24, 80331 München, Germany

www.ingramcontent.com/pod-product-compliance
Lightning Source LLC
Chambersburg PA
CBHW081431270326
41932CB00019B/3167